VIOLENT RACISM:

Victimization, Policing and Social Context

Revised Edition

Benjamin Bowling

OXFORD

UNIVERSITY PRESS

Great Clarendon Street, Oxford OX2 6DP

Oxford University Press is a department of the University of Oxford
It furthers the University's objective of excellence in research, scholarship,
and education by publishing worldwide in

Oxford New York

Athens Auckland Bangkok Bogotá Buenos Aires Calcutta
Cape Town Chennai Dar es Salaam Delhi Florence Hong Kong Istanbul
Karachi Kuala Lumpur Madrid Melbourne Mexico City Mumbai
Nairobi Paris São Paulo Singapore Taipei Tokyo Toronto Warsaw

with associated companies in Berlin Ibadan

Oxford is a registered trade mark of Oxford University Press
in the UK and in certain other countries

Published in the United States
by Oxford University Press Inc., New York

© Benjamin Bowling 1998

The moral rights of the author have been asserted

Database right Oxford University Press (maker)

First published 1998

First published in paperback with revisions 1999

British Library Cataloguing in Publication Data

Data available

Library of Congress Cataloging in Publication Data

Bowling, Benjamin.
Violent racism: victimization, policing, and social context / Benjamin Bowling
p. cm.—(Clarendon studies in criminology)
Includes bibliographical references.
1. Minorities—Crimes against—Great Britain. 2. Hate crimes—Great Britain.
3. Racism—Great Britain. 4. Police—Great Britain.
5. Discrimination in law enforcement—Great Britain.
I. Title. II. Series.
HV6250.4.E75B68 1998 364.1—dc21 97–47464

ISBN 0–19–826252–3
ISBN 0–19–829878–1 (Pbk.)

1 3 5 7 9 10 8 6 4 2

Printed in Great Britain
on acid-free paper by
Biddles Ltd., Guildford and King's Lynn

For Samson, Johannes and Frederik

'The idea that blacks comprise a problem, or more accurately a series of problems, is today expressed at the core of racist reasoning. It is closely related to a second idea which is equally pernicious, just as popular and again integral to racial meanings. This defines blacks as forever victims, objects rather than subjects, beings that feel yet lack the ability to think, and remain incapable of considered behaviour in an active mode. The oscillation between black as problem and black as victim has become, today, the principal mechanism through which 'race' is pushed outside of history and into the realm of natural, inevitable events' (Gilroy, 1987: 11).

'It is neither healthy, nor desirable to spend one's whole European life aware of 'colour', and I have yet to meet a single black person who enjoys it, but the curiously warped logic of the European continually attempts to force this upon us' (Phillips, 1987: 125).

General Editors' Introduction

The *Clarendon Studies in Criminology* series was inaugurated in 1994 under the auspices of centres of criminology at the Universities of Cambridge and Oxford and the London School of Economics. There was a view that criminology in Britain and elsewhere was flowing with interesting work and that there was scope for a new dedicated series of scholarly books. In particular, there was a recognition that authors of research monographs, the life-blood of any subject, face growing difficulties in publishing their work. The intention, declared Roger Hood, its first general editor, was 'to provide a forum for outstanding work in all aspects of criminology, criminal justice, penology, and the wider field of deviant behaviour.' We trust that that intention has been fulfilled. Fourteen titles have already been published, covering policing; prisons and prison administration; gender and crime; the media reporting of crime news, and much else; and others will follow.

Violent Racism is an important addition to the Clarendon series. Few subjects are more laden with *a priori* assumptions and sharply contested standpoints. Bowling's own mixed race background sensitises him to the issues involved to an unusual degree, and has also heightened his awareness of the pitfalls facing the sociologist who seeks too readily to gloss over profound conflicts of experience and interpretation. His study combines a detailed analysis of the complex history of developing strategies to combat racism and violence with the story of one project in the East End of London that aimed to curb violent racism by multi-agency co-operation. It is a story of halting progression from official denial that any such problem existed to one of partial but limited success in agency partnership. His analysis illuminates the immensity of the task by making such subtle yet profound distinctions as that between violent racism and racist violence, and builds on the pivotal difference between the event-based logic of policing and the experience of cumulative victimization which eludes it. Only as strategies are evolved which take such constraints into account will the real potential for proactive partnership against violent racism take more effective shape.

The fact that *some* progress has been made carries the danger of complacency and a lack of preparedness for the sudden upsurge of violent racism, which remains immanent. The book ends with the words 'more *must* be done'. Its substance provides invaluable insights into what forms that should take.

David Downes and Paul Rock

Preface

The name of Stephen Lawrence, a black teenager, murdered in cold blood on an ordinary English street, hit the world news headlines on 24 February 1999.[1] In Britain, his name dominated terrestrial and satellite television, radio, and print media for several days, with some of the national newspapers the following day publishing 'pull-out' special editions, many running to double-figure full-page spreads. A curious thing about this frenzied interest, and its reverberations across the whole of the British body politic and beyond, was that Stephen Lawrence's death occurred nearly six years earlier on 22 April 1993.

Stephen Lawrence and his friend Duwayne Brooks were on their way home, waiting for a bus in Eltham, South East London when a group of five or six white youths crossed the road towards them. One shouted 'what, what nigger?' and the group 'literally engulfed Stephen'. Stephen Lawrence was stabbed twice in the chest and arm; both stab wounds severed arteries and Stephen was probably dead by the time an ambulance arrived. An Inquest jury returned a unanimous verdict in 1997 that 'Stephen Lawrence was unlawfully killed in a completely unprovoked racist attack by five white youths'. The police investigation, which failed ultimately to bring the killers to justice was condemned as 'palpably flawed' and incompetent. A second investigation was launched but could not salvage the errors and omissions of the first, and could not compensate for the time which had been wasted.

Why Stephen? one television documentary demanded, the question concealing myriad questions: Why was Stephen Lawrence murdered? Why, of all the mothers' sons was this young man targeted and felled with strokes from a long blade? Why did the police fail to investigate

---

[1] The international news agencies and some papers around the world included reports on 24 February including: *Frankfurther Allgemeine Zeitung, Le Monde*, Reuters, The Associated Press, Agence France Presse, Asian Intelligence Wire. On 25 February coverage included: *Sueddeutsche Zeitung, Frankfurter Allgemeine Zeitung, Vancouver Sun, Los Angeles Times, The Columbian, Pittsburg Post-Gazette, The Arizona Republic, The Record, Northern New Jersey, The Salt Lake Tribune, Chicago Sun-Times, Washington Post, Sydney Morning Herald*; and 26 February: *Le Monde, Sueddeutsche Zeitung, Fankfurter Allegemeine Zeitung, The Toronto Star, Los Angeles Times, China Daily, Greensborough News and Record, International Herald Tribune*, and the *Sydney Morning Herald*.

the murder with sufficient competence for a prosecution to be laid? Why did the criminal justice system fail to deliver justice—the conviction of guilty men? Why did it take six years to bring the facts to light? Why, of all the racist killings that have occurred over the past four decades, did the murder of Stephen Lawrence become the one which would shame a nation?

The hardback edition of *Violent Racism* did not examine the details of the murder of Stephen Lawrence even though it had become the best-known instance of violent racism in recent British history. For reasons which I have yet to fathom, I felt unable to describe the details of this brutal and untimely death. I felt that I could not do justice to the horror of the stabbing, to the pain of the families and friends, or the disbelief and incredulity at the ineptitude and arrogance of the police. This extraordinary tale of terror, error, and misjudgement which can never been compensated for requires books of its own. Perhaps it was that the scale of the task that defeated me. The published works that examine the Lawrence case in fine detail will certainly illustrate its enormity.[2] And yet this book describes, often with the barest of details, many other racist murders, each of which deserves its own volume. Perhaps there are deeper, more personal reasons that I felt unable to describe the experience of Stephen Lawrence, and his family and friends. Perhaps it was 'too close to home' for me to be able to relate with any semblance of detachment. After all, I too had been a black teenager accosted by a racist gang on an ordinary English street at night.[3] And yet I have lived to tell, even *forget*, the tale. Perhaps to work through the Lawrence's case was too painful and the risk too great that it might unpick my sense of security.

This book cannot answer questions arising directly from the Stephen Lawrence case; and yet, those who wish to understand why young black men are murdered by young white men shouting racist epithets should find some clues here. Since the murder of Kelso Cochrane in 1959 there have been more than ninety murders where racism is known, or widely believed, to have focused violence on black or Asian people,[4] and where racist individuals and organizations have crowed

---

[2] See Sir William Macpherson of Cluny (advised by Tom Cook, The Right Reverend Dr John Sentamu & Dr Richard Stone.) *The Stephen Lawrence Inquiry*. CM 4262-I. Also available on the internet at *http://ww:official-documents.co.uk/document/cm42/4262/4262.htm.*; Richard Norton-Talyor (ed.) (1999), *Colour of Justice*, London: Theatre Communication Group; Brian Cathcart (1999), *The Case of Stephen Lawrence*, Viking.

[3] See pp. 8–12, this volume.

[4] See p. 59, this volume.

and gloated over the deaths and desecrated their memorials. Murder is among *the* most horrendous of crimes, but any discussion of violent racism must link the extreme with the 'everyday'. In that sense, the murder of Stephen Lawrence symbolizes not only the scores of black and Asian people who have been murdered by racists in Britain, but also the thousands of others who, day-in, day-out, are intimidated, abused, and assaulted just because of the colour of their skin.

Although *Violent Racism* does not examine the details of the failed investigation, reinvestigation, internal review, or public inquiry into the murder of Stephen Lawrence, readers familiar with the Lawrence case will experience *déjà vu*. The tale of inept investigation, unwillingness to arrest perpetrators, failure to provide information to victims and their families, denial and dismissal encountered by Neville and Doreen Lawrence is anticipated by the experience of other families and the wider communities who have been the targets of violent racism over the decades. One is forced to ask: 'how much has changed?' The image of the resolute protesters outside the Houses of Parliament in 1959 holding placards asking 'Who Killed Kelso Cochrane?' still resonates powerfully today, forty years later. As the evidence in the book shows, the collective failure of the authorities to respond effectively to the racist murder of Stephen Lawrence, far from being an isolated incident, is part of an enduring pattern.

The extent to which the Lawrence Inquiry, or the Macpherson report, will be seen as momentous, a 'turning point', or 'watershed' will be judged by history. It may be that the content of the report is far less significant than its symbolism. Irrespective of the content of the report, the extent of media coverage both during the inquiry phase,[5] the extraordinary level of public debate around the issues involved probably made the arrival of the report momentous. Although the publication of the report is a defining moment, the journey was more important than the destination. The breadth of issues that the murder of Stephen Lawrence drew into the debate also gives the report a presence. It covered not only racist violence but police powers, competence and personnel; the handling of witnesses and suspects, serious crime investigation, corruption, surveillance, eye witness testimony, first aid, stop and search, prosecution practice, balancing the rights of victims

---

[5] The entire process took 18 months from July 1997 when the inquiry was announced until the publication of the report in February 1999. During this period, the inquiry regularly made front page news in British daily newspapers and filled column inches of editorial, commentary and letters to the editor.

and suspects, training, police accountability, and leadership. It examined, most fundamentally of all, the basic conceptions of fairness and justice. The Lawrence Inquiry report has acted as a lightning-rod, drawing down and focusing energy from diffuse, private grievances and frustrations, transforming them into highly charged issues of public policy.

Of all the issues tackled by the inquiry, those which form the subject matter of this book—violent racism, victimization, and policing—were placed under a spotlight of unprecedented intensity. Of course, there have been moments before when anxiety about some of these issues has become the focus of great public debate, as this book shows, 'moral panic' about 'race' and policing has flared sporadically. In the recent period, the Scarman Inquiry is probably the nearest equivalent examination of policing practice. Both were set up under relevant Police Acts[6] which allow a panel of inquiry to take evidence orally and in writing. They require police officers and other public officials to account for themselves in an open forum. They also provide a focus for individuals and organizations, local and national, to articulate their experiences in writing and submit them for examination. For both Scarman and Lawrence, the issues of central concern related in some sense to a failure in policing. Each inquiry probed established police procedures and the extent to which paper policies have been carried out into practice. They have brought to the surface fundamental issues concerning police powers, competence, accountability, personnel, and training.

The events which triggered the inquiries are quite different, however. The Scarman Inquiry was ordered by then Home Secretary, William Whitelaw, two days after some of the most serious riots on mainland Britain this century. During the 'temporary collapse of law and order' in Brixton on 10–12 April 1981, at least 350 people were injured, 107 vehicles and 145 premises were damaged or destroyed, many by fire. Scarman's deliberations were given added urgency by the rioting that flared again across the country that July. That inquiry was concerned primarily with the police failure to handle conflict and public disorder that resulted from oppressive policing and the collapse of consent. By contrast, the Stephen Lawrence Inquiry came about five years after the murder[7] not because of any governmental sense of

---

[6] Scarman was authorized by William Whitelaw under Section 32 of the Police Act 1964 (see Scarman, 1981). The Lawrence Inquiry is the first public inquiry authorized under section 49 of the Police Act 1996.

[7] The Lawrence Inquiry started taking evidence on 16 March 1998, a month short of five years after the murder.

urgency but through the relentless campaigning of Neville and Doreen Lawrence and their supporters in the face of official indifference and denial.

The publication of the Lawrence inquiry is, for many people, a land-mark during a period of unprecedented introspection, examination, reflection, and catharsis. It has been a painful process, not least for the Lawrence family. The six years after Stephen's death have been a con-stant struggle to unearth details of their son's last moments and what went wrong with the investigation. All right-thinking police officers will feel ashamed at what has been revealed. No one who aspires to be professional or even workmanlike could desire to fail so abjectly. Some, if not all, of the apologies given by senior police officers suggest that this has been a humbling experience for them. It is surely right that the police—indeed any public body—should be subject to close exam-ination of their policies, procedures, and practices when things go wrong. It must also be right that in the search for explanations, not only are acts and omissions carefully scrutinized and documented, but also the attitudes, beliefs and ethos of the organizations upon which all of us, ultimately, may have to rely upon for protection.

The Lawrence Inquiry took evidence from 88 witnesses over 69 days of public hearings and received 148 written submissions amounting to more than 100,000 pages of documentary evidence. The report concluded that the failure of the investigation was the result of 'professional incompe-tence, institutional racism and a failure of leadership by senior officers'.[8] It documented failing in the provision of first aid, lack of direction and orga-nization in the initial response, lack of imagination, coordinated action, and planning to search for suspects, insensitive, and unsympathetic treat-ment of Mr and Mrs Lawrence as the victim's family and Duwayne Brooks as a victim of attack. In short, there was a series of fundamental flaws in the conduct of the investigation. Widening its scope to focus on the 'matters arising' from the murder of Stephen Lawrence, the report identified an absence of confidence and trust between the police and ethnic minority communities. This was a consequence of not only a failure to respond properly to violent racism, but more widespread concern about the inequitable use of stop and search powers, deaths in police custody, racial discrimination, and a lack of openness and accountability. In summary, the experience of the black community was described as being 'over policed . . . and under protected'.[9]

[8] *The Stephen Lawrence Inquiry*, 317.
[9] David Muir, representing Black Church Leaders, cited at paragraph 45.7, p. 312.

The report made seventy recommendations, which, taken together, amount to one of the most sweeping sets of proposals for reform in the history of British policing, certainly the most extensive in the history of the relationship between the police and ethnic minority communities. Its starting-point was a recommendation that a ministerial priority should be declared to 'increase trust and confidence in policing among ethnic minority communities' through the elimination of racist prejudice and disadvantage, and the demonstration of fairness in all aspects of policing. To achieve this a long list of recommendations followed including an invigorated inspection regime, and the application of freedom of information and anti-discrimination legislation to the police service. The report recommended improvements in the definition, reporting, recording, investigation, and prosecution of racist incidents; in first-aid training, family liaison, the handling of victims and witnesses, and training in awareness of racism and cultural diversity. Further recommendations concern employment, recruitment and retention policies, handling discipline, and complaints; and the regulation of stop and search powers. Finally, it went beyond the police service to make recommendations for prevention of racist violence in the wider sense, including the role of education. In an *Action Plan* published by Home Secretary's in response to the Lawrence Inquiry, 56 of the 70 recommendations were fully accepted, five were accepted in part and seven are to be subject to further examination.[10]

Recognition and acceptance of the challenges emerging from the Stephen Lawrence inquiry provides a starting-point to build a safer and fairer society. But it is only a starting-point and the success of the strategies' implementation cannot be predicted with any certainty. The Lawrence inquiry has generated new thinking about the principles of policing and of the standards by which we treat one another. It has provided evidence—from interview, observation and documentation—of quite extraordinary levels of incompetence compounded by institutional racism. The reporting of the evidence submitted to the inquiry, the television documentaries, interviews with key personnel, and the theatrical reconstruction of the inquiry have all involved the white population in a process of self-examination which will have been a unique experience for many people. Racism, after all, has created a barrier preventing white people from getting to know people of colour as personal friends and family.

[10] Home Office (March 1999) *The Stephen Lawrence Inquiry: The Home Secretary's Action Plan*. London: Home Office.

For the black and Asian communities, however, the inquiry has dis-covered little that was not already known or at least suspected. As *Violent Racism* shows, the experiences of assault and the failure of polic-ing have a long history. One can sympathize with Doreen Lawrence who said 'I was looking forward to the report, thinking that it would be a watershed for centuries to come, but instead it has only scratched the sur-face and has not gone to the heart of the problem.' There are also weak-nesses in the report. It has been characterized as poorly written, repetitive, and containing unnecessary evidentiary weaknesses. There are question marks remaining about the process of the inquiry and even the preparation and presentation of the report. The distribution of the report's Appendices including names and addresses of informers was a terrible mistake. Most of the people who toiled over the thousands of pages of evidence (often painstakingly researched) to submit to the inquiry will have been shocked to see the six pages that comprised Part II of the document. This material was replete with statements of principles, evidence, and recommendations for action that are not reflected any-where in its 335 pages.

Most fundamentally, however, the Lawrence Inquiry lacks a coherent analysis of the problem of violent racism and the failures of the state response to it. Despite the extraordinary amount of evidence taken orally and in writing, and the extensive list of 'publications seen by the inquiry', the report fails to set the murder of Stephen Lawrence in context. No account is taken of the history of violent racism or of the experience more generally of the ethnic minority communities in Britain. There is no analysis of the meaning of racism as a political ideology, as a 'common sense' set of beliefs nor of the discrimination and disadvantage that result. Consequently, the reader is forced to turn to other sources to fill the analytical void. It is my hope that this book will provide a context for the Lawrence Inquiry report and its recommendations.

*   *   *

Shortly after the hardback edition of *Violent Racism* was published, I was contacted by two police Superintendents charged with drafting Scotland Yard's response to Part II of the Lawrence Inquiry who asked for my advice. Their first question put me on the spot: 'In your book you say that police officers need to be *anti-racist* in order to provide a fair response to ethnic minority victims in general and to victims of violent racism in particular.' 'What do you mean,' I was pressed, by 'anti-racist policing?' What indeed? It was one of those terrifying moments in academic life when a practitioner signals their intention to act on your advice. Since then, I have thought hard about the question of what is to be done to remove racism from policing. My tentative recommendations are set out below.

The first requirement for the development of anti-racist practice must be a recognition and acknowledgement that racist prejudice exists among individual police officers and its organizational culture, and that such prejudice results in racist discrimination in routine operational practices. Some police officers have sympathy with extreme racist political movements and there are probably some racist activists within the service who have simply been careful who they reveal their activities to. Although the observational study of the police in action conducted by the Policy Studies Institute (PSI) is now nearly two decades old,[11] many of the police officers who were freely expressing extreme racism in 1981 are probably still in the job. Some will be experienced constables and sergeants guiding the next generation, while others will have moved into middle and senior management positions.

Looking beyond the dispositions of individuals, there remains evidence of the existence of widespread racist assumptions, prejudice, and stereotyping in the culture of the organization. The evidence set out in this book suggests that many police officers are not only *not opposed* to racism, but actually share the values of the racists who are making life hell for black and Asian people.[12] Some empathize with the white man who 'resents having *his* area taken over', and, to a lesser extent, with white 'yobs' who feel that 'the system' which should be working for *them* was working also for black communities.[13] Some officers think it is 'despicable' when Asian people speak their mother tongue, and that 'failing to adapt' to English customs and appearance—wearing traditional clothes, for example—renders them both 'threatening' and 'vulnerable'.[14] These racist attitudes and prejudices are clearly reflected in the behaviour towards black and Asian victims, witnesses, suspects, employees, and the general public.[15]

Compounding the effects of individual and cultural racism, is the racism which is built into the policies and practices of the organization—*institutional racism*. This is the systematic discrimination against people from ethnic minorities irrespective of the intent of individuals. It is to be found in the way in which colour is viewed as grounds for suspicion, in the stereotyping of African Carribean people as lazy, dangerous, and

---

[11] See Smith and Gray (1983).   [12] See pp. 253–6, this volume.
[13] See p. 253, this volume.   [14] See pp. 254–5, this volume.
[15] See pp. 294–8, this volume.

criminal, and Asian people as shifty, untrustworthy, and devious. And it can be seen in such outcomes as black and Asian victims being left dissatisfied with how the police handled their cases, about how well informed they were, and what action (or lack of it) is taken.[16] The consequence of individual, cultural, and institutional racism is a failure to deliver either a *quality service* or *equality* of service.

Formally at least, the problem of institutional racism has been recognized by Chief Police Officers and the Home Office. As the Home Secretary commented, in response to the inquiry finding that the Met was institutionally racist: 'In my view, any long-established, white-dominated organization is liable to have procedures, practices and a culture that tend to exclude or to disadvantage non-white people. The police service, in that respect, is little different from other parts of the criminal justice system—or from Government Departments, including the Home Office—and many other institutions.'[17] In a confessional style, John Newing, President of ACPO and Chief Constable of Derbyshire, wrote to the Lawrence Inquiry to admit not only institutional racism within the police service, but also his own personal racist attitudes and his own unfair, discriminatory behaviour.[18]

Having recognized that a problem exists, a second precondition for change must be an acknowledgement that there is no middle ground to the subject of racism. You are either for it or against it: to be neutral is to collude with racism. As bell hooks has so eloquently put it: 'all our silences in the face of racist assault are acts of complicity'.[19] Those police officers (and anyone else) who are not explicitly against racism, are implicitly for it. This does not mean that all claims to anti-racism can be accepted at face value. On the contrary, a questioning and critical approach to all such claims is needed. The point is that the neutral position, for so long that of the British state, has left black and Asian people unprotected and vulnerable to victimization. It has allowed such fundamental human rights as life, liberty and safety to be violated and has failed to provide redress when violations have occurred. Over the decades, as this situation has slowly come to light, it has seriously damaged the institutions of British society in the eyes not only of the black communities, but of the wider public in Britain and abroad.

[16] See pp. 235–8, this volume.
[17] *Hansard* 24 February, column 391.
[18] *The Stephen Lawrence Inquiry*, p. 32.
[19] hooks (1995: 19).

Now that individual, cultural, and institutional racism within the police service has been acknowledged, it must be addressed. Obviously, overtly racist individuals have no place in the British police and efforts to remove such people should be sustained and strengthened. It beggars belief that only six of the 444 complaints of racially discriminatory behaviour reported to the Police Complaints Authority in 1996/7 were sustained.[20] There is a need to challenge and change an occupational culture that tends to see ethnic minorities as 'a problem', subscribes to notions of racial superiority, inferiority and exclusion, sustains racial prejudice and stereotyping, and denies ethnic minorities' experiences of racism. Most fundamentally, there is a need to tackle insititutional racism in policing in order to stop police practices from disadvantaging people from ethnic minorities. The challenge is to develop anti-racist practice by articulating the principles against which the organization is to be judged and then holding police leaders rigorously to account on its record in adhering to those principles.

Anti-racist practice is founded on the ethical responsibility for institutions to act in ways consistent with the democratic principle of *equity*, enshrined in Article 14 of the 1950 European Convention on Human Rights (ECHR)[21] and the 1965 International Convention on the Elimination of all forms of Racial Discrimination (ICERD).[22] This principle requires public authorities to examine all aspects of organizational policies and practices to assess whether the *outcome* of the application of police powers, resources or discretion is to create or sustain patterns of discrimination. Where it is evident—from management statistics, for example—that the outcomes of organizational practices impact differently on people from ethnic minorities, this constitutes a *prima facie* case of discrimination. The burden of proof, for any organization claiming to be anti-racist, falls on the organization to demonstrate that the practice in question is *not* discriminatory and can be justified. Even if such a justification is demonstrated, it is still necessary to show that there is no alternative, but equally effective practice that is less likely to create or sustain disadvantage. Where practices are shown to be discriminatory, there is an ethical responsibility to take action, in the words of the

---

[20]   Home Office Statistical Bulletin 21/97 (Cotton and Povey).

[21]   The Council of Europe *Convention on Human Rights and Fundamental Freedoms (ECHR)*, 1950.

[22]   United Nations (UN) *International Convention on the Elimination of all forms of Racial Discrimination* (ICERD), 1965. See, for a detailed overview, Michael Banton (1996) *International Action Against Racial Discrimination*, Oxford: Clarendon Press.

ICERD, to 'amend, recind or nullify' such practices.[23] By definition, organizations seeking to be 'anti-racist' must actively work towards eliminating racism. Tackling systemic discrimination requires a systemic analysis and transformation of taken-for-granted principles and institutional practices.

In order to re-orient policing towards the human rights values and the principle of equity, policing skills, competencies, and 'operational common sense' need to be examined rigorously to ensure that services to a diverse public are *appropriate*, *relevant* and *accessible*.[24] Colour-blind' practices must be adapted so that they recognize that public institutions serve a diverse society in which people have different needs and experiences. This commitment means reinventing the notion of 'police professionalism' emphasizing that 'quality of service' must meet the needs of a diverse society through creating genuine partnerships between the police and all sections of the community.

There is a clear and direct link between equality of opportunity within the organization and the quality of service delivered to the public.[25] Developing a police service which more closely reflects the population it serves is an important goal in its own right, but is also a means to the end of improving service provision. This implies the need for a new ethos, based on the values of democracy, respect for human rights, quality and equality of service, diversity, continuous improvement, and openness.

The 'post-Lawrence' environment provides an exceptional opportunity to enhance and invigorate the accountability of the British police service. The Lawrence Inquiry called the police, government, and many others to account for their actions in this individual case. The future holds the possibility for that degree of accountability, on an ongoing basis. Systems of monitoring and accountability are needed to enable managers to explain what actions are taken in specific cases, why operational (both tactical and strategic) decisions are taken and what results are achieved. When something goes wrong, those affected should be informed and receive apologies and redress without having to spend years campaigning.

Creating a fully independent complaints authority or ombudsman must surely now be an urgent priority. The Government's *British Social Attitudes* survey showed that only 3 per cent of the public disagree that

[23] ICERD Article 2 (c).
[24] See: Bowling, B. (1991), 'Ethnic minority elderly people: helping the community to care', *New Community*, vol. 17, no. 4. July (1991), 645–52.
[25] Her Majesty's Chief Inspector of Constabulary (1997), *Winning the 'Race': Policing Plural Communities* London: Home Office. Black Police Association (1998), *Submission to part II of the Stephen Lawrence Inquiry*. London: BPA.

the police should be investigated by an independent body rather than the police themselves.[26] It has been said that complaints procedures are the 'touchstone' of police accountability. The ability to complain and to receive redress when officers behave badly, abuse their powers or simply make mistakes, is central to future good practice as well as confidence and trust in the organization. There should be the capacity to complain to a fully independent authority and complainants should have direct access to the legal process. A new independent authority, staffed with trained investigators, should be charged with enforcing anti-discrimination law by responding to complaints and through its own self-generating investigations. When inappropriate or unlawful practices are uncovered, systems for redress should be open, accessible and speedy.

The post-Lawrence environment also creates new opportunities for real openness. Such processes as lay oversight of recruitment, promotion boards and training, police policy-making, implementation, compliance, complaints, and discipline, must be enacted. There is an opportunity for lay advisors to be introduced at all levels and in all areas of specialization. There is no reason for the police to be a closed organization. The decisions taken affect everyone, and we all have a stake in good policing. If the doors of the organization are being opened up to people who are outspokenly critical to observe, monitor and scrutinize police practices, then surely there must be a responsibility on the critics to respond to that opportunity.[27]

Of course, the bottom line of an anti-racist policing strategy is effective service delivery to, and equal protection of, a diverse public. Improvements in the way in which victims are treated, their satisfaction with the service provided, and confidence in the police and local authorities as guardians of community safety will be the ultimate tests of success. As I argue towards the end of this book, however, there is a need for a fundamental shift in focus from victims to offenders. This is not to undermine the efforts to improve victim services, but to suggest that in terms of crime reduction, offender-oriented strategies are required. It is encouraging that academic research has now turned its attention to racist offenders and the context within which offending occurs.

The Metropolitan Police Racial and Violent Crime Task Force led by Deputy Assistant Commissioner John Grieve, has taken on board many

---

[26] Tarling, R. and Dowds, L. 'Crime and Punishment' in Jowell, *et al.*, *British Social Attitudes* (1997: 206). London: National Statistics.

[27] For an alternative, and more sceptical view, see Eugene McLaughlin and Karim Murji, 'Drawing Lines in the Sand: The Stephen Lawrence Report', *Critical Social Policy*, Summer 1999.

of the lessons described above and has adapted to the 'new agenda' of anti-racist practice, commitment to principles of human rights and ethical policing.[28] Central to the Task Force approach to tackling offending is the use of an intelligence-led model.[29] In this context it enables the police to identify who are responsible for violent racist acts, how they operate, how they relate to each other and how they select their victims. With this information to hand, it may be possible to identify where attacks are most likely to take place and where preventive resources should be targeted. A wide range of sources of intelligence can be drawn on—internal and external. Recorded crime and emergency call data can be mapped geographically and mined to search for patterns of repeat victimization and offending. External sources—particularly 'open' sources of publicly available information—can also be drawn into this ambit. Research and intelligence, properly collected, evaluated, synthesized, and disseminated within clear protocols can assist in developing new knowledge about prevention. This process may also lead to détente between the police and monitoring groups who hold in their files detailed information about violent racists as well as the effectiveness, integrity and equity of policing.

*   *   *

I am sceptically optimistic that the vision of an 'anti-racist police service' will become a reality. I am sceptical because the talk about change within the police organization has come about after too much reluctance, resistance, and denial to accept the stated commitments at face value. Moreover, the political will properly to protect black and brown-skinned English people has been unreliable. Even once we have gone beyond dismissal and denial to acknowledgement, acceptance, and a willingness to change, organizations, their cultures, and practices rarely transform as planned. Even with the clearest of mission and all the will in the world, plans fail, are blocked, have unwanted consequences, and get overtaken by events. I am optimistic because a commitment to anti-racist practice

[28] Metropolitan Police (1999), *Action Guide to Race/Hate Crime*. Consultation Draft, April 1999, London: Metropolitan Police.

[29] Intelligence is the organization of verifiable information, known in advance, based on specified assumptions, drawn from various sources, which can initiate a course of action. See n. 28 (above).

[30] See, for example, the commitments made by Paul Boateng, MP (Minister of State), Sir Paul Condon, Commissioner of Police of the Metropolis and Denis O'Connor, Assistant Commissioner with responsibility for policing diversity reported in Metropolitan Police *Working Together Towards and Anti-Racist Police Service*, Report of Conference 18 December 1998. London: Metropolitan Police.

has now been made at the highest level,[30] and there is some evidence that change is already in progress. The lay advisory group to the Metropolitan Police Racial and Violent Crime task force has the potential for external scrutiny along the lines I have suggested and it could be replicated at all levels within that organization and in police services elsewhere. If we are to see change in the way in which policing is delivered, those committed officers who are champions of change need support and encouragement.

As I was writing this Preface in April 1999, three nail-bombs exploded in central London, each one targeting the centre of a minority community, leaving three people dead and more than one hundred people injured.[31] Such explosively violent racism underlines the need to envision and shape a police service which meets its responsibility to protect everyone according to their needs.

[31] The first bomb exploded at 5.36 p.m. on Saturday, 17 April 1999 in a crowded market in Brixton, south London, centre of one of London's African Caribbean communities; 39 people were injured (news report: *The Independent on Sunday*, 18 April 1999). The second bomb exploded almost exactly a week later at 5.57 p.m. on Saturday, 28 April in a market in Brick Lane, east London, centre of one of London's Asian communities; at least six people were injured. The third bomb exploded at 6.37 p.m. on Friday, 20 April in the Admiral Duncan pub, Soho, centre of London's gay community; three people were killed, 60 people injured, six critically (news report, *The Guardian*, 1 May 1999. A man was arrested on 1 May (news report: *The Observer*, 2 May 1999).

Acknowledgements

Without the help of a great number of people, this book would never have been written. First, I have to thank London School of Economics Professors David Downes, Michael Mann, Terence Morris, Robert Reiner, and Paul Rock, who saw me through the seven years I studied there. I would also like to acknowledge the financial support during this period provided by an LSE scholarship, the students' union hardship fund, the Home Office, and those who employed me as van driver, wine salesman, office cleaner, hospital domestic, research assistant and gerontologist. Special thanks are due to Jim Sheptycki, friend and constant intellectual travelling companion for more than a decade. He discussed every thought and read every word in the book, and almost turned me into a sociologist.

The North Plaistow Racial Harassment Project, which provided much of the material for the book, was made possible by the staff of the London Borough of Newham, West Ham Division of the Metropolitan Police, Newham Council for Racial Equality, and Newham Victims Support Scheme. Among the many helpful and informative people I met over the three years spent working in Newham, Scott Ballintyne, Mary John Baptiste, Cath de Concilio, Eltaz Bodalbhai, Monika Dixon, Dave Robertson, Jeff Jones, and Bill Ibbotson were among the most supportive. My greatest debt of all is to Bill Saulsbury who co-ordinated the project and co-authored its final report, supervised my work, and mentored my progress as journeyman through the no-man's land between the state and academia.

Throughout the period of the project and afterwards many colleagues in the (now defunct) Home Office Research and Planning Unit provided practical help and support in a variety of ways. Alec Ross deserves a special mention for his help with transcribing verbatim the experiences of the victims in the survey. The librarians at Queen Anne's Gate—especially Francis McCann—provided invaluable assistance. In preparing the book for publication, I am also grateful to colleagues at John Jay College of Criminal Justice, City University of New York and the University of Cambridge Institute of Criminology for their advice and support. Many of those already mentioned read various parts of the book and I am also grateful for the detailed comments made by Louise Brogan, Marian FitzGerald, Janet Foster, Loraine Gelsthorpe, Paul Gordon, John Lowman, Brian MacLean, Karim Murji, Robert Reiner, Eugene McLaughlin, Coretta Phillips, Justin Russell, Alice Sampson, Rae Sibbitt, David Smith, Kevin Stenson, Sandra Walklate, Colin Webster, and Rob Witte. Few, if any, of the academics, civil servants, local government officers, police officers, and others mentioned above will agree with everything I have written. I hope they will forgive me for the occasions on which I have failed fully to take account of their advice and criticism. Of course, I alone am responsible for the errors of fact and interpretation which remain.

To my family—particularly Claire Spencer, Chris Postins, Frank Bowling, Rachel Scott, Dan Bowling, Sacha Bowling, Ushi Bock, Humpty Sahmland, and Runi Hoffmeier—a massive thank you for providing me on various occasions with space, place, and time to write as well as encouragement and belief in me over the years. Loving thanks are due to my wife, Susanne Sahmland, for being the rock to which I am anchored.

Above all, I am indebted to the people whose experiences are described here and particularly to Ms J. and Mr A. I hope that sharing your experiences will enable others to understand the destructiveness of racism and its expression in violence. Above all, I hope it will promote a willingness to combat violent racism by whatever means is necessary.

BENJAMIN BOWLING
Cambridge, July 1997

Permissions

The author is grateful to the following copyright holders for their kind permission to reproduce work previously published in journals and edited collections. Chapter 2 is a revised version of 'The Emergence of Violent Racism as a Public Issue in Britain 1945–81' in P. Panayi (ed.) (1996) *Racial Violence in Britain*, reproduced by permission of Leicester University Press (a Cassell imprint), London. All rights Reserved. Chapter 5 is a revised version of 'Racial Harassment and the Process of Victimisation: Conceptual and Methodological Implications for the Local Crime Survey', originally published in the *British Journal of Criminology*, Vol. 33, No. 1, Spring (1993) (Crown copyright. Reproduced with the permission of the Controller of Her Majesty's Stationery Office. The views expressed are those of the author and do not necessarily reflect the views of Her Majesty's Stationery Office, the Home Office or any other government department.) The map in Figure 6.1, Chapter 6 is based on Ordnance Survey mapping with the permission of The Controller of Her Majesty's Stationery Office © Crown copyright Licence Number 399612. Some of the material presented in Chapter 7 appeared in 'Racial Harassment in East London' in Hamm, M. (ed.) (1994), *Hate Crime: International Perspectives on Causes and Control*, Cincinnati, OH: Anderson Publishing Co. and Academy of Criminal Justice Sciences.

Contents

Detailed Contents

List of Figures

List of Tables

1

Introduction

People differ about Quality, not because Quality is different, but because people are different in terms of experience. . . . to take that which has caused us to create the world and include it within the world we have created, is clearly impossible. That is why Quality cannot be defined. If we do define it we are defining something less than Quality itself [Pirsig, 1974: 244–5].)

I firmly believe that reality can be constructed in different ways, that these constructions may be incompatible and that there is no final way to determine which is truer and no procedure for choosing among these constructions of reality, because they are ideologies—that is, frameworks of interpretation where knowledge, values and ways of organising the world are inextricably interwoven [Rein 1976: 256].

As this book was researched it became apparent that almost everything about the subject of study was contested. There was even controversy over what it should be *named*. Here, Sir Kenneth Newman (Commissioner of Police of the Metropolis 1982–6) succinctly distinguishes the police-prefered terminology from that used by the Home Office and local authorities, respectively:

It has become common in discussing this subject for reference to be made not only to 'Racial *Incidents*' but also to 'Racial *Attacks*' and 'Racial *Harassment*'. I have therefore set out the present definition of a Racial Incident . . . in order to remove any existing misconceptions [Metropolitan Police, 1986a: 1, original emphasis].

Alternatives not mentioned by the Commissioner (but widely used at the time) include 'racist violence', 'racist attacks, or 'racist harassment' and 'racial terrorism', all terms preferred by anti-racist and police monitoring organizations as well as some academic researchers. At first the issue seems to be one of semantics: these nouns do sound similar, and it is tempting to proceed on the assumption that, really, 'we all know we are talking about' and that terminological differences are irrelevant.

It is contended in this book that the terms 'racial incident', 'racial attacks', 'racial harassment', and 'racist violence' are, for conceptual and practical purposes, as different from each other as the police, the Home Office, local government, and anti-racist organizations are themselves different. The process of naming the problem is not simply a matter of semantics but reflects the intensely political process of conceptualization. Reading the policy documents produced by various statutory agencies, one is struck by the way in which the issue of violent racism has been transformed by each agency into its own image (see Chapters 2 and 3). The discourse used by these agencies and their officers (see Chapter 6) indicates that these competing terminologies have deep micro-cultural roots, have emerged historically within different social spaces, and are indicators of quite different frameworks of language and experience.

The most extraordinary example of this transformation is the rudimentary police definition of a 'racial incident'—in existence from 1978 but not made public until 1982—which covered 'an incident involving concerted action by or against members of an ethnic group [including] *such* action which is directed against the police' (Home Office, 1981, emphasis added). At first this may seem bizarre. How could the police (apart from ethnic minority officers) be targets of violent racism? Are police officers, as a group, confronted with ideologies that cast them as racially inferior, a 'social problem', and objects of racial hatred. Are they faced with practices of exclusion, harassment, intimidation, and expulsion that have been the cumulative experience of ethnic minorities in Britain? The evidence would say no to these questions, and yet it is clear from official reports of the early 1980s that the police *did* actually conceive of themselves, and indeed the white community as a whole, as target for 'racial' violence. 'Racial', for the police, did not denote the existence of racist ideologies of practices, but simply the involvement of people from ethnic minorities. Any incident involving such people thus became 'racial', or *racialized* in the terms used by sociologists of racism.[1]

The problem of defining the subject recurred throughout the period of study. For example, while the local authority at a corporate level defined the problem in a different way from the police, further definitions existed among different local authority agencies—such as housing, social services, and the schools. Reviewing research studies

[1] See, e.g., Miles and Phizacklea, 1984; Solomos, 1988, 1989; Smith, 1989; Miles, 1989.

and reports led to a proliferation of concepts and definitions; every organization commenting on the subject conceptualized the problem differently, each perspective implying different causes and prescriptions. Evidently, there exist competing versions of reality within each local and central state agency and looser social groups within the community. These 'different realities' ('true' in their own terms perhaps) are in conflict with one another.

Observations of this kind and the implications they have for an objective science of society have been grappled with by many researchers, theorists, and novelists. Both Robert M. Pirsig and Martin Rein, quoted at the beginning of this Introduction, suggest that the personal biographies, ideologies, frames of reference, values, and experiences of the observers inevitably influence the way in which they construct reality—how they define what is *good* and what is *not good*, for example. This suggests that it is important to investigate subjective experience (Ellis and Flaherty, 1992), but does not resolve the problem of determining which of several competing discourses is 'true' or, at least, 'truer'. Martin Rein (1974) argues that there may be no procedure for choosing among different versions, or constructions, of reality 'because they are ideologies' (Rein, 1974). The existence of multiple paradigms or value frameworks upon which a social problem is constructed poses a problem for the notion of neutral or value-free social science and policy analysis. If it is accepted that the observer—researcher included—*inevitably* (and usually *implicitly*) brings to a subject his or her own conceptualization of a particular substantive matter the distinction between objective and subjective reality becomes very problematic. Social science, it might be alleged, simply objectifies or reifies the specific subjectivity of its author.

The question then becomes how do I, the researcher, or you, the reader, choose between competing social constructions of the problem and their attendant terminologies? How do we interpret information or suggest a course for future policy or practice when groups of individuals understand the social world in conflicting frameworks of interpretation? How is social action to be evaluated—its *value* determined—when value itself is contested? How, for example, is 'quality of service' to be assessed if quality cannot be defined?

One possibility is that 'in practice whatever group is dominant imposes its ideology upon others. Differing definitions and solutions are resolved by power' (Rein, 1974: 257). This is obviously problematic.

Notions of fairness and justice are negated if power is the final arbiter in conflicts of value and experience. It is especially important that a criterion for choice other than power is used in relation to violent racism because, as will become clear, there is often a great gulf between accounts of violent racism as experienced by its victims and as related by third parties. Since victims are frequently less powerful than those to whom they turn for help, it is clear that those who suffer would be the losers if selection among conflicting definitions, explanations, and solutions is made on the basis of power. Another possibility is to accept as natural and inevitable that there will be multiple paradigms, each providing a different system for interpreting truth and with only limited communication between those who hold different perspectives. Social science is then forced to make 'brute choice among them, without the benefit of criteria for choice' (Rein, 1976). Rein's suggested alternative is to 'tell relevant stories' emanating from each paradigm:

Advice giving is essentially a matter of choosing a relevant story which is about the circumstances and the particular values espoused by the person who needs to make decisions. This may take the form of supplying supporting evidence for what the policy makers want to do, or reassurance. More often the essential role of advice is to supply contradictory evidence, pointing out the limits of the policy makers' ideas or programmes, or speculating and, better still, supplying evidence, about the possibility of unanticipated consequences. Story-telling extracts the insights of particular paradigms from the paradigm itself and thus makes possible a multi-paradigmatic approach to policy analysis [Rein, 1976].

These stories can inform both the institutional communities about which they are told (i.e. police, central, and local government) and those non-institutional communities which would wish to bring about change in the response of those institutions.

Taking a leaf out of Rein's empirically and theoretically useful work,[2] this book attempts to explore the definitions, perceptions, and practices of different groups with a stake in the social construction of violent racism. In this book, information from different viewpoints is set out and an attempt is made to extract insight from the points where the accounts agree and where they conflict. In one sense this amounts to triangulation. Certain facts are argeed on by most, if not all, participants. It is a fact, for example, that the London Borough of Newham has consistently had among the highest number of

---

[2] See (1976) and (1983).

Table 1.1 *Racial incidents recorded by the police in Newham (1986–96)*

Year	Number of incidents
1986	208
1987	364
1990	249
1991	498
1992	525
1993	629
1994	599
1995	579
1996	502 (until end of October)

recorded racial incidents in the country (see table 1.1). It is also a fact that the number of racial incidents recorded by the police has increased steadily since such records were first published (see table 1.2). The explanation of what each of these facts means and how they are to be explained, however, are essentially contested and it is here that one can learn from convergent viewpoints.

To accept that there are many different 'versions of reality' does not mean to retreat into value relativism. Rein argues that the question marks which hang over the notion of value-free social science imply, and perhaps even require, that policy analysts and other social scientists make explicit their value framework and be specific about the values of the audience for whom their advice is intended. To this end this book is for people who believe that no individual should be judged, limited, or placed at risk of violence by his or her 'race' (aspects of his or her physical appearance and genealogy). In short it is for those who hold human rights paramount. In specific:

Universal Declaration of Human Rights Article 3: Everyone has the right to life, liberty and the security of persons[3].

Universal Declaration of Human Rights Article 2: Everyone is entitled to all the right and freedoms set forth in this Declaration, without distinction of any kind, such as race, colour, sex, language, religion, political or other opinion, national or social origin, property birth or other status.

---

[3] Universal Declaration of Human Rights, Arts. 2 and 3. See Brownlie, 1992; cited in Lapido, 1997.

Table 1.2 *Racial incidents recorded by the police in England & Wales, and Scotland*

| Year | England and Wales | | Scotland |
	Recorded incidents	Number of forces	
1984	1329	15	–
1985	1626	20	–
1986	4519	28	–
1987	2965	38	–
1988	4383	40	–
1989	5044	43	376
1990	6339	43	636
1991	7782	43	678
1992	7734	43	663
1993	9218	43	756
1993/94	10997	43	791(1994*)
1994/95	11878	43	–
1995/96	12199	43	832

*After 1994, Scottish forces move to recording these figures by financial year

To explain my position, it seems appropriate to acquaint the reader with specific aspects of my biography, to describe my personal orientation toward violent racism, and how this has changed during the period of study.

* * *

At the start of this study of violent racism, my conceptual vignette would comprise an Asian mother being stoned by a group of young men and boys somewhere in the East End of London or other distant and declining 'inner city' areas. My view at the outset was that violent racism occurred in places I had never been to, and involved people I had never met and with whom I could not identify. It was a problem from which I, personally, was distant and insulated. Although I had read what little I could find on the subject, I found it difficult to visualize what the violent racism consisted in and to put the research evidence into perspective. Indeed, in the first introduction to the study—which I naïvely wrote at the beginning—I commented that the distance between social researchers (including myself) and the subjects of their study tended to undermine insight into violent racism as it is *experienced*. Understanding that experience, I thought (and still think), is the key to understanding what the problem consists in from the point of view of the person affected. From a 'victim-oriented perspective', this experience *is* the problem for all practical purposes.

Over the period of study my understanding of racism and violence changed for a number of reasons, some directly related to conducting the research, others concerned with everyday life and reflection on past experience.

First, my perspective changed as a result of members of my family and me being confronted by racist insult and neo-fascist propaganda. During the period of the study my son (in the company of his mother), brother, and I were, on separate occasions, called 'nigger' on the street or underground. My father's studio was broken into and sprayed with a foot-high NF symbol in silver paint. On one occasion a man walked into Dixons on Victoria Street and yelled 'niggers!' at the top of his voice at the numerous black staff and shoppers. Conversations with colleagues and friends indicated that these were by no means isolated experiences. Forms of racism of this nature which lie on the border line of everyday understandings of 'violence'—call it incivility, aggression, or threat—appear to be part and parcel of everyday life for ethnic minorities even in relatively affluent parts of central London. Other forms—racist graffiti, for example (NF, BNP, Nordic symbols, and swastikas) may be observed and their message expressed and absorbed across the country on lavatory walls and railway bridges.

In 1990 my home in central London was leafleted by the Choice organization. The newspaper, *Choice*—sidelined 'Racialism is Patriotism'—was mainly composed of rants against any possible 'influx of Jews' from Eastern Europe, 'alleged Nazi War Crime' trials, and the 'Zionist ONE WORLD conspiracy' [*sic*]. Its aims, stated clearly on its back cover, however, relate mostly to opposing 'the full scale multiracial INVASION [*sic*] . . . of socially, culturally and racially incompatible people' which Britain is to be 'rid of . . . for all time' through a policy of repatriation.[4] Later in the same year my workplace at the Home Office in Queen Anne's Gate was leafleted by the same organization. This time *Choice* contained flyers from an

---

[4] This is a position roughly equivalent to that of the British National Party. Its manifesto reads: '[w]e are wholly opposed to any further non-white immigration into Britain, and we are pledged to carry out a programme whereby those immigrants and their descendant now living here are humanely resettled in the countries of ethnic origin' (BNP, 'Where we stand', leaflet undated but circa 1989/90).

organization called English Solidarity—another splinter of the extreme right. Among these leaflets were those which shouted in bold capitals 'Who's for repatriation?' and the one which touched the rawest nerve: 'multiculturalism mongrelises: half-castes are outcasts in all lands and all nations are degraded by it'.

These almost incidental experiences of racism in London together with the process of conducting the research for this book alerted me to experiences of violent racism from my youth. I am not sure now whether these experiences had been hitherto repressed or forgotten, or whether I had simply failed to recognize their significance or connection to the academic study in which I was engaged. Let us say simply that until conducting this research these childhood memories seem not to have occurred consciously to me since my late teens.

*   *   *

I was born in London in 1962 to a (black) British Guyanese father and a (white) English mother. I grew up in Clent, a small village in rural Worcestershire, with my mother in a flat perched on a hill look-ing south towards Malvern and the Welsh Black Mountains to the West. I remember my early childhood as being happy and carefree, nurtured in the relative prosperity of middle England in the affluent 1960s. I am almost certain that the facts that my skin is brown and my hair curls were quite irrelevant to the vast majority of those I came into contact with in Clent. Although I could not fail to notice the difference in physical appearance between myself and most of my friends, it was not until much later in life that I became aware of the significance of my appearance to other people. At first, I assumed I was an English boy no different from any other. Like many English children I sang 'I vow to thee my country' in school assembly and learned the national anthem. In the scouts, I swore allegiance 'to God and to my Queen' and carried the English flag in the St George's Day parade.

I think that racism was absent in my junior school experience. The head teacher was a firm and fair man who made it clear that bully-ing of any kind was unacceptable in his school. I do remember a cou-ple of playground rhymes, however, which are related below. The first is a cautionary tale and the second an adaptation of a football chant:

I was walking in the park one day,
in the merry, merry month of May,
I was taken by surprise,
by a skinhead twice my size,
so I kicked him in the balls and ran away.

Patched up Levi's, clip on braces,
Doctor Martins, leather laces,
We are the boys who'll smash your faces,
We are the Clent boot-boys!

At middle school, aged 11 or 12, I have the first clear memory of being silenced by a racist remark—'black bastard!'—by a school friend in an argument during a football game. From around this time, and certainly by the time I was at high school, references to my skin colour were common among friends and enemies alike. From friends the racist insults were jocular, ironic, and apologetic—'got a black milkman?', 'don't take any notice of him, he's black', 'he is a nig-nog but don't hold it against him', 'shut up or I'll give you a white eye and a thin lip'. Throughout my secondary schooling, a constellation of racial epithets was used on a daily basis. The use of 'blackie', 'chocolate drop', and 'jungle bunny' were used often casually and even without malice, though they had the power to demean and exclude and were used instrumentally at times. More obviously exclusionary were the countless times I was told to 'go back to the jungle!' or 'back to your own country!' I even became known variously as 'Kunte Kinte' or 'Chicken George' after Alex Haley's epic mini-series 'Roots' was shown on British TV for the first time. I suspect that these experiences are common to many black people of my generation, especially those who were relatively isolated from other people of colour (see Troyna and Hatcher 1992).

Whatever the pain these casual, even 'friendly', remarks may have caused me, the everyday racism of my enemies was far more violent and vicious. I have strong memories of three bullies in particular who had an extraordinarily wide vocabulary of racism which drew on the language of Enoch Powell, the National Front, 'Till Death Us Do Part', 'Love Thy Neighbour', and other TV shows, skinhead songs and the white racism of the US Confederate south. Among their repertoire were 'Sambo', 'coon', 'boy', 'wog' and 'nigger'. Accompanying their verbal abuse were kicks, jostles, and punches and 'dead-legs'—sometimes delivered playfully, sometimes to hurt.[5] I should add that although these violent forms of racism were perpetrated by other pupils, I did encounter explicit racism from school staff. The instance which sticks best in my memory is being asked early in my French GCE 'O-Level' oral examination 'Quand veux-tu revenir à votre pays d'origine?'. I understood the examiner's words, but not at first what he meant. As his question sank in it delivered a shattering blow. Even adults, even teachers, echoed 'go back to your own country'. But this *is* my country! I was born here. I *am* English.

In 1979, I was 17, the NF was at its strongest politically, and skinhead style was enjoying a revival as the sub-cultural expression of youthful violent racism. Walking to the pub one evening with about eight male and female schoolfriends on Stourbridge high street we were confronted by a group of, perhaps, ten skinheads. They were dressed in Harrington jackets (black or red with tartan lining), eleven-hole Doctor Marten boots which were met at the top of the calf by jeans hitched up by clip-on braces. Shaven heads and hard as nails. They barred our way, gathering around us menacingly. "What is *that?*" asked the one of the group, pointing to me. "What the fucking hell is *that!?*" We all stood still and silent. Seconds ticked by painfully. Then the tension broke and the skinhead who had spoken laughed a raucous and hateful laugh and struck up a song consisting of one line repeated over and over to tune from the terraces—"what the fucking hell is that?!"

The third sense in which this research has caused me to re-evaluate my own experience as a brown-skinned English person is that the study itself meant the investigation of the history and cultural life of ethnic minorities in Britain and the reaction to them from politicians, the media, and the white public. To read English history is, as an English person, to read the history of oneself. To learn the history of England in the 1960s and 1970s, for example, is to gain insight into what influences during this period shaped one's own experience culturally, socially, economically and politically. The closer the history to one's own experience the greater the likelihood of finding references to oneself in that history. I could not avoid, therefore, seeing my 6-year-old self as one of Powell's 'grinning piccaninnies' living somewhere in the West Midlands in 1968. Reading about the politics of race and the violent expression of racism during the 1970s led me

---

[5] These bullies had other targets too—on one occasion they hospitalized a tall boy they said was 'a poof' (i.e. homosexual) with a vicious kick in the testicles.

for the first time to understand fully the wisdom of my mother's caution to avoid Wolverhampton and Smethwick, where racism was so rife and vicious. Similarly, confronting (no less today) disgusted references to racial impurity and plans for repatriation of the 'descendants' of the 'invasion' is a disturbing experience.

There have been times during the study that reading often frightening and offensive material and listening to people's experiences of violent racism has led to feelings bordering on paranoia. Any sense of complacency about the problem of violent racism and the vulnerability to it of me and my family has gone. Reconnecting my experiences with the history of English racism and with contemporary black experience is both disturbing and empowering.[6] Gaining some understanding of the connections between 'personal troubles' and public issues is a source of power in the sense that it is no longer neccessary to face these troubles in isolation. But the process is disturbing because of the implication that English ethnic minorities (and white people who associate with them) will remain vulnerable to violent racism for the foreseeable future.

The ultimate conclusion from these diverse but interconnected experiences is that whatever my claim to Englishness (and that of other black and brown English people), there is a substantial body of opinion which would refute it—and is prepared to use violence to do so. Indeed, the very notions of blackness and Englishness remain today mutually exclusive social and cultural categories (Gilroy 1993:58; cf Mullard, 1973). Without recourse to Englishness or another of Britain's national identities—which privilege claims to *belong*, to be *of* Britain, 'one of us', only to white British people, the tenure and safety of ethnic minorities in specific localities and in the country as a whole remains conditional on the goodwill of the white majority.

I find myself therefore at the end of the journey into the heart of racist politics and practice, having learnt something about the public response to violent racism and something about myself. It was part of my social scientific training to conduct *objective* research: impartial, accurate, valid, and reliable, and this is what I have sought to

---

[6] I was struck, in particular, by newspaper articles relating the experience of black people and 'mixed-race' couples who are in the public eye. To take only a few examples, Bernie Grant has described the quite extraordinary stream of hate mail, excrement, and other offensive material that he received in the late 1980s as leader of Brent Council and later as MP. Lenny Henry and Dawn French were subjected to a campaign of hate mail and offensive material from the Ku Klux Klan, the National Front, and 'ordinary' racists. In January 1997, mixed-race couples were targeted with letter bombs by Combat-18 and Scandinavian neo-Nazis. Zerbano Gifford commented that to be a black person in the public eye is to be a target for racist violence.

achieve in this book. Objectivity and subjectivity are not mutually exclusive and the presence of one does not necessarily imply the absence of the other. For example (subjective) experience can be recorded (objectively). Moreover both subjective and objective knowledge are required to make sense out of the world. Facts—numerical and narrative records of occurent events—are unavoidable in daily life. And yet what they mean to a specific individual—*you the reader*, for example—is not knowable from the facts themselves. Meaning, interpretation, and emotion lie in the realm of lived experience, which is, by definition, subjective.

In my view, knowing something about the biography of the author and his or her personal perspective only makes it more obvious that the quantitative and qualitative data he or she presents must be accurately, rigorously and systematically recorded. Since the reader may—in his or her own interpretation of the research—take account of the researcher's distance from, or proximity to, his or her research subjects he or she will know where to look for bias.

* * *

Of course, this still leaves the question of choosing a terminology, which could amount to taking a position in the discursive battle among state and non-governmental organizations about what the problem is to be called and how it is to be defined. Instead of selecting among the terms listed (or ommitted) by Sir Kenneth Newman, I have used the each agency's prefered term when refering to its discourse or practice. That is: the term 'racial incident' is used when reporting on the ideas and actions of the police; 'racial attacks' when examining central government; 'racial harassment' for local government; and 'racist violence' when refering to non-governmental bodies such as police monitoring groups.

These terms—racial incidents, racial harassment, racial attacks, and racist violence—all draw attention to the sense that the problem is a specific form of incident, harassment, attack, or violence. In each case, the typology is concerned with a racial or racist *form* of a more general phenomenon that can take other forms—domestic, sexual, political, sectarian, ethnic, mysogenistic, homophobic, etc. This is one way of looking at the problem, and it is to be expected that agencies—such as the police—would be concerned about broader phenomena—crimes and other incidents—of which the '*racial*' or '*racist*' ones would be among several different types. The police are charged with responding to generic incidents (of violence), and for many practical purposes, the precise *type* of violent incident (e.g. what motivated its perpetrators) is irrelevant. Similarly, local authorities are responsible for dealing with many different kinds of harassment among which specifically *racial* harassment is only one. This is not to say that 'racist' or 'racial' violence has nothing to do with other forms of violence. On the contrary, there are manifest connections between various forms of violence. The point is that this book is not centrally concerned with racist violence as a sub-category of violence. Indeed, it does not advance a theory of violence *per se*. That would be quite a different, and much more ambitious, project. Instead, this book is centrally concerned with *racism in its various forms, especially its violent form*. In other words, this book is about a specific form of racism rather than a specific form of violence.

The choice of the term *violent racism* is intended to reflect this shfit in contextual, descriptive, and explanatory focus. Specifically, the notion of violent racism allows the connections between racist discourses, exclusionary practices, and experiences of violence to be explored. Subtle forms of racism, such as casual epithets, racist jokes, and other forms of subtly exclusionary behaviour, can thus be reconnected with racism expressed in the form of aggression and violence. What unites all of these experiences is their root in the language and behaviour of racist exclusion.

* * *

In 1988 I gained employment as a researcher on what became known as the North Plaistow project. The project involved the Home Office, the Metropolitan Police, the London Borough of Newham, Victim Support, and the local Council for Racial Equality working 'in partnership' to develop and co-ordinate a comprehensive response to racial harassment in a small study site. The job would entail, at the start of the project, acting as a 'technical resource' to the project—feeding in research information to the decision-making process. At the end I would, with the project facilitator, evaluate the effectiveness of the new 'multi-agency approach' and write a final report (see Saulsbury and Bowling, 1991). Within a short period of time I found myself collecting information from police records, interviewing police and local government officers, and designing a victimization survey.

After a few months, on the advice of my supervisors at the London School of Economics and Home Office, I decided to use material collected in east London for my doctoral research. I was in the field, at last. However, combining (and separating) the roles of academic resarcher with project researcher was not straightforward. Using the experience and material gathered during involvement in an action-research project for the basis of an academic study limited my ability to control the conduct of the research. The data-collecting process—the design of instruments, methods of data collection, the mode of analysis, interpretation, and (initial) presentation—was strongly influenced by the organizations involved in the project. Much of this work was conducted by, or at least originated in, a committee comprised of representatives from each of the state and voluntary organizations involved. These combined tasks ruled out the use of a one-dimensional methodological approach or theoretical framework. An eclectic and pragmatic approach was called for: one that could utilize material collected using a range of methods from a number of sources; that could use theory from several disciplines, particularly those examining micro-social processes; and that could evolve with the development of the job which I was employed to do[7]. The guiding social scientific principles were rigour in the collection, coding, analysis, and interpretation of data; and clarity and openness concerning its strengths and limitations.

*   *   *

Because of its genesis the aims and objectives of this research were not laid out in advance, but emerged and developed as it progressed. Indeed, it was not until the research was well advanced that it became clear how the subject of study was to be defined and what were the most relevant research questions to ask.

---

[7] The eclectic theoretical and methodological approach of this study may disappoint or irritate the purist. In borrowing ideas from various disciplines one runs the risk of over-simplification, misrepresentation, or failure to take account of the academic traditions from which theories and methods have emerged. Thus, sociologists, political scientists, social historians and others whose work I have drawn on will be able to identify weaknesses in the way in which I have used their work. Equally, statisticians, ethnographers, historiographers, and others will have methodological bones to pick with the approach adopted. In response, I can submit only that the nature of the research process in this instance required flexibility, pragmatism, and eclecticism. A consequence of exploring a tightly defined subject matter drawing on various methods and theories is that the researcher remains a theoretical and methodological generalist.

Clearly, the central concerns of the study are strongly influenced by the aims and objectives set out for the North Plaistow project and by the data collected during its life. As a consequence, an account of the phenomenon of violent racism and an analysis of the police response to it form the body of empirical data presented in the book. This material is used as a basis upon which to address such questions as: what is the extent and nature of violent racism? Who are the offenders and their victims? Is the police response effective? As I explored the subject independently, however, a range of secondary questions began to emerge. Among these were: why did government policy in this area begin to develop only in the 1980s? How are the striking contradictions between various accounts of the problem to be reconciled—particularly that between the police and black and anti-racist community organizations? Why did consensus that violent racism could be tackled only using a multi-agency approach emerge at this time, whose idea was it, and what was it supposed to achieve?

It became obvious that in order to understand the contemporary phenomenon, historical context was needed. And in order to understand the quality of the police response to the problem, an examination of the history and development of the policies which were currently in place was required. In order to make sense of the data, it was also necessary to examine the findings from east London in the light of previous academic studies. To provide this context, Part I comprises four chapters which review historical and sociological literature on violent racism and policing in the recent period; describe the events and pronouncements recorded in the national and local press during the 1980s; and examine the policy documents published by various statutory agencies from around the beginning of the 1980s.

Chapter 2 presents a history of racism and its expression in violence in Britain. It charts the racialization of political and policy debates after the Second World War and examines the emergence of violent racism as a public issue. This chapter shows that specific forms of racism are woven into the discourses and practices of British society. A core idea of 'new right' political discourse is that the British people constitute a 'race' or 'ethnic group', of which 'non-white' (i.e. dark-skinned) people from Britain's former colonies and elsewhere cannot be part. 'Ethnic minorities' have, in this formulation, no legitimate claim to belong to the island or to live on it. The extreme view asserts that 'racialism is patriotism' and advocates the 'humane resettlement' or repatriation of 'socially, culturally and racially incompatible people' to their countries of ethnic origin. These advocates of 'ethnic cleansing' for England may now seem to be very extreme, and yet in many ways they are not. The Dowager Lady Birdwood who was convicted in 1991 for distributing racist pamphlets and was alleged to be their author has the outward appearance of an ordinary little old English lady. On the other hand, recall that in the late 1960s, Enoch Powell, a former Conservative cabinet minister, advocated the creation of a Ministry for Repatriation to oversee the 're-emigration' of 700,000 British citizens. Although Powell's parliamentary career was irreparably damaged by his racist rhetoric of fear, loathing and rivers 'foaming with much blood', popular support for him and his ideas was widespread (Holmes, 1988: 265). The key 'race' issue in the 1960s and 1970s was which political party was most likely to keep immigrants out. As late as 1978, one in five electors regarded immigration as one of the two most urgent problems facing the country. The adoption of a strong stance against immigration was seen as a key reason for the success of the Conservative Party from 1978 onwards and of the electoral failure of the extreme right (Husbands, 1992).

Evidence from opinion polls in the 1950s and 1960s and survey research in the 1980s and 1990s suggest that a significant section of public opinion holds or agrees with racially exclusionary views (Husbands, 1983). At a local level this racial exclusionism has taken many forms, including active discrimination in public- and private-sector housing markets, for instance (Smith, 1989). The existence of an explicit (and later implicit) 'colour bar' in employment, places of entertainment, and in all areas of social life is well documented (Brown, 1984; Fryer, 1984; Hiro, 1991). The legacy of this discrimination on the basis of 'race' is evident in the segregated patterns of settlement across the country which exist to this day (Smith, 1983, 1993). Racism is imbued into the very fabric of English, British, European life, indeed into the ideas and acts of the entire territory of the European diaspora. The notions of superiority and inferiority are built into the very languages which (in)form personal and organizational practice. It is in this context that the instances of 'racial violence' must be understood.

Chapter 3 describes the 'discovery' of violent racism by central and local government and the police, and how each of these statutory agencies defined and constructed the problem during the early 1980s. This historical material offers some answers to the question why it was that violent racism became a public issue at the beginning of the

1980s. Certainly, there is evidence that during the period immediately preceding its gaining official recognition as a specific form of crime, the extent and ferocity of violent racism was unprecedented. The expression of public protest—in the form of the anti-racist and self-defence movements—also exerted an effect on public opinion and policy debates. Undoubtedly, the urban unrest which occurred at the end of the 1970s and early 1980s, the moral panic which surrounded it, and the public pronouncements which followed were influential. The end of the 1970s and early 1980s is also a period in which policing was politicized to an extent unknown in the twentieth century. The apparent failure to deal effectively with violent racism was only one issue among many for which the police were being criticized. In particular, ethnic minority communities were expressing considerable concern about policing in general. Moreover, the whole question of how the police should be held accountable to the community gained prominence. The legitimacy of the police claim to protect and serve impartially all members of society, and the legitimacy of their use of force to do so faced a serious, and often physical, challenge at this juncture.

Chapter 4 describes how this challenge to police legitimacy continued into the mid-1980s and examines the emergence of the multi-agency approach to racial violence, and of 'community policing' and 'co-ordinated crime prevention' more generally. The history of this development indicates that each of the agencies involved in the development of this approach—the police and Home Office at first, then, later, community relations councils and local authorities—had quite different aims and objectives for advocating co-ordination and collaboration. The stated objectives of the Home Office, local authorities, and community organizations were to improve police effectiveness, prevent police inaction and denial of the problem, and prevent violent racism itself. The key objectives for the police were to restore the confidence of, and to increase the exchange of information with, central government and local authorities, and to release the police from the position of sole or main responsibility for creating the social conditions which make racial incidents less likely. This chapter also examines the academic discussion of co-ordination in criminal justice and considers the likelihood that these competing objectives will be realized.

Drawing on literature in criminology, victimology, and the sociologies of 'race' and policing, Chapter 5 presents a conceptual frame-

work for the empirical study. Here it is argued that while victimization surveys, crime statistics, and the criminal law tend to treat racial
harassment and other forms of crime as though they were static
events or incidents, racist victimization does not occur in an instant
and is more dynamic and complex than the notion of a 'racial incident' can imply. The 'events-orientation' fails to capture the experience of repeated or systematic victimization; the continuity between
violence, threat, and intimidation; or the complex relationships
between all the social actors involved. It is argued that if racial
harassment and other forms of crime are to be described and
explained adequately and controlled effectively, they should be conceptualized as processes set in their geographical, social, historical,
and political context. Thus, surveys need to be complemented with
other methods of inquiry if the underlying social processes of victimization and policing are to be revealed.

Part II of the book comprises an empirical study of violent racism
and the police response to it, preceded by an introduction to the geographical, demographic, social, and economic characteristics of the
locality (Chapter 6). Chapter 7 presents the results of the analysis of
police records, interviews with local officers, and the victimization
survey conducted as part of the North Plaistow project. It describes
the nature, experience, and effects of the problem, patterns of victimization, and explores its relationship with racism and racial discrimination more generally. This chapter shows that the experience
of victimization is widespread among the ethnic minority communities. For some groups—notably Asian women—the effects of this victimization are profound. Only one in ten Asian women were not at
all worried about either themselves or their families being victimized.
It is evident that violent racism has a significant impact on how the
minority community in east London thinks, feels, and acts. The survey also discovered that white people reported victimization that they
saw as racially motivated. This finding and its implications are
explored and an attempt is made to set the experiences of different
ethnic groups into a broader social context.

Chapter 8 presents an analysis of policing policy and practice concerning racial incidents in the locality, drawing on police records,
group and individual interviews with police officers. It examines the
processing of racial incidents from attending the scene, investigation,
and follow up, through to prosecution and the calculation of clear-
up rates. These data are used to evaluate police performance with

respect to law enforcement, order maintenance, crime prevention, and the production and distribution of information. A consequence of legal, cultural, and organizational constraints—and the fact that these cannot be changed within local democractic structures—is that police protection of ethnic minority communities is precarious at best. Nonetheless, changes in police policy which have prioritized racial incidents have improved performance indicators such as clear-up rates. The implications of this paradox are explored.

Chapter 9, the conclusion, considers the extent to which policy and practice implemented in the late 1980s and early 1990s achieved the various objectives stated by the organizations which began to respond systematically to violent racism in 1981. An Epilogue, written after re-visiting the research site, brings the book up to date.

* * *

It is important to be clear at the outset where the boundaries of the study lie. The research consists principally of a case study of violent racism and the police response to it in an east London locality between 1988 and 1991, set in the context of recent history and policy development concerning this social problem in England. Comments on racism are restricted specifically to an English variant, though this should not be taken to mean that other *racisms* do not exist; they obviously do. The research does not look closely at the experiences of the Jewish community in Britain, neither at the violent racism to which its members have been subjected, the strategies which they have developed to defend themselves from it, nor the relationships which exist between the police and Jewish community leaders (see Factor and Stenson, 1989; Stenson and Factor, 1993; Jenkinson, 1996). Similarly, the book does not deal with attacks directed against white ethnic minority groups such as the Irish, Germans during the First and Second World Wars, or the eastern and southern European communities in the post-war period (see Sponza, 1996; Panayi, 1996). Homophobic violence, which also has its roots in notions of racial superiority and inferiority, was not examined in the present study. The book does not look specifically at the police as perpetrators of violent racism except to the extent that their failure to act may be construed as such. Although the study is concerned centrally with ideas of racial exclusionism, it contains few empirical data on the perpetrators of violent racism. Thus, the nature of the offenders' racism, and the connections between their behaviour, racist political parties, social movements, and notions of race and nation are not fully explored. Racism, racial exclusion, and violent racism are conceptualized from the victim's, rather than the offender's, perspective. Finally, the book says much less than it should about class and gender, and their inter-relationships with 'race'.

To what extent is it possible to generalize from a single case study? Like any case study, there are a series of atypicalities that make the present study distinctive and idiosyncratic (Yin, 1989). Undoubtedly, violent racism, policing practice, and co-ordinated action will differ where other social and political factors exist. It seems probable, nonetheless, that much of what was observed in this study will be found in other places in Britain and elsewhere. It is only by documenting such experiences that this will become clear. As Robert Yin (1989) argues, case studies require replication no less than surveys. Indeed, evidence from North Plaistow has confirmed observations from other research on violent racism (Hesse *et al.*, 1992), policing practice (Sheptycki, 1993), and co-ordinated crime-prevention initiatives (Hope, 1985; Weatheritt, 1986). Rather than claiming to have produced a definitive account of how violent racism is policed in all places at all times, on the basis of the North Plaistow experience pointers are offered—suggestions where both potential for, and constraints on, effective action may lie. As Martin Rein suggests, 'understanding . . . depends upon telling relevant stories: that is, deriving from past experience a narrative which interprets the events as they unfolded and draws a moral for future actions, suggesting, for example, how the future might unfold if certain steps were taken' (Rein, 1976: 265–6).

It is now for the reader to judge whether this book tells 'relevant stories' about violent racism, and what can be done about it.

I
Context, Concepts and Method

1

Context, Concepts and Method

2

The Emergence of Violent Racism as a Public Issue

Accepted wisdom about violent racism is that after a period of relatively successful integration of large numbers of black and brown people arriving in Britain from the former Empire, there was a sudden flare-up of violence between whites and 'non-whites' in the second part of the twentieth century. Identifying exactly when it became an issue of public concern—occurred for the first time, say—is not easy, though dates including 1958 and 1981 have often been suggested. Sadly, however, violent racism has a much longer history than this (Panayi, 1996). Records suggest that racism has taken a violent form—lynching, murder, fire-bomb, assault, harassment, intimidation, expulsion—throughout the history of ethnic minorities in Britain. Drawing on an analysis of English discourses of race and nation, the process of migration to Britain from the New Commonwealth and Pakistan, the development of explicitly racist and anti-racist political movements, the influence of racism on the political centre, and the extent of violent racism itself, this Chapter describes the 'prehistory' of violent racism and how it was eventually recognized to be more than simply a personal trouble of a few 'paranoid' and 'unreliable' immigrants.

Minorities, Racism, and Violence in Early British History

Historical documents indicate that white Britons have been ambivalent about the presence of dark-skinned minorities living on 'their' island. At various points in history significant numbers of people with origins in the Middle East, Africa, and Asia have settled here and have contributed to its economic, political, and social life. For at least 1000 years black and other ethnic minority people have lived here as merchants, soldiers, sailors, musicians, craftspeople, and domestic servants. In this sense British people have welcomed these people and have valued their contribution to the British economy and culture. At times, however, white Britons have turned against these minority individuals and communities. Black and brown people have been physically attacked by individuals and mobs, while the British government has gone as far as to expel them from the island. Some authors have suggested that the roots of this phenomenon are deep:

attacks have been inflicted on minority communities since they settled in this country. The massacre of 30 Jews in a riot in London after the coronation of Richard I in 1189 was followed by similar attacks in York, Bury St Edmunds, Norwich and Lincoln until the small Jewish community was expelled in 1290 [Nicholson, 1974; cited in Klug, 1982].

People of African, Asian, and Middle Eastern descent have formed a continuous presence in Britain since the reign of Elizabeth I. Towards the end of the sixteenth century, at the advent of the slave trade, it was beginning to be fashionable to have a black slave among the household servants of the titled and propertied classes in Britain. Other black people lived in Britain at this time as musicians and court entertainers. In 1596, Elizabeth I expressed her disapproval of the presence of black people by ordering their deportation: 'Her Majestie understanding that there are of late divers blackamores brought into this realme, of which kinde of people there are allready here to manie. . . . Her Majesty's pleasure therefore ys that those kinde of people should be sent forth of the land' (cited in Fryer, 1984: 11). It seems that this attempt to expel black people from Britain was unsuccessful, for again in 1601 Elizabeth issued a proclamation in which she commanded that the 'negars and Blackamoores . . . which are crept into this realme' should be 'with all speed' banished and discharged out of Her Majesty's dominions (Fryer, 1984: 12). Again, this attempted expulsion was largely unsuccessful and black people have lived in Britain ever since (Fryer, 1984; Hiro, 1991). The experiences of these early settlers from the British colonies of being seen as a people apart from the 'indigenous' British, being defined as a 'problem' and being threatened with repatriation are echoed in the history of 'race' and violent racism which unfolds in twentieth century.

Violent Racism 1919–48

Although dark-skinned people have been present in Britain in increasing numbers since the reign of Elizabeth I, it is with the outbreak of the First World War in 1914 that large numbers came to live and work in Britain. People from the British colonies worked in munitions and chemical factories, and in the British merchant fleet, while troops from the West Indies, Africa, and India fought against German forces in Africa and France. By the end of the war in 1918 there were about 20,000 black people in Britain, and 'the war-time boom for black labour fizzled out as quickly as it had begun' (Fryer, 1984: 298). A large proportion of the black people living in Britain in 1918–19 were unemployed soldiers and sailors, many of whom lived in the ports of London, Bristol, Liverpool, Glasgow, and Cardiff.

In February 1919 Middle Eastern seamen, all British subjects, were attacked by white sailors in South Shields and Liverpool. In May of the same year black men peacefully walking Liverpool streets were being 'attacked again and again' (Fryer, 1984: 300). After a clash between West Indian and Scandinavian seamen at the beginning of June, police raided boarding houses used by black seamen in an effort to arrest those involved. In a subsequent fracas, a West Indian, Charles Wotton, was allegedly lynched by the mob. According to Fryer (1984: 300):

Wotton ran from the house, closely pursued by two policemen—and by a crowd of between 200 and 300 hurling missiles. The police caught him at the edge of Queen's Dock, but the lynch mob tore him from them and threw him into the water. Shouting 'Let him drown!', they pelted him with stones as he swam around. Soon he died, and his corpse was dragged from the dock. No arrests were made.

After this incident 'an anti-black reign of terror raged in Liverpool' (*ibid.*). According to a police report to the Colonial Office, mobs of youths in 'well-organized' gangs, their total strength varying from 2,000 to 10,000, roamed the streets 'savagely attacking, beating and stabbing every negro they could find' (May and Cohen, 1974). 'Whenever a negro was seen he was chased, and if caught, severely beaten', reported *The Times*. The assault increased in ferocity, culminating in the wrecking and burning of boarding houses occupied by black people. In the face of such an onslaught at least 700 of the black people living in Liverpool sought sanctuary in police and fire stations.

At the same time South Wales was experiencing 'one of the most vicious outbreaks of racial violence that has yet occurred in Britain' (Evans, 1980; Jenkinson, 1996). During a week of anti-black rioting, three men were killed and dozens injured in Newport, Barry, Cadoxton and Cardiff. In Newport, houses occupied by black people, a Greek-owned lodging house, and Chinese laundries were wrecked by a mob of several thousand. 'We are all one in Newport and mean to clear these niggers out', one rioter told a reporter (quoted in Fryer, 1984: 303). Cardiff's black population had increased from about 700 in 1914 to around 3,000 in April 1919, about 1,200 of whom were unemployed seamen. During the violent outbursts which occurred in Cardiff in June 1919 the black quarter of the city (referred to by *The Times* as 'nigger town') was brought under virtual siege. The police responded to these attacks in South Wales by offering the black sailors passage out of Britain, an option taken up by around 600 sailors. There were also anti-Jewish riots in South Wales (Alderman, 1972; Evans, 1980) and anti-black riots in Glasgow (Jenkinson, 1985; 1996) during the summer of 1919.

Although there are few reports of serious outbreaks of violent racism in the period between the end of the First World War and the end of the Second World War, what was known as the 'colour bar' was in effect in Britain. This meant that black workers found it difficult or impossible to get work in British industry because of the attitudes and exclusionary practices of white employers, workers, and trades unions. The colour bar also meant 'the refusal of lodgings, refusal of service in cafes, refusal of admittance to dance halls, etc., shrugs, nods, whispers, comments, etc., in public, in the streets, in trams and in buses' (Little, 1943; see also Constantine, 1954; Fryer, 1984: 356–67).

The inter-war years also saw the rise of British fascism and anti-Semitism. Although the first extreme right-wing party, the British Brothers' League (BBL), was formed in 1902, it is in the 1920s that specifically fascist movements grew in Britain (Taylor, 1982). These movements, which grew in the wake of the fascist revolution in Italy, included the British Fascists, the National Fascisti, and the Imperial Fascist League. In 1932 Oswald Mosley founded the British Union of Fascists (BUF) which had, at its peak during the 1930s, between 17,000 and 40,000 members (*ibid.*: 7). The BUF became increasingly involved in violence (often clashes with anti-fascists), the culmination of which was the 'Battle of Cable Street' in October 1936. In this incident 'anti-BUF demonstrators refused to allow the BUF to march and became involved in a fight with the police who were trying to clear a path, ultimately unsuccessfully, for the Fascists' (*ibid.*). Although the fascists of this period were not concerned with migration from the colonies, anti-semitism was a central theme in their political platform, as was the 'defence' of the British nation from the large numbers of Jewish people fleeing European fascism, referred to as the 'alien menace'.

'Race', Racism, and Immigration in the Post-war Years 1945–58

The period following the end of the Second World War marks an important juncture in the history of Britain's black population, of debates about 'race' and immigration, and, therefore of the context within which violent racism takes place.

The most important development over this period was the onset of mass migration to Britain from the countries of its former empire. This migration occurred for numerous reasons which can only be touched on here. First, there was no legal restriction on the rights of British subjects to travel to or from the United Kingdom and elsewhere in the empire. Under colonial rule, there was no distinction between British subjects born in the United Kingdom and those born elsewhere in the empire; all had the right to enter the United Kingdom, find work, and settle permanently. The 1948 British Nationality Act, which drew a distinction between citizens of the Commonwealth and those of the United Kingdom and Colonies, upheld the right of people born in such newly independent countries as India and Pakistan to come to Britain and had no impact on those countries which remained British. That colonial subjects enjoyed an inclusive British citizenship had implications that went beyond the possession of a legal right. For many, especially those who had contributed to the war effort, travelling to Britain was 'coming home' to the 'mother country'. The colonial education system had inculcated an inclusive notion of Britishness which was taken seriously. Many of the settlers from the colonies 'regarded themselves not as strangers, but as kinds of Englishmen. Everything taught in school . . . encouraged this belief' (Deakin, et al.: 1970).

Secondly, Britain was experiencing a shortage of labour in the effort to rebuild its infrastructure and economy. The most important source of migrants to Britain from 1945 to 1951 was Europe, whence came as many as 300,000 people. During that period between 70,000 and 100,000 Irish people, some 128,000 Polish ex-servicemen, and around 85,000 people from other east European countries settled in the United Kingdom (Solomos, 1989: 44; Rees, 1982: 83). The arrival, in 1948 of the *Empire Windrush* at Tilbury docks in London carrying 492 Jamaicans, has come to symbolize the onset of migration from the Caribbean (Solomos, 1989: 45; Miles and Phizaklea, 1984: 25; Fryer, 1984: 372). However, although this migration from the Caribbean represented an unprecedented growth in Britain's black population, by 1958 migrants from the Caribbean still totalled only about 125,000. Between the mid-1950s and mid-1960s, migration from the Caribbean, and later from the Indian sub-continent, increased in volume. People who were facing economic uncertainty in the colonies and encouraged by British industry began to come to Britain in large numbers.[1]

It is during this period that the 'problem' of black immigration was constructed (Miles and Phizacklea, 1984: 24; Layton-Henry, 1984: 16–30; Solomos, 1989: 40–9). The political debate about immigration which had begun in the late 1940s began to focus increasingly throughout the 1950s on the need to control 'coloured' immigration. This debate, Solomos suggests, turned on two themes: first, revision of the 1948 Nationality Act so as to limit the number of black workers who could come and settle in the United Kingdom; and secondly, a parallel debate about 'the problems caused by too many coloured immigrants in relation to housing, employment and crime' (Solomos, 1989: 46).

The hostility of ordinary white Britons to the arrival of black migrants over this period does not seem to have been particularly extreme at first. Surveys cited by Banton (1983, 1985) suggest that during the early 1950s British people did not identify black people as a threat. Although racial prejudice was widespread, this tended to be based on beliefs about black people in the colonies, rather than in Britain itself. One survey found that two thirds of Britain's white population held a low opinion of black people or disapproved of them. Those who were prejudiced saw black people as:

heathens who practised head-hunting, cannibalism, infanticide, polygamy and 'black magic'. They saw than as uncivilised, backward people, inherently inferior to Europeans, living in primitive mud huts 'in the bush', wearing few

---

[1] It is worth noting that during the period 1951–81 699,000 more people migrated out of Britain than migrated in. After net in-migration of 12,000 during 1951–61 more than 700,000 people left Britain between 1961 and 1981. See Tompson, 1988: App. 2 for further information.

clothes, eating strange foods, and suffering from unpleasant diseases. They saw them as ignorant and illiterate, speaking strange languages, and lacking proper education. They believed that black men had stronger sexual urges than white men, were less inhibited, and could give greater satisfaction to their sexual partners [Richmond, 1955; cited by Fryer, 1984: 374].

Half of this prejudiced two-thirds were 'extremely prejudiced'. These people (comprising one in three white Britons):

strongly resisted the idea of having any contact or communication with black people; objected vehemently to mixed marriages; would not have black people in their homes as guests or lodgers; would not work with them in factory or office; and generally felt that black people should not be allowed into Britain at all [*ibid*.].

These attitudes are reflected in the practices of employers, trades unions, landlords, and local authorities over this period. On arrival in Britain, African/Caribbean and Asian people faced active discrimination in their search for jobs and homes, were ostracized socially and unrepresented politically. Colonial racism was transformed into indigenous racism.

Violent Racism 1948–58

By 1958 there is evidence that violence was increasingly inflicted on black individuals and communities. Clearly, with attitudes such as those expressed above being widespread, together with the enforced maintenance of the colour-bar, violence inflicted upon individual black people may well have been more prevalent than that which is recorded. Undoubtedly, there is scope for research to explore the oral history of violence among the first generation of black British and English people. What documents there are focus on the several occasions in the late 1940s and throughout the 1950s when violence flared into visible public disorder.

In Birmingham in May 1948 a mob of between 100 and 250 white men besieged and stoned a hostel where Indian workers were living (Layton-Henry, 1984: 35). In August of the same year violence directed against unemployed black sailors broke out in Liverpool (Fryer, 1984: 367–71). In July 1949, Deptford in south east London was the scene of a serious disturbance which culminated in a siege of a black men's hostel by a white mob (Hiro, 1991: 38). In 1954 there were two days of violence in Camden Town, north London, during which the home of a black family was petrol-bombed (Glass, 1960; cited in Layton-Henry, 1984: 35; Hiro, 1991). Sporadic attacks on black people and their homes were reported during the 1950s in Nottingham, Dudley, and London.

By far the most serious outbreaks of violent racism during this period were the riots in Nottingham and west London in 1958 (Fryer, 1984; Miles, 1984). In Nottingham, where about 2,500 West Indians and 600 Asians were living, the violence which broke out in August quickly developed into a national news story. In the weeks before violence erupted 'at least a dozen black men were beaten up and robbed by Teddy Boys', with the police showing little interest in catching the culprits (Hiro, 1991). On 23 August, a fight which lasted ninety minutes occurred between a group of West Indians and whites (Fryer, 1984: 377; Miles and Phizacklea, 1984: 33). Police claimed that this was 'a reprisal by coloured people for previous incidents recently when some of their number were attacked by white men' (quoted in Fryer, 1984: 377). After this fight, in which six white people were said to have been stabbed, a large mob then set about attacking any West Indian in sight (Miles and Phizacklea, 1984: 33). Within a few days, thirty-five reporters had descended on Nottingham which acted as 'a magnet for would-be anti-black rioters the following weekend' (Fryer, 1984). On the evening of Saturday, 30 August a crowd of white people—estimated to be as large as between 1,500 and 4,000 people (Layton Henry, 1984: 35; Hiro, 1991: 39)—were on the streets shouting, 'Let's get the blacks' (Fryer, 1984: 377). However, the entire black community stayed indoors under a self-imposed curfew from Friday evening to Monday morning (Hiro, 1991: 39).

The outbreaks of disorder in Notting Hill and other parts of north Kensington in west London, which occurred between 23 August and 2 September, were, if anything, even more violent than those in Nottingham. An important feature of the events in London was the involvement of far-right organizations. Several racist political organizations, including the Mosleyites (Hall *et al.*, 1978: 333–4) were based in the area, and had been active for some time distributing leaflets, scrawling slogans, holding indoor meetings, and 'generally inciting the white people to "Act Now" to "Keep Britain White" ' (Hiro, 1991: 39). In north Kensington sporadic attacks had occurred throughout the summer, many of which were attributed to gangs of 'teddy boys' who 'on weekend evenings . . . cruised the streets looking for West Indians, Africans or Asians' (Fryer, 1984: 378). In

Shepherds Bush a black-owned café was wrecked in July, and on 17 August a white crowd smashed the windows of a house occupied by black people. On 23 August gangs of Teddy Boys—probably influenced by the national radio and newspaper coverage of the Nottingham 'riots'—went 'nigger hunting' with iron bars, table legs, and knives, leaving 'at least five blacks unconscious on the pavement' (Hiro, 1991: 39). As the *Manchester Guardian* put it, 'they chose streets where only an occasional black person was seen and then attacked in the ratio of six to one'. On 30 August widespread and vicious violence against black people and property occurred including setting houses on fire (Hiro, 1991: 40). By the end of August:

brawls, disturbances, and racist attacks were a daily, and nightly feature of life in north Kensington. A Jamaican was shot in the leg. Petrol bombs were thrown into black people's homes, including the homes of pregnant women. Such attacks were often preceded by a threatening letter or a shouted warning: 'We're going to raid you tonight if you don't clear out'. Crowds hundreds strong shouted abuse at black people. A young African student, a stranger to the area, emerged from an Underground station to find himself chased by a hostile crowd shouting 'Lynch him!' [Fryer, 1984: 379].

The climax came on the night of 1 September and in the early hours of the 2nd. After an open-air fascist meeting on Sunday 1st, a crowd of between 500 and 700 surged through north Kensington shouting 'Let's get the niggers', 'Lynch the blacks', and 'Give 'em to us and we'll string 'em up'. Attacks were also reported in other nearby parts of London, including Latimer Road, Harrow Road, Kensal Green, and north Paddington; they were also reported further afield in Southall, Hornsey, Islington, Hackney, and Stepney. 177 people were arrested in all (Fryer, 1984; Hiro, 1991). By mid-September 1958 things had subsided to a 'normal' incidence of racist violence (Fryer, 1984: 380), though further tragedy occurred the following year in north Kensington when in May 1959 a West Indian carpenter, Kelso Cochrane, was stabbed to death by a gang of white youths (Layton-Henry, 1984: 112).

The 1958 riots are cited by many authors as a watershed in the politics of 'race'.[2] The riots and the media coverage which surrounded them brought the presence of black people and the problems 'associated' with them to the centre of the political stage. The riots also

[2] e.g. Solomos, 1989: 48; Layton-Henry, 1984: 35; Hiro, 1991: 38–49; Miles and Phizacklea, 1983: 33–8.

served to politicize the black settlers. Four main constructions of the problem of the riots and solutions to them have been identified and should be mentioned here. The problem was identified, first, as a lack of respect for law and order by an unrepresentative section of British society, and, in particular, by the Teddy Boys. Although the Teds had been around since 1953 and had already become something of the 'folk devil' by 1956, it was this violence that fuelled one of the first 'moral panics' defining youth as a problem (Cohen, 1972; Cashmore, 1984). There was widespread condemnation of the riots by politicians, church leaders, and leader writers in the press. Gaitskell, the Labour Prime Minister, wrote in *The Times* (4 September 1958), 'Whatever local difficulties there may be, nothing can justify the riots and hooliganism of the past few days'. The response to this 'hoolinganism' was to be found in strict enforcement of the law. Nine youths were convicted of assault during the disturbances and were given 'deterrent' sentences which gained widespread public satisfaction.[3]

A second reaction to the riots 'was to assume that they were a response by host populations who felt under pressure from the new immigrant population and that the answer was immigration control' (Layton-Henry, 1984: 36). For some observers, the large number of people involved in the riots suggested, first, that it was not only young thugs who were involved in the violence and, secondly, that they represented only the most extreme manifestation of more widespread racial resentment of, and hostility towards, coloured immigration. Several commentators, most notably Cyril Osborne, Conservative MP for Louth, had been campaigning for immigration control since the mid-1950s. Osborne had been active in Parliament, within the Conservative party, and in the media on the issues of disease and crime among black immigrants and advocated immigration controls as the solution. On 27 August, *The Times* printed a story under the headline 'Nottingham MPs Urge Curb on Entry of Immigrants' in which two Nottingham MPs criticized the 'open door policy'. The following day, *The Times* followed this up with a story headlined 'Renewed Call for Changes in Immigration Law', which

---

[3] On conviction Salmon LJ condemned the actions of those convicted saying: 'You are a minute and insignificant section of the population who have brought shame on the district in which you lived and have filled the whole nation with horror, indignation and disgust. Everyone, irrespective of the colour of their skin is entitled to walk through our streets erect and free from fear. This is a right which these courts will always unfailingly uphold' (cited in Rose *et al.*, 1969: 214).

reported the views of Norman Pannell and Cyril Osborne calling for restrictions in coloured immigration. Lord Salisbury stated that he was 'extremely apprehensive of the economic and social results, for Europeans and Africans alike, that were likely to flow from unrestricted immigration of men and women of the African race into Britain' (*Guardian*, 3 September 1958). It was not only those on the right of the Conservative party who favoured controls, however. Mr George Rogers, Labour MP for North Kensington, told the *Daily Sketch*: 'The government must introduce legislation quickly to end the tremendous influx of coloured people from the Commonwealth . . . Overcrowding has fostered vice, drugs, prostitution and the use of knives. For years the white people have been tolerant. Now their tempers are up' (*Daily Sketch*, 2 September 1958).

Most of those on the left condemned the riots as hooliganism, while others offered a third—'rarely heard, yet most accurate'—explanation for the riots—racial prejudice (Miles and Phizacklea, 1984: 34). Its proponents called for action to eliminate discrimination from British society (*ibid.*). For example, the Labour party chairman, Tom Driberg, told the Trades Union Congress:

People talk about a colour problem arising in Britain. How can there be a colour problem here? Even after all the immigration of the past few years, there are only 190,000 coloured people in our population of over 50 million— that is, only four out of every 1,000. The real problem is not black skins, but white prejudice [*Report of Proceedings at the 90th Trades Union Congress . . . 1958*, 326].

Fourth, the riots spurred the formation of black self-defence organizations and the development of community-support networks. Once black people had overcome their initial shock, alarm, and despondency about the assault that they had experienced, they began to organize to help themselves. They provided escorts for those black employees of London Transport who had to work late-night or early morning shifts and formed vigilante groups who patrolled the area in cars (Hiro, 1991: 40). Black community organizations had begun to emerge in the years prior to 1958, but the riots served to forge a new-found black community identity. In the immediate aftermath of the riots, Norman Manley, Prime Minister of Jamaica, and Carl Lacorbiniere, Deputy Chief Minister of the West Indian Federation, flew to London for a tour of the riot areas, with the specific objective of reassuring the West Indian migrants and for consultations with the British Government (Hiro, 1991: 41). Later, in December 1958, officials of the West Indian Federation helped to organize the West Indian Standing Conference to act as an umbrella for British West Indian organizations which was inaugurated in Birmingham a year later (*ibid.*).

'Race', Racism, and Immigration 1959–67

The period between 1959 and 1968 is that in which British political debates became 'racialized' and in which 'race' became politicized. Immigration control was not an issue in the 1959 General Election and neither was there provision for a debate about immigration at the 1960 Conservative Party annual conference (Layton-Henry, 1984: 38). At this time the majority of the Conservative government and the Labour opposition considered the Commonwealth an asset and were reluctant to take any action which might undermine the principle of the Commonwealth or Britain's moral authority at its centre. During 1960, however, the campaign for the control of black immigration within the Conservative Party, Parliament, and the media gathered strength. This debate, which focused on the dangers of unrestricted migration and the problems associated with the presence in Britain of black people, led to introduction of the Commonwealth Immigrants Bill in 1961 (Solomos, 1989: 51). The Bill was fiercely opposed by Gaitskell and the Labour shadow cabinet who accused the government of betraying the Empire and the Commonwealth.

The Act which came into effect on 1 July 1962 was only a mild measure of control, introducing a system of employment vouchers for Commonwealth immigrants (Layton-Henry, 1984:42). Although immigration from the New Commonwealth fell after the Act was passed, public concern over immigration was not allayed for long. Rather, 'the salience of immigration as an issue was greatly raised by [the Act's] controversial passage' (*ibid.*). Between 1962 and 1964 'the mood of the Conservative Party swung strongly in support of tougher controls', while the Labour Party abandoned its principled opposition to anti-immigration legislation. In 1963, the new leader of the Labour party, Harold Wilson, said that Labour did not contest the need for immigration control, but that it should be negotiated with Commonwealth countries. This position, together with a promise to 'legislate against racial discrimination and incitement in public places and give special help to local authorities in areas where immigrants have settled' formed the basis for their 1964 election manifesto (Labour Party, *Manifesto*, 1964).

The 1964 General Election, and in particular the nature of the campaign fought by Peter Griffiths in the West Midlands town of Smethwick, had 'a deep impact on both the local and national political scene' (Solomos, 1989: 53). Although immigration control was not an important issue in the national campaigns of the parties, the issue of black immigration was frequently raised. But it was when Peter Griffiths dramatically unseated Patrick Gordon-Walker, the Labour Shadow Foreign Secretary, that the electoral impact of the issue became clear. Griffiths had fought the election largely on a platform of defending the local white majority against the 'influx of immigrants'. When commenting on the slogan, 'If you want a nigger neighbour, Vote Labour', which had been used during the campaign Griffiths is reported to have said, "I think that it is a manifestation of popular feeling. I should not condemn anyone who said that" (*The Times*, 9 March 1964). The result, which showed clearly that racial prejudice could be exploited for electoral advantage, was a 'shattering result and a disaster for race relations' (Layton-Henry, 1984: 57).

The Labour Government, which was returned to power in 1964 with only a small majority, seemed vulnerable on the issue of immigration. In response, the government worked hard to establish a 'bipartisan consensus' on the issues of 'race' and immigration. This consensus consisted of a dual policy of strict immigration controls, on one hand, and positive measures to assist the integration of those immigrants already settled in Britain, on the other (Layton-Henry, 1984: 62). In an effort to consolidate this consensus and to offset the anti-immigration feeling which was growing in certain parts of the country, the White Paper, *Immigration from the Commonwealth*, was published. The Race Relations Act, which outlawed racial discrimination in places of public resort and created the offences of incitement to racial hatred was also passed in 1965.

In 1967 a renewed campaign for control was instigated by Enoch Powell, among others, which focused around the growing influx of British Asians from Kenya. This campaign reached a climax in February 1968 when, amid a media-generated moral panic, the second Commonwealth Immigrants Bill was introduced. This was designed specifically to control the flow of East African Asians holding British passports, restricted immigration to those with close ties to the United Kingdom by birth, naturalization, or descent. During this period, Labour were forced further on to the defensive by Powell's 'rivers of blood' speech in Birmingham in April 1968. In highly emotive language Powell warned of what he saw as the dangers of immigration leading to a 'total transformation to which there is no parallel in a thousand years of British history' and of the increasing racial tensions that would result. According to Powell, the long-term solution to this problem went beyond immigration control to include the repatriation of immigrants already settled in the United Kingdom. Although he was sacked from the Shadow Cabinet as a result of this speech, Powell and his campaign became very popular with the electorate, inspiring demonstrations of poplar racism all over the country, such as the strike by dockers and porters from London's Smithfield Market who marched to Westminster in his support.

Violent Racism 1959–67

Although violent racism was not a particularly salient political issue between 1959 and 1967, attacks and disturbances were reported in key areas across the country. Anti-black riots occurred in the West Midlands towns of Dudley and Smethwick in 1962, in Wolverhampton in 1965 (Reeves, 1989: 44), and in Accrington and Leeds in 1964 (Hartley, 1973; cited in Pearson, 1976).

One of the more serious incidents in Dudley in 1962 was triggered by a fight outside a public house in which three black men were injured. Subsequently, 'a chanting mob of white people brandishing sticks, chair legs, coshes and bottles marched "like a pack of wolves to their prey" into a street where a number of black people lived' (Reeves, 1989). Over the following two nights crowds 300 strong gathered to hunt for, and beat up, black people. In Wolverhampton in 1965 a crowd of about 150 white people attacked a house occupied by Jamaicans (*ibid.*).

In 1964, there were around 250 Pakistani residents in Accrington, whose population was around 37,000. Geoff Pearson witnessed the 'trouble' which flared up after a white man died, allegedly stabbed by a Pakistani in a fight outside a coffee bar. Pearson describes seeing a gang of between 100 and 200 white youths and men aged between 15 and 30 moving down the main street of the town in search of 'Pakis'. Many of the gang carried chains, belts, and sticks, and others had large, menacing dogs 'most of which seemed to be Alsatians'. As the 'mob' moved down the street, Pakistanis were knocked down, beaten, and trampled on:

On one occasion as the gang passed a bus-stop, a 'paki' who had not been visible from within their ranks, emerged from under their feet—as if he had been 'heeled' from a rugby pack. 'The lads' were literally walking on 'the pakis'. Whites at the same bus queue stood by watching this. The 'paki' lay on the floor, bleeding from the head and face, dazed and struggling to get off the floor [Pearson, 1976: 52].

A couple of police cars hovered about, but made no attempt to interfere. Over the next few days there were sporadic attacks on immigrants. The streets in which they lived were invaded, windows broken, the curtains of their houses set on fire, Moslem food-shops were wrecked and vandalized. Finally, several men were arrested when they appeared in the centre of the town with a double-barrelled shotgun shouting, 'Black bastards. Stop or we will shoot you'. When the gun was stuck into the ribs of one Pakistani there was a struggle and the police intervened. According to the *Accrington Observer*, the police were told: 'You — nigger lover. They all want shooting' (Pearson, 1976: 52–3).

Eight of 'the lads' were charged with, and four gaoled for, a range of offences including threatening behaviour, behaviour likely to cause a breach of the peace, possession of an offensive weapon, assaulting a police officer, damage to the door of a police cell. However, they were not charged with assaulting the Pakistanis. Indeed no one was charged with assault during the 'brief season of paki-bashing' in Accrington (Pearson, 1976: 52).

Powellism: 'Race', Racism, and Immigration 1968–77

The speeches made by Enoch Powell and others, and the tremendous publicity which they generated after 1968, changed the terms of political debate about black people and race relations, thereby destroying the fragile 'bipartisan consensus' on race and immigration created by the Labour government. First, the debate was shifted further towards the need for firm immigration controls; secondly, the debate shifted to focus on 'repatriation' of Commonwealth migrants already living in Britain; thirdly, the moral panic which was generated about immigration and the presence of black people provided the political space for the emergence of new and explicitly racist political forces.

Powell delivered his 'rivers of blood' speech three days before the parliamentary debate on the Race Relations Bill. The Bill, the purpose of which was to establish equality of treatment in housing and employment, was supported by the liberal wing of the Conservative opposition as well as some members of the Shadow Cabinet, though the majority of back-bench and constituency opinion was opposed to it. Powell attacked the Bill, playing on fears that it would place black immigrants in a privileged position. Using reported incidents and conversations he raised fears of immigrant invasion and take-over of streets and areas, and fears that old people would be harassed by 'grinning piccanninies' (Layton-Henry, 1984: 71). Despite the opposition which Powell had generated, the Act, which outlawed discrimination, expanded the Race Relations Board, and established the Community Relations Commission was passed in November 1968 (Layton-Henry, 1984: 72; Gay and Young, 1988).

The campaign waged by Enoch Powell and the public support which he generated during the summer of 1968 forced the Conservative Party leadership to abandon the ideal of Commonwealth citizenship to which it had been firmly committed ten years previously. In response to Powell, Edward Heath, Leader of the Opposition, gave several speeches calling for an end to immigration, demanding that a check should be kept on Commonwealth immigrants during their first four years, and reaffirming the party's policy of financial assistance to those migrants who wished to return to their country of origin. By now Powell was going further, arguing in November 1968 for a Ministry of Repatriation which would embark upon 'a programme of large scale voluntary but organised, financed and subsidised repatriation and re-emigration' of Commonwealth settlers. By June 1969 Powell had devised a scheme to repatriate 700,000 coloured immigrants which he costed at £300 million. In the run-up to the 1970 General Election the Conservatives were seen as the party most likely to 'keep immigrants out' (Butler and Stokes, 1974) reflecting the Conservative Manifesto, which proposed still tighter control on Commonwealth immigrants along the lines proposed by Heath (Hiro, 1991: 251).

One of the early tasks of the newly elected Conservative Government was the passage of the 1971 Immigration Bill. This replaced all the legislation of the 1960s, based immigration control around a single distinction between 'patrials' and 'non-patrials'. A patrial refers to persons born, adopted, naturalized, or registered in the United Kingdom, or were born of parents one of whom had UK citizenship, or one of whose grandparents had UK citizenship. Patrials had the right to live in Britain, while non-patrials holding British passports did not (though there was a system of vouchers which allowed a limited number of non-patrial British and Commonwealth passport-holders to enter the country). The hope of the Conservative leadership that this legislation would finally end the immigration debate and defuse the 'race issue' was shattered, however, in August 1972 when General Idi Amin, President of Uganda, announced the expulsion of all Asians living in his country (Layton-Henry, 1984: 81). As most of these people were eligible for British passports, it was clear that Britain was primarily responsible for them. The announcement that 50,000 Asians might head for Britain was received with a large amount of hostile media coverage and racist rhetoric from some politicians, particularly Powell. Despite the Powellites lobbying MPs and the Home Office with reference to election promises, the Heath government decided that Britain would have to accept these British passport holders and 27,000 people from Uganda subsequently arrived in the United Kingdom. What became known as the 'Ugandan Asians crisis' received a great deal of media attention and acted as a major boost to anti-immigrant organizations, both within the Conservative Party (such as the Monday Club) and further to the right (such as the National Front) (*ibid.*). This panic about immigration and the presence of black people, together with what many on the right saw as Heath's betrayal of the British nation, signalled a new development in British right-wing politics.

The National Front and Anti-fascism in the 1970s

The National Front was a direct descendant of the far-right parties of earlier periods.[4] In late 1966 the leaders of the British National Party (BNP) and the League of Empire Loyalists (LEL) agreed the terms of a merger, and in February 1967 the National Front (NF) was

---

[4] Its origins may be found in the pre-war British Brothers League; Mosley's British Union of Fascists and the Imperial Fascist League of the inter-war years; and A. K. Chesterton's League of Empire Loyalists (LEL), the Racial Preservation Society, The National Labour Party, and the White Defence League of the post-war years (Hiro, 1991: 254; Tomlinson, 1981; Taylor, 1982). In 1960, the White Defence League and National Labour Party merged to form the British National Party (BNP), from which splintered off, in 1962, the more openly fascist National Socialist Movement (from which John Tyndall later split to form the Greater Britain Movement).

formed from these two organizations together with a section of the Racial Preservation Society. Later the Greater Britain Movement, led by John Tyndall, merged with the NF.[5] The aims of the party, led by A.K. Chesterton, were to provide a new arena for far-right activism outside the Conservative party as an independent political organization. It declared a commitment to parliamentary democracy, opposed entry to the European Economic Community, advocated a strengthening of 'law and order' and a 'reconstruction' of the Empire (Miles and Phizacklea, 1984: 121). In particular, the National Front 'enthusiastically adopted the Powellite idea of repatriating black and Asian immigrants' (Hiro, 1991: 254).

Powell's campaign brought direct benefit to the National Front by giving tremendous publicity to the race issue, which was their major *raison d'être*, and by legitimating consideration and support for policies like repatriation (Layton-Henry, 1984: 92). The National Front began to field candidates in the 1969 local elections and put up ten candidates in the 1970 General Election, where they averaged only 3.5 per cent of the vote. The 'Ugandan Asians crisis' of 1972 stimulated rapid growth for the National Front which, by 1973, claimed a membership of 14,000 organized into thirty-two branches and eighty groups (Nugent and King, 1977: 175). In the May 1973 by-election in West Bromwich the NF candidate, Martin Webster, gained 4,789 votes, 16 per cent of the poll. In the General Election of February 1974 the National Front fielded fifty-four candidates, all of whom lost their deposits. In the second General Election of that year (in October) the National Front fielded ninety candidates, thus gaining television and radio broadcasting time. The election brought poor results averaging only 3.1 per cent of the vote, with only their best results in London, Leicester, Wolverhampton, and West Bromwich gaining more than 4.5 per cent of the vote.

In May 1976 a new immigration scare erupted when small numbers of Asians from Malawi began to arrive in Britain as a result of restrictive measures taken against them by the Malawi government. These people were UK passport holders, entitled to come to Britain under the quotas established for non-patrials in 1968. The news that some of these migrants were being put up by West Sussex Council in a four-star hotel prompted a rash of headlines such as 'Scandal of

---

[5] See Walker, 1977; Fielding, 1981; Tomlinson, 1981; Taylor, 1982; Solomos, 1989: 130; Miles and Phizacklea, 1984: 120; Layton-Henry, 1984: 87–107; Edgar, 1978; and Billig, 1978 for a discussion of the emergence of the National Front.

£600 a week immigrants' (*Sun,* 4 May), 'New Flood of Asians in Britain (*Daily Mirror*), '4 star Asians run up £4,000 bill' (*Sun*, 7 May). This panic led to further scare stories about the supposed extent of illegal immigration, 'Immigrant racket row' (*Daily Express*, 25 May), and about the scale of future immigration from the Indian sub-continent, 'New Asian invaders' (*Sun,* 17 May) (cited in Gordon and Rosenberg, 1989: 23). The National Front responded to this opportunity by organizing symbolic acts of 'territorial reoccupation' in the form of demonstrations and meetings in areas populated by New Commonwealth migrants and their children (Miles and Phizacklea, 1984). In the local elections which followed this panic in 1976 and 1977, the NF obtained over 10 per cent of the vote in twenty-five districts and just over 20 per cent in two. In the 1977 Greater London Council election, the NF contested ninety-one of the ninety-two seats. The East End provided nearly one third of its total vote, the party gaining more than 20 per cent of the vote in some constituencies. After this success, however, the NF began to decline in importance as a political force, and in the 1979 General Election the party suffered electoral disaster and eventual fragmentation and collapse.

The National Front and the racism which it propagated did not go unchallenged during this period. During the mid-1970s, new movements began to develop from the self-defence and anti-racist organizations of the 1950s and early 1960s, and from left-wing anti-fascist action. In June 1974 anti-fascists organized a march to Conway Hall in Red Lion Square, central London, to picket a National Front meeting. In the resulting clashes between the NF, anti-fascist demonstrators, and the police, a demonstrator, Kevin Gately, was killed (Gilroy, 1987: 118; Scarman, 1975). Between 1973 and 1976 a network of anti-fascist/anti-racist committees was formed, a development which gathered momentum after the 1976 elections in most towns and cities with large black populations (Gilroy, 1987: 119; Layton-Henry, 1984: 101). In February 1975 the anti-fascist magazine, *Searchlight,* was founded to challenge the electoral and popular support of the NF. Rock Against Racism was formed in August 1976 by a small group of activists associated with the Socialist Workers' Party, and in November 1977 the anti-Nazi League was formed (Gilroy, 1987: 120–30).

Opposition to the NF was also growing within the Labour movement during this period. Following an internal report on the growing electoral success of the National Front in September 1976, the

National Executive Committee (NEC) of the Labour Party agreed to launch a campaign against racism jointly with the TUC. The 1976 TUC Annual Conference of that year passed numerous resolutions against racism, while the Labour Party conference which followed passed resolutions demanding the repeal of the 1968 and 1971 Immigration Acts. Both the TUC and Labour Party conferences passed resolutions calling for a campaign against racialism, and advising all Labour councils to ban the use of council property by the far right and to lend their support to the formation of local anti-fascist committees (Layton-Henry, 1984: 100; Miles and Phizacklea, 1984: 103).

Violent Racism 1968–77

During the period following Powell's speeches at the end of the 1960s racial tension reached a peak and violent racism was reported in many locations across Britain. Although the term 'wog-bashing' has been used to describe violence such as that inflicted on black communities by the Teddy Boys in the late 1950s, the label 'Paki-bashing' is said by several authors to have emerged at some point in 1969 or 1970 (*Race Today* 1969–71; Pearson, 1976; Layton-Henry, 1984: 112). It seems that at the turn of the decade there was a real upsurge in violent racism and also 'the emergence of a "moral panic" when the official and semi-official view of "public opinion", the mass media, the courts and the police found a new word to describe acts of "unprovoked assault" on people who are said to be racially inferior (Pearson, 1976: 50). The violence itself can be associated with three inter-related developments during a wider moral panic about immigration and 'race' stimulated by the Powellites, the emergence of, and widespread public support for, the National Front and the emergence of a new, violent, and explicitly racist youth culture—the skinheads.

The skinheads emerged at the beginning of the 1970s, first in the East End of London and then elsewhere in Britain. 'Skins' adopted a uniform with half-mast trousers, braces, 'bovver boots', and close-cropped hair which seemed to be 'at one and the same time, both a caricature and a re-assertion of solid, male, working-class toughness' (Mungham and Pearson, 1976: 7). The skinhead style, with its 'severe and puritanical self-image [and] formalized and very 'hard' masculinity' (Clark and Jefferson, 1976: 156), lent itself to an overtly violent stance towards 'Pakis' and 'queers'. The skins had a strong sense of class and geographical location: '[t]he importance of one's own

patch, one's own football team, and the defence of working-class territory and neighbourhood loomed large in the skinhead's lifestyle'
(Mungham and Pearson, 1976: 7). This territorial defensiveness is
closely linked to Paki-bashing as a 'ritual and aggressive defence of
the social and cultural homogeneity of the community against its
most obviously scapegoated outsiders' (Clarke, 1975: 102; cited by
Cashmore, 1984). Ironically while Asians were the explicit focus of
skinhead violence, the first skinheads listened and danced to West
Indian music—rock-steady and ska (Cashmore, 1984: 32–3).

In 1970 in the East End of London, over a three-month period, 150
people were seriously assaulted, and in April, Tosir Ali, a kitchen
porter, was stabbed to death only yards from his home in Bow
(Gordon, 1990/1986: 2). On one day in April 1971 arson attacks
against West Indians were reported in Forest Gate and on an Asian
family in Manor Park (Newham Monitoring Project, 1991). Violent
racism was also reported in schools in East London, two schools in
particular gaining notoriety as those 'where "Paki-bashing" and
"Nigger bashing" were the norm' (Newham Monitoring Project,
1991: 26). In 1972, a young Sikh boy was stabbed at one of these
schools by a white youth who told him, 'Unless you cut your hair and
stop wearing your turban, we will kill you'. In another incident an
11-year old boy, Sohail Yusaf, was beaten on his way home from
school and left unconscious on a building site (ibid.).

In 1973 there were three apparently racist killings in Coventry,
Leicester, and Birmingham (Gordon, 1990: 8). In south London in
1975 a black bus conductor was fatally injured after a row over a fare
for a dog. In Glasgow in the same year a West Indian man was shot
dead by Brian Hosie, a National Front member who claimed to be
pursuing his policy to 'boost emigration [and] start extermination'.
At the time he told the police, 'Niggers mean nothing to me. It was
like killing a dog' (Searchlight, 'The Murderers are amongst Us': 5).
Violent racism hit a new peak in the wake of the anti-immigration
reporting of the arrival of Asians from Malawi in May 1976.
Following this media coverage black people's shops, homes, and
community organizations were stoned and set on fire in east London
and Southall (Gordon and Rosenberg, 1989: 23). In the same month
two Asians, Dinesh Choudhury and Ribhi Al Haddida, were killed in
Essex; in June, Gurdip Singh Chaggar was murdered in Southall and
Emmanuel Allombah was murdered in west London; and in August,
Mohan Gautam was murdered in Leamington Spa (Gordon, 1990: 8).

There is little doubt that while these killings were the most extreme form of violent racism, less extreme variants of the same phenomenon were felt by minority individuals and communities across the country. Some of the violence afflicted on black and other ethnic minorities over this period can be directly attributed to members of far-right political parties and fascist sympathizers (*Searchlight*, 'The Murders are amongst Us). However, much of the violence seems more easily attributable to the mobilization of white community hostility against black people. In some instances, this hostility was mobilized specifically by low-visibility activity of the far-right. But it was mobilized and legitimated more generally through the racist rhetoric of the news media and right-wing politicians.

Evidence of the direct involvement in violent racism of far-right groups such as the National Front was gathered during the mid-1970s by Paul Rose, MP. In February 1975 he founded an organisation to combat fascist and racist groups, and in August that year he presented evidence of over 1,000 incidents of far-right political violence to the Home Secretary (Fielding, 1981: 177). This violence, Rose suggested, was not an organized campaign, but rather emerged from a culture in which violence was accepted or approved of. Nigel Fielding's detailed study of the National Front also provides evidence of 'covert action by the NF' (*ibid.*). Fielding notes that there is a difficulty in separating out covert attacks actually carried out by the NF against the 'coloured community' from 'those done by local residents in situations of racial harassment'. Considering the level of local support for the NF over this period, however, the distinction should not be overdrawn. Fielding cites evidence linking the NF to a series of fire-bomb attacks, racist leafleting, and attacks on a Community Relations Office in London during the mid-1970s (Fielding, 1981: 177–85). In 1974 an NF member who recruited outside West Ham football ground, speaking to *Skin*, a London Weekend Television programme, said, 'We used to buy the kids a few drinks, then wind them up and send them off to smash up a Paki's home. We just sat back. They did it all for us.'

There is some evidence of direct links between racially inflammatory media reports and the incidence of violent racism. For example, the sensationalist reporting of the arrival in Britain of Asians expelled from Malawi was followed by an upsurge in racial attacks. Within twenty-four hours of the *Sun* reporting '3,000 Asians flood Britain', an Asian-owned newsagent's shop in east London was daubed with the slogans '3,000 moor [sic]' and 'Packie Patel' and the following week the offices of the Joint Council for the Welfare of Immigrants narrowly escaped serious damage after an arson attempt (Gordon and Rosenberg, 1989: 10). At the time the journalist Paul Foot commented:

Race hate and race violence does not rise and fall according to the numbers of immigrants coming into Britain. It rises and falls to the extent to which people's prejudices are inflamed and made respectable by politicians and newspapers ['What the Papers Say', Granada TV; cited in Gordon and Rosenberg, 1989: 23].

Racism and Anti-racism 1978–80

Several important political developments occurred in the period between 1978 and 1981 which should be mentioned at this point. First, between 1976 and the 1979 General Election the rhetoric of the Conservative party, and particularly of the leader of the opposition, Margaret Thatcher, took an increasingly anti-immigration stance. Secondly, in the late 1970s anti-racist organizations grew in strength and visibility, opposing the National Front wherever they marched. Thirdly, a new cross-party group, the Joint Committee Against Racialism, was formed, which was to play a crucial role in bringing official recognition to the problem of racial attacks. Fourthly, in the 1979 General Election the National Front suffered complete electoral disaster followed by political decline and fragmentation.

After narrowly losing the 1974 General Election, the Conservative Party became more aware of the electoral importance of white resistance to black immigration (Layton-Henry, 1984: 103). The success of the National Front during the mid-1970s gave a clear indication that 'race' and the fears of the white electorate could be exploited for political purposes. Anti-immigration feelings were clearly evident within the Conservative Party, which, for example, brought forward 140 resolutions on immigration at the annual party conference in October 1976, following the Malawi Asians panic earlier that year. Mrs Thatcher, the new Leader of the Opposition, decided that the party should harden its attitude towards immigration, and the Home Secretary, William Whitelaw, said that the party would develop a policy which would end 'immigration as we have seen it in the post-war years' (Layton-Henry, 1980: 67; Layton-Henry, 1984: 104). On 30 January 1978, Margaret Thatcher stated in a television interview that '[p]eople are really rather afraid that this country might be rather swamped by people with a different culture', and '[w]e do have to hold out the prospect of an end to immigration except, of course, for compassionate cases'. She said that, while the Conservatives would not be highlighting immigration in the forthcoming election, it was important for major parties not to neglect people's fears about immigration, which otherwise would drive them to the National Front. When George Burns, the interviewer, asked, '[s]o, some of the support that the National Front has been attracting in recent by-elections you would hope to bring back behind the Tory party?', she replied, '[o]h, very much back, certainly, but I think that the National Front has, in fact, attracted more people from Labour voters than from us. But never be afraid to tackle something people are worried about. We are not in politics to ignore people's worries; we are in politics to deal with them' (Granada Television, *World in Action*, 30 January 1978; cited in Layton-Henry, 1984: 104). Although Mrs Thatcher's comments were condemned as pandering to popular prejudice and even as 'giving aid and comfort to the National Front' (*Sunday Times*, 26 February 1978), their effect was to boost support for the Conservatives and to undermine popular support for the NF (Hiro, 1991: 257). While Labour and the Conservatives had been neck-and-neck in the opinion polls conducted in January 1978 prior to this speech, immediately afterwards the polls showed an increase of 9 percentage points in electoral support for the Tories over Labour. Moreover, those who regarded immigration as one of the two most urgent problems facing the country leapt from 9 to 21 per cent (*ibid.*).

The Conservative Party entered the 1979 General Election campaign committed to tightening immigration controls. The manifesto promised: a new British Nationality Act (1981) to define entitlement to British citizenship; an end to allowing permanent settlement for those coming for a temporary stay; limits on the entry of the families of those already settled; restrictions on the issue of work permits; and the introduction of a quota system to control all entry for settlement. Although there could be 'no question of compulsory repatriation' the Conservatives promised 'firm action against illegal immigrants and overstayers and help those immigrants who genuinely wish to leave this country' (Conservative Central Office, *Party Manifesto*, 1979). This tough line on immigration was accompanied by rhetoric which emphasized the dual approach to race relations,

namely that racial harmony was possible only with effective immigration control (Layton-Henry, 1984: 151).

Although the Conservatives had become aware of the importance
of the black electorate and made efforts to attract black voters during this period, these met with little success (Layton-Henry, 1984:
152). In opposition, the Conservative Party had begun to recognize
that black people were an important potential source of political support and part of the future of British politics. The formation of
Anglo-Asian and Anglo-West Indian Conservative societies were just
part of the Conservatives' attempt to become attractive to black voters. The decision not to oppose the 1976 Race Relations Act showed
an awareness of the need to tackle racial discrimination and that the
Conservatives were prepared to take some steps to avoid alienating
British blacks. That William Whitelaw gave personal endorsement to
the Federation of Conservative Students' campaign against racialism
in the autumn of 1977 also indicated that the party was opposed to
incitement to racial hatred and the activities of the National Front
(Layton-Henry, 1984: 149).

The 1974–9 Labour government suffered more acutely than did the
Tories from 'facing in opposite directions'. It 'maintained the structure of immigration control which had been established to keep
'coloured immigrants' out of Britain, and yet campaigned against
racism' (Miles and Phizacklea, 1984: 94). Although it had opposed
the 1971 Immigration Act, the government did not regard its repeal
as a priority. The Labour government did make some concessions,
however, allowing, for example, the entry of husbands and fiancés of
women living in Britain, and increasing the number of vouchers for
UK passport holders denied the right to enter Britain. The government also introduced the Race Relations Act 1976 which strengthened legislation against racial discrimination and set up the
Commission for Racial Equality to replace both the Race Relations
Board and the Community Relations Commission (Miles and
Phizacklea, 1984: 95). Over this period, the Labour Party began to
lose some of the political initiative, partly as a result of its small
majority in the House of Commons and partly as a result of the
onslaught from the Powellites (and eventually Mrs Thatcher), whose
accusations that Labour was 'soft on immigration' were fuelled by
media panics about 'race'. The proposals devoted to immigration
and race relations by the Labour Party in its 1979 election manifesto
concentrated on the need to strengthen anti-discrimination and

race-relations legislation. These were to promote equality of opportunity in employment in the public sector; to help those whose first language is not English; to introduce monitoring; to clarify the role of the Public Order Act 1936 and to widen the scope of the Race Relations Act; and to review the 1828 Vagrancy Act with a view to repealing section 4 (commonly known as 'sus') (Labour Party, *Manifesto*, 1979: 29).

More direct opposition to racism and to the racist violence associated with the National Front was to be found in other spheres of left-wing politics. Paul Gilroy charts the development of the anti-racist movements such as the Anti-Nazi League (ANL), Rock Against Racism (RAR), and the Campaign Against Racism and Fascism. These movements grew from 1976 onwards, RAR in particular drawing on the emergence of and growth of the anti-authoritarianism and cultural style of Punk (1987: 120–30). From 1978 onwards RAR co-operated with the ANL in organizing several large demonstrations/rock concerts in various parts of the country. The first of these 'carnivals', as they were called, in London in May attracted 80,000 people. At this time the Asian self-defence movements were also becoming better organized. For example, in the wake of the murder of Altab Ali, on 14 May 1978, 7,000 people, mostly Bengalis, marched from Whitechapel, where he had been murdered, to a rally in Hyde Park and a protest at 10 Downing Street. This was one of the biggest demonstrations by Asians ever seen in Britain (Bethnall Green and Stepney Trades Council, 1978: 56). The ANL and RAR formed part of a loosely formed anti-racist alliance which was willing and able to take swift, direct action to prevent the National Front from marching (cf. Webster, 1980). For example, the ANL organized, in conjunction with local Bengali community organizations, a protest demonstration for 18 June, a week after an 'organized racist rampage' down Brick Lane in the East End of London. Over 4,000 people, black and white, joined the demonstration (Miles and Phizacklea, 1984: 104; Bethnall Green and Stepney Trades Council, 1978: 57). Further action was taken against the National Front demonstrations in Brick Lane on Sunday, 9 and Sunday, 16 July, and the next day 8,000 workers stayed away from work in response to the Hackney and Tower Hamlets Defence Committee call for a Black Solidarity Day (Bethnall Green and Stepney Trades Council, 1978: 57).

At the Old Bailey on 19 July 1978 four Sikh brothers from East Ham, Mohinder, Balvinder, Sukvinder, and Joginder Singh Virk, were found guilty of causing grievous bodily harm and were sentenced to a total of twelve years' and three months' imprisonment. The incident had occurred a year before when, on 23 April 1977 (St Georges Day, the same day as a National Front march through Wood Green), five drunk white youths approached the brothers shouting racist abuse, provoking, and then attacking them. During the ensuing fracas, one of the white youths was stabbed. The Virks telephoned the police, who, when they arrived, arrested and charged the brothers. In court, the police chief prosecution witnesses were the white youths who had attacked them, and Virks' lawyer's attempts to establish the racist nature of the attack (by questioning whether they were members of the NF or had been at the Wood Green demonstration) were ruled out of order. For the black community it seemed that the victims of an attack were the ones arrested and the 'offence' of self defence was the one punished (Bethnall Green and Stepney Trades Council, 1978: 59; Newham Monitoring Project, 1991: 35–6). The Virk case and the subsequent result was an important catalyst in the development of black self-defence organizations such as the Standing Committee of Asian Organizations and the Newham Defence Committee.

Throughout the summer of 1978 anti-racists and black communities in east London and in Southall organized against the National Front and racist attacks. Union leaders visited Brick Lane to express their concern. David Lane, Chairman of the Commission for Racial Equality, visited, promising a major investigation into the situation in the East End. Other visitors included the High Commissioner of Bangladesh and Arthur Latham MP, Chairman of the Greater London Regional Council of the Labour Party, who called for a public inquiry into the events in Brick Lane (Hansard, vol. 955, No. 166). The Labour Home Secretary, Merlyn Rees, declined repeated requests to visit the area and expressed his total confidence in the police (Bethnall Green and Stepney Trades Council, 1978: 60).

In the 1979 General Election the National Front fielded an unprecedented 303 candidates. Not only did this give the impression that the NF was able to contend as a national political party, but also entitled it to radio and television air time and free postal distribution of electoral material. In response, the Anti Nazi League and its supporters opposed the National Front wherever it held election meetings. On 23 April the Anti Nazi League and the local Asian community mobilized to prevent a National Front meeting in Southall. It was estimated that 10,000 anti-fascists demonstrated against a meeting of only fifty National Front supporters. Clashes occurred between demonstrators (who were determined that the NF should not be allowed to meet) and the police (who were determined to keep the path clear for the National Front supporters to attend the meeting). In the outbreak of serious disorder which ensued, Blair Peach was killed, allegedly by the Metropolitan Police Special Patrol Group (SPG) (Layton-Henry, 1984: 105).

The Conservative victory in 1979 marks the decline of both the NF and the ANL. The National Front won only 0.6 per cent of the vote in October 1974, despite its massive increase in candidates from ninety to over 300 in 1979. Even in its traditional strongholds in the East End, the National Front achieved little more than 5 per cent of the vote, against a swing to the Conservatives averaging 14.2 per cent. As Layton-Henry suggests, '[i]t seems clear that the major reason for the electoral reverse was the public identification of the Conservative Party with a tough line on immigration' (1984: 106). The defeat was a shattering blow to the NF. It had lost much prestige and resources fighting the election campaign, and the mobilization of the ANL against it 'had shown the National Front that it was unlikely to ever achieve its goal of becoming a respectable political party' (ibid.). The demise of the National Front as a contending national political party may have led to an upsurge in street-level racist activity.

From the mid-1970s community-based organizations such as the Steering Committee of Asian Organisations, the Newham Defence Committee, the Southall Youth Movement, the Bangladesh Youth Movement, and the Asian Youth Movement became increasingly well organized in response to violent racism and to the way in which it was being dealt with by the police. These organizations and their offshoots were galvanized into a new phase of action after the murder of Akhtar Ali Baig in Newham in July 1980. In the immediate aftermath of this murder, 150 Asian and some Afro-Caribbean youths held an impromptu march to Forest Gate police station, and later to the spot where the murder had taken place (Newham Monitoring Project, 1991: 40–4). During these demonstrations sixteen people were arrested, which further politicized the young people and led to the formation of the Newham Youth Movement (ibid.). On 19 July, 2,500 people marched through Newham in protest, which resulted in a further twenty-nine arrests being made after clashes with the police. A second march was organized by the Newham Youth Movement and the Steering Committee of Asian Organisations which was supported by over 5,000 people (*ibid.*). In 1980, representatives from these organizations came together around the issue of racial harassment to form the Newham Monitoring Project (Newham Monitoring Project, 1991: 44).

Although demonstrations against the National Front and against racist attacks served to raise the profile of the issues involved, it is the activities of interest groups with greater political influence which led to the government giving official recognition to the problem of 'racial attacks'. The Joint Committee Against Racialism (JCAR) was formed in the autumn of 1977 and formally launched in December 1978. This committee included the Conservative, Labour, and Liberal Parties, the British Council of Churches, the Board of Deputies of British Jews, the National Union of Students, the British Youth Council, and leading immigrant organizations. Nominees from the Labour and Conservative Parties acted as joint chairmen. Although Mrs Thatcher vetoed the appointment of John Moore MP to JCAR (which was seen as an anti-racist organization involving not only the Labour Party but the far-left as well), Mrs Shelagh Roberts, a prominent Conservative from outside Parliament, was appointed (Layton-Henry, 1984: 150).

During 1980 and early 1981 some of the organizations associated with JCAR, in particular the CRE, the Board of Deputies of British Jews, and ethnic minority organizations, were lobbying the Home Secretary to act against racial attacks. In January 1981 JCAR presented to the Home Secretary a dossier of over 1,000 racial attacks, and in February met with him to discuss what they saw as an increasing degree of violence being inflicted on ethnic minority people and their property in Britain. The Home Secretary, William Whitelaw, was 'impressed' by the detailed evidence compiled by JCAR and was concerned with the contention that the 'frequency of racial attacks was increasing and that this was not entirely attributable to sporadic incidents of hooliganism but was the result of organised attempts at intimidation by extreme right-wing movements' (Layton-Henry, 1984: 114). In response to JCAR's approach the Home Secretary agreed to set up a Home Office inquiry into racial attacks and the activities of the racist organizations alleged to be responsible (see Chapter 3).

Violent Racism 1978–80

In 1978 Bethnal Green and Stepney Trades Council published its report on racial violence in the East End of London. Drawing on the

records of the Bangladesh Welfare Association, the Bangladesh Youth
Movement, and Tower Hamlets Law Centre it looked in some detail
at over 110 attacks on Asians and their property that had occurred
between January 1976 and August 1978. Together with evidence from
individuals, trade union branches, community and ethnic minority
organizations, the community relations council, anti-racist bodies,
the churches, and councillors, they produced the first in-depth report
on the problem to be published in Britain.[6] The report uncovered an
'appalling catalogue of violent crime' which appeared to be targeted
directly against the Bengali community and which had often led to
the hospitalization of the victims. This violence included hammer
attacks, stabbings, slashed faces, punctured lungs, clubbings, gunshot
wounds, people beaten with bricks, sticks, and umbrellas, and kicked
unconscious in broad daylight. The report concluded that:

While the East End is traditionally a 'high-crime' area, there is clear evidence
that the local Bengalee community has suffered physical attacks and harassment over recent years on a totally different scale from that inflicted on the
rest of the community. There is a danger in assuming that this violence is
confined to the occasional isolated incident or outburst that finds its way into
the headlines. . . . Behind the headlines is an almost continuous and unrelenting battery of Asian people and their property in the East End of London.
The barrage of harassment, insult and intimidation, week in week out, fundamentally determines how the immigrant community here lives and works,
how the host community and the authorities are viewed, and how the
Bengalee people in particular think and act [Bethnal Green and Stepney
Trades Council, 1978: 3–4].

In addition to attacks on individuals, the report also reported on
what it referred to as 'serious mass outrages' by racist groups in the
area against the black community. The most serious of these
occurred after a National Front meeting in Brick Lane on Sunday, 11
June 1978, when:

50 white youths ran down Brick Lane shouting 'Kill the Black Bastards' and
smashing the windows of a dozen shops and the car windscreens of Bengalese
shop keepers. 55-year-old Abdul Monan was knocked unconscious by a hail
or rocks and stones hurled through his shop window. He ended up in hospital where he needed five stitches in his face. He lost two of his teeth
[Bethnal Green and Stepney Trades Council, 1978: 41].

---

[6] Hunte's (1965) earlier work catalogued racist violence penetrated by the police.

Elsewhere in the East End, in London, and in the country as a whole between 1978 and 1980 there were a number of apparently racist killings,[7] and also growing evidence that violent racism was, as in Tower Hamlets, a persistent feature of the lives of members of the black and Asian communities. In April 1978, 10-year-old Kennith Singh was murdered near his home in Plaistow, east London. The murderer was never found. The same month, a 9-year old Asian boy on his way home from school for lunch was stopped outside his front gate by five white boys armed with a knife. They pinned him to a wall and '[o]ne of them shouted, "Stab him now." "No, lets just take his eye out", another replied. They cut open his face from his left eye across to his left ear' (Newham Monitoring Project, 1991: 38). The best-known of the racist murders over this period was that of Akhtar Ali Baig on East Ham High Street on 17 July 1980 by a skinhead gang. Two boys and two girls aged 15 to 17 stopped him in the street, abused him, and spat in his face before one of them, 17-year-old Paul Mullery, pulled out a sheath knife and stabbed him in the heart (Newham Monitoring Project, 1991: 40). Although the police described the incident as a 'mugging gone wrong', the evidence of racism was overwhelming. During the trial it emerged that some local youths who had witnessed the killing had followed the skinheads to a house, and called the police, who subsequently arrested those involved. Two of the skinheads were known by teachers at Plashet school who had heard racist remarks and seen them attacking Asians at school. The police told the judge that on searching the bedroom of one of the gang, they had found material with swastikas, the letters 'NF' and 'Pakistanis Out' written on it. The judge in the case ruled that the murder was 'plainly motivated by racial hatred'. The killer, Paul Mullery was said to have boasted at the time of the murder, 'I've just gutted a Paki'. As he was led from the court, 'he gave

---

[7] On 4 May 1978 Altab Ali was murdered in Whitechapel; in June Ishaque Ali was murdered in Hackney; in July Benjamin Thompson and Michael Nathaniel were murdered in north-west London; Vernon Brown was murdered in Birmingham in September; and Michael Ferreira was murdered in east London in December. In January 1979 Abdul Aziz was murdered in Peterborough; in August Kaymarz Anklesaria was murdered in east London and Sawdegar Khan was murdered in Birmingham. In January 1980 Mohammed Arif was killed in Burnley and Sewa Singh Sunder was killed in Windsor; Famous Mgutshini was killed in London in March; Pala Majumbar was killed in Greenwich in June and Louston Parry in Manchester in September. While the murderers were never found in most of these cases, each was widely believed by local communities to have been carried out for racist motives (see Gordon, 1986: 8; Newham Monitoring Project, 1991: 40).

the nazi salute and shouted "Seig Heil" and "All for a fucking Paki" '
(Newham Monitoring Project, 1991: 42–3).

Summary and Conclusion

The literature reviewed above indicates that violence has been an
enduring feature of the white British reaction to the presence of
'blacks', 'Pakis', and Jews who have settled on this island. This is not
to say that violent racism is an unchanging, trans-historical phenomenon, fixed either in the psyche of the British or in some characteristic of the victimized individuals or communities. Rather, at various
historical junctures racist ideas have identified black and brown
people as a 'problem' on the basis of which white Britons have sought
to attack, harass, and terrorize them, often with the stated goal of
expelling them from specific localities and, indeed, from the country
as a whole. Exactly how violent racism becomes manifest in particular locations at particular times depends on such factors as local tradition, the health of local and national economies, and prevailing
ideologies of race and nation. The first explicitly 'anti-black' riots in
1919 illustrate that during periods of crisis, the presence of black
people may be seen not only as a problem, but also as an explanation for other, broader, social problems. In this case, the crisis of the
post-war slump and soaring unemployment in certain sectors of the
economy (particularly shipping) was identified with the presence of
black sailors and Jewish merchants in British ports. The most prominent interpretation of the events at the time was that these black
people were themselves the cause of the violence inflicted against
them. Correspondingly, the solution which was advocated by the
authorities was their evacuation and eventual repatriation.

Violent racism was not a new phenomenon in late 1981 and it was
'on the political agenda' before this time (see Witte, 1996). From the
point of view of black and brown-skinned people, violent racism has
formed an integral part of their politics, ever since specifically 'black
politics' existed in Britain (see Sivanandan 1982). And even prior to
the development of British black self-organization in the 1950s, the
experience of violent racism formed part of the political consciousness
of individual black people and their communities of formation. The
experiences of the pre- and post-war colonial settlers has, by and
large, not been recorded in history books and their oral histories have
yet to be written. However, drawing on the evidence that we do have

of British racism in the colonies and of the colour-bar at home, it seems likely that the early colonial migrants met considerable hostility and violence as they looked for work, homes, and places to socialize. The riots of 1958 brought home to black people that, whatever their views about their relationship to Britishness, the fact of their 'race' could be used as the basis for exclusion, attack, and terrorization. The 1958 racist riots, and the sense of threat which they engendered, were important catalysts in the development of black political organization (Hiro, 1991: 26–43).

The riots of 1958 also placed violent racism on national political agendas. They were covered by national newspapers and drew commentary from individuals from all the major political parties as well as from the judiciary, the church, and other moral entrepreneurs. However, as was the case in the aftermath of the racist riots of 1919, the dominant explanation for their occurrence was the presence of black people themselves. Indeed, the politics of 'race' which emerged after the 1958 riots led to an increasing focus on the problems 'associated' with black people and on the 'dangers' of unrestricted immigration. Rather than addressing the racism which had given rise to, and focused, the violence of large numbers of white people against the small black communities in Nottingham and London, commentators used the riots as an example of the problems 'caused' by the presence of black people. After 1958 an inclusive notion of Britishness which encompassed the entire empire was abandoned in favour of one defined in terms of British 'blood and bone', subsequently institutionalized through immigration legislation of 1960s and 1970s.

Racist outbursts serious enough to merit news media attention occurred sporadically throughout the 1960s and early 1970s. Little is known about the daily experiences of African, Caribbean, Asian, Jewish, Arab, and other dark-skinned minorities as they struggled to take their place in Britain over this period. But the colour-bar did not crumble as soon as anti-discrimination legislation was passed. Rather, explicitly whites-only residential neighbourhoods, places of entertainment, and sections of the employment market persisted long after the Race Relations Acts of 1958, 1968, and 1976. The vestiges of the colour-bar are still evident in some places to this day. As a consequence, individual black people had to learn where they could and could not work, what pubs and clubs it was safe to attend, and where it was safe and unsafe to live. The colour-bar, like any other ban, needed coercion, the threat of violence, and actual violence to keep it in place. Throughout this period, racism was made respectable and institutional through the rhetoric of politicians such as Powell and through immigration controls that discriminated one British passport holder from another on the ground of their 'race'. The dominant theme that runs through the racialized discourses of this time is that black people are a problem the solution to which is halting, and then reversing, migration from the Commonwealth.

During the mid- to late-1970s violent racism became more open and explicit than hitherto. Several murders of Afro-Caribbean and Asian people were carried out by people explicitly identifying themselves as racists. Numerous other murders occurred in a context of racist antipathy, which black communities believed to be the work of racists but for whom no one was caught. In some localities, such as the West Midlands, parts of London, the North West, and elsewhere, racist harassment and attacks became a daily reality for black individuals and communities. Again, the racialized rhetoric of politicians and media panics about immigration and the problems associated with (black) immigrants served to justify the 'territorial defensiveness' of the 'host' community. The rise of the National Front and the popular support which it gained over this period served to strengthen the resolve of those committed to resisting and repelling the settlement of black people. Moreover, there is good evidence that the NF was actively organizing racist attacks, and through its demonstrations and distribution of literature was inspiring sympathizers to take direct violent action against their black neighbours.

By the end of the 1970s, a fairly well articulated moral panic had emerged about the National Front and the violence with which it was associated. More problematic from the viewpoint of the media, the police, and central government, however, was the resulting conflict between the NF, anti-fascists, and the police. The most visible manifestation of this conflict were the events which occurred in Southall in 1979. For many commentators, the anti-fascists were as much to blame for the resulting public disorder as the National Front.

Violent racism seems to have been on the agenda of central government, albeit at the periphery, long before being acknowledged as such. Clearly, the racist riots of 1919 and 1958 and the activities of the National Front during the 1970s were government concerns, even if this did not constitute the existence of an issue on the public agenda (see Witte, 1996). From the mid-1970s, concern about violent racism had begun to reach a critical mass, particularly on the left but also among those on the liberal wing of the Conservative Party. Both Conservative and Labour governments were forced to respond to lobbying on the issue of violent racism by MPs, black organizations, and anti-racist groups. However, it was only when the all-party Joint Committee Against Racialism (JCAR) was formed and began to influence government thinking at the very end of the 1970s that a route was found to communicate the experiences and fears of Britain's black communities to central government politicians.

*   *   *

For the British ethnic minorities, violent racism has always been on the political agenda. For central and local government and the police, however, such violence was seen (at best) as a personal trouble, or (at worst) as a problem emanating from the presence of black people themselves. Indeed, as the Home Office itself points out, violent racism was not 'on the agenda' for central government until 1981. Having belatedly 'discovered' the problem from 1981 onwards, activity directed at the problem of violent racism on the part of local and central state agencies increased dramatically. The product of this activity in the form of defining the problem, conducting research, developing policy, and attempting to change state practices is explored in Chapter 3.

3

Violent Racism and Policy Formulation (1981–4)

1981 marks a turning-point in the history of the state response to violent racism. As the central government Inter-Departmental Racial Attacks Group commented in 1989, 'the 1981 Home Office study, with the advantage of its official status, put racial attacks on the political agenda for the first time' (Home Office, 1989: 1). In November 1981, the Home Secretary, William Whitelaw, announced that 'racially motivated attacks' were 'wicked crimes', that were 'more common than we had supposed' and had not been recognized before simply because of a 'lack of reliable information' (Home Office, 1981). Until then, as the problem did not exist, there was no publically stated police or government policy to deal with it (Witte, 1996). Within two years, this situation had changed fundamentally. A range of governmental agencies, among them the House of Commons, Home Office, Metropolitan Police, Association of Chief Police Officers, and Greater London Council, each elevated violent racism to the status of urgent priority. This Chapter describes how, and in what form, official policies developed between 1981 and 1984. It examines the diverse ways in which various statutory organizations defined the problem of violent racism and how they decided what it consisted in, who its victims and perpetrators were (and were not), its relationship to politically organized racism, and to the wider problems of racial disadvantage, public disorder, and policing.

The 1980s: A Turbulent Decade

The recognition in 1981 that violent racism was a genuine social problem came about partly because many believed that it had escalated to an unprecedented level of intensity and ferocity between 1979 and 1981. The view that violent racism was on the increase was expressed in every report on the subject published at the time. Certainly, 1981 marks a peak in instances of racist murders (see Table 3.1). However, 1981 is a critical year in the history of the relationship between the police and ethnic minority communities more generally.

Table 3.1 *Racist murders in Britain 1970–92*

Year	Murders
1970	2
1971	1
1972	0
1973	3
1974	0
1975	2
1976	5
1977	0
1978	8
1979	3
1980	6
1981	26
1982	0
1983	0
1984	1
1985	6
1986	5
1987	2
1988	1
1989	4
1990	–
1991	1
1992	8
1993	2
1994	3

Source: Gordon (1986/1990); Anti-Racist Alliance, *Bulletin*; Pimpinella (1995); press accounts. Defined where it was known or widely believed to have involved some element of racial motivation.

The issues of racism, violence, and policing were in newspaper headlines, not only because of the high incidence of racist attacks, but also because of the widespread outbreaks of violence between the police and young (and frequently) black and Asian people which occurred during the spring and summer of that year.[1] Behind the riots were factors such as the economic resession, which affected young people in the inner cities the hardest; racial prejudice (Brown, 1984), fear of crime, and police misconduct and mistreatment of ethnic minorities. Among the events of 1981 were the disorders in London, Manchester, Birmingham, and elsewhere. The riots in Brixton, London, in April occurred in the aftermath of 'Operation Swamp' and resulted in the injury of seventy-nine police officers and forty-five members of the public. There were further riots in Toxteth and Southall in July, and in numerous cities and towns across England and Wales. Most of these riots involved black and white youths confronting the police. The only casualty was the death of a young white disabled man, hit by a police car during a riot in Toxteth at the end of July.

These 'almost American-style riots' alarmed the British public, the government, and police managers. The British police, historically a source of great pride and still respected by the great majority of the population, came under critical scrutiny. They had hitherto also been politically protected by a bi-partisan approach by government, though by 1981 the Labour Party was already beginning to adopt a more critical stance (Sked and Cook, 1993: 353). Among the most critical reports on the Metropolitan police was the Policy Studies Institute (PSI) Report which, according to one review, condemned them as "bigoted, racist, sexist, bored, dishonest and often drunk" (Sked and Cook, 1993: 353).

1981 was a bad year for the police in other ways. There were corruption scandals in London and elsewhere (Reiner 1992). Crime continued to rise (it had risen from 1.6 million in 1970 to 2.8 million in 1981). Spending on the police rose by 5 per cent a year, while the pay of a police constable had risen in real terms by over 30 per cent between 1979 and 1983 with the result that the number of police in England and Wales had increased by 9,500 to more than 120,000 during Mrs Thatcher's first term of office. Labour MP Jack Straw introduced a Private Member's Billl which would have made local police forces responsible to committees of local councillors. The Labour Group that took control of the Greater London Council 1981 immediately set up a police committe with staff to oversee the running of

---

[1] A discussion of the conflict between the police and young people over this period can be found in Kettle and Hodges, 1982; Benyon and Solomos, 1987; Solomos 1988; Hiro, 1991 Cashmore and McLaughlin, 1991; Keith, 1996.

the police, and provided funding for local monitoring groups (Keith and Murji, 1990; Sked and Cook, 1994; Reiner, 1992: 238–9).

The clashes between anti-racist demonstrators, organized racists, and the police, evident throughout the latter part of the 1970s, continued into the 1980s. Violent clashes between Asian young people, far-right political groups, and the police occurred in Southall, Bradford, and Coventry during the spring and summer of 1981 (Hiro, 1991: 175–6). A long overdue public policy response to violent racism and policing became a political necessity in 1981.

Racism, Violence and Policing 1981–4

Before looking in detail at how the police and central and local government agencies defined violent racism during the early 1980s and what types of policies were developed to respond to this policy development, it is necessary to acquaint the reader briefly with the violent racist activity which occurred during this period and with the concerns about policing policy and practice which emerged at this time.

The New Cross and Walthamstow fires

On 18 January 1981 thirteen young Afro-Caribbean people died and thirty others were injured in a fire in Deptford/New Cross, south London (Ramdin, 1987; Smith and Gray, 1985: 328–434, Layton-Henry, 1984: 114). Although the cause of the fire was never established beyond doubt (the inquest arrived at an open verdict), there was circumstantial evidence which led many people to believe that it was started by racists. In particular, during the period leading up to the fire, the black community of Deptford had been the focus of National Front activity and racist attacks and harassment (Layton-Henry, 1984: 114; Smith and Gray, op. cit.). In the immediate aftermath of the fire, Mrs Rudock (whose house was burnt down and who lost a son and daughter in the fire) received 'highly offensive and racialist [letters which] gloated over the deaths and saw the fire as a first step in ridding Britain of black people' (Smith and Gray, 1985: 430). At the inquest it was revealed that an unexploded incendiary device was found outside the house (Smith and Gray, 1985: 433). A mass demonstration organized by a 'Massacre Action Committee' was held on 2 March in which an estimated 10,000 to 15,000 people took part (ibid.). During the march from Deptford to central London clashes occurred between the police and demonstrators and at least twenty-eight arrests were made (Smith and Gray, 1985: 428; Small, 1983).

During a spate of attacks on black people and their property in Walthamstow in March, a school was smeared with five foot high swastikas and National Front daubings (Hesse *et al.*, 1992: 5). On 10 April a young black man, Malcolm Chambers, was murdered in Swindon in an 'anti-black riot' (Layton-Henry, 1984: 115). On 18 April Satnam Singh Gill, a 20-year-old student, was stabbed to death in Coventry city centre by skinheads (*ibid.*). At around the same time a Sikh temple was petrol bombed and the Indian and Commonwealth Club in London suffered an arson attack (Layton-Henry, 1984: 115). In the early hours of 2 July the home of the Khan family in Walthamstow was set ablaze after petrol was sprayed through the letter box (Hesse *et al.*, 1992: 10). Mrs Parveen Khan and her three children died in the fire and Mr Yunus Khan was seriously burned. The inquest verdict of unlawful killing confirmed that four murders had taken place but failed to address the concern that this had been a racist arson attack[2] (*ibid.*).

The London Borough of Newham was a particular focus of violent racism during the early 1980s. Attacks and harassment were directed, in particular, against the homes of Asian families and against Asian schoolchildren, though attacks were also reported on ethnic minority workplaces and places of worship (Gordon, 1986: 8–16; Tompson, 1988; Newham Monitoring Project, 1991). Newham was also a site of community self-defence and vigorous organized opposition to violent racism over this period. In 1980 the Newham Monitoring Project (NMP) was formed and presented a dossier of cases to local MPs. In 1982 NMP set up an advice centre in Forest Gate and launched a twenty-four-hour emergency help-line for black people experiencing violent racism or police harassment (Newham Monitoring Project, 1991: 44–5). Violent racism, policing, and the question of self-defence organization became in Newham issues of national concern in 1982 as a result of the 'Newham 8' case[3].

---

[2] Other murders believed to have had racist motives during 1981 include Amil Dharry in Coventry in April; Fenton Ogbogbo in south London and Charan Kaur and Poran Singh in Leeds in June; Asif Ahmed Khan Shamsuddin in north London in July; and Mohammed Arif in Bradford in November (Gordon, 1990: 8).

[3] The Newham 8 case arose out of an incident on 24 September when a group of Asian young men were 'sworn at . . . and racially abused [by] three white men, scruffily dressed in jeans, bomber jackets and trousers' whom the Asian youths took to be racists (Newham Monitoring Project, 1991: 51). A fight broke out and within minutes

Non-government Reports on Violent Racism 1982–4

Evidence of somewhat less serious, but often persistent, racially motivated attacks and harassment which were affecting black individuals
and communities across the country was also gathered during the
early 1980s.[4] For example the Joint Committee Against Racialism
report (JCAR, 1981) presented to the Home Secretary the day after
the Deptford fire provided evidence of attacks directed specifically
against ethnic minorities in areas where there was strong evidence of
far-right activity and recruiting.[5] The report found among the hundreds of cases across the country numerous attacks on Synagogues,
Temples, and places of burial. Another report published in 1981 by
the Union of Pakistani Organizations suggested that racist attacks
had grown from an average of twenty-five a week in 1980 to fifty to
sixty a week in 1981 (Layton-Henry, 1984: 116).

Evidence from various independent organizations confirmed that
violent racism continued to be as serious a problem during 1982–3 as
it had been at the turn of the decade. Some argued that it continued
to escalate; few believed that the situation was improving. The Policy

uniformed police officers, dog handlers, and a police helicopter were on the scene. The
'scruffily dressed men', it turned out, were plain clothes police officers, members of a
locally based District Support Unit. The 8 Asian youths, many of whom were badly
beaten, were taken to Forest Gate police station (*ibid.*). In response to the arrest of the
8 youths, 500 people attended a public meeting and thereafter began to organize a campaign in their defence and to oppose violent racism. One year after the original incident 2,000 people marched through Newham on a 'National March Against Racism
and Fascism'. When the case came to court in November 1983, 500 schoolchildren
staged a school strike and picketed the courts, a picket which was maintained throughout the 6-week-long trial at the Old Bailey (*ibid.*). The outcome of the trial was that
4 of the 8 youths were found guilty of affray. However, because the trial had focused
media attention on the issue of violent racism and provided the media 'with a worm's
eye view of the non-accountable and aggressive way in which black inner-city communities are policed', the result, according to the Newham Monitoring Project, was a
'victory for community self-organisation' (*ibid.*).

[4] Other reports published over this period included those compiled by Ealing
Community Relations Council on Racialist Activity in the London Borough of Ealing
(1981), the Commission for Racial Equality (1981), and the Runnymede Trust (Klug,
1982).

[5] JCAR drew on information from Community Relations Councils, informants, and
publications from ethnic minority organizations, Searchlight magazine, local law centres, and community organizations. They provided detailed case studies of attacks in
High Wycombe, Oldham, and Lambeth and noted that a similar story could be told
of many other London boroughs (such as Greenwich, Hackney, Tower Hamlets,
Lewisham, Camden, Barking, or Hounslow) as well as London suburbs, towns in the
north-west (such as Blackburn), and major cities (such as Bristol and Manchester). See
Chap. 1 for further details on the formation and activities of JCAR.

Studies Institute (PSI) survey of racial attacks, carried out as part of its study of *Black and White Britain*, concluded that the frequency of such attacks at that time could have been as much as ten times that estimated by the Home Office (Brown, 1984 see pp. 154–5, below). A poll conducted by the Harris Research Centre for London Weekend Television found that one in four Asians in the east London boroughs of Tower Hamlets, Redbridge, Waltham Forest, and Newham said that they or a member of their family had been racially attacked, one in ten of them seriously (cited in Gordon, 1986: 6). Towards the end of 1983, the Board of Deputies of British Jews reported that there had been an average of between twenty and twenty-five anti-Semitic incidents each month in London during the previous two years (cited in Greater London Council, 1984: 19).

The Police and the Public: Legitimacy, Consent, and Accountability

The feature of the police organization which unifies all of its disparate activities is the ability to use coercive force to 'define and enforce collectively binding decisions on the members of a society in the name of a common interest or general will' (Jessop, 1990; cited in Sheptycki, 1995). As Bittner put it, 'the policeman and the policeman alone is equipped, entitled and required to deal with every exigency in which force may have to be used' (Bittner, 1970: 35). However, as Bittner argues, the capacity to use force, and in particular the actual use of force, is antithetical to the goals of peace in modern society. Therefore, the police, and the legitimacy of their use of coercive force in the name of the 'general will' requires justification.

In other words, outside a specific normative framework, the police, as *the* organ of state coercive authority, cannot be taken as a given. This is evident from the fact that blue-uniformed police were not established until well into the nineteenth century in London (and later still in the United States), after most other structures of the modern democratic state, such as the prison were in place (see Bittner, 1970; Emsley, 1983; Foucault, 1977). When Peel pushed through the Metropolitan Police Act in 1829, he did so in the face of considerable opposition from across the social-class spectrum, and it was only successful through inspired and careful justification of the police institution. This justification included such principles as the prevention of crime and preservation of public tranquility, the dependence of public approval of the existence, action, and behaviour of the police, the willing co-operation of the public in voluntary observance of the law, impartiality and fairness, the minimum use of force, the notion that the 'police are the public and the public are the police' and that their role should not extend to judging guilt or punishing the guilty (see Reiner, 1985; Lee, 1901, cited by Radlet and Carter, 1994). We might refer to this process of justification as a form of hegemony, meaning the construction and maintenance of ideological predominance of some groups over others (Milliband, 1969: 162). However, this justification is not simply something which happens. Rather it is the result of a permanent and pervasive effort to create a 'national supra party consensus' or 'higher order solidarity' (*ibid.*).

*   *   *

The quality of the relationship between the police and the people whom they have a mandate to protect transformed radically in the period to 1981. The ephemeral post-war 'golden age' passed into the more fractious and conflict-ridden 1970s to a period characterized by frequent violent conflict between the police and public and sense of 'crisis' at the beginning of the 1980s (Reiner, 1985; McLaughlin, 1991). The policing of industrial disputes, black and Asian communities, students, feminists, political protest, transformed into open (and physical) conflict in the 1970s and 1980s. At the same time, the failure of the police to reduce crime—and in particular specific crimes such as rape, racial attacks, domestic violence, child abuse—was drawn into question through academic, institutional, and political inquiry. British and American social science began to indicate that established modes of policing practice were ineffective in solving, preventing, and reducing crime; and that the reasons for this lay at the very core of the way in which the police institution is organized (Weatheritt, 1986; Goldstein, 1990).

Although the twentieth century and even the post-war period were not as tranquil as they have been characterized (Benyon, 1987: 27), the riots during the 1980s were certainly the most serious disorders on mainland Britain since the Second World War. By 1981 it appeared that some sections of society were willing to challenge the legitimacy of the police to an extent unprecedented in the twentieth century. It is in this context that the statutory response to violent racism developed, and so it is relevant to consider the nature of the challenge to the idea that the police are the legitimate protectors of all members of the public and the sole possessors of the legitimate use of force.[6]

The change in the relationship between police and public noted above has been characterized as the breakdown of 'legitimacy' (Reiner, 1985), 'consent' (Morgan, 1989), and 'accountability' (McLaughlin, 1991). Reiner argues that each of the factors which had led to the de-politicization of the police from the 1830s to the 1950s and created the notion of 'policing by consent' had, by the end of the 1970s, come into serious question.[7] The image of the police as an efficient, disciplined bureaucracy eroded through numerous corruption scandals in the 1970s. Reiner summarizes the elements of the 'crisis' facing the police as follows. There was evidence of police violations of legal procedures when dealing with offences which undermined the idea that they simply upheld the rule of law; the development and deployment of paramilitary policing techniques replaced the use of minimal force; the overtly political stance of increasingly vocal police managers and professional associations belied the idea of non-partisanship; the 'service' and 'preventive' roles of the police were overshadowed by the role of the police as crime fighters; it became increasingly evident that the police did not and perhaps could not effectively control crime; and the impact of police powers on marginalised sections of society became increasingly visible as conflicts between diverse social groups including the young, political protesters, strikers, and, most relevant here, ethnic minorities, flared into violence (Reiner, 1985: 64–82).

Morgan separates 'the component strands of meaning in the idea of "policing by consent" ' (1989: 217). *Contractual* consent, he suggests, is created between the police and government and comprises legal consent and political consent. *Legal* consent is maintained through 'the

---

[6] Bittner (1970) concludes that the core function of policing—that of maintaining order—relies on the potential use of legitimate (legally sanctioned) force: 'the policeman, and the policeman alone, is equipped, entitled and required to deal with every exigency in which force may have to be used'.

[7] Reiner (1985: 52–61) argues that 7 specific policies, laid down by the architects of the 'New Police'—Rowan and Mayne—established the legitimacy of the police institution. These were: (1) the creation of the image of police officers as 'disciplined members of a bureaucratic organisation of professionals'; (2) the strict regulation of the use of discretionary legal powers; (3) the use of 'minimal force'; (4) non-partisanship; (5) the cultivation of the 'service role'; (6) preventive policing; (7) a belief in the policing effectiveness in controlling crime; and (8) the incorporation of the working class.

rule of law' and *political* consent through the parliamentary mechanism. Thus, the law does not determine key aspects of policing policy and neither, directly, do politicians (1989: 218). *Social* consent—that between the police and public—also has two dimensions: attitudinal consent and operational consent. *Attitudinal* consent, Morgan suggests, may be measured by opinion surveys. *Operational* consent—deference to police authority—may be measured by the extent to which the police feel the need to resort to defensive strategies or force during their work. Morgan concludes that during the 1980s the claim was seriously challenged that there existed an acceptable level of consent, in all four senses of the term (Morgan, 1989: 219).

McLaughlin (1991) argues that the legitimacy of the police use of force, and of the institution itself, rests on its accountability—its obligation to explain and justify its conduct in public (McLaughlin, 1991: 110; McLaughlin, 1994; Lustgarten, 1986). The 1964 Police Act formalized the tripartite structure of governance of the police consisting of police authorities comprising (outside London) members from local government, central government, and the police. In London, the police authority is the Home Secretary alone. The peculiar position in London derives from Peel's Metropolitan Police Act of 1829 which made the Secretary of State responsible for approving the size of the force, the regulations guiding it, and empowered the commissioners in command of the force to execute specific duties (Lustgarten, 1986). This situation has remained largely unchanged by subsequent legislation. Outside London, the police authorities have a range of responsibilities including the appointment of senior police officers, but have no mandate over 'operational' matters. Under the 1964 Act (and remaining basically unchanged by the 1976 Police Act and 1984 Police and Criminal Evidence Act) Chief Constables have responsibility for 'direction and control', which embraces police practice relevant to 'operational matters'—such as legal duties and the use of police powers in general and in specific (Jones, Newburn and Smith, 1994: 217–25).

It has been argued that the 'tripartite' system after the 1964 Act shifted power towards central from local government and made it difficult to open the police institution to both scrutiny and outside pressure. In his review of the changes in the extent of accountability of the police specifically to black communities McLaughlin argues that, as a consequence of the failure of the 1964 Police Act to resolve the problem of accountability to the public in general, policing was placed back on the political agenda as it became more controversial at the end of the 1970s (McLaughlin, 1991: 111). Concern was expressed about an increasing gap between the police and the community. In 'technocratic' mode, the police, it appeared, felt no need to 'negotiate their presence in neighbourhoods, to cultivate the consent of the community or to take into account the needs of the community. Policing strategies were decided upon, implemented and changed without consultation' (ibid.). The situation was exaggerated in London, where the Home Secretary and Metropolitan Police Commissioner had no statutory requirement to take account of locally elected bodies, such as the Greater London Council.

The criticisms to which McLaughlin refers were part of a wider debate about police accountability at the beginning of the 1980s which focused on malpractice, corruption, brutality, and racial prejudice. In November 1979 and March 1980 Labour MP Jack Straw attempted to introduce legislation to strengthen the powers of police committees and create an elected police authority for London. In 1981 the London Labour Party included demands for a police authority for London in its manifesto (Sheptycki, 1991; McLaughlin, 1991: 114). In May 1981, a new Labour left administration took control of the Greater London Council (GLC). Its platform included, among other issues, a campaign for democratic accountability for the police, and race equality and equal opportunities policies (Keith and Murji, 1990: 124–5). The Council immediately established a Police Committee 'with the central aim of campaigning for a new Police Authority for London, comprised wholly of elected councillors to replace the existing arrangements' (ibid.).

McLaughlin argues that as a consequence of the high degree of autonomy of the police and of the powerlessness of black communities to voice their experiences of oppressive policing, political and (frequently) violent conflict intensified during the 1980s. Moreover, the lack of accountability of the police is reflected in the evidence which emerged over this period of the failure of the police to protect black individuals and communities against racial attacks and for police officers actually to engage in oppressive practices themselves. Numerous research studies and reports on the policing, racism, and racial violence were produced between the middle 1960s and the early 1980s.[8] This literature is characterized by criticism of the police for

---

[8] For a useful analysis of developments over this period see McLaughlin, 1991. See also Commission for Racial Equality, 1979; Institute of Race Relations, 1979/1987; Home Office, 1981; House of Commons, 1982; Smith and Gray, 1983.

their failure to respond adequately to reported instances of racist violence and allegations of discrimination towards those harassed or attacked and hostility towards ethnic minorities in general. Although some reports find evidence of positive and effective police action, most criticize the police as complacent and ineffectual at best and, at worst, as hostile towards the victims they are charged with protecting. Table 3.2 summarizes the specific criticisms levelled at the police by government and non-government organizations over the period.

Table 3.2 *Criticisms of the police response to violent racism*

Issue	Criticism of police	Report
Protection	Not protecting Asian community	IRR 1979; Scarman, 1986: 31.
Prevention	Not preventing racial offences	Home Office, 1981
Definition of the problem	Redefining attacks (as street crime, burglary, juvenile crime, hooliganism, or neighbourly disputes)	IRR, 1979/1987
	Defining criminal assaults (actual bodily harm) as non-criminal (common assault)	GLC, 1984
Identifying racial motivation	Refusal to recognize racial dimension or denying racial motivation	IRR, 1979; Home Office, 1981
Prioritziation	Playing down attacks; the police do not treat racial harassment seriously (i.e. as a crime)	IRR, 1987; Hesse *et al.*, 1992: 70
Immediate response	Delay/slowness in responding to calls for help	IRR, 1979; GLC, 1984; HAC, 1986
	Unresponsive/non-response/failure to arrive	Home Office, 1981; GLC, 1984; HAC, 1986
Victim Support	Hostile questioning and unsympathetic treatment of victims (sometimes leading to the arrest of the victim)	HAC, 1986
	Misguided advice to victims (such as advising victims to bring private prosecutions or civil action when criminal proceedings were appropriate)	IRR, 1979: Home Office, 1981; GLC, 1984; HAC, 1986
	Hostility to complainants	IRR, 1979
	Treating victim as aggressor; the police treat the victims as the problem	IRR, 1979, 1987; GLC, 1984: 12–17; Hesse *et al.*, 1992
	Failure to keep victims informed of action taken	HAC, 1986

cont.

Table 3.2 *Cont.*

Issue	Criticism of police	Report
	Arrest or harassment of victims (for example, asked to produce their passports in confirmation of their immigration status)	Home Office, 1981
	Unwillingness to provide interpreters	HAC, 1986
Law enforcement (investigation)	Unwillingness to investigate/not following up cases; where the police do respond there is no follow up	IRR, 1979, 1987; GLC, 1984; Hesse *et al.*, 1992
Accountability	Unrepresentative of the community	Home Office, 1981
	Not doing enough to respond to the problems experienced by the ethnic minorities	Home Office, 1981
	Lack confidence from ethnic minority communities	Home Office, 1981
	Criminalizing self defence	IRR, 1987; Newham Monitoring Project, 1991
Police racism	Unequal treatment of ethnic minorities	Home Office, 1981
	Direct police harassment of the community	Hunte, 1966; IRR, 1979
	Commonplace use of racist language	GLC, 1984
	Racially discriminatory policing such as: illegal entry into black people's homes, stop and search targeted specifically against black people; assault and racist abuse during arrest; 'blatant racism' and harassment when dealing with black juveniles; treating black victims of crime as criminal; and speculative passport checks (referred to as immigration 'fishing raids') directed against black people.	Hunte, 1966; GLC, 1984: 9–12

Note: the 1986 Home Affairs Committee report commented that 'The extent to which each of these characteristics is typical of the police response to racial incidents is difficult to assess, although for most of them there is evidence that they occur in some cases' (House of Commons, 1986: viii, original emphasis). See also reports by GLARE, 1988; Murji and Cutler, 1992; Hesse *et al.*, 1992; Commission for Racial Equality (CRE), 1979–87; Dunhill, 1989; NMP, 1991; NMP Annual reports.

The failure to take account of the concerns of ethnic minority communities, to explain and justify the weakness of the police response to violent racism in public and the related conflict in the relationship between the police and ethnic minority communities at the beginning of the 1980s may be characterized as a breakdown in consent, a collapse of accountability or crisis of legitimacy. The alternatives offered during the 1980s by the police, central and local government, and community organizsations to bring about a more effective response to violent racism all included some reference to the transformation of the formal relationships between police and public. Thus, the question of police legitimacy and the attempts made to re-establish it during the 1980s recurs throughout this Chapter and, indeed, the remainder of the book.

Redefining Violent Racism

In the two years between November 1981 and October 1983, the Home Office, the House of Commons (Home Affairs Sub-Committee on Race Relations and Immigration), the Association of Chief Police Officers (ACPO), the Metropolitan Police, and the Greater London Council issued policy statements on the issue of violent racism. In each case, the seriousness of the problem and the inadequacy of existing responses was acknowledged (grudgingly in the case of the police, who had been criticized most fiercely). In the policy statements published during this period, each agency provided a definition of the problem, outlined measures that would be taken to tackle it, and suggested measures that other agencies should pursue.

Reviewing these documents one is struck by the extent to which agencies differed in the way in which they defined and conceptualized the problem. Definitions differed in respect of: the terminology used; the types of acts or activities which were included; the role of racism and extreme right-wing political movements; and in the role of policing in combating and perpetrating racist violence. Table 3.3 illustrates the various conceptualisations of violent racism evident between 1978 and 1984.

Metropolitan Police Definition 1978–81

Although the Metropolitan Police had no publicly stated policy aimed specifically at violent racism until 1982, they had established

Table 3.3 *Conceptualizing violent racism 1978–84*

Institution:	Central government	Police	Local Government	Black community organizations
Reports:	Home Office, 1981 Lord Scarman, 1981 House of Commons HAC (1982)	Metropolitan Police Force Order (1978); ACPO evidence to HAC (1982); Metropolitan Police evidence to HAC (1982)	Greater London Council (1984)	Institute of Race Relations, 1979; Newham Monitoring Project (annual reports); Community Relations Councils
Victims:	Principally ethnic minorities; Asians most affected; Afro-Caribbeans also affected; Some white people	All parts of the community; Ethnic communities; Elderly white women	Black people	Black people
Perpetrators:	White youths/skinheads	White youths Black youths	White youths Skinheads Far-right Police officers	White youths Skinheads/far-right Police officers
Role of extreme right wing	Little concrete evidence of direct involvement Create a climate in which attacks flourish	No evidence of direct involvement	Deeply implicated in organizing and orchestrating attacks	Responsible for carrying out attacks Implicated in organising and orchestrating

an 'operational definition' and a recording system for 'racial inci-dents' in 1978. In a memorandum submitted to the 1981–2 Home Affairs Committee, the Metropolitan Police (Met) explain that, for the purposes of notifying serious incidents and disturbances to local senior officers, the Community Relations Branch, Public Order Branch, and Special Branch, a definition of a 'racial incident' had been developed. The Met's definition provides an interesting insight into how the police conceptualized 'racial incidents' during the latter part of the 1970s. It is worth citing the definition in full:[9]

A 'racial incident' is:-

   (a) An incident involving premises, individuals or organisations associ-ated with the furtherance of community relations; or
   (b) an incident involving political movements which arises from their involvement in community relations; or
   (c) an incident where there is some indication that the offender was in some way motivated by racial prejudice; or
   (d) an incident involving concerted action by or against members of an ethnic group. This will include such action which is directed against the police.

The police defined the problem as 'racial *incidents*', reflecting the basic recording unit of the police organization. All 'crimes', 'distur-bances', 'disputes', and other 'events' which come to the attention of the police are defined and recorded as incidents. The police record-ing system is based on events fixed in time and space, and all infor-mation systems—despatch, Incident Report Books, message pads, crime forms, etc.—are incident-based.

The rather opaque mention of 'community relations' and 'political movements' in (a) and (b) may be seen as references to the conflict involving the police, the extreme right, anti-racist, and community organizations during the 1970s. Individuals and organizations associ-ated with the 'furtherance of community relations' include the gov-ernment-funded community relations councils (crcs) and other groups representing ethnic minorities. 'Political movements' involved in 'community relations' almost certainly refers to anti-racist organiza-tions, though it might be taken that the National Front and other extreme racist organizations are also 'involved' in community rela-tions, even if this is a negative involvement.

---

[9] Metropolitan Police, *Force Order on Racial Incidents 1978*, cited in Home Affairs Committee, 1982: 17).

Point (c), concerning the offender's motivation, requires that an event coming to the attention of the police (e.g. a crime, dispute, or disturbance) would become a racial incident if there were any indication that the offender was motivated by racial prejudice. However, no guidance was provided on how 'racial prejudice' should be defined, nor how and by whom this motivation should be ascribed. It became clear that this was to be decided by a police officer only when the Met presented evidence to the 1981–2 Home Affairs Committee, discussed later in this Chapter.

Item (d) is undoubtedly the most surprising inclusion in the 1978 definition of a racial incident, particularly the inclusion of the police as possible targets for 'racial' violence. Here the 'racial' nature of the incident is defined by the involvement of 'concerted *action by or against an ethnic group*'.[10] Thus the Brixton riots and the numerous 'mini-riots' which preceded them in the late 1970s, and indeed any incident involving collective action by black people could have been recorded as a 'racial incident'.[11]

Between 1978 and 1982 the way in which the police formally defined a racial incident only partially matched the violent racism experienced by ethnic minorities at this time and is as interesting for what it included as well as for what it excluded. As well as 'racially motivated' incidents, the police definition *included* reference to incidents involving anti-racist political movements, activity in defence of black communities, and also more general instances of conflict between the police and 'ethnic' communities. Surprisingly, however, it *excluded*, or at least failed to refer specifically to explicitly violent racism perpetrated by far-right political organizations (such as the National Front) or explicitly racist social movements (such as the skinheads).

The 1981 Home Office Report

The inquiry into racial attacks ordered by the Home Secretary in February 1981 (see also Chapter 4) took the form of a survey of

---

[10] Note that the term 'ethnic' is used here by the police interchangeably and with equivalent meaning to the term 'ethnic minority'. The contemporary police discourse uses the term 'ethnic' when referring to groups or individuals in the same way that the word might be used to refer to, for example, 'ethnic food'. There is no sense in the police discourse that Englishness, or even Jewishness, is an ethnicity. Ethnicity therefore becomes a feature possessed only by black people, rather than a feature of all people.

[11] Such as Brockwell Park 1978; riots at Carnival in the 1970s etc. (see Hall *et al.*, 1978).

reported incidents in selected areas across the country and interviews with informants from local authorities, the police, and ethnic minority communities. The team of statisticians and researchers who undertook the study conceptualized the object of analysis for their study as a 'racial incident' for which a working definition was adopted as follows: 'an incident, or alleged offence by a person or persons of one racial group against a person, persons or property of another racial group, where there are indications of a racial motive' (1981: 7).

This definition bears a close resemblance to point (c) of the 1978 police definition in its use of the notion of a 'racial *incident*' as its unit of analysis and in that it is based on an indication of the perpetrator's 'racial' motive. A legalistic terminology (incident, alleged offence, motive) was used because the primary source of data for the study was police records. Unsurprisingly, perhaps, the Home Office definition reflected the police understanding of the problem. It should be noted that this undermined an understanding of the context of racism and violent racism and maintained the police definition of certain forms of crime committed by black people as 'racial'. Thus, the Home Office also included inter-racial incidents involving theft committed by blacks against whites, and found that both victims and the police perceived such incidents to have a 'racial motive'. However, the Home Office also found that the rate of incidents involving ethnic minority suspects and white victims where there were indications of a racial motive were fifty times less frequent than attacks by whites against Asians and thirty-six times less frequent than white attacks on Afro-Caribbeans. When comparing different forms of crime committed between 'racial' groups, it is important to note that racist attacks against ethnic minorities closely parallel the propaganda of the far-right and popular racist ideologies, while no evidence of such a relationship has ever been cited in the case of crime committed by ethnic minorities people against whites.

The Police Response

The conflict between the views of ethnic minority and police informants became clear when the report turned to the question of the police response to racial attacks. The report found that 'both individually and collectively' ethnic minorities lacked 'confidence in the capacity of the police to respond to offences of a racial character' and believed that 'the police should do far more to respond to the problems experienced by the ethnic minorities and to prevent racial offences' (Home Office, 1981: 17). Ethnic minority informants told the researchers that the police were unresponsive to their needs and unrepresentative of the community. When they reported violent incidents to the police they said they 'were liable themselves to be arrested or harassed by the police (for example, asked to produce their passports in confirmation of their immigration status) [and] even if the police found the offenders, they did no more than give a word of warning not to repeat the offence' (*ibid.*). It was believed, further, that 'in some cases, the police must be aware of the identity of the offenders, who were well known locally, and could take action if they wanted to but nevertheless did not' (*ibid.*). What the ethnic minorities wanted, the report concluded, was not preferential treatment, but treatment equal to that which they considered was received when members of the majority community were victims of criminal offences (*ibid.*).

The police, for their part, were concerned that the ethnic minorities lacked the full confidence of the police and were taking 'positive steps to secure the trust and co-operation of the ethnic minorities' (*ibid.*: 18). However, the police argued that 'with the best will in the world, it would never be possible to prevent racial incidents' (*ibid.*). This, they argued, was because 'the nature of many racial incidents made investigation and detection very difficult': sometimes when the perpetrator was known to the victim there was no evidence to prove his involvement.[12]

The report concluded that while racial attacks were only one manifestation of crime and could not claim an automatic priority, 'there was . . . a tendency on the part of the police to underestimate the

---

[12] The report explained the difficulty the police faced as they saw it: 'Often members of the ethnic minorities who have been attacked may identify the attacker and call the police in the expectation that the alleged offender will be immediately arrested. They fail to recognise that the police cannot make an arrest unless there is evidence of involvement in an offence for which there is a power of arrest. In the absence of such evidence, the police may feel that they can do no more than issue a word of warning to the alleged offender or advise the victim to take out a private prosecution. On the other hand, we were told of several cases in which the police insistence on thoroughly questioning the victim or witness at the scene of the incident had resulted in the escape of offenders who had been identified to them. The ethnic minorities interpret responses of this kind as denoting a lack of police interest in their problems, and as likely to give some white youths the impression that they can commit such offences with impunity. For their part, the police consider it important that the ethnic minorities should understand the limits which the law imposes on their ability to take summary action' (Home Office, 1981: 18).

significance of racialist incidents and activities for those attacked or threatened' (*ibid*.: 32). In response to this, training, in the form of 'giving police officers a greater awareness of ethnic minorities', was thought to be of benefit. Special police squads were said to have been rejected by the majority of both the police and ethnic minority informants primarily because 'Responding to racialist offences should be the responsibility of all operational officers, and it was important that all officers, and not just a select few should be made aware of the problems of and show sensitivity towards the ethnic minority communities' (*ibid*.: 20).

The report commented that the police invariably regretted that ethnic minorities were unwilling to apply to join the police force. The study team noted that some ethnic minority informants regarded the police as a hostile institution and would therefore have nothing to do with it. Some would not join as long as the police were unsympathetic to their problems, while others thought that those ethnic minorities who joined the police could no longer devote themselves to the interests of, and would risk coming into conflict with, their own community (*ibid*.: 23). The study team noted that in areas where ethnic minority communities had lost the confidence in the ability of the police to protect them, 'considerable pressure is likely to develop for the formation of self-help or vigilante groups, particularly to protect places of worship'. The report cited evidence of younger Asians in particular being willing to take action to ensure the protection of their community, by retaliation against white youths in some cases. The report found that although retaliation was not condoned by most minority communities, they were told of cases in which 'the police had arrived at the scene of a racial incident and arrested the ethnic minority people, who claimed to be acting in self defence, and not their attackers' (*ibid*.: 23). In other cases, having held onto a person responsible for regularly attacking their premises until the police arrived, the victims were themselves arrested for forcibly detaining the alleged offender (*ibid*.).

The Local Authority Response

The Home Office report noted that local authorities were also affected by racial attacks in housing, social services, and education, but were without the necessary information or policies to respond effectively. Local authority housing departments, for example, felt that it was difficult to take action beyond repairing damage. They also found themselves in a double bind with respect to requests to transfer racial attack victims from addresses at which they were being victimized. On one hand, transferring the victim might give encouragement to racists while, on the other, victims found it difficult to understand why they should have to remain as targets for racial harassment (1981: 26). While some authorities claimed to have a policy of forcibly transferring families known to engage in racial attacks, they found it extremely difficult to find evidence actually to do so in practice (*ibid.*).

Police Liaison Committees

Two issues regarding the relationship between the police and public, and the need for 'liaison', cropped up in the Home Office report. First, the report suggested that the response to victims of racial attack should be swift and co-ordinated between local authority services and the police. While relationships between local authorities and the police were good at a senior level, the report found, there was 'scope for more regular contact between police officers at more junior levels and housing managers, teachers etc.' (1981: 34). Secondly, the report suggested that liaison committees which allowed communication between the police, community relations councils, and other representatives of the ethnic minority communities could be a valuable form of regular contact (ibid.: 37). The study team, however, were 'disappointed to find that even in areas with significant ethnic minority populations, either no formal machinery for liaison existed or such machinery was inadequate' (*ibid.*). On this point, the Home Office report concluded that:

Greater co-operation between the minority communities, the police and local authorities is a first and essential constructive step, and where this has been achieved (as, for example, by the Jewish community) a positive and effective approach can be adopted to the whole problem of racial attacks [*ibid.*].

Unfortunately, the report does not detail the experience of liaison between the police and the Jewish community.[13] Neither does it state how liaison committees have been, or could be, a constructive, positive, or effective approach to racial attacks.

[13] The relationship between the police and the Jewish community *vis-à-vis* racial attacks was cited as a model on several occasions over this period. However, the police seemed reluctant to be precise about what arrangements actually existed (HAC, 1982: 6, para. 7); see also Factor and Stenson, 1989; Stenson and Factor, 1993).

Policy Proposals

Although the 1981 Home Office report did not make any recommendations, in the foreword to the report, William Whitelaw, then Home Secretary, identified a number of lines of action which would be pursued. First, because it was the opinion of the study team that the failure to appreciate the seriousness of violent racism hitherto had been 'largely due to a lack of reliable information about it', the police would now collect information about the incidence of this form of crime. Secondly, arrangements for liaison between the police, local authorities, and ethnic minority communities would be explored. Thirdly, the police would receive training to enable them to develop a greater sensitivity to the problem of racial attacks. Fourthly, ethnic minority groups would assist with 'on the job' training for the police; this would also provide opportunities for the police to explain matters of evidence and law to community leaders. Fifthly, the report called for racial incidents to be reported immediately and directly to the police (though a means to achieve this was not specified). And sixthly, the report noted that ways of combating racist activity and propaganda among young people, particularly in schools and football grounds, were needed, though what this would entail was not specified (Home Office, 1981: iii–iv).

The Scarman Report

A week after the publication of the Home Office report on racial attacks, Lord Scarman's report on the Brixton riots was published (Scarman, 1981/1986). This report has received a great deal of attention elsewhere (Kettle and Hodges, 1982; Cowell, *et. al.*, 1982; Reiner, 1985/1992; Benyon and Solomos, 1987; Howe, 1988; Keith, 1993), so comments here will be restricted to those aspects of the inquiry that bear directly on the problems of violent racism and policing.

The 1981 Disorders

The disorder which occurred in Brixton between 10 and 12 April and in Southall, Manchester, Liverpool, the West Midlands, and numerous other locations in July may collectively be seen as the culmination of a deteriorating relationship between the police and black communities in Britain over the previous three decades. In a sense, then, what Scarman was expected to do, and set out to do, was to describe the nature of the crisis of policing the inner city black communities and prescribe solutions to it.

Scarman concluded that a significant cause of the hostility felt towards the police in Brixton and elsewhere in the country was a loss of confidence in the police by significant sections of the population. This, he argued, was due to: a lack of communication between police and public in the areas affected; the use of 'hard' vigorous policing methods without consulting community representatives; a distrust of the official complaints procedure; and unlawful and racially prejudiced conduct by some police officers when stopping, searching, and arresting young black people on the street.

Disorder in Southall

The violence which occurred between the police and young Asians in Southall on Friday 3 July started after 'a large group of white skinhead youths, mainly from the East End of London, who were on their on their way to attend a concert at [a] public house,[14] began smashing shop windows in [Southall] Broadway' (Scarman, 1981: 30). Scarman's comments on the conflict between the police and Asian youth in Southall tie together three key themes concerning racism, violence, and policing—the (in)ability of the police to protect Asian communities against attack from racists and far-right activity, the police conceptualization of violent racism and the role of police racism.

Police (In)action Against Violent Racism

Scarman commented that while the Afro-Caribbean community complained principally of police harassment, the Asian community complained that the police were 'not sufficient' to protect their community from racist attacks. The disorder in Southall, Scarman concluded, was an indication:

not only of racial tension but of relations between Asian youths and the police which were at best characterised by lack of communication and at worst by outright hostility. It seems clear that the Asian youths were prepared to take the law into their own hands rather than rely on the police to protect them and, when the police got in their way, to attack them [Scarman, 1981: 31].

---

[14] The band—the 4-Skins—were part of the explicitly racist Oi! movement.

Here, Scarman reflects the findings of the Home Office study, *Racial Attacks*, and the experiences of the Asian community. From the perspective of the latter, the police had consistently failed to protect the community from attack which had led to community-based strategies of self-help and self-defence. As Scarman noted, alleged police inaction influenced the attitude of the Asian community towards the police. In the context of a long history of racist provocation and violence directed against Southall's Asian community, many thought that the role of the police should have been to protect and defend the minority community from attack and to take a firm stance against racism. The approach of the police, however, was to turn the event on its head by describing it as an attack by an Asian gang on innocent young followers of a 'pop group'.[15]

Police Racism—The Bad Apple Thesis

Scarman's discussion of police racism was what has become known as the 'bad apple' thesis (Pearson *et al.*, 1989; Howe, 1988: 24). Rather than seeing racism as systemic or institutional, Scarman considered only that '[r]acial prejudice [manifests] itself occasionally in the behaviour of a few officers on the streets' (Scarman, 1981: 105). Racially prejudiced behaviour is not common, he wrote, but even its occasional display 'goes far towards the myth of a hostile police force' (*ibid.*: 106). Some allegations of police harassment were true, he said, but this was the result of the 'ill-considered and immature' actions of the same few individual officers (*ibid.*). The shortcomings in the behaviour of the police towards the ethnic minorities, either in their apparent failure to provide protection from attack or in the oppressive way in which black people were dealt with as suspects, were not based in 'deliberate bias or prejudice'. Scarman specifically rejected the allegation that the police force was 'institutionally racist', which he understood as being discriminatory 'knowingly, as

---

[15] Contrary to Scarman's evidence and other independent accounts (e.g. Hiro, 1991: 174), Metropolitan Police Deputy Assistant Commissioner Radley commented to the 1981–2 Home Affairs Committee that: 'As I understand that particular incident, it was in fact the supporters of a particular group who went to the particular licensed premises where the group was playing' . . . there is nothing we can do about a pop group appearing at a public house and nothing we can do about the followers of that pop group. . . . As far as I am aware there is no intention of anyone attacking anyone on that occasion . . . I am not of the opinion that that was in any way a concerted, organised or planned form of attack on the inhabitants of Southall' (House of Commons, 1982: 29).

a matter of policy' (1986: 28). Reiner (1985: 205) argues that, within this 'subjective rather than objective' definition of institutionalized racism, the evidence supports Scarman's assertion. There is, as Reiner points out, no evidence to point to an official (e.g. written) policy of discrimination against ethnic minorities. Even the practice of demanding passports when questioning black suspects cited by the GLC to refute Scarman occurs in 'disregard of official policy statements' (GLC, 1982; cited by Reiner, 1985: 205).

Accountability and Relationship Between Police and Black Communities

Scarman made a number of recommendations to solve the problems of conflict between the police and ethnic minority communities as he saw them. In policing recruitment policy he urged 'vigorous efforts' to recruit more black people into the police and recommended the development of 'scientific ways' to identify racial prejudice so as to avoid prejudiced officers entering the police service (1986: 199). He recommended changes in the way that police officers were trained, supervised, monitored, and disciplined, endorsing the Commission for Racial Equality (CRE) proposal that racially prejudiced or discriminatory behaviour should be included as a specific offence in the Police Discipline Code (Scarman, 1986: 200–1). He recommended that methods of policing, especially in inner-city areas, should be re-examined, with particular reference to the balance between 'hard' and 'community' policing methods.

Of particular relevance to the developments described in Chapter 4, Scarman recommended that consultative arrangements between the police and the community should be imposed by statute on Police Authorities and on Chief Officers of Police (ibid.: 202). While he did not recommend any substitution for the Home Secretary as the sole police authority for the Metropolitan Police, he did recommend a statutory framework that would require local consultation between the Metropolitan Police and the community at the Borough or Police District Level (ibid.). Despite the disapproval of Scarman's recommendation of statutory consultative arrangements by the Home Secretary and ACPO, such a statutory duty was later built into the Police and Criminal Evidence Act (1984). A key question arising from Scarman's proposals was whether such arrangements for 'consultation' would have the effect of bringing about the changes in the policing of ethnic minority communities (or indeed the 'community' as whole) that Scarman felt were necessary.

The Home Affairs Committee 1982

During December 1981 and January 1982, the House of Commons Home Affairs Committee (Race Relations Sub-Committee) met to consider both the *Racial Attacks* and *Scarman* reports, and to take evidence from the Association of Chief Police Officer (ACPO) and the Metropolitan Police (House of Commons, 1982). The actual report of the Sub-Committee, presented to Parliament on 27 January 1982, consisted simply of an endorsement of the Home Secretary's proposals set out in the Home Office Report. The document is of interest, however, because it provides insight into the police conceptualization of violent racism and their views about the nature of, and changes to, the police response that were being debated at the time. In particular, the cross-examination of police witnesses during the Committee proceedings provided an opportunity for the police to express aspects of their conceptualization of a racial incident that were hitherto (and subsequently) hidden from public view.

Racial Attacks Affect 'All Parts of the Community'

The police considered that racial attacks were a form of crime inflicted on white as well as black people. The Metropolitan Police written submission to the Committee concludes that:

Although the [Home Office] report highlights the impact of racial attacks on the ethnic minority communities, it should be remembered that racial attacks affect all parts of the community and the impact of street crime committed by black youths on elderly white women cannot be passed over lightly [House of Commons, 1982: 17].

The issue of theft committed by black people against whites—popularized through the use of the term 'mugging'—had been a concern of the police for some time (Hall *et al.*, 1978). Indeed, tackling 'street crime' was one of the primary motives for conducting 'Operation Swamp' that had triggered the Brixton riots (Kettle and Hodges, 1981; Scarman, 1986; Benyon and Solomos, 1987). The idea that theft committed by black youths against vulnerable white women was a form of 'racial' crime had also been articulated previously by Enoch Powell, among others in the late 1960s (Solomos, 1988: 108). It also formed a component of the political action of the National Front, for example in the form of the marches 'against mugging' through areas of ethnic minority settlement during the mid to late 1970s (Hall *et al.*, 1978: 333–4; Gilroy, 1987: 120; Solomos, 1988: 111). The Home Office study also included inter-racial thefts in its definition of a racial incident. The study included a number of black-on-white robberies in the category of incidents with strong evidence or some indication of a racial motive, noting that '20 of the 24 victims of handbag snatches or theft from persons, which were judged to be racially motivated, were white' (Home Office, 1981: 12).

The tendency to define theft perpetrated by black on white people as *racialist*[16] crops up again in a discussion of racial motive or motivation. Mr Goodson, Chief Constable of Leicestershire, representing ACPO, explained to the Home Affairs Committee that the reporting officer (the first police officer attending the scene) would be the person who would first decide whether the incident was 'racial' or not. There was a problem facing this officer, however:

It is not easy to identify what is and what is not a racial attack. If a woman has her handbag snatched by a coloured person this could be a racial attack but it might not be. The coloured man may have said to himself that he will attack the next person that comes round the corner and it happened to be a white person. Inevitably there is a certain amount of personal judgement [House of Commons, 1982: 5].

As this quotation indicates, defining an incident as 'racial' hinges on a police officer's subjective interpretation of the offender's motivation. The fact that a black-on-white robbery rather than a neo-Nazi skinhead attack on a mosque is used as an example is also revealing.

Metropolitan Police Policy

In their memorandum to the Home Affairs Committee, the Metropolitan Police responded to the Home Secretary's recommendations outlined in the Home Office report. The Metropolitan Police accepted that 'the nature of racialist crime, the [Home Office] report

---

[16] It is important to distinguish between different uses of the term 'racial' by the police in this context. In some instances the term is used simply as a coded way of referring to the presence of black people, in the sense of the 1978 definition of a racial incident, for example. In other instances the term is used to refer to 'racialism' or racial prejudice. It seems that the term 'racial' is used by the police to mean 'racialist', or racially prejudiced, when referring to theft committed by black people against white people.

itself and the remarks in the foreword by the Home Secretary place a heavy responsibility on the police . . . a responsibility that we have already assumed' (House of Commons, 1982: 17). However, both the Metropolitan Police and (particularly) ACPO also emphasized that 'there is a high level of crime affecting all communities which markedly detracts from the quality of life of those it touches' (*ibid.*: 2). The problem, therefore, was one of 'the effects of crime upon the community generally and the injured party in particular', while 'racially inspired crime' was a 'most wicked additional burden faced by ethnic groups resident within already high crime areas'. Bear in mind that for the police both crime and 'racial incidents' affected *all parts of the community*. What shortcoming there were in police performance were explained to be because of the lack of evidence of racial motivation and the problem this posed in defining specific crimes as 'racial': 'What constituted a racially motivated crime is the most difficult to identify and the criticism that too often the Police have sought to deal with *all crime on a general level* perhaps reflects that difficulty'. (*ibid.*, emphasis added).

The police also claimed that they were already 'implementing many of the proposals in the report'. They noted that problems concerning training, explaining matters of law to ethnic minority communities, and changes in public order legislation that were already in train would meet the Home Secretary's concerns. The two issues most relevant to the present study were proposed changes in recording and monitoring procedures and the development of structures for police-community liaison.

The Police Re-conceptualize Racial Incidents

Although the police had an operational definition of a 'racial incident' in 1978, the Home Office report and the deliberations of the Home Affairs Committee forced the police to shift some ground on how the problem was to be defined.[17] The new system for the reporting and collating of racial incidents proposed by the Metropolitan Police and introduced into the force as a whole in April 1982 was a

---

[17] In a memorandum to the Home Affairs Committee the Met commented that 'Although the Metropolitan Police Force has an existing system of identifying racial attacks, it is accepted that a revision of the system is necessary both for operational purposes and to engender confidence in minority communities that this Force has the willingness and ability to respond to the particular problems facing them' (House of Commons, 1982: 15).

revision of the system in operation since 1978. The principal differ-ence was the way in which a racial incident was defined. A racial inci-dent was now defined as 'Any incident, whether concerning crime or not which is alleged by any person to include an element of racial motivation or which appears to the reporting or investigating officer to include such an element' (Metropolitan Police, *Force Order*, 1982).

This shed all of the 1978 definition's references to 'community organisations', 'political organizations concerned with community relations', or 'concerted action by and against an ethnic group'. What remained was that aspect of the Met's former definition that most closely related to that used by the Home Office in its 1981 study.

The new procedure required that racial incidents would now be reported to the District Community Liaison Officer, who would be responsible for collating, analysing, and disseminating the informa-tion produced. Follow-up visits to the victims of racial attacks would be made by the local Home Beat Officer. It would be this officer who would complete the details of the incident on a special racial incident form. The Community Liaison Officer was also required to compile a weekly statistical return of the incidence and type of attacks to the Community Relations Branch at Scotland Yard who would 'centrally monitor all such incidents to discern trends and pass information back for operational purposes where necessary'. The Community Relations Branch would be immediately notified of those incidents 'which would have a serious impact on the ethnic community, or receive national publicity'. The stated aim of the new system was a greater awareness of the problem at all levels which would lead to a 'greater confidence being shown by the ethnic communities, which may in turn lead them to reporting all attacks promptly' (House of Commons, 1982: 15).

With respect to the need for formal liaison identified by Scarman, the Metropolitan Police noted that liaison arrangements already existed 'at all levels' (*ibid.*). The Commissioner had meetings 'with bodies such as the Commission for Racial Equality and the London Boroughs Association', while meetings were held on a District and Divisional basis with representatives of the ethnic minority commu-nities, and 'extensive contact' existed with 'youth clubs, tenants asso-ciations, neighbourhood groups and the like'. Building on an existing model, this 'community contact' would be extended.[18]

[18] The Metropolitan Police submission noted that 'In 1979, 2 officers were posted to each of ten racially sensitive Districts in an effort to extend community involvement,

The GLC Inquiry into Racial Harassment

In August 1982 the GLC Police Committee constituted a Panel of Inquiry into Racial Harassment. The report and recommendations of the Inquiry were adopted by the GLC in October 1983 and published early the following year (Greater London Council, 1984). In defining racial harassment, rather than attempting to pinpoint 'where or when racist motivation becomes dominant in the intentions of those who inflict harassment', the GLC Panel of Inquiry adopted a 'subjective or victim-centred perspective'. This was a radical departure from the definitions of the police, who had argued that the reporting or investigating officer should identify the presence of a racial motive, and the Home Office which had argued that 'the only reliable information on racial motivation would be from the offender' (Home Office, 1981). Defining racial harassment in terms of the victim's experience rather than the perpetrator's motivation, argued the GLC:

was not only inevitable but also a desirable way of approaching the problems of definition. This has the effect of displacing the burden of proof in harassment cases away from the victims, who, it is argued, should be believed first and investigated second rather than the other way round [GLC, 1984: 1].

Drawing on the evidence of seventy organizations and one hundred individuals, the report examined four aspects of racial harassment in London. It looked: firstly, at the police system of recording racial harassment cases; secondly, at the 'pattern of racial harassment', specifically 'racial harassment by the police' and 'police harassment in their response to victims'; thirdly, at racial harassment and the extreme right; and fourthly, at racial harassment on local authority housing estates. The report concluded with recommendations for policy to address each aspect of racial harassment.

Police Recording of Racial Harassment

The report noted that the Metropolitan Police recording system had been improved as a result of the April 1982 Force Order, and that this may have been responsible for the increase in its recorded incidence between 1981 and 1982. Evidence submitted to the inquiry

particularly with regard to *the problems engendered by the presence of ethnic minority communities.* In August this year, the option to employ officers in this capacity was extended to all [District] Commanders' (House of Commons 1982: 15, emphasis added).

suggested that 'at the top' of the police organization, at least, 'there is a recognition that racially motivated crime exists'.[19] The report concluded, however, that despite these improvements, police statistics remained inadequate 'not only because people do not report offences, but because the police are still not systematically recording all incidents reported' (GLC, 1984: 6). In response to the perceived weakness in police records, the report drew mainly on cases reported directly by victims to the Panel of Inquiry and on the 'information held by those organisations which had close links to the local community and to whom the victims of racial violence might go for assistance or support' (GLC, 1984: 7).

Racial Harassment by the Police

The GLC report parted radically from the previous reports of the Home Office, police, and House of Commons in that it brought racist behaviour *by the police themselves* within a definition of racial harassment. That the police did not include such behaviour in their definition of a racial incident is hardly surprising. The Home Office found that allegations of harassment or improper treatment were 'apparently groundless' (Home Office, 1981: 19). That the GLC included police harassment undoubtedly reflects the Council's broader concern with racism in the Metropolitan Police and its goal of bringing the police under local democratic control. Bringing police behaviour into this ambit also reflects the concerns of community organizations presenting evidence to the Inquiry: 'a great many of the organisations and individuals who submitted material to the Panel identified police conduct itself as a source of both overt and indirect harassment' (GLC, 1984: 9).

The racial harassment said to have been perpetrated by the police in evidence presented to the Inquiry consisted first of *direct* harassment. Informants identified the police use of racist language as being 'commonplace' and mentioned examples of apparently racially discriminatory policing such as: illegal entry into black people's homes; stop and search targeted specifically against black people; assault and racist abuse during arrest; 'blatant racism' and harassment when dealing with black juveniles; treating black victims of crime as criminal; and speculative passport checks (referred to as immigration 'fishing raids') directed against black people (GLC, 1984: 9–12).

[19] Evidence of Ealing Community Relations Council, cited in GLC, 1984: 4.

These issues were hardly new, least of all to London's black and Asian communities. Evidence that the police were engaged in widespread harassment of ethnic minority communities in London and elsewhere had been published since the mid-1960s.[20] That black people, and especially the young, had been the targets of discriminatory policing practices such as the use of stop and search and 'sus' had been known for some time and had recently become the subject of research reports funded by the Metropolitan Police (Smith and Gray, 1983) and conducted by the Home Office (Willis, 1983). What was new, however, was the explicit definition of these forms of behaviour as 'racial harassment', at least in an official local government report.

Secondly, the GLC report found evidence of *indirect* harassment relating to the conduct of police work once a complaint of racial harassment had been made; this included non-response, delay, unwillingness to investigate or to prosecute, defining criminal assaults (actual bodily harm) as non-criminal (common assault), giving misleading advice—such as advising victims to bring private prosecutions or civil actions when criminal proceeding were appropriate, and treating victims of racial attacks as criminal (Greater London Council, 1984: 12–17). Again, most of these allegations of 'non-response' had been voiced on earlier occasions. The 1981 Home Office report had commented on many of them and had, indeed, criticized the police for their failure to treat the problem as seriously as was necessary. The police themselves admitted that they frequently advised victims to take out a private prosecution, rather than instituting criminal proceedings. What was new here also was the Panel's endorsement of the view of several submissions to the Inquiry who 'define[d] these patterns of police practice as a *distinct form of harassment*' (GLC, 1984: 12, emphasis added). Damningly, the report concluded that:

The result of these abuses is that London's police are viewed by many blacks with fear, suspicion and hostility. They are seen, not only as potential perpetrators of racial harassment, but also as sympathetic to the individuals and groups who carry out harassment unchecked by the law [GLC, 1984: 18]

Although the GLC also saw the police as crucial in responding to racial harassment, the council took a quite different view of the

[20] See, e.g., Hunte, 1965; Hall *et al.*, 1978; Gordon, 1984; Howe, 1988; Institute of Race Relations, 1979; 1987.

problem from that of the police and central government. First, the police were themselves 'deeply implicated in London's racial harassment problems' both as perpetrators of racial violence and in a systemic failure to respond to racial attack victims. Secondly, the 'police failure could not just be put down to the attitudes of a few individual police officers or to general inefficiency. Rather it was necessary to tackle the *institutional* racism within the police force' (GLC, 1984: 2). Thus the failure of the police was related to the low priority afforded to the problem of violent racism in overall police policy and a low status in the occupational culture of the officers who ought to be dealing with it (*ibid.*: 52). The solutions to the problem included those advocated by Scarman and the Home Office, such as training and identifying racism during recruitment. More fundamentally, however, bringing about an effective response to racial harassment concerned the resources, organization, and management of the police organization. For the GLC, this was rooted in questions of what kind of police force could meet London's needs and how it should be accountable to the community it served (*ibid.*: 52). In particular, authority was concerned with making the Metropolitan Police accountable to an elected police authority (see also GLC, 1983).

Racial Harassment on Local Authority Housing Estates

Twenty-five of the GLC report's fifty-six pages dealt with the problems of racial harassment on local authority housing estates. It focused, in particular, on those estates in Tower Hamlets which the GLC owned. Evidence presented to the Inquiry indicated a very serious level of violent racism being directed against ethnic minorities, and particularly the Bangladeshi community, resident in dwellings owned by the GLC and Tower Hamlets. Particularly badly affected were the Asian families living away from the main centres of ethnic minority settlement in the borough. Rather than seeing racial violence as comprising only one-off events, the GLC saw them in the context of racism in the provision and use of public housing. Attention focused on the allocation policies of local council housing departments and the racial segregation of local authority housing that had resulted. A key factor was the role that violent racism played in maintaining 'whites only' estates and neighbourhoods (see also Smith, 1989: 158–63).

The report concentrated on GLC and borough housing policies and practices which came in for a good deal of criticism. In particular, both authorities were criticized for the failure to develop a fair and consistent policy for allocating or transferring black tenants (GLC, 1984: 29–30, 33–4), the failure to take seriously or respond adequately to victims reporting racist attacks (*ibid.*: 32–3), racist attitudes among senior council housing staff (*ibid.*: 34); suspicion of tenants' motives in reporting racist attacks (*ibid.*: 36); playing down attacks or referring to them as 'child's play' (*ibid.*: 37); and denying that attacks had a racist motive (*ibid.*: 38). Similar problems with both racial harassment and the response of the housing department were also faced elsewhere in London boroughs.

The report concluded that many of the criticisms of the housing department were justified and that what was needed was 'not in new policies, but in the effective implementation of those already on paper' (*ibid.*: 43). Drawing on policies being developed in other London boroughs, the report also made suggestions for recording and monitoring procedures, transfer of racial attack victims, and action against perpetrators. It was noted that while taking legal action against tenants on grounds of racial harassment was 'extremely problematic', some local authorities were testing their powers in this regard; the London Borough of Camden was at that time in the process of taking a case for repossession through the courts (*ibid.*: 46; see also London Borough of Camden, 1988).

Co-operation with the Police

The GLC report on racial harassment was ambivalent on the issue of the extent to which local authorities should work together with the police in racial harassment cases. On one hand, evidence presented by local authority housing departments to the Inquiry suggested that 'in some areas regular meetings with the police specifically on this issue could serve a useful, though limited purpose' (GLC, 1984: 47). Such meetings, experience in Camden and elsewhere suggested, could prevent police inaction and denial of the problem, provided a forum in which ethnic minority organizations could make demands on both police and housing officials and, potentially, could lead to co-ordinated action.

Against these benefits, however, the Panel presented a number of dangers of co-operating with the police and concluded with a sceptical appraisal of future possibilities. The principal danger they suggested was the threat to individual liberty. 'Low grade information' offered to the police might be used for purposes other than that for which it was intended. Moreover, the Panel held the view that the police remained unwilling to take the issue of violent racism seriously and held little possibility of the police giving many real concessions to those wishing to see an improvement in the police response. Again, the GLC's response to the question of co-operation with the police is tied up with their concern that the Met be brought under democratic control (GLC, 1983, 1984, 1986).

Violent Racism and the Extreme Right

An issue discussed by each of these state agencies was the relationship between violent racism and the racist ideologies and 'anti-immigrant' strategies of extreme right political parties.

The Police View

The view of the police was that there was little concrete evidence that the extreme right were responsible for organizing or orchestrating racist attacks. For example, the Metropolitan Police were prepared to acknowledge 'a correlation' between racist propaganda, distributed at football grounds for instance, and the incidence of violent racism, but denied that there was evidence that attacks were organized. Mr Radley, Deputy Assistant Commissioner said, for example:

I would say that there is a relationship but I do not know how direct that relationship is. Obviously if groups of very impressionable youngsters do hear some of the racialist propaganda . . . then yes there is a correlation between that and racist attacks. . . . I am sure that some of the young skinheads who run down Brick lane smashing windows are in fact copying or carrying out in their minds—and they are not the most intelligent of people—the wishes of others. I do not think it is organised. I have certainly got no evidence and I do not think this Committee found there was any evidence of this being organised, but I think that it does have an effect, yes. [House of Commons, 1982: 26].

The ACPO representatives went further, specifically denying that there was any evidence of a link between the extreme right and violent racism. In taking oral evidence from Mr Goodson (Leicestershire Constabulary and ACPO representative), Labour MP, Alf Dubbs, asked questions relating to this issue in various ways. The exchange is worth quoting in full:

[Mr. Dubbs] Do you feel that there is a relationship between that type of racist publicity and so on in association with certain football grounds and racist attacks?

[Mr Goodson] I can only speak of my own experience in Leicestershire. Certainly, from time to time literature is distributed outside the Leicester City football ground but I have no reason to think that this relates directly to the incidence of racial attacks.

[Mr Dubbs] Might it not incite young people to commit a racist attack because of the pressure they are under from these sort of things at and near football grounds?

[Mr Goodson] It might do, but on the other hand I have got no evidence that it does.

[Mr Dubbs] If bits of paper are put about which encourage people to hate those whose skins are not white, is it not at least likely that some of the people at football grounds might later on, not necessarily that day, be so incited by this literature?

[Mr Goodson] Indeed. Clearly, the people who distribute the literature think that this is the case. It may well be but that is not my experience.

[Mr Dubbs] Therefore would you concede that one possible aim of this literature is to provoke such attacks?

[Mr Goodson] I understand that the object of the literature is to make propaganda for the people who are seeking to put forward a view. If indeed an offence under the (sic) racial law were taking place we would take action in this. I cannot really look into the minds of the people who are distributing the literature. I have no evidence myself that the distribution of this literature goes directly to the incidence of racial attacks in my area [House of Commons, 1982: 8].

Similarly, when discussing violence occurring in a context where racism is explicit, ACPO drew short of confirming any direct relationship by focusing on evidence (in the narrowest, legal sense) of the direct relationship between racist propaganda and racial incidents. The exchange between select Committee Member, John Wheeler MP (Conservative), and Mr Goodson is informative:

[John Wheeler, MP] Do you think that extremist organisations incite racial attacks . . .?

[Mr Goodson] . . . we have on occasions had walls sprayed with political slogans, hoardings daubed with political slogans which clearly indicate the origin of the party that is putting forward this view. But that could well be one individual who may or may not represent that party. The National Front is a good example. You see 'NF' on walls but you have no guarantee that the person who put it up there was a National Front member, or indeed that more than one person did it [House of Commons, 1982: 8].

[Mr Hunt, MP] I am intrigued to know who is likely to spray NF on a wall who is not a member of the National Front.

[Mr Goodson] I suppose that if there are other organisations that feel strongly against an immigrant community and they wish to make a point they could certainly put NF up even if they are not members of the National Front.

[Mr Laugharne, Chief Constable, Lancashire] Not everybody who writes 'Kilroy was here' is in fact called Kilroy. I do not wish to be flippant but there is a good deal of the 'copycat' element in things of this sort, particularly by youngsters. You find many, many young people who have seen an 'NF' and know that it creates some disturbance so they go and spray it on walls. A lot of that goes on. It is very difficult to discern which slogans are in fact motivated by the National Front [House of Commons, 1982: 9].

The need for direct evidence was so stringent, it seems, that senior police officers felt able to state that even 'NF' slogans may not have been *motivated* by the National Front. While the 'influence' should not be confused with the 'involvement' of the far right, the police view fails to consider fully the role of politically organized racism in the expression of violent racism.

The Home Office View

The Home Office endorsed the police view, but added that racist organizations produced a 'climate' in which racial attacks could flourish. The Home Office study team found that while there was a widespread belief among ethnic minorities that racist attacks were instigated or carried out by particular extremist organizations, they noted that the police considered that there was rarely any concrete evidence to substantiate this belief (Home Office, 1981: 23). This is not to say that the report found no evidence of explicitly racist right-wing political activity or provocation or the actual involvement of such groups in violence. On the contrary, the report cites a great deal of evidence from the police, local authorities, and ethnic minority community organizations concerning organized racist activity in localities where racial violence was a problem. The report notes that in many areas extremist organizations were actively recruiting young people in football grounds, pubs, pop concerts, and schools (*ibid.*: 23), and pointed to 'overt provocation by right-wing groups [through] their attempts to march, or otherwise demonstrate, in areas of relatively high ethnic minority populations (*ibid.*: 30). The study team found evidence of increasing racist activity in schools including the distribution of racist leaflets, and racist badges and insignia (*ibid*.: 23). The report also acknowledged the existence of links between international neo-Nazis and the British far-right (such as reports of conferences and exchange visits) (*ibid*.: 30). Concerning the direct involvement in violence of racist organizations, the report notes that 'over the past few years there have been major instances of the prosecution and conviction of members of the National Front, the New National Front, the British Movement and other extreme right wing groups' (*ibid*.: 29).

However, the approach which the study team adopted in analysing the role of racist organizations was to separate the evidence that the far right directly organized racist attacks from the evidence that the activity of extremist groups provided a 'climate' in which racist attacks might flourish (Home Office, 1981: 29). Using the word *evidence* as a strictly legal term, the study team concluded that there was ample evidence that the far-right played a role in the latter sense, but little evidence of their involvement in the former. Thus:

Even the presence of slogans at the scene of an incident does not necessarily prove that the offender belonged to a particular grouping: slogans were sometimes daubed by children who were far too young to appreciate the significance of their actions. For their part, the police believed that most racial incidents were the work of young whites influenced by racist propaganda but not connected with any racialist organisations. On the other hand, many members of the ethnic minorities considered that, even if those who engaged in racial attacks had no formal connection with extremist organisations, the latter should be regarded as responsible for creating a climate in which racial violence was becoming increasingly prevalent [Home Office 1981: 23].

What this formulation overlooks is, first, covert action by the National Front and other far-right political parties, and, secondly, the possibility of direct provocation of racist attacks and harassment by such groups. As the evidence outlined in Chapter 2 suggests, one strategy used by National Front activists was to encourage young people to carry out attacks on their behalf. While such a practice would still not constitute a 'direct connection', it goes beyond the creation of a climate of racism.

The GLC View

The GLC voiced the views of the Board of Deputies of British Jews and representatives from *Searchlight* who argued that racist organizations were much more deeply implicated in promoting racist violence. One of the GLC Inquiry's 'greatest concerns' was the role of the extreme right in perpetrating racial harassment in London. It reported that submissions from the Centre for Contemporary Studies, the Board of Deputies of British Jews, and *Searchlight* magazine (GLC, 1984: 19) supported the idea that 'individuals *directly inspired or encouraged* by these organisations were responsible for a significant proportion of racial harassment cases' (*ibid.*, emphasis added). This was evidenced by the systematic nature of attacks in some locations, the targeting of institutions (e.g. community relations councils and places of worship) for racist attacks, and the parallel between the language used by racist organizations and the graffiti painted on Jewish cemeteries and on local authority housing estates (*ibid.*). The report also noted that although extreme right-wing groups relied on only a core group of individuals, their activities had a much broader impact, particularly the fascist activity around football grounds and pop concerts which influenced young people (GLC, 1984: 20).

The GLC report strongly criticized the police investigations into and prosecution of right-wing racist activity and also the existing law of incitement to racial hatred. The report cites cases of arson attacks resulting in death (such as those on the Khan family in Walthamstow and on an elderly Jewish couple in Enfield). In each case the police denied the possibility of racist motivation, despite local histories of racist violence and agitation. In the Enfield case, racist activity included the circulation of hoax letters, attacks on the local synagogues and Sikh temple and a large number of street attacks. In the same locality members of the "Ku Klux Klan" were arrested after carrying out a "cross burning", though the Director of Public Prosecution (DPP) decided against proceeding with the case. The report cites evidence of the failure of the police and DPP to proceed against the distribution of racist material, which was in their view, partly to do with the inadequacy of the law itself: "The spread of [racist] propaganda alone represents a form of harassment of sizeable dimensions which cannot be dealt with inside the framework of existing law" (GLC, 1984: 22)

The Academic View

Several academics have also focused on the role of the extreme right over this period. Layton Henry (1984: 118) argues that a major weakness of the Home Office report was its failure to examine the evidence of the attempts by the far right to 'promote violence by its actions as well as indirectly through its propaganda and language'. Citing Fielding (1981), Layton-Henry points to the involvement of the far right in paramilitary activities, illegal possession of firearms, and violent provocation. As Fielding (1981) suggests, violence is functional for the extreme right as it provides new recruits and publicity and can generate negative publicity for their opponents (Layton-Henry, 1984: 117–19). During the period of National Front electoral success there remained an emphasis on street politics in the form of marches, demonstrations, and inflammatory propaganda campaigns. While committed members are prepared to be involved in electoral activity with little chance of success, those on the periphery are more attracted to such direct action as provocative marches in areas of ethnic minority settlement (Fielding, 1981). In the period following the failure of the National Front in the 1979 General Election and its subsequent collapse and fragmentation, there is evidence of a shift towards more violently oriented groups (such as the British Movement) and towards direct action more generally (Hiro, 1991; *Searchlight*, June 1982; Layton-Henry, 1984: 118).

Criticism of Agencies Other Than the Police

Although the spotlight was turned largely on the police response to violent racism, other agencies were also coming in for criticism. Local authority services, housing in particular, were also identified as being implicated in London's racial harassment problems. The Home Office report noted that local authorities often had as much difficulty as the police in identifying the problem and taking effective action to combat it. Authorities, the report noted, often had no policy or guidelines for the practices of housing officers, social workers, or teachers, who would be confronted with the problem. The Home Secretary urged local authorities to think about their responsibilities and to appreciate the significance of racial attacks. 'Co-ordination between services', he stated, 'should make possible a swift and coherent approach to the problems produced for those services for racial attacks' (Home Office, 1981: iv).

The GLC report also focused on the failure of local authorities in tackling racial harassment. It noted that racist violence was particularly prevalent on the estates for which the GLC and other authorities (such as Tower Hamlets) were landlords. The roots of this problem lay in poor management of the estates which had become increasing run down. White tenants had identified the Asian population of the estates as the cause of the deterioration and had made them the scapegoat for the councils' failures. A second root cause lay in the council's allocation policies which had led to the ghettoization of Asian communities in particular localities and the development of 'whites only' neighbourhoods. Other problems included a failure to record racial harassment cases, inadequate training of housing staff, a lack of family accommodation, and prejudiced attitudes with the housing department that led to dismissing or playing down attacks. The GLC report concluded with recommendations to tackle each of these problems. Nonetheless criticisms of public housing agencies continued to be voiced throughout the 1980s (e.g. London Borough of Camden, 1988).

Conclusion

The principal reasons that violent racism moved from the periphery towards the centre of police, central, and local government concerns during the early 1980s were the activities of black and Asian communities and anti-racist organizations which shifted public and official opinion, an apparent upsurge in racist activity and a 'moral panic' about 'race', violence, and policing which reached a zenith in this period. The agencies which began to respond to the problem (variously defined) also had a number of stated and unstated reasons for prioritizing this issue at this time.

The Home Office was the agency to which most criticism of the police was articulated. As the Department of State responsible for both policing and 'race relations', it was to the Home Office that the ethnic minority and anti-racist organizations made their representations. The Home Office had to react to this pressure by being seen to attempt to bring about a more effective police response. The Home Office was also concerned about broader issues concerning the relationship between the police and 'the community' in general, and ethnic minority communities in particular. Questions surrounding racial disadvantage, public order legislation, and Lord Scarman's inquiry into the Brixton riots were of key Home Office concern. Thus, the *Racial Attacks* report offered an opportunity to exhort the police to tackle racial discrimination within the ranks of the police and to introduce more professional methods of training. Of particular relevance to this study was the Home Office advocacy of liaison arrangements between the police, local authorities, and ethnic minority communities, and co-ordinated action between the police and local authorities (see Chapter 4).

The publication of the Home Office and Scarman reports put the police in a position where they too had to respond publicly to the issue of violent racism. The events of 1981 had brought into high visibility questions surrounding the relationship between the police and black community, and a public response to violent racism was a political necessity. As the police put it, a new policy was necessary to 'engender confidence in minority communities that [they had] the willingness and ability to respond to the particular problems facing them'. Reiner (1985) identifies 1981 as the year in which the legitimacy of the police organization was at its lowest ebb in the post-war period. The promise of an improved response to racial incidents was an essential step in restoring some of that lost legitimacy.

From 1981 the Greater London Council began to campaign for an elected police authority for London. The focus on the failure of the police response to violent racism and the accusations that police officers themselves were responsible for racist acts illustrated perfectly for the GLC the unaccountable and discriminatory way in which London's communities (and especially the black communities) were policed. The GLC was also facing a legitimacy crisis of its own with regard to ethnic minorities and racial harassment. Much violence occurred in public housing and the GLC, too, was implicated in both setting the conditions for, and failing to respond to, it. A public response was both a political necessity to offset its own problems of legitimacy and expedient in pursuing a policy to make the police accountable to local government.

I am not claiming that officers of the state at central and local level simply used violent racism cynically as a vehicle to pursue other agendas. Nonetheless, it does appear that the issue was used to articulate and advance other political concerns. For each agency involved, violent racism (variously conceived) embodied specific political solutions. The crucial point is that the emergence of violent racism as a 'new' crime symbolized the need for new relationships between the police, local and central state agencies, and the 'community'. Policy activity generated around the issue of violent racism brought to the fore issues of accountability, consultation, liaison, co-operation, and co-ordination.

Although it was apparent that the Metropolitan Police were outside local democratic control, in that they were accountable only to the Home Secretary as sole police authority for London, the accusation that they were not meeting the needs of the community was now explicit. The ability of the police to resist a shift in the constitutional or administrative arrangements for their control had weakened. The Home Office cautiously advocated 'consultation', 'liaison', and 'co-ordination' as means of bringing about change without going so far as to support the calls for the Metropolitan Police to be answerable to an elected police authority, a proposal which was widely perceived by the police and the Conservative government as giving undue control to local authorities. The 1985 Local Government Act, which abolished the GLC along with the other metropolitan authorities, shows what the Thatcher government thought of the involvement of local government in policing, education, housing, and other areas of social policy. As McLaughlin puts it, the Act was 'a convenient means of putting to an end the unceasing demands for democratic accountability of the police' (1991: 117). As we shall see in the next Chapter, the Home Office was more concerned, as it had been for many years, to emphasize the role of agencies other than the police in responding to and preventing crime. The Greater London Council (and other local authorities) rejected the ideas of consultation and liaison, identifying them as a hopelessly weak alternative to local 'democratic accountability' (Legal Action Group, 1982).

In the early 1980s, the police and central and local government took up specific political and ideological positions on the issues of violent racism and the relationship between police and community. Beneath superficially similar languages invoking the terms of racism, violence, and policing were clear conceptual and political conflicts. Between 1981 and 1986, as violent racism continued to make headlines and, arguably, the 'crisis of legitimacy' worsened for both the police and local authorities, the conflicts between state agencies became more obscure, submerged beneath an newly emergent consensual discourse of co-ordination and collaboration. Chapter 4 explores the development of this consensus, built around the idea that the solution to violent racism would be found in the 'multi-agency approach'.

4

The Evolution of the Multi-agency Approach to Violent Racism

Coordination (like other kinds of reorganisation) can become a tool in out-right power struggles over control, priorities, or resources within the social service system. Each group with a stake in how social services are organised is interested in coordinated linkages that operate to its own relative advantage. Naturally, ideas about appropriate and effective coordination conflict. . . . Sometimes these conflicts are really over questions of coordination. At other times the call for reform premised on the assumption of coordination is simply a way to fight other battles [Martin Rein, 1983].

Violent racism did not cease as a result of official policy formulated in the early 1980s. Indeed, many commentators believed that the extent and ferocity of attacks and harassment simply got worse. The problems facing the police and other governmental organizations did not ease either. If anything, the apparent failure of the police to 'do something' about violent racism became more obvious and more public towards the middle of the decade. Specifically, there was a strong current of public opinion that the failings of the police justified violence in the cause of community self-defence. Some went further, claiming that police use of force was being used to victimize rather than protect ethnic minority communities. The basis of police legit-macy—their lawful right to use force—was bitterly contested in the mid-1980s. As this 'crisis of legitimacy' reached its zenith, however, a new governmental consensus began to form, centred on the idea that the solution to violent racism would be found through co-ordination among the police, local government organizations, and the community. By the late 1980s, police–community conflict had melted into the 'multi-agency approach', marginalizing those who were crit-ical of the police. This Chapter describes and explains how this trans-formation took place.

Violent Racism 1984–5

Violent racism continued to be a problem facing ethnic minority individuals and communities in Britain during the mid-1980s (Rose,
1996). The period has been characterized as one in which extreme
racist views and everyday exclusionary practices were widespread,
though not as politically organized as at the turn of the decade
(Gordon, 1990; Hesse *et al.*, 1992). Extreme variants of nationalism,
localism, and exclusionism were diffuse rather then mobilized around
a specific political party, although the National Front and the various splinters which emerged from it after its electoral failure at the
beginning of the 1980s were still collecting hundreds of votes in local
elections. Specific localities, such as Newham South, continued to
have both numerous National Front supporters and a high rate of
racist attacks.[1]

Instances of violent racism occurred sporadically in the London
Borough of Newham during 1982–4. For example, during June and
July 1984 mosques in Manor Park and Canning Town, respectively,
were fire-bombed, the latter incident resulting in serious damage.[2]
Also in July 1984 in Custom House, Mr Ade Ogunsanya was beaten
with a snooker cue and then stabbed in the back and chest in an
unprovoked attack by a 'white gang'.[3] As well as these extreme cases,
it is clear that many families were suffering campaigns of harassment
which led to them 'becoming prisoners in their own home[s]' as one
report put it.[4] In January 1985, for example, the *Newham Recorder*
reported that adults were encouraging children to conduct a 'terror
race hate campaign' against an Asian woman, Mrs Maryam Jawaid,
and her three children in Canning Town. Over a three-year period
'gangs of up to 20 children [threw] missiles at her on the street while
chanting racist slogans'.[5] The attacks culminated in rocks and stones
being thrown at the family's flat, one of which hit 18-month-old
Irfam in the face, causing a deep cut.

Hesse *et al.* describe 1985 as the year of 'the burning of the houses'
because of the unprecedented number of arson attacks on the homes
of Asian families which occurred in east London (1992: 24). On

---

[1] Gordon, 1990; Pilger, 1988; Tompson, 1988. See also *Searchlight*, and *Race Today*
over the period.

[2] *Newham Recorder*, 5 July 1984.   [3] *Newham Recorder*, 17 July 1984.

[4] *East End Express*, 22 September 1984.

[5] *Newham Recorder*, 31 January 1985.

numerous occasions black people died or narrowly escaped death after burning petrol was poured through their letterboxes. The London Borough of Newham was also affected by this spate of attacks. For example, at 1.30am on 2 July 2 1985 fifteen members of an Asian family escaped after their home in Custom House, in the south of the borough, was set ablaze as they were sleeping. The fire, started by setting alight petrol or paraffin poured through the letterbox into the hall, gutted the first floor of the house.[6] The most tragic of these arson attacks during the summer of 1985 was the petrol-fire attack which resulted in the deaths of Shamira Kassam and her three sons aged 6 and 5 years and 14 months at their home in Seven Kings, Ilford, on 13 July 1985 (Hesse *et al.*, 1992: 28). This attack was the third arson attack on the Kassams' house in three years and came only three weeks after a similar arson attempt in which petrol was poured through the letterbox and ignited.[7]

In August 1985 a Bangladeshi family of nine, including a 70-year-old man and a 10-month old baby, were rescued by the police after an arson attack on their home in the early hours of the morning. The family were asleep in the first floor of a block of flats in Bow Road[8] when petrol was poured through their letterbox and set light. According to the *East London Advertiser*, three white youths were seen and heard 'laughing gleefully' shortly after the arrival of the firemen.[9] On 10 August, three weeks after the Kassam murders, the Kayani family home in Leyton was set ablaze at about 2 am. Although all fourteen people, including several young children, who were sleeping in the house at the time escaped, there were several minor injuries including cuts and burns. Mr Kayani suffered a deep cut in his arm after he broke a window to enable the other occupants to escape.[10] Around the same time, on the Isle of Dogs, an 11-year-old boy was set alight by white youths, who sprayed inflammable liquid into his face and threw a lighted match at him.[11]

In August 1985 violent racism directed against the Jewish community appeared to escalate. On 7 August youths hurled bricks and stones at Ilford Jewish Primary School after anti-Semitic daubings earlier in the year. In East Ham, the gates of the Jewish cemetery were daubed with the words 'nazis are back'. According to

---

[6] *Newham Recorder*, 11 July 1985.   [7] *The Guardian*, 16 July, 1985.
[8] Bow Road is in Tower Hamlets bordering Newham.
[9] *East London Advertiser*, 9 August 1985.   [10] *Guardian*, 16 August, 1985.
[11] Anne Dummet in *New Society*, 23 August 1985.

Searchlight magazine, members of the Jewish community in the east London Borough of Redbridge 'received letters telling them to report to the local police station for instructions for deportation to their own or their parents' lands of "ethnic origin" ', a tactic used against the Asian community on earlier occasions. Elsewhere in London synagogues were daubed with anti-Semitic slogans.[12]

As the preceding paragraphs illustrate, both national and local newspapers took an interest in violent racism over this period (see also Rose, 1996). They reported not only the most serious instances, but also patterns of harassment and intimidation which appeared to be affecting whole communities. Indeed, newspapers of all political hues published strongly worded articles and editorial comments condemning violent racism during 1984–5.[13] Even the *Sun*, not usually known for its anti-racist views, commented that:

The spate of arson attacks on the homes and properties of Asians in London is highly alarming. The police have an open mind on the motives and other sickening attacks. But the Asians are convinced they are the victims of a hate campaign by extremists. They deserve the sympathy and support of all decent people.[14]

Violent Racism and Community Self-defence: The Newham Seven Case

The media interest in, and condemnation of, racist attacks during this period were overshadowed by reports of confrontation between the police and Asian youth claiming to be acting in defence of their communities and by police reports claiming to have improved their response to racist attacks. These issues moved towards the centre of the political stage during 1985 as a result of the trial of the 'Newham Seven'. This case, which was to become a *cause célèbre*, arose out of a series of racist attacks and counter attacks in April 1984 (Rose, 1996).

Although there are conflicting accounts of what actually occurred, it is possible to draw out the key facts of the case.[15] During April 1984 a number of attacks had been perpetrated by white youths

[12] *Searchlight*, October 1985: 9–11.

[13] e.g. *Newham Recorder*, 14 January 1984, 31 January 1985; *Guardian*, 16 July 1985; *Asian Times*, 29 August 1985; *Time Out*, 24 October 1985.

[14] *Sun*, 14 August 1985 (cited in Hesse *et al.* 1992).

[15] Sources: *East End News*, August 1984; *Newham Recorder*, 30 May, 6 June 1985; David Rose in the *Guardian*, 11 July 1985; *Daily Telegraph*, 11 July 1985.

against Asians in Newham. On 7 April a group of ten to fifteen Asian youths assaulted a white youth believed to be responsible for earlier attacks, after he had verbally abused the Asians in a hamburger bar. The white youth then bought a claw hammer with the intention of seeking 'revenge' on the Asian youths who had attacked him. The white youth, together with several others, then cruised the area in a car and kidnapped five Asians in turn, dragging them into the car and attacking them with the hammer. One Asian boy was taken to Wanstead Flats (a nearby large open space), was forced into a ditch, and subjected to further assaults. He sustained serious head injuries but was saved from anything worse only by the intervention of a passer-by. Another boy jumped from the moving car to escape. On hearing about these attacks a large group of Asians then went to the Duke of Edinburgh public house which they believed was the base for, and might still be sheltering, the gang which carried out the assaults from the car. By 5 pm a group of about fifty Asian youths had gathered outside the pub, armed with bottles, batons and bricks. They then threw missiles at the pub, smashing its windows. Fifteen to twenty white youths charged out of the pub, confronted the Asians, and pelted them with billiard balls. The police arrived almost immediately and arrested one of the Asians. Over the next week six more young Asians were also picked up. The white youths who had attacked the Asians in the Ford Granada were arrested a year later.

When the case came to court at the Old Bailey in April 1985, the seven Asians were charged with affray and conspiracy to cause criminal damage, and three white youths with affray and criminal damage.[16] In response to the charges against the Asian youths the Newham 7 Defence Campaign was formed. (It subsequently received GLC funding.) On Saturday, 27 April the Defence Campaign organized a demonstration marching to Plashet Park (passing Forest Gate police station *en route*) which was attended by a crowd variously estimated at between 1,500 and 2,500. During the march, violence flared between police and demonstrators resulting in thirty-three arrests and the injury of fifty protesters.

The demonstrators claimed that after stopping to protest outside the police station for five minutes a marcher was pulled over a barrier separating them from the police and was dragged into the police station. The police claimed that marchers began throwing objects at

---

[16] *Newham Recorder*, 18 April 1985.

them, prompting them to enter the crowd to make arrests.[17] Police managers were criticized by both anti-racist organizers and local police officers. Unmesh Desai of the Newham Monitoring Project accused the police of over-reacting,[18] a sentiment echoed by several commentators who laid the blame with 'members of a police snatch squad [who] were seen jumping over a barrier, lunging into the crowd'.[19] Local police officers accused their managers of 'surrender[ing] the streets to the demonstrators'.[20]

Two weeks later a second demonstration organized by the Newham 7 Defence Committee ended in violence, the injury of fifteen police officers, and the arrest of fifteen demonstrators. On this occasion marchers in the 1,500 to 2,000-strong demonstration clashed with police, including mounted and riot police in full riot gear.[21] During these clashes, the local press carried numerous news stories and letters to the editor. Although the stories included comment from both the police and the Defence Campaign, the content and language of the articles tended to promote a police perspective. The headlines referred repeatedly to the demonstrators as a 'mob', and used apocalyptic language such as 'violent chaos'. A particularly vivid example was another Hugh Muir article in the *Newham Recorder* on 4 May: '30 arrests as demo mob lay siege to cop station', with the subheading: 'Missiles hurled at police as violence flares on anti-racist march'. Although an article in the same edition included a comment from a local councillor that the police 'picked on marchers at random', the tone of the two articles lent plausibility to Commander Jones' opinion that 'The march was used by a malicious minority to provoke violence and disorder'. This viewpoint was reflected and intensified by three letters to the editor published on 9 May under the headline 'Disgusted by race demo aggro'. One reader wrote:

The trouble at the anti-racist demonstration last week was disgusting. How dare these people attack the police just for wanting to keep law and order. The militants were also present stirring them up. Newham Council pamper them and give them money for their various projects but these people are liberty takers.

In the same vein another wrote:

[17] *Newham Recorder*, 2 May 1985.   [18] *Stratford Express*, 2 May, 1985.
[19] Amarit Wilson and Zubaida Motala in *New Statesman*, 3 May 1985.
[20] *Newham Recorder*, 2 May 1985.
[21] *Newham Recorder*, 16 May 1985; Amrit Wilson in *New Statesman*, 17 May 1985; *Stratford Express*, 18 May 1985.

Various missiles were thrown at the police during the march by the Newham Seven Defence Campaign. This was supposed to have been a peaceful march. Could the people of Newham explain to me why this march was allowed to go ahead? Had this been a demonstration by the National Front there would have been a public outcry.

Although the Newham 7 Defence Campaign accused the police of sabotaging what were intended to be peaceful demonstrations, one result of the clashes between police and demonstrators was that national news media attention was focused on the trial when it finally came to court on 23 May 1985. The story became even more news-worthy when, in the afternoon of the first day of the trial, one of the Asian defendants, Parvais Khan, appeared in the dock with a black eye. According to Khan's counsel, during the lunch time adjournment prison staff had subjected Khan to an 'unprovoked attack' and racial abuse. It was alleged that they beat him badly after he refused to eat a pork pie because he was a Muslim.[22]

The trial ended after eight weeks on 10 July 1985 with the conviction of three whites for common assault, four Asians for affray, and the acquittal of three others. The three whites were each fined £100 immediately. The four Asians who were convicted were remanded for social inquiry reports and a week after the trial ended were each sentenced to 100 hours' community service. This is a very lenient sentence considering that affray carries a maximum penalty of ten years and that some of the defendants had previous convictions. When sentencing the four Asian youths Judge Neil Dennison commented that they had acted under 'extreme provocation'. The judge added that he had received many letters urging him to show leniency, and before passing sentence had been handed a 10,000-signature petition. He said:

I take the view that you over-reacted to long-standing and extreme provocation. One has only to read the newspapers, watch television and listen to the radio to realise what is going on. There are people still there in Newham who commit offences far more serious than yours. If you can help bring these people before the court so they can be properly dealt with it will be a great service to your community

The trial verdict gained wide news coverage on the day after the trial finished. One of the key issues highlighted by the trial and referred to in almost every article was Newham Seven's claim to have

[22] *Daily Telegraph*, *Guardian* (David Rose), 23 May 1985.

been acting in self-defence. The *Daily Telegraph* report, 'Asians and Whites Guilty of Race Fight', commented that the Newham Seven 'enjoyed a hero status as the champions and defenders of the Asian population in the East End'. The article reported that throughout the trial supporters of the Seven had been outside the Old Bailey shouting, 'Newham Seven to save the day, self defence the only way. The Newham Seven are innocent, self defence is no offence'. The *Telegraph* article pointed out that the Seven were said to have retaliated after their community had suffered one race attack after another, quoting the trial defence barrister Leonard Woodley: 'Older Asians may be prepared to tolerate Fascists but the younger generation is going to stand up and fight'. The article concluded by quoting defence lawyer Rudy Narayan, who told the jury how frightening it was for Asians living in the Newham area who were subject to 'blind racist fury' at that time. Across the country local newspapers carried syndicated reports on the trial verdict all of which cited Narayan's claim that the Asians acted in self-defence.[23] The day after the trial had finished, the *Guardian* carried two articles. A news report, 'Seven convicted in "racism" trial', outlined the details of the case and highlighted the 'vociferous and active' Newham 7 Defence Committee and their assertion that 'the Asian defendants were innocent of anything other than protecting their community from racialist attacks'. The second article, written by David Rose, then *Guardian* crime correspondent, was entitled 'Newham, a powder keg set to blow'. Here, Rose spelled out most clearly the implications of the case:

The issue on which the case turned was whether the response of the young Asians, who soon learnt of the attacks on the efficient Newham Grapevine, was justified. There was good reason to believe that the gang, or part of it was indeed inside the pub. One of those attacked gave evidence that he had seen one of his assailants playing a vigorous part in the later affray at the pub. But the central question was the justification or otherwise of the Asians belief, which Kallisher [the prosecuting counsel] conceded was strong and deeply rooted, that the police would not pursue the Granada gang with speed or vigour. . . . As the details of the extent of racial attacks and alleged police indifference to them emerged, the essence of the case came to be expressed in the defence campaign's slogan: 'self defence, no offence'.

---

[23] 'Seven Convicted over race clash', *Scotsman*; 'Four Asians, three whites guilty of fight', *Western Mail* (Cardiff); ' "Race clash" jury finds seven guilty', *The Times*; 'Newham Seven: Four guilty as rest go free', *Daily Post* (Liverpool); 'Seven convicted after battle in East End street', *Yorkshire Post* (Leeds); 'Seven guilty of street clash', *Birmingham Post*; 'Cheers for three cleared by "race war" jury', *Voice*.

The most important question in this complex debate is whether the lack of confidence in the police to investigate racist attacks was justified, and whether any failure which might exist on the part of the police justified direct violent action in defence of minority communities. At the risk of over-simplifying a complex situation, the debate which was played out in the media during 1984 and 1985 may be polarized into two camps. In one camp there are those from black and Asian communities such as the Newham Monitoring Project (NMP) and commentators sympathetic to their standpoint who argued that the failure of the police to protect black communities justified self-defence. NMP's most vocal spokesperson, Unmesh Desai, was widely quoted by the news media, arguing the case for community self-defence and criticizing the police for failing to respond to, and playing down, racist motives in reported attacks. In an article in the *East End News* entitled 'The right to "self defence" under attack', Desai was quoted saying that the arrest of the Newham Seven had to be seen in the context of 'the unprecedented increase in the number and ferocity of racist attacks in East London . . . and the total lack of police response to these attacks'. The theme of the failure of police protection and the necessity of community self-defence was echoed in numerous articles in ethnic minority publications and those such as the *New Statesman*. But it was not only the left-of-centre publications that argued on the side of the Asian community, but rather publications across the political spectrum. *The Economist*, for example, commented in an article entitled 'Now catch the real criminals', that:

The Asian communities do not riot and threaten nobody; it is they who are under threat. They live in specific areas and have identifiable problems. To them the police must now turn their utmost energies. That means getting among, identifying and prosecuting, not the Asians but the white thugs who attack them.[24]

Perhaps the most strongly worded comment on the events during the summer of 1985 was published by Arif Ali, editor of the *Asian Times*, in the form of an open letter to Margaret Thatcher.

Prime Minister, you must surely be aware of the acute plight that faces the Asian community in Britain today. Within the course of just one week recently there were three serious arson attacks in London alone that could easily have claimed over twenty lives. Three weeks earlier a young Asian

[24] *The Economist*, 17 August 1985.

mother—eight months pregnant—and her three young children were burnt to death.

In present day Britain the majority of the Asian community lives in fear. How could it be otherwise when every day brings new cases of assault, when for many daily life is simply one long round of abuse, threats and violence, when scores of our people have died as a result of racially motivated attacks?

Your election campaign of 1979 was fought not least on a platform of law and order. You have consistently claimed that you will stand up to those whom you choose to call 'terrorists'—a point that you have returned to repeatedly in recent months . . . With all this concern for 'law and order' and the 'resolute approach' . . . we feel entitled to ask—What about us? Are we not entitled to live free from the threat of terrorism? . . .

. . . as you know we are a peace-loving and law-abiding community. But our patience is not inexhaustible. If the authorities will not protect us we will be reluctantly forced to defend ourselves. This has nothing to do with becoming 'vigilantes'—it is simply about survival.

Perhaps were you to visit the areas where our people live, were you to meet the people who must live in fear and are assaulted daily, were you to meet those bereaved as a result of racist murders, perhaps you might at least begin to accord this problem the seriousness it deserves.

Our patience is wearing thin, Prime Minister, and we are expecting a serious response.[25]

In the opposing camp in this debate there were the police and sympathetic commentators who argued that the police response to racial incidents was adequate and under no circumstances was there a justification for taking the law into one's own hands. Commander Jones, Deputy Assistant Commissioner for Area 2 (East London), for example, argued at the end of the Newham Seven trial that:

The police performance in dealing with racial incidents means that the residents of Newham do not need to take the law into their own hands. The police will enforce the law with fairness and firmness to all parties irrespective of race and colour. The number of instances where groups take the law into their own hands in this locality is minute.[26]

Nigel Spearing, then Conservative MP for Newham South, congratulated the Newham police for their 'greater sensitivity' in dealing with racial incidents. Commenting on the annual report of the Commissioner of Police, he said that:

---

[25] *Asian Times*, 23 August 1985.   [26] *Guardian*, 11 July 1985.

In this context I pay tribute to the greater sensitivity shown by the police in my part of Newham. These matters depend on the sensitivity and local links which may not necessarily be formal, and the confidence and co-ordination between the police and leaders in the community. That is something for which one cannot legislate and which cannot be created by writing enlightened paragraphs into annual reports or making enlightened speeches on the subject. It has to be worked on, people have to take initiatives, and the police are in a central position because it is they who are able to take initiatives which count. So I offer my congratulations.[27]

Some went further, equating the Newham 7 Defence Committee with 'left-wing extremism' and placing blame on them for the deterioration of the relationship between the police and the Asian community. The *Newham Recorder,* for example, informed the reader that 'The GLC have admitted they gave £5,800 to the Newham Seven Defence Campaign'[28] and implied that the Newham 7 Defence Campaign was a politically motivated 'campaign against the police'. Mr John Wheeler, Conservative MP for Westminster North and Chairman of the House of Commons Home Affairs Select Committee, also said that he was 'concerned about the extremism of the left-wing of the Labour Party in London', which 'preached aggression against the police and non co-operation', a tactic which did nothing to reassure the ethnic communities. The extremism of both the far left and far right were '[b]oth equally evil' he believed.[29]

Contradictions in Policing Discourse

In August 1985, the Metropolitan Police worked hard to offset the criticism levelled at them concerning their response to violent racism. Responding to a *Guardian* leader comment which called for the police to stop denying the presence of racist motives for the arson attacks, and for more serious and systematic policing, Hugh Colver, the Met's Deputy Director of Information, quoted the Commissioner's report for 1985 as an indication of how seriously the problem was taken:

no serious observer of inner city life could fail to be concerned by the nature and frequency of racial incidents which are as socially damaging a problem as can be imagined. . . . A symbol of our serious approach to this problem is that the Commissioner made racial attacks one of three new priority areas

[27] *Newham Recorder,* 11 July 1985.   [28] *Newham Recorder,* 18 July 1985.
[29] *Guardian*, 13 August 1985.

within the Force goal for 1985, and has instituted pilot schemes aimed at identifying best practice in prevention and response. In addition, in the areas worst affected every incident receives personal attention from an Inspector as well as the home beat officer, and every case is reported directly to the divisional Chief Superintendent.[30]

Ten days later, Commissioner Sir Kenneth Newman made his clearest public response to the spate of allegedly racist arson attacks which had occurred during the preceding months. Significantly, he did not make any promise to change operational police tactics. The problem was not any unwillingness on the part of the police to investigate. Rather, it was that racial attacks were more difficult to target than many other forms of crime—'often there was no identifiable pattern in the attacks other than the fact that they took place near to the homes of the victims'.[31] The Commissioner added that the number of racial attacks had 'fallen substantially' over the previous two years, a view strongly contested by the Commission for Racial Equality.[32] The main theme in Newman's statement concerning an improved police response was to call on voluntary race relations groups and local authorities to 'set aside their disagreements with the police to combat racial violence'. As we shall see later in this Chapter, this call for a co-operative approach was to emerge as Newman's key response to racial incidents the following year.

A rather different perspective on the police response to violent racism over this period can be found in the editorial comments of the *Police Review* over this period. In the first of three articles on this subject in 1985, 'Protection from racial attacks', the editorial argued that the police were unable to act in many cases of racial harassment:

The Asian who feels threatened, with good reason, by the mere presence of white youths, the family whose window is broken by a brick thrown by one of 20 children, the householder whose life is made a misery by a racialist neighbour, are still beyond effective help from the police. There are numerous minor crimes and nuisances in which police cannot afford to become involved, and in which the victim is deprived of help unless he can be certain of the identity of his attacker.[33]

Moreover, the editorial comment went on, some crimes, 'classed as racial attacks by the police . . . have only a tenuous racial connec-

---

[30] *Guardian*, 6 August 1985, letters to the editor.
[31] *Guardian*, 13 August 1985.   [32] *Guardian*, 16 August 1985.
[33] *Police Review*, 5 September 1985.

tion'. Asian businesses were attacked for profit, and because the hours they were open laid them open to attack. Some incidents became defined as racist because 'all communities have their share of paranoiacs who are quick to interpret the accidental shove or routine rudeness as actions aimed only at them'. The article went on to argue that when 'genuine' racial attacks occur, the police 'can and do take extra steps to protect those in danger'. The article made an important point about the type of resources that the police had at their disposal to protect individuals and communities in danger—para-military policing. As the editorial comment observed:

the deployment of the Special Patrol Group in East London must be producing all sorts of dilemmas for those who demand its abolition. If there are insufficient police resources devoted to this particular area, the far left thugs from the Anti-Nazi League and the Socialist Workers Party who roamed the area 10 years ago posing as vigilante groups will have yet another opportunity to alienate the police from the community.[34]

A second *Police Review* article, headlined 'The "truth" of "racist" attacks', consisted almost entirely of the unexpurgated views of a sergeant in a police station in an area with a large Asian population. The officer, who 'wasn't prejudiced when I came here . . . but now I'm not so sure', was 'under constant attack from the local Asian community—and its many supporters—for failing to deal with racial attacks'. However, opined the sergeant, '[t]he trouble is that they expect more then we can give, and they see fascists and racists behind every crime'. In the editorial the sergeant complained that racial attack victims 'get all our attention while the other victims get too little'. He claimed that 'racial incidents' frequently had no racial motive, that they were often perpetrated by other Asians because of 'caste or money', and that the motive for claiming that incidents were 'racially motivated' was to get better council houses. The article concluded that:

Yes, there have been petrol bombs. But we know that in at least four houses, the fires have been started inside—the seats of the fires show that. But if we say that openly we're accused of racial prejudice. [This] makes it more difficult to deal with the genuine attacks, there has to be an initial period in which we waste time, trying to discover whether we have been told the truth. For heaven's sake, we don't want women and kids burned to death while we do nothing about it, but there are a lot of factors within the Asian

---

[34] *Police Review*, 5 September 1985.

community that make it convenient for them to allege racial motivation when it's simply caste or money at the root of the problem. We could find the real racist much more quickly, if we were told the truth every time.[35]

Whatever the 'truth' of the police sergeant's views quoted at such length in this editorial comment, it is clear that there is wide gulf between the views of the rank-and-file police officers and that of the Commissioner. Further evidence of the contradiction between the discourses of the upper echelon of the Met and those at the coal-face can be found in a further *Police Review* article published in October. This piece, written by DC Noel Bonczoszek, one of the officers involved in the Newham Seven trial, was entitled 'Gradually losing the war with the left' and was preceded by a statement that 'The views expressed below are representative of a number of letters and phone calls we have received'. The article argued that the 'propaganda war fought by the left wing, aided and abetted by vacillating politicians, indifferent legislators, naive police officers, and ably assisted by judges and magistrates' was motivated by those seeking to form a wedge to drive between the police and the community. To this end they had finally latched onto a sufficiently 'nebulous' and emotive subject:

The subject I refer to is, of course, the new fad, the latest 'in' word— racism—and the blanket, catch-all smear which goes with it and can be thrown at anyone who fails to comply with left-wing points of view. I do not believe that we have a severe problem of racism either inside or outside the police force: it is merely a fabrication constructed by the left to divide the community. . . . The method they employ requires calculation, effort and dedication. First of all they isolate an ethnic section of society by telling it that it is beleaguered—eventually it will believe that it is, no matter what the truth is. . . . Having estranged that section . . . they convince them by words or fear that local criminals are martyrs to be looked up to as defenders of the ethnic minority. . . . That just leaves the coup de grace—they tell the ethnic minority that the people whose duty it is to deal with crime, i.e. the police, are racists picking on them for racist reasons, and they cite the arrest of criminals within that section as proof of racism. . . . Every poisoned ounce of propaganda put forward by the left is dripped into public opinion by the press and pounded into their subconscious memory by a daily diet of TV. Isn't it about time that the Police Federation put the truth into this war we find ourselves in by using all forms of the media to show the general public what the truth is—advertising, television, newspapers etc. even if it costs a considerable amount of money?[36]

[35] *Police Review*, 11 August 1985.   [36] *Police Review*, 25 October 1985: 2154.

The Challenge to Police Legitimacy Continues

The material presented above illustrates that, by the mid-1980s, it was possible to speak of a 'crisis of legitimacy' for the police over the issue of their response to violent racism. Although the police had strong support from the government, there were strong challenges from various quarters that alleged that they were unable to respond effectively and, therefore, that 'self-defence' was legitmate. The next task is to chart the development of policies aimed at reforming the state response to violent racism. The remainder of this Chapter will cover the period from the discovery of the problem in the early 1980s to the point in the late 1980s when the case study which forms the basis for Part II was undertaken.

The key theme to be examined in the remainder of this Chapter is how, in spite of the apparent conflicts between the police and other state and community agencies, what became known as the 'multi-agency approach' emerged as the dominant paradigm in discourses concerning the statutory response to violent racism. It charts the origins of the idea that the most effective means of tackling violent racism (and other forms of crime) is to prevent its occurrence through preventive intervention co-ordinated between the police and other agencies and involving the active participation of the community. The Chapter examines the evidence upon which the multi-agency approach was believed to be effective, its stated rationale and the second agendas which were pursued through its development. What follows is a narrative account of the origins and development of the multi-agency approach, and a review of the academic literature on the subject.

The Origins of a Co-ordinated Approach to Crime Prevention

The idea that responsibility for tackling crime was not that of the police alone emerged at some point in the 1950s[37] (Home Office,

[37] The first centrally organized crime-prevention campaign was mounted following an approach to insurance companies by the Home Office in 1950 (Home Office, 1982: 1). References to similar initiatives on a local level may be found in Reports of the Commissioner of Police for the Metropolis during the 1950s. Morris (1958: 190) notes that 'in 1949 the Ministry of Education and the Home Office sent a joint Memorandum to the Charimen of County Councils, Lord Mayors and Mayors of County Boroughs in England and Wales on the subject of juvenile delinquency . . . The Memorandum suggested that meetings be called to discuss the problem and that these might be transformed into standing committees'.

1982: 1). This led the Home Office to call for a co-operative effort to prevent crime involving 'every part' of the community. The 1965 Cornish Committee on the Prevention and Detection of Crime suggested that the police should work with other agencies, such as the motor trade, retail traders, local authorities, and welfare organizations, towards the goal of crime prevention (Home Office, 1965). This was followed by the creation of the Home Office Standing Committee on Crime Prevention, with the purpose of bringing together 'persons and organisations who have a common interest in crime prevention for an exchange of ideas and a stimulus to further effort' (Home Office, 1965). This led to the development of new strategies of 'situational crime prevention' (such as security measures and environmental design improvements) and the production and distribution of 'crime prevention information' (such as *Crime Prevention News*). The Home Office *Review of Criminal Justice Policy* spoke specifically of a need for a 'co-ordinated approach' to crime prevention which would involve the police, government departments, local authorities, and agencies outside government in the crime-prevention field (Home Office, 1976; Gladstone, 1980).

Preventing Vandalism in Manchester

Although the idea had been kicking around for some time, one of the first systematically evaluated 'feasibility studies' of the co-ordinated approach was a project aiming to reduce vandalism in schools involving the Greater Manchester Police, Manchester City Education Department and the Home Office (Gladstone, 1980; Hope, 1985). An evaluation of the project found that levels of vandalism were unaffected by the initiative because of the practical problems of co-ordinating and implementing the joint initiatives which were proposed (Hope, 1985: 35–6). Despite the disappointing results of this project, the fact that the research had been carried out at all acted as a stimulus for the further development of co-ordinated crime prevention (Home Office, 1982; Weatheritt, 1986).

Police–Community Involvement in Social Crime Prevention

Over the same period police agencies were developing 'community involvement' and 'social crime prevention' policies. During the 1960s many police forces set up community relations departments initially as a response to problems perceived to be 'posed by the presence of ethnic minorities', though their remit rapidly broadened to a more general public-relations function (Pope, 1976; Weatheritt, 1986). The activities of these specialist 'community relations' or 'community involvement' police officers and departments included developing and sustaining contacts with local statutory and voluntary agencies, establishing 'schools involvement programmes' and work with juveniles. This activity facilitated formal means of communication and co-operation between the police and other agencies and the development of joint-agency initiatives. The Home Office encouraged these developments arguing that 'improved co-ordination and joint activity' between police, probation, education, and social services would increase police effectiveness (Home Office, 1978, 1980).

These ideas were given particular impetus within policing circles by the Chief Constable of the Devon and Cornwall Constabulary, John Alderson, through the activities of his Crime Prevention Support Unit (CPSU). For Alderson, community policing required three elements: 'Community Police Councils, inter-agency co-operation, and community constables appointed to localities' (Alderson, 1982: 136; Alderson, 1979). The Exeter Community Policing Consultative Group, set up at the end of the 1970s, was composed of officers and elected members of the local authority, representatives of churches, trades unions, the magistracy, the Department of Social Security, and the Department of the Environment. It aimed to improved co-operation and co-ordination between the police and local authority agencies to reduce crime by 'social as well as police action and for sharing respective problems and initiatives' (Moore and Brown, 1981: 53). Although the initiative was hailed as a success, the impact on crime of the forum's initiatives was not demonstrated empirically. Weatheritt, reviewing the evaluation of the initiative notes that the authors of the evaluation 'periodically flirt with the notion that crime was prevented by the CPSU's activities, only to draw away from the full implications of accepting that this might be the ultimate test of the Unit's effectiveness' (Weatheritt, 1986: 79).

By the beginning of the 1980s, both the police and the Home Office had well-developed ideas about the need for co-ordination between the police and other agencies. For the Home Office, co-ordination was an integral part of a *crime prevention* policy based on a rational model of crime analysis, policy development, implementation, monitoring, and evaluation. For the police 'inter-agency co-operation' was a component of a *community policing* policy. The latter idea, which was more ambitious, though (at this time) less clearly defined within a rational model, focused on regaining public support for the police and setting up formal lines of communication with other agencies.

Both the police and the Home Office were becoming increasingly committed to their own versions of a co-ordinated approach, though there was a good deal of interchange of ideas and collaborative effort in each of these strands of policy development. Both were also putting resources into encouraging, even exhorting, other agencies to participate. On one hand other central government and police agencies were encouraged to participate and to disseminate the idea of collaboration within their own areas of responsibility. On the other, it was necessary to encourage those that were the target of the co-ordinated approach—local authorities, the private sector, voluntary and community agencies. As John Alderson put it: 'It is "pie in the sky" to expect community policing to be brought about by voluntary agreement. Neither the Home Office nor police authorities are able to guarantee to bring about change without some form of coercion' (1982: 137).

Clearly, coercion had to be applied to all participants in the new model—police, local statutory and voluntary agencies, and 'the community' alike. Indeed, as we shall see later in this Chapter, inducement, subtle and not-so-subtle coercion in the form of government circulars, research, and other resources would continue to be used throughout the 1980s.

A Co-ordinated Approach to Violent Racism

Given that the idea of co-ordinated action was well developed by the beginning of the 1980s, it is hardly surprising that such an approach should have been advocated when the Home Office published the first government report on *Racial Attacks* in 1981. The Home Secretary exhorted other authorities 'with a responsibility for local services which affect ethnic minority communities' to give 'due weight' to racial attacks in 'their arrangements for co-ordination between services'. This would 'make possible a swift and coherent approach to the problems produced for those services by racial attacks' (Home Office, 1981: iv). More specifically, the Home Office study team pointed to the need for co-ordination between local authority officers (such as teachers and housing managers) and the police. With the acknowledgement of racial attacks as a political problem came the advocacy of co-ordination as a policy solution (see also Chapter 2, above).

The idea of collaboration between the police and other agencies dovetailed neatly with the recommendations arising out of Lord Scarman's report on the Brixton riots (Scarman, 1986) and the discussion of the issues surrounding policing and race relations in the 1981–2 Home Affairs Committee Report (House of Commons, 1982; see Chapter 2 above). Scarman emphasized the need for 'community policing', involving community constables and mechanisms by which the police could maintain contact with the people of the locality in which they worked. To this end, Scarman recommended improved co-ordination between all bodies concerned with crime in the community and a statutory framework for consultation and liaison between the police and local communities. Both these strategies can be seen as a stimulus to the development of co-ordinated policy or joint initiatives, particularly because of the formal structure to which they gave rise. It is important to bear in mind, however, that both the Home Secretary and the police were resistant to the idea of police–community consultative mechanisms at the time that Scarman published his findings. This is reflected in the caution evident in the form and structure of the consultative mechanisms which emerged. The June 1982 circular to Chief Constables, for example, makes it quite clear that police–community consultative mechanisms would be for consultation only, leaving the police independence in enforcing the law unaffected (Gordon, 1987: 136).

The response of the Metropolitan Police to the Home Office Report on Racial Attacks and Scarman in 1982 was to point to the existence of formal and informal liaison arrangements at all levels within the organization (see Chapter 3). At this time, however, although the Metropolitan Police were 'willing to talk', as they put it, there was little that they could point to *in practice* that would constitute a co-ordinated approach to racial violence in the guise either of a community policing or co-ordinated crime prevention strategy.

The Co-ordinated Approach to Crime Prevention Goes Public

In September 1982, the Home Office organized a seminar to discuss crime-prevention issues at the Police Staff College at Bramshill which was attended by very senior police officers and local government officials.[38] In the report of the proceedings published later that year, Sir Brian Cubbon, Home Office Permanent Under Secretary, introduced the idea that a new, 'co-ordinated approach', to tackling crime was necessary because patterns of crime were changing (Home Office, 1982). In particular, he said, street crime, burglary, and racial attacks appeared to be increasingly prevalent. The ideas that circulated at the Bramshill seminar informed a series of circulars, the most important of which was Circular 8/84 issued jointly by the Home Office, the Department of Education and Science, the Department of the Environment, the Department of Health and Social Security, and the Welsh Office (Home Office, 1984). This circular emphasized the importance of crime-prevention measures and sought to promote a greater awareness of their potential. In particular, it drew attention to the relevance of the crime-prevention activities of agencies other than the police and stressed 'the need for a locally co-ordinated approach' (*ibid.*).

These circulars, which have been referred to as the 'cornerstone of most subsequent official policies on crime prevention' (Bottoms, 1990: 3), acted as a catalyst in the development of a co-ordinated approach. Over the following years, the theme of co-ordination in crime prevention was elaborated in policy documents and embodied in a number of practical initiatives such as the Five Towns Initiative and Safer Cities Programme (Bottoms, 1990; Liddle and Bottoms, 1991).

Community Policing and the 'Multi-agency Approach'

Emerging in parallel with the development of the Home Office discourse of 'co-ordinated crime prevention' was a discourse of community policing within police circles. This development was given a new impetus with the arrival of Kenneth Newman as Commissioner of the Metropolitan Police in October 1982 (Reiner, 1985; Gordon, 1987). Newman became Commissioner at a crucial juncture. In the preceding eighteen months the Metropolitan Police had been in the full glare of public and media attention in the aftermath of the 1981 riots. Numerous reports (including the *Scarman Report, Racial Attacks,* and the Policy Studies Institute report, *Police and People in*

[38] This seminar occurred one month prior to Kenneth Newman leaving his post as Commandant of Bramshill to assume the post of Commissioner of the Metropolitan Police.

London) had criticized London's policing strategy and had concentrated attention on police racism. The Greater London Council had, within the previous year, formed a police committee with the expressed aim of making the Metropolitan Police accountable to an elected police authority. The GLC had by that time started to publish documents illuminating what it saw as the consequences of the lack of accountability of the Metropolitan Police to the people of London.[39] Ideas about community participation, co-ordination between agencies, and the need to find new ways of preventing crime and re-establishing public support for the police had germinated within the Home Office and within numerous police forces, including the Metropolitan Police under McNee. Indeed, McNee had introduced what he termed 'neighbourhood policing' experiments in 1981. However, these initiatives were crystallized and given renewed impetus by Newman. For example, in January 1983, shortly after taking up his post in the Metropolitan Police, he presented a report to the Home Secretary which outlined his plans for reorganizing the Metropolitan Police. Newman emphasised what he termed the 'multi-agency approach' in which '[p]roblems identified locally will be tackled systematically by co-ordinating the contributions of police, public and local agencies. The concept of a corporate strategy is vital' (Gordon, 1987: 138).

In developing new strategies of community policing and the newly coined 'multi-agency approach', Newman drew on the ideas of Herman Goldstein, a US police researcher (Goldstein, 1979, 1990; Eck and Spelman, 1987). Goldstein's theory grew out of research which indicated that the three basic elements of traditional 'incident-driven policing'—random preventive patrol, rapid response, and reactive investigation—were an ineffective means of tackling crime.[40] The entire orientation of traditional policing methods, with its emphasis

[39] In addition to the report on *Racial Harassment in London*, referred to in chapter 3, the GLC and its successor, the London Strategic Policy Unit, published reports on the Police Bill (which became the Police and Criminal Evidence Act) 1984, Public Order Bill 1985, police complaints, policing domestic violence, the Irish community, and a range of other issues (see GLC, 1986; LSPU, 1987a). Most importantly, the GLC argued consistently for a democratically elected police authority for London (GLC, 1983; LSPU, 1987b).

[40] On the basis of experiments such as the Kansas City Preventive Patrol Experiment (Kelling *et al.*, 1974), Eck and Spellman go as far as to state that: 'Incident-driven policing is obsolete. The police can no longer restrict their tactics to preventive patrol, fast response to calls, and reactive investigation; such tactics are incapable of preventing most crimes' (1987: 31).

on response to reported incidents, failed to tackle the root causes of crime. Effective crime control, Goldstein argued, required the replacement of reactive, incident-based policing with a means of solving the local community problems that give rise to incidents requiring police attention. In order to bring this about, Goldstein argued that 'problem-solving', a rational approach to transform reactive policing into a more community-based form, was necessary.

In 1983 Newman sent officers from his newly created Management Services Department (MSD) to meet Goldstein at the University of Winsconsin in the United States. On their return in November 1983, the Metropolitan Police's MSD undertook a feasibility study of the applicability of the problem-oriented approach to their operations (Hoare, Stuart, and Purcell, 1984). This exercise took the form of four pilot studies aiming to tackle four specific problems (*viz.* prostitution, theft from cars, shoplifting, and teenage gangs). Although the evaluation of the projects found little evidence that these problems had actually been solved using this method, or indeed that incidents had been reduced, the report concluded that police effectiveness and performance had been improved. The report also noted that there would be some difficulty in implementing a problem-oriented approach in the Metropolitan Police:

The present structure of the Metropolitan Police is probably out of step with the approach, and its adoption would involve risk taking and the abandonment of some of the traditional expectations of line managers. The 'Problem Oriented Approach' is more a matter of attitude than skill, and an idea which would have to be progressively assimilated rather than being imposed [Hoare, Stewart, and Purcell 1984, summary page].

This notwithstanding, the report noted that the idea of problem oriented policing was in tune with Newman's strategy to reorganize the structure and function of the Metropolitan Police. In particular, Hoare *et al.* argued that it 'reinforces the current strategies of local, effective, multi-agency initiatives'. As Goldstein subsequently noted (1990: 55), Newman's commitment to problem solving is reflected in his (1985) modernized restatement of Rowan and Mayne's *Principles of Policing*:

Many of the apparently isolated incidents to which the police are called are symptoms of more general substantive problems with roots in a wide range of social and environmental conditions. The aim of the Metropolitan Police will, therefore, be to work with other agencies to develop what is known as a 'situational' or 'problem-solving' approach to crime prevention, where, rather than merely dealing with individual acts of law-breaking, careful analysis is made of the total circumstance surrounding the commission of types of crime, taking account of wide-ranging social and environmental factors, in order better to understand—and counter—the causes of those acts [Metropolitan Police, 1985: 12].

This passage from Newman's 'little blue book' (distributed to all the Met's serving officers) neatly encapsulates Goldstein's argument, utilizes his terminology, and incorporates the solution which he advocated. It also ties together Goldstein's theory with the Home Office thinking on co-ordinated crime prevention. The result was Newman's 'multi-agency approach'—an apparently rational solution in which the police work with other agencies to understand and tackle the causes of crime through 'problem-oriented', 'situational', and 'social' crime prevention.

The Multi-agency Approach to Racial Incidents

Community Relations Department 'Pilot Studies'

In a separate initiative, begun in 1984, the Metropolitan Police Community Relations Department (then A7) carried out what it termed a 'pilot study' to apply the 'problem solving technique in an effort to generate a range of new approaches by police to the problem of racial incidents'. Although the Community Relations Department utilized the terminology of problem-solving, the methods adopted in this initiative bear little resemblance to those advocated by Goldstein. What the Department did was to trawl for new responses in five police districts[41] by asking local Community Relations Officers to adopt a 'problem solving/multi-agency approach towards racial incidents'. The responses returned by Divisional Community Relations Officers were then translated into policy recommendations. The communication between the Community Relations Departments of Scotland Yard and K Division (which includes the London Boroughs of Newham, Barking, and Havering) provides a useful insight into the form the problem-solving approach took and into the existing relationship between the police and community in east London.

Between January 1984 and January 1986 a series of memoranda passed between Scotland Yard and K Division requesting and returning

---

[41] The districts were H, X, S, R, and K.

information on strategies used to communicate with 'the community'.[42] In reply to a question concerning the existing degree of multi-agency involvement, the Community Liaison Officer (CLO) replied that good liaison and communication existed between the police and the housing department. Referring to collaboration over the eviction of the McDonell family in Newham in 1984, the CLO commented that the housing department was capable of 'appropriate positive interference'. With regard to education, the CLO referred to 'an easy relationship with all schools' which provided 'a reciprocal exchange of helpful information'. It was also possible to point to the provision of information in the form of a 'composite bulletin of racial incidents reported to the police' which was supplied to the Councils for Racial Equality, Borough Race Relations Units, and other race relations organizations. The CLO reported that the post-Scarman Consultative Committees were in operation in the London Borough of Barking and Dagenham, at an advanced stage of negotiation in Havering, and at a preliminary stage of negotiation in Newham. Perhaps the most revealing comment was provided in response to the question of what methods of 'general public participation' were in operation. The CLO replied candidly: 'Good relations with the local press promote a police perspective to be simultaneously countenanced [sic] in the majority of articles or reports concerning racial matters. In addition, police initiatives in the area generally receive an indulgent report in the local press.'

The dialogue between Scotland Yard and K Division shows that the police community relations specialists were putting a good deal of effort into establishing relationships with agencies such as local authority service departments, schools, and the media. Although there are grounds to suggest that the quality and utility of these relationships were gradually 'talked up' as the 'problem-solving' initiative progressed, there is no doubt that the police saw them as successful. It is also clear that there was a good deal of information flowing between the police and other agencies.

While there was a two-way flow of information, the flow was not

[42] (1) Memorandum from Commander A7 to Divisional Chief Superintendents and CLOs Reporting Racial Incidents (9 January 1984); (2) Memorandum from DAC 'A' (ops) to Commanders H, X, R, S, and K Racial Incidents (15 January 1985); (3) Memorandum from Commander 'K' District to DAC 'A' (ops) Racial Incidents: interim report on the problem-oriented approach (30 January 1985); (4) Metropolitan Police (1986), *Recording and Monitoring Racial Incidents Guidelines*, published by A7 Branch, January 1986 (London: Metropolitan Police).

really reciprocal. While the police were able to collect varied information from many sources, the outflow of information was restricted to composite reports on recorded racial incidents and briefings provided to the press. It is significant that the Divisional CLO pointed to the relationship with the media as the police's primary involvement with the 'general public'. As press reports over this period illustrate, the local media (particularly the *Newham Recorder*) did indeed provide an 'indulgent report' on police initiatives and promoted a 'police perspective' (see sections at the beginning of this Chapter).

Community Liaison Officers in other districts also reported more concrete results from their multi-agency/problem-solving initiatives. In particular H District (Tower Hamlets) police were able to report an increase in the 'arrest/clear up rate . . . from eight per cent in 1984 to 31 per cent in 1985, and in the number of arrests from 54 in 1984 to 140 in January–November 1985' (House of Commons, 1986). This was attributed to 'gaining the confidence of the community to a greater extent, gaining the confidence of the various agencies in the borough, and a commitment on the part of the police to take firm action' (*ibid.*). Specific measures included local training, more Home Beat officers, a twenty-four hour help-line, use of volunteers from the local Bangladeshi community, and a multi-agency forum for discussing cases[43] (*ibid.*).

Policy Formulation

Between January 1985 and January 1986 information from the five, pilot study districts was analysed to produce a range of policy initiatives. In particular, the theme of the multi-agency approach was well developed. The result of the 'pilot studies' was the *Recording and Monitoring Racial Incidents Guidelines* ('the *Guidelines*') published by A7 Branch in January 1986 (an edited form of which appeared as an appendix to the 1986 Home Affairs Committee Report). In this document, the police policy on racial attacks is stated to be as follows:

[43] In April 1985 Commander Sullivan, head of H district which covers Newham's neighbouring borough—Tower Hamlets, together with Chief Inspector Pat Prididge and PC Dereck Noblett (Sullivan's Community Liaison Officers) returned from a 3-week 'fact-finding tour of Bangladesh aimed at improving police effectiveness in London' (trip to better understanding, the *Job* 19 April 1985). Sullivan's initiative was to put together what was described by the *East London Advertiser* in an article headed 'Police "team" to cut race crime', as a 'new-style anti-crime "panel"'. The panel, to which a range of local agencies would be invited, was, according to Sullivan, still in its infancy. He explained that '[t]he idea is that people involved should be able to speak frankly about racial problems, where they stem from, what are their causes—and also, they should be able to do more than just talk about them'.

Force policy on racial incidents . . . falls into two parts:

a) A continuing effort to develop and refine internal procedures for recording, reporting, investigating and monitoring incidents.

b) Fostering and encouraging multi-agency approaches toward the search for
solution to the problem involving other agencies, local and central government, voluntary organisations and the community as a whole.

The second, *and more important part* of Force policy recognises that police
action alone cannot be expected to reach the causes of the problem. Indeed
it could be argued that the achievement of the social changes needed to bring
about a reduction in racial incidents is a matter *almost certainly outside the
area of police responsibility* [Metropolitan Police, 1986a: 3, emphasis added].

Thus was formulated a twin policy of refining administrative and
investigative procedures on the one hand and fostering and encouraging the multi-agency approach on the other. It is interesting to note
a contradiction evident in this policy. The Metropolitan Police argue
that the more important part of the policy entails fostering the multi-
agency approach and, yet, prevention—the rationale for the
approach—is argued to be 'almost certainly outside the area of police
responsibility'. The document lists other 'distinct advantages [which]
accrued from a multi-agency approach'. These were (1) the establishment of confidence and understanding between agencies; (2) the
establishment of common ground; and (3) the increased exchange of
information.

This document quite candidly outlines the police objectives in
establishing the new approach. It is evident throughout this key policy document that the multi-agency approach is in no way intended
to impact on operational police procedures outside the community
relations specialism. The multi-agency approach—initiated, fostered,
and encouraged by the police—is seen as a mechanism by which
responsibility for reducing violent racism may be off-loaded from the
police to other agencies. At the same time, the police benefit by
restoring the confidence of other local agencies with which they find
'common ground'. These agencies provide information to the police
and are recipients of police-generated information.

Multi-agency Options

The new policy suggested nine multi-agency options that could be
pursued by local police Community Relations Officers. These
included such *ad hoc* measures as the production of joint publicity

and the use of schools involvement and a range of more structured multi-agency initiatives. Preferably, it was stated, such an initiative would be free-standing and independent from the police. The *Guidelines* suggest an initiative that would 'assume a corporate nature, perhaps with an independent chairmanship, thus releasing the police from the position of sole or main responsibility for creating the social conditions which make racial incidents less likely' (Metropolitan Police, 1986a).

Two options were favoured. First, the formation of Racial Incident Panels: these would take the form of a panel comprising representatives of the local authority, other agencies, and voluntary organizations which would review reported racial incidents to assess what action should be taken. The benefit of this was said to be 'widening the options available for remedial action in individual cases as well as ensuring that the nature and scope of the problem is fully understood outside the police service'. It is clear from a note of caution which accompanied this suggestion that 'widening the options available' did not include changing police operational practices. The *Guidelines* note that:

[d]ifficulties may be encountered when there is a lack of understanding amongst panel members of the legal and constitutional position of the police in relation to law enforcement procedures etc., and care should be taken therefore to clarify these issues prior to the setting up of panels [Metropolitan Police, 1986a: 12].

In other words, it should be made clear to local authorities and community groups that the police were accountable only to the law and to the Home Office. Racial Incident Panels were quite clearly not intended to be a means to influence police operational decision-making.

The second favoured multi-agency option was the formation of a sub-committee of the police–community consultative groups recommended by Scarman and made statutory through their inclusion in section 106 of the 1984 Police and Criminal Evidence Act (see Morgan, 1989). This was thought to be 'preferable in most circumstances', and in particular 'where police commanders judge there is little local consensus on the issue'. This forum would facilitate the type of discussion suggested for the racial incident panels. The key police contribution would be to 'supply details of incidents and to discuss police activity to deal with them'.

Local Authorities and Community Organizations: Were They Pushed or Did They Jump?

This Chapter has focused so far on the push coming from the police and the Home Office towards community policing and co-ordinated crime prevention and the eventual fusion of these discourses into the 'multi-agency approach'. Both the police and the Home Office were actively pursuing these policies, seeking sites on which to assess their viability and putting resources into communicating the worth of the new approach to a wide audience. Before moving on to look at the advancement of the multi-agency approach from the mid-1980s onwards we must first turn to the question of where the agencies which were the target of multi-agency co-ordination—i.e. local authorities and community organizations—stood at this time .

London Race and Housing Forum 1981

Some of the earliest statements published by community relations councils (crcs) on the subject of violent racism include a call for co-ordinated action which echoed that of central government at the time. In its 1981 report on racial harassment on local authority housing estates, the London Race and Housing Forum (funded by the CRE) recommended that 'in conjunction with all relevant agencies in its area, the local authority [should develop] a coherent strategy to combat racism which should not just deal with individual incidents but should also move towards overcoming the causes of racial harassment (1981: 18, recommendation 2).

To advocate that local authorities and other relevant agencies should develop a 'coherent strategy' and attempt to deal with *causes* mirrors the Home Office idea of, and rationale for, a co-ordinated approach. It is evident in the report that there is some support from within community relations councils for them to have a co-ordinating role between the police and other agencies in a broad response to racial harassment. The London Race and Housing Forum report cites the experience of the crc in Camden where:

acknowledgement of [the seriousness of the problem] has been gained through a long process of *regular meetings (organised by the community relations council*, but there is no reason why other bodies should not take similar steps) between the Community Liaison Officer, homebeat officers, social and community workers, housing department staff and crc workers, At these meetings, both individual cases and general policy/action is discussed and in the two years that they have been convened, it has become less and less difficult to persuade the local police stations to take action, and visits are made almost immediately after notification [London Race and Housing Forum, 1981: 14, emphasis added].

It is not clear how these ideas filtered into the discourse of the crcs, but the motivation for advocating a co-ordinated approach is clearly stated. In essence, it is a means of gaining more police and local authority resources to tackle the problems faced by ethnic minority communities. By establishing a forum of the kind suggested, the police and the local authority may be called upon to take action where they were formerly reluctant to do so. It is interesting to note that Camden crc claims to have organized these meetings. There is no evidence available on which to confirm or refute this claim, but it is apparent that such meetings were possible only because of the existence of a police Community Liaison Officer and home beat officers whose job it was to initiate and participate in such forums (Philips and Cochrane, 1989).

The Greater London Council 1982–4

In March 1982, the GLC Housing Committee responded to the London Race and Housing Forum report published a year earlier, 'accepting its recommendations with some reservations'.[44] One particular reservation concerned the suggestion that the local authority should work with the police, although the GLC report acknowledged the potential for joint action, where such action had met with some success in London authorities. Interestingly, the panel cites Camden as a locality where co-ordination had showed some promise:

In Camden, *the housing department had initiated a series of meetings* on estates where harassment was particularly bad, involving the local police, officials from housing and social services, the tenants associations and local councillors. These meetings have now developed into regular working groups involving local community organisations and youth workers. Their purpose is to discuss anti-racist work on particular estates. A spokesperson from the council considered that within the limitations already described these meetings had enabled officials, the police and local organisations to work together effectively [GLC, 1984: 47 emphasis added].

[44] This was the point at which the GLC ceased to consider racial harassment as simply a 'management issue' for the housing department and began to develop polices specifically targeted at the problem (GLC, 1984: 31; see also Chap. 2).

The rationale for the approach here seems to be concerned less with gaining more resources for the community than with administrative effectiveness. Note here that the housing department not only advocated co-operation but claimed to have organized the same meetings previously attributed to the crc. What makes these conflicting claims more interesting is that in an oral submission to the GLC Panel of Inquiry Camden crc criticized the views of Camden housing department for being 'too optimistic' (GLC, 1984: 47).

The GLC concluded that 'in some areas regular meetings with the police specifically on this issue could serve a useful, though limited purpose'. It cited the benefits as: (1) preventing police inaction, (2) preventing denial of the problem, and (3) providing a forum in which local organizations working in support of victims could make demands on both police and housing officials with the possibility of 'co-ordinated action . . . if necessary'. Set against these potential benefits, the panel presented a number of dangers and a sceptical appraisal of future possibilities. The principal danger, it argued, was the threat to individual liberty. It was possible, it suggested, that low-grade information offered to the police might find its way onto the index cards of the collator's office at the local station. 'There is', the report warned, 'a fine line between co-operating with the police in effective action, and simply serving as a source of information for police purposes' (GLC, 1984: 47).

The main thrust of the GLC's opposition to working with the police is its view that the police were unwilling to take the issue of racial harassment seriously. This view is based on the experience of making demands on the police in Tower Hamlets and, in particular, on the Shadwell Gardens estate. There, two strategies that were employed by groups (such as tenants' associations) were to make demands on home beat officers and at a senior level of the local police. With respect to the home beats, evidence was given that 'while people may get to know and gain confidence in their local home beat officer, the police officers who eventually come when they need help are strangers from elsewhere'. The tenants' association drew four lessons from its attempts to make demands on the police through a 'multi-agency forum': the seriousness of the problem was played down by the police; demands were rejected on grounds to which only the police and housing department were privy (e.g. resources), precluding further discussion and justifying lack of action; there was a failure on the part of the police to provide alternative proposals in those areas where it could act. Finally, there was:

a tendency for statutory agencies to play-off responsibility against each other. With the police and housing department this happens both at the level of individual cases—the housing department leaving the case to the police, and the police to the housing department—and in terms of policing policy [GLC, 1984: 50].

On the basis of the experience in Tower Hamlets and elsewhere, the GLC concluded that:

The action of statutory authorities as experienced in meetings like this point to the difficulties of [paraphrasing the London Race and Housing Forum] 'a coherent and effective strategy to combat racism' involving statutory authorities and community groups. In particular the power and autonomy of the local police force is such that, unless there is a change within the local command structure or new instructions from Scotland Yard, there is no reason to believe that it will participate in any coordinated approach, except possibly on its own terms which, to date, have been less than constructive [GLC, 1984: 50].

The GLC's cautious response to the idea of co-ordinating with the police is reflected in its recommendations for future action. It went no further than to suggest that meetings should take place between district housing managers and officers of the GLC Police Committee Support Unit to draw up guidelines on dealing with the police over individual cases and on giving information to the police (GLC, 1984: 54).

Although the GLC was only one local authority among many in London, its ideas had symbolic importance during this period. In particular, the willingness of the GLC to take on the Thatcher Government on a number of fronts, and particularly its pursuit of an elected police authority for London, led to its policies influencing the thinking of other authorities. It was at the forefront of local government policy-making on 'race' and policing issues which it urged other authorities to adopt. As Michael Keith and Karim Murji put it, '[t]he GLC's Police Committee was largely hegemonic because of its command of an extra level of resource and its city-wide remit' (Keith and Murji, 1990: 124). For example, in June 1981, the Chair of the GLC Police Committee, Paul Boateng, wrote to Labour-controlled authorities in London urging them to establish their own police committees and police committee support units, which many subsequently did (Keith and Murji, 1990). For these reasons, and because the GLC report on racial harassment was the first to be published by a local authority, the view that the dangers of co-operation with the police outweighed its limited potential as a means of getting more resources in the community was very influential.

Although the struggle with the police over the question of democratic accountability meant that co-operation was not seen as a viable option by the GLC, other authorities were inclined to respond more positively to the police. A rift developed between the GLC, which wanted the boroughs to 'retain a critical pressure group approach to the police', and those authorities which felt that 'until there was proper accountability there was much to be achieved by a critical engagement with the police' (Keith and Murji, 1990: 125). Authorities such as Islington and Newham may be seen as taking the latter 'realist' approach.

The London Borough of Newham

Initially, the London Borough of Newham followed the GLC's lead by forming its own Police Committee and Police Committee Support Unit (PCSU). During the early to mid-1980s the authority remained strongly critical of the police and took only tentative steps towards active co-operation with them.

By the time that the London Borough of Newham Council submitted evidence to the 1986 Home Affairs Committee, however, it is evident that it had come to accept the idea that it should play a part in preventing crime and supporting victims. Indeed, the Council pointed to various measures that it had taken in this regard, such as the appointment of a 'community safety officer', changes in procedures in its housing department, its funding of a local Victim Support Scheme, and the development of support for victims. With respect to dealing with perpetrators, although it pointed to its success using its powers of eviction (i.e. in the McDonnell case), it argued that 'the lynchpin in ensuring that action taken is the police service' (House of Commons, 1986: 46) and it remained strongly critical of police action. It provided a list of specific criticisms of the police response to racist violence, many of which echo those made by community groups and anti-racist organizations since the end of the 1970s (see Table 2.2).

Newham's PCSU was also strongly critical of the police overtures *vis-à-vis* the multi-agency approach. It stated that 'the increasing and prevalent belief is that police calls for a "multi-agency" approach in dealing with racial violence in Newham are a smokescreen for police inaction' (House of Commons, 1986: 47). In particular, it pointed to

the experiences of attempting to establish multi-agency practice between council services and the police, which, interestingly, the council claimed responsibility for initiating: 'in 1984 the Housing Department *persuaded local police to join them in two multi-agency pilot projects* where there were particular problems of racial harassment in local authority area (House of Commons, 1986: 44, emphasis added). Its experience of the 'pilot project' was not encouraging, however:

Police commitment to the multi-agency projects, introduced with such high expectations, were seen as crucial to success. Once these projects were set up, however, both Council and Community Groups were astonished to note what police commitment actually meant: On the Clements Avenue Estate in particular such a multi-agency panel was established to deal with racially motivated attacks. At meetings of this panel over a nine month period police representatives had hardly ever bothered to turn up, had never sent apologies when they failed to arrive and when they were present had never initiated discussion on racial harassment or attack in that or any other area of the borough. . . . In the second of the pilot areas . . . although no multi-agency panel exists it was understood that police were carefully plotting incidents of racial harassment in the area. Subsequently this turned out to be merely the plotting of the existence of Neighbourhood Watch Schemes [House of Commons 1986: 47].

Despite the strength of its criticisms, it is clear that Newham Council had grasped the potential of the multi-agency approach not only as a means of improving the police response to the problem but also as a means by which the council might possibly exert some influence over police operational decision-making. Raising the moral stakes, Newham Council concluded that:

Racial harassment can only be tackled on a multi-agency basis, but co-operation on anything can only work when all sides are *genuinely* co-operating with each other and are genuinely committed to the objectives of the task in hand. . . . We feel that with regard to these other agencies action is a matter of will and that will has yet to be found [House of Commons, 1986: 52, original emphasis].

The 1986 Home Affairs Committee Report

The 1985–6 Home Affairs Committee Report, *Racial Attacks and Harassment* (House of Commons, 1986), marks an important juncture in the development of the public-policy response to racist

violence. Although there had been a good deal of activity involving central government, the police, and other agencies, this report was the first government statement on the problem of violent racism since the Home Affairs Committee report on the subject four years earlier (House of commons 1982). The report drew on written and oral evidence from an array of agencies including the police (ACPO, the Metropolitan Police, Greater Manchester Police, and West Midlands Police), the Department of Education and Science, the Association of Metropolitan Authorities, Manchester Community Relations Council, and the London Borough of Newham.

The Problem of Racial Attacks and Harassment

The report condemned racial attacks and harassment as 'the most shameful and dispiriting aspect of race relations in Britain' (House of Commons, 1986: iv) citing a range of evidence which illustrated the nature of the onslaught of violent racism directed against British black communities. The report quoted from a report of the GLC race and housing team, which said that this harassment included:

racist name calling, rubbish, rotten eggs, rotten tomatoes, excreta etc. dumped in front of the victims' doors, urinating through the letterbox of the victims, fireworks, burning materials and excreta pushed through the letter-box, door-knocking, cutting telephone wires, kicking, punching and spitting at victims, serious physical assault, damage to property, e.g. windows being broken, doors smashed, racist graffiti daubed on door or wall. Dogs, cars, motorcycles are still being used to frighten black people. Shotguns and knives have also been used occasionally [House of Commons, 1986: iv].

The report noted that such violence was concentrated in parts of London and other cities, but that it also occurred in areas where ethnic minorities were fewer and were 'therefore more vulnerable'. The proportion of people suffering racial attack or harassment ranged from 23 per cent of Asian families in the London Borough of Newham to 'every household' among some Asian groups in Glasgow and Manchester. The 'typical victim' of racial violence, the report found, was an Asian, often a woman or child, though 'Afro-Caribbeans, Chinese and white people (some of the latter, Irish, Jewish or of mixed race)' were also victimized. The 'typical perpetrator' was a white teenager, 'often part of a gang and sometimes encouraged by parents'. Afro-Caribbeans, the Committee reported, sometimes perpetrated racial attacks but were "more likely to be vic-

tims than perpetrators" (*ibid*.: v). The effects that racial violence was having on individual, family, and community life were profound. The Committee cited Manchester Council for Community Relations (1986), which pointed to:

the reality which lies behind all of these cases—an individual or family living in fear, subject to humiliation, stress and physical danger, frequently too terrified for their safety to allow children to play outside, driven to tranquillisers and sleeping pills, constantly at the alert wondering if tonight will bring a brick through the window, or tomorrow morning the letters "NF-Pakis go home!" on their front door. Family life is destroyed as the parents and children, almost invariably, show their frustration, anger and fear to each other. What was a home becomes a prison [House of Commons, 1986: v].

The Police Response

As well as speaking in the strongest language about the scale and impact of the problem, the report acknowledged that 'the response to racial incidents by the police and other official bodies has been widely criticised as inadequate' (House of Commons, 1986: vi). This was attributed in part to the problem of detecting and prosecuting perpetrators, but also to the view that white people found it difficult to imagine the 'constant fear and the experience of attacks upon one's self, one's children and one's home motivated solely by racial hatred'. This lack of understanding and awareness, the Committee argued, went 'far to explain why policies and measures to counter racial attacks have developed slowly and on an *ad hoc* basis'. What was necessary was a recognition that racial violence 'challenge[d] the right of ethnic minorities to live in Britain at all'. It concluded that much more emphasis was needed from the highest political levels to demonstrate that racial violence was unacceptable and urged effective action against it. To this end, the Committee recommended that police forces covering areas with appreciable ethnic minorities should follow the lead of Sir Kenneth Newman in the Metropolitan Police by making it clear that tackling racial incidents was regarded as one of their priority tasks. It was noted that the police response was variable, though complaints were frequently made. These included:

slowness in responding to calls for help (or failing to arrive at all), hostile questioning and unsympathetic treatment of victims (sometimes leading to the arrest of the victim), unreasonably denying the racial motive of attacks, unwillingness to provide interpreters, failure to act against perpetrators even to the extent of giving informal cautions, advising the victim to take out private prosecutions, and failure to keep victims informed of action taken. The extent to which each of these characteristics is typical of the police response to racial incidents is difficult to assess, although for most of them there is evidence that they occur in some cases [House of Commons, 1986: viii].

The Committee believed that a reasonable measure of the effectiveness of the police response was the 'clear up or detection rate'. The report singled out problems in the Metropolitan Police area to be *'the most worrying . . . where the clear up rate for racial incidents was only 13 per cent in 1984 and 15 per cent in 1985'* (House of Commons 1986: vii, original emphasis). However, the report pointed to new procedures and policies in Tower Hamlets, where the 'arrest/clear up rate' more than tripled from 8 to 31 per cent. This 'dramatic increase' was attributed to 'gaining the confidence of the community . . . gaining the confidence of the various agencies in the borough . . . [and a decision to] take very firm action to tackle the problem'.

The Committee also recommended that the police should initiate prosecutions themselves (including common assault cases where appropriate), disseminate information on improved effectiveness, introduce training on racial incidents, allocate officers to be responsible for monitoring incidents, ensure that victims were kept informed about the progress of their cases, and ensure that interpreters were available if necessary.

Advocating the Multi-Agency Approach

One of the main thrusts of the report was to advocate strongly the multi-agency approach. The Committee noted that the Metropolitan Police had made the approach central to their policy and reviewed the evidence from their pilot studies. On the basis of this information and the advocacy of Newham Council and Manchester CCR, the Committee argued that:

A multi-agency approach is not simply a way of making the police more effective and more aware of the problem, but should also promote action by other agencies and in particular a co-ordinated approach towards racial incidents in general and towards individual cases. . . . We regard a multi-agency approach as crucial in developing an effective response to racial incidents, and we pay tribute to those who have worked to establish such an approach [House of Commons, 1986: xiv].

The Committee also noted that there was no guarantee that multi-agency schemes would work well and that they could be no substitute for each agency developing its own policy. It also noted that both the police and local authorities had criticized the role of each other in such forums. These problems notwithstanding, the Committee recommended that:

all police forces and local authorities whose areas contain an appreciable ethnic minority population give serious consideration to the establishment of a multi-agency approach to racial incidents, and that the Home Office ensure that knowledge acquired as to the best ways of organising a multi-agency approach is disseminated [*ibid*.: xv].

In order to establish such an approach, the Committee stressed the importance of the post-Scarman consultative arrangements under section 106 of the Police and Criminal Evidence Act 1984. Emphasizing that the provisions of section 106 were mandatory the Committee recommended that 'the Secretary of State use his powers under Section 106 to ensure that police authorities make the necessary arrangements and that in so doing he seek an explanation in writing for any failure by any party to give effect to such consultation agreements' (*ibid*.) This clearly coercive posture was intended to bring any reluctant local authorities into line. Additional pressure was placed on local authorities by the Select Committee by raising the moral stakes:

Since there is no possibility of effective action against racial incidents independently of the police, and at the same time little chance of the police being successful without the co-operation of other agencies and the community at large, we regard refusal to co-operate with the police as political self-indulgence from which the sufferers will be the ethnic minorities [*ibid*.].

In order to take the multi-agency approach still further, the Home Affairs Committee moved outside the specific areas of Home Office responsibility to make a number of recommendations for local authority action on racial harassment. In particular, it recommended that there should be a statutory duty on housing authorities to monitor and record offences, to develop policies concerning them, and to designate officers to be responsible for dealing with them. The Committee also took the unusual step of recommending that local authorities test their legal powers of prosecution in racial harassment cases and that the Department of the Environment should encourage them to do so in 'appropriate cases'. The Committee also recommended that social services departments and local education authorities recognize their responsibilities and adopt training policies and procedural guidelines.

The Inter-departmental Racial Attacks Group

The central government commitment to the multi-agency approach as a key policy response to racial attacks was forged and elaborated in the 1986 Home Affairs Committee report. But despite this advocacy, at that time there was little research or practical experience that would indicate how such an initiative might be set up, what its terms of reference might be, how safeguards, checks, and balances might be incorporated, what the responsibilities of each constituent agency might be, or on what basis its effectiveness might be assessed. The Home Affairs Committee went little further than to note the model adopted by the Metropolitan Police in its 'pilot studies' and to urge the Home Office to carry out further research.

In response to the recommendation that a multi-agency approach should be adopted to tackle racial attacks and harassment, the Ministerial Group on Crime Prevention[45] established an inter-departmental working party—the Racial Attacks Group (RAG)—with the following terms of reference: '[t]o consider the scope for greater co-operation between the police and other agencies in preventing and dealing with racial attacks and to give support to the development of local multi-agency approaches to combating such attacks [Home Office, 1989: paragraph 3].

The Group, which met for the first time in February 1987, was composed of representatives of the Home Office (Research and Planning Unit, Race Relations Division, and Police Department), the Scottish Office, the Departments of Health, Environment, and Education and Science, the Metropolitan Police, ACPO, ACPO (Scotland), the Commission for Racial Equality, and the Joint Committee Against Racialism.

One of the topics raised at the beginning of the life of the group was how to stimulate and evaluate new initiatives to deal practically with the response to and the prevention of racial attacks (Home Office, 1987). At its second meeting in March 1987 the RAG decided that a multi-agency action project should be initiated and asked the Home

---

[45] This group, comprising ministers from 13 government departments, was formed in Spring 1986.

Office RPU to produce a paper reviewing relevant practical initiatives which might be applied to the prevention of racial attacks. The paper which was produced reviewed a range of initiatives including those initiated in the Metropolitan Police by Sir Kenneth Newman, the Home Office Crime Prevention Unit study of crime and racial harassment against Asian shopkeepers (Ekblom and Simon, 1988), and the North Peckham multi-agency initiative. The paper concluded that although there was some potential in these prior experiences, it was:

very difficult to set up in a rational manner an action project whose primary aim is the amelioration of complex community problems. Apart from the problems of getting all interested parties together, there is also the question of how to develop solutions to the problem in hand which are both practicable and viable [Home Office, 1987].

As a means of resolving these problems, the paper advocated using Herman Goldstein's problem-oriented approach citing the experience of applying the approach in Britain and the United States.[46] The paper lists the elements for the practical application of Goldstein's theory as: tackling specific practical problem in a well-defined local area; abandonment of legal definitions of incidents in favour of describing underlying problems; collection of information from all available sources; and a genuinely broad search for solutions, unshackled by traditional definitions which have influenced their responses in the past. The authors concluded that '[t]he problem-oriented approach provides the essential mechanism of involving the *rationality of research* in the search for feasible preventive action' (Home Office, 1987, emphasis added).

The proposal for a 'problem-oriented multi-agency approach to prevent racial attacks' suggested that an evaluated action project should be set up. A steering group would be established comprising all local statutory, voluntary, and community groups concerned with racial harassment. The stimulation, management, and administration of such a group would be organized by an independent co-ordinator employed by the Home Office, who would be 'in a good position to over-come difficulties which may exist between participating agencies'.

The resulting North Plaistow Racial Harassment Project was initiated later in 1987. The project, on which I worked as 'action-researcher' forms the basis for the case-study which will be described in Part II of this volume (see also Saulsbury and Bowling, 1991).

[46] The paper cited Hoare, Stewart, and Purcell (1984); Spelman and Eck (1987); Goldstein (1979).

Academic Studies of Co-ordination

Martin Rein: Policy into Practice

Co-ordination is often seized upon as a management strategy when other solutions have been unsucsessful in solving problems at which they are directed. Martin Rein (1983), drawing on the experience of the US government's attempts to co-ordinate policy and practice for services to children in the 1960s, argues that it is essential to analyse the (explicit and implicit) reasons for advocating co-ordination in order to understand the apparent paradox that, while the call for co-ordination is frequently made, attempts to co-ordinate are rarely successful. He argues that:

Clients, professional practitioners, administrators, planners and politicians may all want to see more coordination in the delivery of services, each group for its own reasons, from the vantage point of its own positions. Any general movement toward coordination is likely to be an amalgam of the various motivations and definitions of the problem that these groups bring to their advocacy. It is often difficult to clarify and separate these motivations and therefore to understand just what problems coordination is expected to alleviate [1983: 60].

He goes on to argue that while the plea for co-ordination may arise simply from a concern with administrative efficiency or an 'inchoate longing for control and certainty in a disorderly environment', co-ordination is usually advocated for quite concrete reasons. He suggest a number of potential reasons:

(1) the sense of working at cross purposes; (2) perceived overlap and duplication of coverage; (3) gaps or discontinuities in available services; (4) felt need for comprehensive or holistic treatment for clients; (5) frustration with limited service technologies; (6) clients desires for more resources; and (7) political and organisational needs for reform and control [ibid.: 61].

The complexity of the problem of violent racism, the multidimensionality of the perspectives brought to bear upon it, and the diversity of the constituencies calling for co-ordination provides the potential for many of these goals to be cited in this context. Certainly, the sense of working at cross-purposes, gaps in existing services, the need for comprehensives, clients' desire for more resources and organisational reform are evident in the discourses of those advocating the co-ordinated approach to racial violence. 'Frustration with limited service technologies' could be seen as an analogy for the shift in the focus of policing discourse from detection to crime prevention. Having identified the limits of the police ability to control crime using the methods upon which routine policing was based, co-ordination with other agencies suggests itself 'naturally', almost as 'common sense'. As Rein argues:

> Professionals may call for co-ordination because they feel the service they provide is inadequate to the human problems they are charged with solving. . . . [for managers], if social problems persist, there is a natural tendency to believe that either more resources or better coordination of activities will more effectively attack those problems. Managers are held responsible for fulfilling their responsibilities. Faced with severe resource constraints, their impulse is to cast about for ways to do more while spending less. As a result, coordination is frequently seized upon as a primary management strategy (*ibid.*: 64).

Economic and Social Research Council-funded Research

Since the mid-1980s increasing academic interest has focused on the theory and practice of co-ordination between state agencies, community participation, crime prevention, and other related issues. The contributors to this debate come from a wide range of theoretical and political perspectives and institutional affiliations. One of the most important recent studies was that carried out by a team of researchers from Lancaster University and Middlesex Polytechnic with Economic and Social Research Council (ESRC) funding (Pearson *et al.*, 1989; Blagg *et al.*, 1988; Sampson *et al.*, 1988). Reviewing the literature concerning the multi-agency approach, Sampson *et al.* (1988) identify two dominant perspectives which they term the 'benevolent' and 'conspiracy' approaches.

For Sampson *et al.*, the conspiratorial model sees the multi-agency approach as the means by which 'the police co-opt other agencies and even the entire community, to pursue police-defined goals and objectives'. This approach, they argue, 'invariably rests upon an analysis of the state and its agencies as monolithic entities', the policies of which 'are portrayed as inevitably both instrumental and coercive' (*ibid.*: 480). For authors such as Paul Gordon, Lee Bridges, Phil Scraton, and others, the multi-agency approach is a component of a wider 'community policing strategy' which 'seeks to penetrate communities to break down community resistance, to engineer consent and support for the police, and to reinforce social discipline'

(Gordon, 1987: 141; Scraton, 1985). The 'benevolent' approach, on the other hand is characterized, for Sampson *et al.*, by a 'paternalistic corporatism . . . whereby "good" managers and "respectable" community leaders can be extracted from their organisations and brought together in moments of crisis to "save" the plight of inner city areas' (Sampson *et al.*, 1988: 481; citing Alderson, 1982; Moore and Brown, 1981; Kinsey *et al.*, 1987). This perspective, which also conceptualizes 'both the state and communities . . . as homogenous units', tends to overlook conflicts within and between communities and state agencies and implies 'an unproblematic consensus on aims and objectives' (Sampson *et al.*, 1988: 481).

The ESRC researchers found evidence which both supported and contradicted these two models, leading them, finally, to reject both. In support of the conspiratorial model, the researchers concluded that 'as the lead agency in so many multi-agency initiatives, the police will often attempt to shape and adapt multi-agency agendas to their own interests and preoccupations' (Sampson *et al.*, 1988: 480). Contradicting this model, however, the researchers found that these attempts at control were often unsuccessful because of strong resistance by other agencies and community representatives, and because they were hampered by divisions within police organizations. Although the researchers found that increased co-ordination did bring about an improvement in the quality of life for some people in some localities, it was less clear what benefits accrued to residents of these localities as a whole. And despite the objectives of the co-ordinated crime prevention model, Sampson *et al.* found little evidence that these joint-agency improvements had an impact on crime in the localities they studied (*ibid.*: 482). Most importantly, they concluded that the 'benevolent state perspective' had to be rejected because of the tendency for inter-agency conflicts and tensions to appear in spite of co-operative efforts, even when there appeared to be 'a solid policy consensus' on a particular issue (*ibid.*).

The binary typology employed by Sampson *et al.* to interpret developments in the multi-agency approach, while useful, is incomplete in certain respects. First, by lumping all the advocates of the multi-agency approach into a catch-all 'benevolent' perspective, important conflicts and contradictions within this advocacy are obscured. In particular, Sampson *et al.* fail to draw a distinction between advocates of the multi-agency approach attached to or associated with central government, local government, and police agencies. This distinction is important because the intended benefits and claims made of the approach are not consistent amongst advocates from different corners of government and non-governmental agencies. There is also some question whether the structural conflicts to which Sampson *et al.* refer are, in fact, as easily glossed over by advocates of the multi-agency approach. It seems, rather, that the naïveté ascribed to such authors as Alderson (1982) is tempered by their concern with the accountability and receptivity of the agencies among whom co-operation is intended to occur (see also Kinsey *et al.*, 1987).

Secondly, Sampson *et al.*'s typology misses two important perspectives which may be characterized neither as benevolent nor conspiratorial, but, crudely, as 'sceptical', and 'rational managerial', respectively. For the purposes of this Chapter, Sampson *et al.*'s typology may be expanded and the perspectives brought to the analysis of the multi-agency approach may be grouped into four perspectives: 'benevolent corporatist', 'rational managerial', 'conspiratorial', and 'sceptical'. The latter perspective (of whom Sampson, Blagg, Pearson *et al.* might be said to belong) may be characterized by healthy scepticism in their analysis of multi-agency initiatives or other attempts at co-ordination, detailed examination of innovation in practice, and close connection with the initiators of such innovations.

Academic Scepticism

This latter perspective is well illustrated by Mollie Weatheritt's *Innovations in Policing*, one chapter of which looks at co-ordinated crime prevention in practice (1986). Weatheritt observes that there is an 'official' history in which 'not only does crime prevention receive strong rhetorical support, [but it] also appears to rest on a sound base of institutional deliberation and activity' (1986: 49). This could also be said of the development of the multi-agency approach described in detail, above. The other history of crime prevention 'goes behind the statements of intention' to look at how innovations have been put into practice and demonstrates that 'the achievements are less impressive' (*ibid.*). Reviewing such initiatives as Alderson's community policing strategy in Devon and Cornwall and the vandalism-prevention project in Manchester schools, Weatheritt concludes that:

research is . . . beginning to suggest that, far from being a panacea, coordination is not only difficult to achieve but may even hinder effective action . . . For the most part, however, the potential problems of coordination are largely unmentioned in official policy pronouncements or in police accounts of their own initiatives. This is hardly surprising given the appeal of coordination as a way out of what might otherwise be a policy impasse, that is, the apparent failure of the institution charged with preventing crime—the police—to make the desired impact [Weatheritt, 1986: 76].

Moreover, the problems to which Weatheritt alludes appear to be quite fundamental, challenging not only the practice, but also the theory, of multi-agency co-ordination. Citing Hope and Murphy's (1983) report on multi-agency co-ordination in Manchester, Weatheritt concludes that:

While it is clearly tempting to recommend even greater communication and liaison between parties to a co-ordinated approach to [the problems which emerged], Hope and Murphy's analysis suggests that in many respects it would be futile to do so. Ensuring greater communication and creating a common approach to a problem not only has resource costs, it also *assumes an agreement about priorities which is often unlikely to obtain in practice.* What may be an important consideration of policy from the viewpoint of one institution may be of minor importance or even irrelevant from the viewpoint of another. *No amount of resort to models of rational decision-making or appeals to the virtue of collaborative effort can obscure the fact that the practice of coordinated crime prevention reveals as many impediments to the implementation of change as it is designed to remove* [1986: 82, emphasis added].

This is hardly the kind of review that would be grounds for optimism for the co-ordinated approach. It is apparent from the sceptical perspective that despite the centrality of research in the discourses advocating the multi-agency approach, the actual findings of the research have largely been unimportant in directing policy. Weatheritt's (1986: 95) comment on the 'research' on the introduction of unit-beat policing that 'far from being designed to test policy assumptions and to provide information to inform policy, was instead largely a fiction which was used to dress a policy necessity in the clothes of virtue', describes the 'research' on the multi-agency approach only too well.

In the face of such conclusions, some authors have suggested that is necessary to distinguish between the substantive and symbolic purposes and outcomes for different decision makers (Morgan, 1989). Blagg *et al.* (1988), for example, argue that '[t]he manifest official enthusiasm for inter-agency co-operation (or some synonym) . . . often remains at the level of rhetoric or sloganising, so that its importance may be symbolic and ideological, rather than indicating much about what is feasible' (1988: 216).

From this perspective it might be said that the research on the multi-agency approach to racial attacks has been useful to illustrate that something is being done and as a point of citation and legitimation for advocates. The Met's pilot project, for example, seems to be a legitimation device rather than research on which policy may be developed, despite its claims of 'rationality'.

Summary and Conclusions

Despite the inauguration of new policing policies in 1981, violent racism continued to be a problem into the mid-1980s, exacerbating the 'crisis of police legitimacy' springing from the manifest failure of the police to prevent it and deal with it adequately when it ocurred. Over the same period, various strands of discussion about violent racism and co-ordinated action emerged on different institutional sites and came together into a complexly interwoven discourse advocating the multi-agency approach.

From the outset there was some common vocabulary among the agencies involved. The issues of racism and racial prejudice, violence, and victimization were of 'common concern' to each. Community Relations Councils not only spoke for the people who were victimized but their offices and staff also encountered violent racism personally. The police were called on to intervene in reported instances of violence and to respond to victims demanding help, protection, and refuge. Local authority housing departments were also called upon to respond to and protect their tenants. A further experience common to statutory agencies—including the Home Office, the police, and local authorities—was the increasingly vocal criticism with which they were faced, particularly from those calling for community self-defence. Although such criticism had been levelled at these agencies for over a decade, by the mid-1980s the challenge to their claims to offer protection made it essential that they respond in some way.

The common concern about racial harassment on one hand, and the challenge to their legitimacy that these agencies faced on the other, is reflected in the establishment of occasional and informal contact between each of these agencies regarding individual cases and problematic localities. Finally, each was confronted by (as well as

Table 4.1 *Claims made for the multi-agency approach by the Home Office, Metropolitan Police, local government agencies (GLC, Newham Council), and ethnic minority community organizations (crcs)*

Home Office	Police	Local government	Minority community organisations*
enable effective action against/ racial incidents	establish confidence and understanding between agencies	enable officials, the police and local organizations to work together effectively	overcome the causes of racial harassment
make the police more effective	establish common ground	prevent inaction	prevent inaction
make police more aware of the problem	increase exchange of information	prevent denial of the problem	to bring about an acknowledgement of the seriousness of the problem among statutory agencies
promote action by agencies other than the police	search for solution to the problem	create an opportunity for local organizations supporting victims to make demands on police and housing	persuade local police to take action
bring about a co-ordinated approach towards incidents in general and towards individual cases	release the police from the position of sole or main responsibility for creating the social conditions which make racial incidents less likely	enable co-ordinated action	
prevent crime	prevent crime	prevent crime	combat violent racism

Sources: House of Commons, 1986; GLC, 1984; London Borough of Newham, 1986; London Race and Housing Forum, 1981.
*The views of the Newham Monitoring Project and other anti-racist and monitoring organizations are not included in this table because of their clear-cut opposition to the idea of the multi-agency approach. Their view has been consistently that this state-sponsored initiative is primarily a means of still furthering the marginalization of ethnic minority community concerns and fails to take account of the central issues as they see it—democratic accountability of, and institutional racism within, the police.

actively propagating) the perception that more systematic modes of communication, co-operation, and co-ordination would improve the effectiveness of their individual responses. Crucially, however, each agency encountered and conceptualized their common concern about racism, violence, and policing differently. Consequently the rationale for and goals of multi-agency co-operation were defined in different and sometimes conflicting ways (see Table 4.1).

Ethnic minority community organizations such as community relations councils (crcs) encountered violent racism most directly. They argued that a co-ordinated approach would bring about a change in the way in which ethnic minority communities were policed, with the ultimate aim of bringing more policing resources to protect black communities. The crcs suggested that the multi-agency approach enabled the persuasion of local police and other agencies to acknowledge the problem and take action against perpetrators. Most optimistically, they saw the approach as a means of combating racism and overcoming the causes of racial harassment.

Local authorities encountered violent racism, first as a 'management issue'; specifically as one that created problems for the allocation and transfer of tenants within public housing (GLC, 1984). The problem subsequently became a political one, wherein ethnic minority organizations placed pressure on local councils, through lobbying, and through such direct action as demonstrations and squatting in council properties. The political temperature was raised through the intensification of black politics in the early 1980s and the use of the issue of violent racism as a weapon with which to fight a battle for democratic accountability for the police, a process seen by many as an essential prerequisite for changing the police response to violent racism. Those local authorities publishing documents on this issue tended to reflect the views of ethnic minority organizations. Their advocacy, therefore, is also based on preventing statutory agencies from denying the problem and taking no action. They also saw this as an opportunity to bring more policing resources into victimized communities, seeing it as an opportunity for local organizations working in support of victims to make demands on police and local authority housing departments. Local authorities also couched their advocacy in terms of improving administrative efficiency, speaking of local agencies working together effectively in a co-ordinated fashion.

The police encountered racial incidents initially as a problem of 'public order' and of community relations. The problem of public order (intensified when anti-racist organizations and ethnic minority people demonstrated on the streets against racist violence and what they saw as a failure of policing) was a sporadic one, and one that could be met with 'public order strategies' (i.e. paramilitary policing involving such units as the Territorial Support Group (TSG)). The community relations problem could be tackled through a range of strategies, one of which was the multi-agency approach. Consequently, in contrast to the crcs and local authorities, the police did not speak about the multi-agency approach as a means of chang- ing the extent of police action in racial harassment cases, although they did invoke the need to search for a 'solution to the problem'. Rather, the policing discourses prioritize the establishment of confidence and understanding between agencies, the establishment of common ground, and the increased exchange of information. Most tellingly of all, they argued that the approach would release the police from the position of sole or main responsibility for creating the social conditions which make racial incidents less likely.

The 1986 Home Affairs Committee fused into one these complex and disparate strands of multi-agency discourse, soldering over the cracks between conflicting conceptualizations of the problem and motives for co-ordinating as it did so. The committee's report spoke to each constituency in its own language by incorporating all of the potential benefits cited by each into the main text and by including evidence presented by each into its appendices. In sum, it stated that the multi-agency approach would bring about an effective and co- ordinated response to racial violence, prevent its occurrence, make the police more effective and more aware of the problem, and pro- mote action by other agencies. This conclusion has tremendous appeal to those wishing to tackle the problem. Its claims made it very difficult to argue against. Who could be against prevention and effec- tive action?

The arguments for establishing multi-agency co-operation did not rest with the appeal to effectiveness and administrative efficiency; powerful moral and legal arguments were also invoked. On the one hand, the Home Affairs Committee reminded local authorities and police forces that the organizational framework of a consultative committee under which a multi-agency approach to racial harassment could develop was now a statutory responsibility—enshrined in sec- tion 106 of the Police and Criminal Evidence Act 1984. On the other, those local authorities who rejected the idea of co-operation with the police were accused of 'political self-indulgence' which would cause ethnic minorities to suffer.

Despite the underlying conflict which existed between the agencies concerned, the combined weight of the advocacy of co-ordination was formidable. Between them, the Home Office, the police, local authorities, and community relations councils monopolized financial, political, communication, and ideological resources. While conflicts among the agencies were barely submerged beneath the language of collaboration, the consensus view that racial violence can *only* be tackled on a multi-agency basis was, by 1986, virtually unassailable. Excluded from this debate were anti-racist and police-monitoring organizations such as the Newham Monitoring Project who argued consistently that the approach was simply a 'smoke-screen for inaction'. Nonetheless the consensus within statutory agencies ensured that the spread of the idea was guaranteed. The creation of the RAG group assured that the multi-agency approach would continue to grow as a major theme in the development of a state response to violent racism and other social problems throughout the remainder of the decade and into the 1990s.

5

Violence, Racism, and Crime Surveys: Capturing the Process of Victimization

There is an obscenity in the functioning and omnipresence of opinion polls as in that of publicity. Not because they might betray the secret of an opinion, the intimacy of a will, or because they might violate some unwritten law of the private being, but because they exhibit this redundancy of the social, this sort of continual voyeurism of the group in relation to itself: it must at all times know what it wants, know what it thinks, be told about its least needs, its least quivers, *see* itself continually on the videoscreen of statistics, constantly watch its own temperature chart in a sort of hypochondriacal madness [Baudrillard 1989: 210].

[s]ome mechanism for testing public opinion is an obvious necessity of modern government and more so in a democratic country than a totalitarian one. Its complement is the ability to speak to the ordinary man in words that he will understand and respond to [George Orwell, *Tribune* 1943; cited by Crawford *et al.*, 1990].

Until the 1980s, British criminology seemed almost unaware that it was relevant to examine the effects of 'race' and racism on victimization or policework. With a few notable exceptions, the discipline remained oblivious to the disproportionate victimization of minority communities, the experience of violent racism, the routine failure of police protection, and police discrimination more generally. The urban riots of 1981 focused public attention on these issues, and criminology was bound to follow suit. The early 1980s also saw the re-emergence of victimology and, with it, the development of a new methodology—the victimization survey. Equipped with questionnaires and improved data-processing, victimologists searched for hitherto overlooked crime victims and began to reveal the extent and nature of racist victimization and of the police response to it. This Chapter describes the contribution of this research and examines some of the conceptual and methodological problems that arise when trying to reconcile the inherently static, events-oriented survey method with the phenomenon of violent racism, a dynamic social process unfolding within a specific historical and social context.

Defining Racial Violence as Crime

In February 1981, the Joint Committee Against Racialism (JCAR)[1] presented a report on racial violence to the Home Secretary. In response, central government acknowledged the anxieties expressed by JCAR and commissioned the first official study of racial attacks and harassment (*Hansard*, 5 February 1981, col. 393). As Chapter 2 illustrated, the report of the Home Office study dramatically altered the status of violent attacks as a policy issue. The study consisted of two complementary research strategies—a survey of reported incidents in selected police areas across the country and interviews with the police, local community organizations and local officials in each area.

The information contained in the report which had the greatest impact was the quantitative 'factual survey of racial attacks' based on incidents recorded by the police (Home Office, 1981: 6). Here, incidents in which victim and offender were of 'different ethnic origin' were collected from eight police forces across England and Wales for two months. The resulting 2,630 'inter-racial incidents' were then categorized on the basis of 'the certainty with which it could be assumed that the primary motive was racial' (Home Office, 1981: 7). In half of the incidents collected, police records indicated that neither the police nor the victim thought that the incidents were racially motivated. In one quarter there was 'insufficient evidence to decide', while in 15 per cent there were 'some indications of a racial motive'. The remaining 10 per cent with 'strong evidence of a racial motive' amounted to 289 incidents.

[1] JCAR is an umbrella organization representing the major political parties and the largest ethnic minority pressure groups including representatives of the Board of Deputies of British Jews. JCAR's representation was the event which precipitated action by the Home Office (see Chaps. 2 and 3). However, pressure had been mounting for some time from a variety of sources. A number of organizations campaigned against racism and racial violence during the 1970s. Organizations such as the Anti-Nazi League and Rock Against Racism were concerned with issues such as police violence, immigration laws, and the rise of the National Front and other neo-fascist organizations. Monitoring groups, such as Lewisham Action on Policing in south-east London and the Southall Monitoring Group, were active specifically in organizing and demonstrating against racial attacks.

This two-month sample of racially motivated incidents is not particularly large, given that the incidents were drawn from police force
areas (including Merseyside, Manchester, Leicestershire, Lancashire,
and London) with a total population of over seventeen million.
Racial incidents, the report estimated, formed less than one quarter
of a per cent of all recorded crime. In total, the report estimated that
there would be '7,000 or so racially motivated incidents . . . reported
in England and Wales in a year' (Home Office, 1981: 14). However,
the report concluded that because of under-reporting, these recorded
racial incidents probably represented only a small proportion of those
that actually took place (*ibid.*).

The finding that has been most frequently cited by reports which
followed (e.g. GLC, 1984; Brown, 1984; Kinsey *et al.*, 1987) was that
the rate of racially motivated victimization was 'much higher for the
ethnic minority population, particularly the Asians, than for white
people. Indeed the rate for Asians was fifty times that for white people and the rate for blacks was thirty-six times that for white people'. The report also commented on the types of incidents suffered by
different ethnic groups:

Figures for Asians were particularly suggestive: 12 of the 13 victims of arson
were Asian, as were 16 of the 25 recipients of abusive telephone calls, and 57
of the 72 victims of racially motivated window-smashing. On the other hand,
20 of the 24 victims of handbag snatches or theft from persons, which were
judged to be racially motivated, were white [Home Office, 1981: 12].

This statistical description overshadowed the qualitative 'views
and opinions' gleaned from interviews with community groups and
local officials. The primacy given to statistical 'fact' directed attention away from the lived experience of racial harassment:

In most places, it was said that the problem had deteriorated significantly
within the space of the last year, and that the main perpetrators were of the
skinhead fraternity. Assaults, jostling in the street, abusive remarks, broken
windows, slogans daubed on walls—these were among the less serious kinds
of racial harassment which many members of the ethnic minorities (particularly Asians) experience, sometimes on repeated occasions. The fact that they
are interleaved with far more serious racially-motivated offences (murders,
serious assaults, systematic attacks by gangs on people's homes at night)
increases the feeling of fear experienced by the ethnic minorities. It was clear
to us that the Asian community widely believes that it is the object of a campaign of unremitting racial harassment which it fears will grow worse in the
future. In many places we were told that Asian families were too frightened

to leave their homes at night or to visit the main shopping centre in town at weekends when gangs of young skinheads regularly congregate [Home Office, 1981: 16].

The impact of the report was considerable. In the foreword to the report, the then Conservative Home Secretary, William Whitelaw, declared that racial attacks were 'wicked crimes which can do our society great harm'. He stated that 'the study has shown clearly that the anxieties expressed about racial attacks are justified. Racially motivated attacks, particularly on Asians, are more common than we supposed; and there are indications that they may be on the increase' (Home Office, 1981: iii).

The study was of particular importance because it demonstrated that although police forces in England and Wales had no means of recording crimes with racial motivation, such crimes could be found in their records. Additionally, by identifying these acts as 'wicked crimes',[2] the Home Secretary ensured that henceforth it was impossible to deny that racial violence was an object for policing. A direct result of the production of this report was the introduction of an 'operational definition' and recording and monitoring procedures within the Metropolitan Police[3] (see House of Commons, 1982).

The publication of this report marks a dramatic increase in police, local, and central government activity directed at controlling racial violence. Indeed, if one were to rely solely on police, central, and local government sources of knowledge, it might appear that at the beginning of the 1980s a new form of crime emerged. This crime—termed variously racial (or racist) violence, racial attacks, racial harassment, and racial incidents—became, quite suddenly, a policy issue. It is only since 1981 that any local or central government

[2] Although this is the first official recognition of racial violence as crime, clearly some of these incidents have been defined as crimes previously. Indeed, the most serious of them (such as murder, arson, and serious assault) would certainly have been recorded as crimes, even if they were not recorded as racial (Institute of Race Relations, 1987). For example, Gordon (1990) lists 74 racist murders in Britain between 1970 and 1990. Many of the more mundane events involved in racial harassment would also come within legal and police definitions of crime. The offences of assault, criminal damage, threatening behaviour are broad enough to cover all types of racial violence. Additionally, although a Private Member's Bill to make racial attacks a specific form of crime within the law was defeated in 1985, the Police and Criminal Evidence Act 1984 (PACE) has defined 'Incitement to Racial Hatred' as a criminal offence.

[3] The Metropolitan Police were the only force to start routinely collecting 'racial incident' statistics at this time. It was not until 1985, when the Association of Chief Police Officers (ACPO) issued guiding principles for the response to 'racial incidents', that other large urban forces began to follow suit (see Home Office, 1986).

agency began to keep systematic records of instances of violent racism or began to develop policies to control it. It is only since this time that any have considered it necessary to ponder the definition of the problem, to carry out research and publish information on the extent and nature of the problem and the effectiveness of the statutory response to it.[4]

Surveys of Racial Violence

In the introduction to the second Islington Crime Survey, Crawford *et al.* state that:

the major purpose of victimisation surveys is to gain a more accurate estimate of the true extent of crime than that provided by the official crime statistics compiled by the police which are subject to widely acknowledged problems of accuracy, the most serious of which is the failure of a high proportion of victims to report criminal incidents to the police [Crawford *et al.*, 1990:2].

Obviously, some forms of crime are more likely to be reported than others. For example, most car thefts are reported because, by law, they must be insured against. On the other hand, official crime statistics reflect only a small proportion of racial attacks because of the unwillingness of victims to report to the police (Home Office, 1981). It seems that the need to look to sources beyond police records to estimate the 'true extent' of crime is particularly relevant for racial violence.

A number of crime surveys have attempted to make quantitative estimates of racial violence. The Policy Studies Institute (PSI) study of *Black and White Britain* was based on interviews with 2,265 white informants, 882 West Indians, and 1,688 Asians. The experiences of those who said they had been physically attacked, assaulted, or molested in the previous year were examined to assess whether they were 'inter-racial'. Those that were were categorized into those

---

[4] Numerous reports on racial violence and the statutory response to it were produced in the 1980s and early 1990s. Many were conducted by Labour local authorities (e.g. GLC, 1984; Hesse *et al.*, 1992), Councils for Racial Equality (e.g. Commission for Racial Equality (CRE), 1981, 1987), anti-racist organizations (e.g. Institute for Race Relations (IRR), 1987; Newham Monitoring Project, 1990), and Central Government (e.g. Ekblom and Simon, 1988; Home Office, 1989). Recent reports have concentrated on police service delivery (Cutler and Murji, 1990), housing policy (Ginsburg, 1989), and services for victims (Kimber and Cooper, 1991). Recent reviews include Gordon (1990), FitzGerald (1989), Virdee (1996).

where (a) the victim specially mentioned a racial motive, a racist organization, or an obvious background of racial hostility; (b) where the attack was unprovoked and where no motive was stated or apparent; and (c) other inter-racial incidents (Brown, 1984: 254). Brown noted that most of the attacks without any stated motive by white on black and Asian people were of a kind where unknown people approached them on the streets and hit, kicked, or threw stones at them where there was no background of prior argument or misunderstanding. A large proportion of those attacks were by gangs of youths often identified as skinheads and were often of a serious nature; one third of attacks by whites on Asians and West Indians involved the use of weapons or missiles including knives, bottles, and stones. On the basis of these findings, Brown estimated that the frequency of racial attacks might be over ten times the figure calculated by the Home Office using police records, bringing the number closer to 70,000 (Brown, 1984: 247–63).

The first Islington Crime Survey estimated that '17% of all assaults which were aimed at Islington residents [in the previous year] were racist in nature', amounting to around 870 cases per year. The authors suggest that despite the fact that this estimate was probably low, only about 4.5 per cent of these cases were recorded by the police. The Newham Crime Survey was undertaken specifically to challenge police statistics which Newham Council believed grossly under-estimated racial violence. The survey included a 'Racial Harassment Questionnaire' that was presented only to Afro-Caribbean and Asian[5] respondents. They found that '1 in 4 of Newham's black residents had been the victims of some form of racial harassment in the previous 12 months' (London Borough of Newham, 1986: 34). They also found that two in three victims had been victimized more than once (*ibid.*: 50) and that the 116 victims of racial harassment gave details of a total of 1,550 incidents which they had experienced in the previous twelve months. Of these eighty-five (or just over 5 per cent) were said to have been reported to the police.

The first two sweeps of the British Crime Survey (BCS) (Hough and Mayhew, 1983, 1985) paid little attention to the problems of racial harassment or attacks. Reflecting growing criticism of this

[5] In the British context the term 'Asian' usually refers to people whose origins lie in the Indian sub-continent. In Newham the largest proportion of Asians are from India, though there are also numbers of Pakistani, Bangladeshi, and Chinese residents.

omission, the 1988 BCS specifically attempted to measure 'ethnic minority risks' including racially motivated offences (Mayhew, Elliott, and Dowds, 1989). Facilitated by a booster sample of Afro-Caribbeans and Asians, the survey found that black people were more at risk than whites for many types of crime, even after taking account of social and demographic factors (*ibid*.: 50). It was also found that 'Afro-Caribbeans and particularly Asians see many offences against them as racially motivated. Being threatened and assaulted because of race is common' (*ibid*.). Forty-four per cent of assaults directed against Asians and a third of those directed against Afro-Caribbeans were thought by respondents to be racially motivated, as were about half of the incidents involving threats. When an incident was thought to be racially motivated:

The use of racist language was the main reason given by both Afro-Caribbeans and Asians, particularly the former. Asians were rather more likely than Afro-Caribbeans to see an incident as racially motivated because they felt that it was something only committed against their minority group, or that it had happened to them before, involving the same people [*ibid*.: 48].

Crime Surveys and the Prioritization of Racial Violence

The nature of the questions asked in the nationwide BCS reflects the change in the prioritization of racial violence which occurred in the 1980s. Since the mid-1980s, the surveys described above have produced quantitative evidence of racial violence and of the degree to which it is under-reported. There seems little doubt that these data and their use as a means to apply pressure on police, local, and central government agencies brought about change in the official view of racial violence.

In 1985 racial incidents became a Metropolitan Police 'force priority' and the Association of Chief Police Officers (ACPO) issued national *Guiding Principles* (Commissioner of Police for the Metropolis, 1985; ACPO, 1985). In 1986 a government Home Affairs Committee report referred to racial attacks and harassment as 'the most shameful and dispiriting aspect of race relations in Britain' (House of Commons, 1986: iv). The prioritization of racial attacks and harassment has been the subject of several Home Office circulars (e.g. Home Office, 1986, 1989, 1991*b*) and Metropolitan Police

Orders (June 1987, November 1990). Most recently, a 'multi-agency approach' to racial violence has been developing which advocates that the police should work in a co-ordinated fashion with other local agencies (Home Office, 1989; Kinsey *et al.*, 1987: 125). Now, racial violence is a priority for six central government agencies, the police, the prosecuting authorities, the courts, and local government services including housing, education, and social services (Home Office, 1989, 1991; Bowling and Saulsbury, 1992).

During the 1980s, surveys contributed to the movement of racial violence from the margins to the centre of national and local political agendas. Now many statutory agencies have recording and monitoring procedures and operational guidelines. But despite these very real changes there is little evidence that statutory policies directed at tackling perpetrators, assisting victims, or preventing racial violence have been effective. In 1989, the central government inter-departmental racial attacks group found 'few examples of effective multi-agency liaison [and] relatively few examples of effective unilateral action by individual agencies' (Home Office, 1989: paragraph 34). Despite a decade of statutory activity there is little evidence that racial violence is being controlled. There is little evidence indeed that it has decreased in incidence, prevalence, or in its effect on minority communities in Britain (FitzGerald, 1989; Ginsburg, 1989; Cutler and Murji, 1990; Gordon, 1990).

Criminal Incidents and Criminology

Until recently, criminology has been content to conceive of crime as a collection of criminal incidents—as events of norm violation (MacLean, 1986). Although feminists and critical criminologists have developed more dynamic accounts of crime (of which more below), the dominant approach to the study of victimization is still events-oriented (Skogan, 1986; Genn, 1988). In this respect both conventional and left-realist surveys reflect the orientation of the criminal justice system. Criminal incidents are the stock-in-trade of the crime-control sector of government and of administrative criminology. Estimates of the size of the problem, and descriptions of where it is located and who the actors are, are necessarily based on such counting exercises as are measurements of police performance such as the clear-up rate. Indeed, the *modus operandi* of the criminal justice system is based upon and shaped by the processing of individualized events.

The criminal justice system attempts to deal with violent racism as individual acts in the same way that it deals with other forms of crime. British law recognizes only the event defined as the criminal offence (Smith and Hogan, 1983; Forbes, 1988). The police definition reflects the legal structure of policework (Grimshaw and Jefferson, 1987: 284) and, like the rest of the criminal justice system, is ordered around the reification of human experience into discrete events (Manning, 1988). To become an object for policing or the courts, an aspect of human behaviour or interaction must be fixed in space and time and be definable as an offence (Young, 1990). Police policy documents stress that the object for policing is a racial *incident* rather than attack or harassment. The policing systems consisting of racial incident forms, incident report books, and methods for calculating response times and detection rates reflect their concern with discrete events.

Racist Victimization as a Process

Despite the primacy of incident-based accounts of crime and racial violence some authors have argued that crime should be seen, not as an event, but as a process. As MacLean suggests, 'crime is not an event or "social fact", but a social *process* which includes a number of social events each of which is inextricably bound up with the other' (MacLean 1986: 4–5, emphasis in original). Conceiving of violent racism (and other forms of crime) as processes implies an analysis which is dynamic; includes the social relationships between all the actors involved in the process; can capture the continuity between physical violence, threat, and intimidation; can capture the dynamic of repeated or systematic victimization; incorporates historical context; and takes account of the social relationships which inform definitions of appropriate and inappropriate behaviour.

Racial victimization is, like other social processes, dynamic and in a state of continuous movement and change, rather than static and fixed. While individual events can be abstracted from this process, fixed in time and place and recorded by individuals and institutions, the process itself is ongoing. Much can be learned from studying criminal events, but, just as it is impossible to understand the content of a film by looking at only one still-frame, 'it is impossible for us to understand crime or any other process by looking at an individual event or moment' (MacLean, 1986: 8).

The process of racial victimization involves a number of social actors each of whom has a dynamic relationship with the others. It is usual, first, to look at victim and offender and at the relationship between them. Obviously, an investigation of violent racism should include an analysis of the characteristics of the people who set out to attack or harass ethnic minorities and of their motivation for doing so. Equally, it should include an analysis of the characteristics of the people under attack and of the effects that victimization has on them. But when an individual is attacked, the process of victimization does not rest with them alone, but may extend to their immediate and extended families, friends, and 'community'. When a serious incident occurs—a racially motivated arson attack or murder, for example—the impact may be felt among people in locations far away from where the incident itself occurred. Similarly, there is a relationship between perpetrators of racial attacks and their families, friends, and community. The expression of violent racism and the victimization to which it gives rise are underpinned by the relationships between different *communities* in particular localities and within society as a whole. Exploring these relationships and the part they play in condoning or condemning racial outbursts seems crucial to an understanding of the process of racial victimization.

Also of importance are the roles of the police and other state agents such as social workers and public housing managers. For those cases that come to be defined as crimes and for which a prosecution is initiated, criminal justice professionals (such as court officials, prosecutors, defence lawyers, magistrates, and judges) play their part. These actors intervene in the process of racial and other forms of victimization in ways which have the potential for escalation as well as amelioration of its effects. A dynamic account of the impact of state action and reaction is important for comprehending the totality of the process of victimization. Finally, local and national news media play their part in communicating knowledge of attacks or about the quality of the statutory response to various sections of the community.

Clearly, the notion of process applies to all forms of crime. Car theft is no less dynamic and bound up with wider social processes than is racial violence. However, the few qualitative accounts that exist point to violent racism often taking the form of repeated attacks (Home Office, 1981) and of a constant (Walsh, 1987) or 'unrelenting barrage of harassment' (Tompson, 1988). In this sense, racial victimization may be compared with wife battery, which is very often prolonged and habitual (Genn, 1988; Stanko, 1988). Victimization which constitutes repeated physical violence or continuous threat and intimidation may be distinguished by its enduring quality. As Betsy Stanko (1990) suggests, these forms of violence create 'climates of unsafety' which transcend individual instances of violence. Attempting to reduce multiple victimization to a series of incidents means that much of this experience will be lost (Genn, 1988: 90; Farrell, 1992).

Thinking about how events may be connected so as to illuminate underlying social processes leads one to a consideration of the connections between different forms of violence in the experience of an individual who is being victimized. Kelly argues that women experience sexual violence as a continuum—'a continuous series of events which pass into one another and which cannot be readily distinguished' (Kelly, 1987: 77). Making these connections seems equally important for the experience of racial violence. As Pearson *et al.* suggest:

For white people for example, racial harassment and racial attacks are undoubtedly merely incidental, one-off events which are rarely, if ever, encountered. For black and minority groups, on the other hand, these are areas of experiences which are part and parcel of everyday life. A black person need never have been the actual victim of a racist attack, but will remain acutely aware that he or she belongs to a group that is threatened in this manner. In much the same way that the high levels of 'fear of crime' among women can be better understood when experiences of subordination and daily harassments, from the subliminal to the blatant are re-connected (Stanko, 1987), so the re-connected experiences of racism from a black and minority ethnic perspective shift the ground of how to define a 'racial' incident and what it is to police 'racism' [1989: 135].

A similar conclusion was reached by Joe Feagin and Melvin Sikes in their excellent study, *Living With Racism*, which examines the black middle-class experience in the USA. They observe that:

Modern racism must be understood as lived experience. . . . Experiences with serious discrimination not only are very painful and stressful in the immediate situation and aftermath but also have a cumulative impact on particular individuals, their families, and their communities. A black person's life is regularly disrupted by the mistreatment suffered personally or by family members. . . . The cumulative impact on an individual of repeated personal encounters with racial hostility is greater than the sum of these encounters might appear to be to a casual observer. . . . the repeated experience of racism significantly affects a black person's behaviour and understanding of life [Feagin and Sikes, 1994: 15–17].

and moreover:

the daily experiences of racial hostility and discrimination encountered by middle class and other African Americans are the constituent elements of the interlocking social structures and processes called 'institutionalized racism' [Feagin and Sikes, 1994: 17].

Although the implications of such an approach have yet to be pursued in research practice, survey research has hinted at its importance. The authors of the ICS, for example, conclude from one interview that 'some segments of the population are so over-exposed to this kind of behaviour [racist assaults] that it becomes part of their everyday reality and escapes their memory in the interview situation' (Jones et al., 1986).

MacLean (1986) argues that crime is underpinned by broader social, political, and economic processes. Of importance for violence directed specifically against ethnic minority individuals and communities are the social, political, and cultural processes of racism and racial exclusion. Susan Smith has argued that forms of political and 'common sense' racism have permeated all levels of British society (1989: 146). Certainly the politics of the New Right have racist ideas at their core (Barker, 1981; Fielding, 1981; Gilroy, 1987: 11; Solomos, 1989). These ideas, some have suggested, influence public opinion in the form of 'low level racism' (Husbands, 1983), 'a sentiment which infuses daily life and is widely but abstractly expressed by a broad cross-section (perhaps a majority) of the population' (Smith, 1989: 148). In a similar vein, Solomos argues that as 'race' became an important variable in British politics, so the terms of debate about migration, civil unrest, crime, and the 'inner city' became subtly infused with racialized stereotypes and symbols (1989; see also Miles and Phizacklea, 1984). As well as 'top down' racism, it has been argued that there are 'bottom-up' influences. This 'experiential racism' is 'a reaction by white Britons to those broad patterns of local socio-economic change that are outside their control and that coincide with (but of course have no necessary causal relationship with) the presence of black people' (Smith, 1989: 149). Clearly, widespread racial antipathy does not determine the expression of violent racism. But, as Smith argues, racist sentiments 'provide a reservoir of procedural norms than not only tacitly inform routine activity, but are also able to legitimatize more purposive explicitly racist practices' (Smith, 1989: 150).

The influences of popular and politically organized racism on the manifestation of violent racism are complex and have yet to be charted fully. It seems that there are many factors which influence the time, place, and form of an 'outbreak' of racial hatred into violence. However, some patterns may be discerned. Some commentators have identified the contiguity of media-generated moral panics about the presence and behaviour of ethnic minority people and spates of racial attacks (Tompson, 1988; Gordon, 1990). Others have identified factors influencing the geographical distribution of violent racism (e.g. the ethnic composition and stability of the local population, changes in local economy, and variations in the strength of local identity (Husbands, 1983)). In some specific locations (such as the East End of London) racial antipathy and territorial defensiveness are deepseated and reflected in support for racist politics (Husbands, 1983). Dick Hobbs describes racism as 'part of East London's ideological inheritance' (1988: 11). The high incidence of violent racism reported in specific locations must be examined in the context of popular and political racist sentiment.

The Process of Racial Harassment: Research and Policy Development

If violent racism is neither expressed nor experienced in an instant, but is more diffuse, contextually bound, and dislocating for its victims than a notion such as 'racial incident' criminological research must address the question whether the events-orientation has offered an understanding of the process of racial victimization or ways to intervene effectively.

Implications for Survey Research

The problem facing the survey researcher is that of developing ways to capture violent racism and victimization *as processes* from the events that surveys describe. This means developing ways of investigating repeat victimization, focusing on all the elements of the crime process and incorporating social context.

The difficulty faced by surveys in capturing repeated victimization has been commented on by numerous authors (Farrell, 1992; Genn,

1988; Kelly, 1987). In a valuable paper on 'multiple victimization', Genn argues that:

Although the experiences of multiple victims ought in theory to represent an important part of the total picture of criminal victimisation and might provide useful insights into the conceptualization of 'crime', victims surveys have largely failed to provide any detailed information on multiple victimisation. This failure stems primarily from the general orientation of crime surveys and partly from the inherent limitations of the survey method as a means of understanding complex social processes [1988: 90].

A survey could attempt to describe repeated racial victimization by rigorously counting every definable event in an episode of harassment or attack. If, for example, an individual or family is being harassed on a regular basis, a complete account could be made of each violent, threatening, or intimidatory act, together with each graffito and other property damage experienced. However, this would create serious methodological problems; victimization surveys are best suited to produce aggregate statistics and do not deal well with statistical outliers[6] (Genn, 1988). Further problems arise in defining how salient an event must be to merit either being mentioned by a victim or recorded by the survey (e.g. Biderman, 1981). Having reached a definition of a relevant event, in some cases the counting task would be a formidable one (Genn, 1988). Some cases of racial harassment span a period of years and include a huge number of salient events (Tompson, 1988). These problems are apparent even for surveys designed sensitively enough to capture racist harassment. If the remit of the survey is broader than this, the chances are that any description of this form of victimization will be submerged beneath aggregate victimization statistics (Genn, 1988). It has to be acknowledged that the general orientation of contemporary victimization surveys has tended to marginalize the experience of those suffering forms of repeated victimization such as racial violence, wife battery, and child abuse.

Surveys of violent racism have mainly focused on the experience of crime victims and on their experiences of reporting to the police. There has been almost no research on perpetrators. While the most basic of descriptions have been formulated (racial attackers tend to be young white men), they remain something of an effigy in the

---

[6] In recent research, this problem has been recognized and attempts have been made to overcome it. For example, shorter recall periods have been used and more sensitive methods have been used to capture the extent and nature of repeat victimization (see Farell, 1992; Sampson and Phillips, 1992, 1996).

criminological literature. In order for a holistic account of victimization to be developed account must be taken of all the actors in the process, and of the relationships among them. While they would be sensitive and difficult to conduct, surveys of perpetrators and their associates could be conducted in parallel with surveys of victims. It might be possible to conduct surveys of offending using the 'self-report method' in localities with high rates of racial victimization. Another approach would be to extend surveys of racist attitudes (e.g. Husbands, 1983) to cover racially motivated violence and attitudes towards it.

Like official statistics, surveys tend to produce static descriptions of crime, and it is not immediately apparent how a dynamic description can be developed from these still images. This stasis has meant the descriptions produced have missed many moments in the crime process. Missing are accounts of the relationship between victim and perpetrator and of their relationships to the communities to which they belong. Also missing are the moments other than the short time-slice that comes to be defined as the criminal event. Notably missing is information about the events subsequent to reporting to the police, such as how criminal and civil justice processes affect both victim and offender. Surveys have told us little about alternative responses to victimization such as self-defence, retaliation, forgiveness, restitution, or conciliation.

While surveys (like any other method) can be presented in their geographical, historical, and social context, most often they are not. As a result, descriptions of patterns of victimization are divorced from wider social processes. Indeed, it may be that the survey research process tends more towards de-contextualization than other methods. Some crime survey researchers (and left-realists in particular) have stressed the importance of both social context and social process to an investigation of crime (e.g. MacLean, 1991). How they are to be incorporated in practice into an empirical research programme has yet to be fully addressed (Walklate, 1989, 1990, 1992).

Implications for Policy Development

With respect to policy development, surveys have had the most influence on the place of the victim in the criminal justice process (Hough and Mayhew, 1985; Rock, 1990: 317–24). Surveys have shown that victims of violent racism are many and that victimization has a debilitating effect on their lives. Now, racial harassment victims may be seen as genuine targets for specialist service provision (see Kimber and Cooper, 1991). However, while surveys have identified the people who are most likely to be victimized, other methods are required to illuminate ways in which people have survived or resisted this victimization. Similarly, while surveys have identified the people most likely to be perpetrators, other methods may be of more help to identify the social, political, and economic factors which give rise to racial hatred, or the factors which lead to its expression in violence.

Because surveys alone cannot capture the dynamic of crime as a social process, the policies to which they have given rise have tended to be one-dimensional, focusing on the event of norm violation. As a result, policies have tended to emphasize reactive police and local authority responses rather than community-based preventive measures. However, there seems to be a contradiction between the idea that racial victimization is a dynamic process and the idea that the problem may best be tackled by responding to a disconnected incident. As Pearson *et al.* (1989) argue, the police definition referring specifically to racial *incidents* is one that implies that 'racial harassment and attacks are "one off" events . . . something which happens casually and which remains disconnected from the dominant forms of life within our society' (1989: 134). This conception, they argue, fails to match with black people's experience of victimization (*ibid.*). This same issue has been noted in the United States by Feagin and Sikes in their analysis of the black middle-class experience. One of their interviewees commented that:

I don't think that white people, generally, understand the full meaning of racist disciminatory behavours towards Americans of African descent. They seem to see each act of discrimination or an act of violence as an 'isolated' event. As a result, most white Americans cannot understand the strong reaction manifested by blacks when such events occur. They feel that blacks tend to 'overreact'. They forget that in most cases, we live lives of quiet desperation generated by a litany of *daily* large and small events, that, whether or not by design, remind us of our 'place' in American society [Feagin and Sikes 1994: 23–4].

The apparent contradiction between police definition and subjective experience partly explains the finding of some research studies that report the police response to victims of racial violence as frequently inappropriate, or even oppressive (e.g. Smith and Gray, 1983: 409–12; Gordon, 1990; Dunhill, 1989: 68–79, Institute of Race

Relations, 1987; Newham Monitoring Project, 1990; Hesse *et al.*, 1992).

There is a similar contradiction between the experience of victim-ization and legal practice. Forbes has identified the limitations to tackling racial harassment imposed by a legal system which under-stands crime only as a single event:

[in presenting a case] only facts relevant to the particular offence which can be proved may be mentioned. Thus, it is not usually permissible to refer to other offences that have been committed by the perpetrator. This means that the offence cannot be set in context of part of a sustained campaign of harassment [1988: 172].

In court, as with policing, the focus on a single event renders the process of victimization invisible. It seems that reducing the complex processes of racial exclusion (Husbands, 1983) and the expression of violence to a racial incident strips it of meaning for the victim and for those to whom the incident must be described (such as a police officer, judge, or jury). By rendering earlier episodes in the process of victimization 'inadmissible evidence' or irrelevant to police investiga-tion, neither the effect on the victim nor the implications for the rest of the 'community' can be described. This undermines the ability of statutory agents to understand the meaning of the event (from the victim's perspective in particular) and, therefore, respond appropri-ately to it. Again, this point applies more broadly than to racially motivated crime. Indeed, it underlines one of the major dissatisfac-tions of victims and communities with criminal justice agencies—that they look only at the incident, not at its history and setting (Genn, 1988; Shapland *et al.*, 1985). If racial victimization (and other forms of crime) may best be conceptualized processually, it follows that the social response to the problem must tackle the underlying processes as well as responding to the reported incidents to which these processes give rise (Goldstein, 1990).

Methodological Approach

In order to explore violent racism as a process, a methodological approach is required which takes account of all moments in the crime process, can capture the dynamic of repeated victimization, and pro-vides geographical, social, historical, and political context. Qualitative as well as quantitative research methods are required to procure an holistic analysis (Bell and Newby, 1977; Walklate, 1989, 1990).

One approach which has been useful in criminology and other spheres is the case study. According to Yin, 'a case study is an empirical inquiry that: investigates a contemporary phenomenon within its real-life context; when the boundaries of the context are not clearly evident; and in which multiple sources of evidence are used' (1989: 23). These features lend themselves to an empirical, holistic, and processual account of crime. Surveys alone can try to deal with phenomenon and context, but by dint of the need to limit the number of variables to be analysed, their ability to investigate context is extremely limited (*ibid.*). Context, history, and process can best be captured using evidence from sources such as historiographical material, in-depth interviews, and observation as well as official records and surveys. In British criminology, case studies have produced some excellent descriptive and theoretical studies (e.g. Smith and Gray, 1983; Grimshaw and Jefferson, 1987).

A case study combining a survey with other methods of inquiry offers the possibility for explanation. Explanation—asking how and why—requires tracing processes over time as well as describing frequencies and incidence. Narrative accounts provided by people interviewed in the survey using in-depth interviews offer some insight in this regard. They offer the opportunity for the research subjects to describe their experiences in their own terms As a means to understand offending, victimization, and state intervention, the actions and experiences of the social actors involved, and the points at which they intersect are indicated. Starting with historical context, data were collected on the events involved in the commission of the offence, its immediate aftermath, and long-term consequences for those involved. Qualitative accounts of the subjective reality of each actor in particular instances aim to flesh out the skeletal descriptions provided by the survey.

Providing a multi-faceted account of the expression and experience of violence offers the potential for evaluating the effectiveness of policing and the criminal justice system. By charting the moments at which criminal justice agents intervene in the processes of racism, violence, victimization, and survival, the impact of their police and court action can be assessed. The police and criminal justice system appear only fleetingly in survey descriptions, and yet both victim and offender may have to interact with them over an extended period (totalling hours, if not days and weeks) after the event.

The Way Ahead

Reading Baudrillard's view of opinion polls or social surveys (during 1989 when analysing survey data collected in North Plaistow) drew my attention to the sense in which statistical simulation does not necessarily increase certainty about the nature of social reality, and indeed may induce uncertainty about the idea of social reality itself. Baudrillard likens opinion polls to meteorology, noting the 'indecisiveness of their results, the uncertainty of their effects, and their unconscious humour' (Baudrillard, 1989: 211). The idea that survey data might 'destroy the political as will and representation, the political as meaning, precisely through the effect of simulation and uncertainty' shook my hitherto acceptance of the axiom of modern social survey research expressed succinctly by Orwell. I saw only the methodological flaws in surveys, their imprecision, uncertainty, the imperfect way in which commercial research agencies conduct their work, and above all the creation of de-contextualized statistics, stripped of meaning. This view was reinforced when I saw a *Sun* report of a 'race relations poll' headlined 'Send us back say Britain's blacks', which proported to show that '[s]even out of ten British black people are in favour of repatriating immigrants'.[7] That a survey could produce such a social 'fact' is surely what Baudrillard refers to as 'statistical pornography' (Baudrillard, 1989: 211).

However, working in a government-funded action-research setting does not allow the researcher the luxury of opting out into the hyper-reality of postmodernism. Survey data are there to be used as best they can as tools in administrative practice. On reflection, the survey was neither designed, conducted, analysed, or written up as well as it could have been. But the data were used nonetheless. Since drafting a report on the survey in 1990, further analysis of the quantitative data and an exploration of the limited qualitative data recorded in the survey have been possible. I am now of the view that survey data are of value, but that they must be seen alongside other forms of data and set in a historical and political context. Using numbers complemented with individual narratives of victims, the police, and others, set in historical context, it is possible to 'tell relevant stories' about racism, violence, and policing.

---

[7] *Sun* 9 October 1989. Respondents were asked, 'If people want to, should they be given financial aid to help to return to their country of origin'. Rather different from 'Send us back' and repatriation, both of which imply expulsion.

II

Racism, Violence, and Policing in North Plaistow: An Empirical Study

6

Introduction to the Case Study

The first part of this book presented a social context for the contemporary empirical research set out in Part II. Chapter 2 presented a history of racism in Britain and its emergence as a public issue. Chapters 3 and 4 described how policy on violent racism was formulated within central government and the police. Chapter 5 described the contribution of criminology to these developments and the theoretical and methodological approach to be adopted in the empirical research. We now turn to east London of the late 1980s and early 1990s and to an examination of victimization and policing based on a detailed case study.

Data Collection

The case study is based on data gathered during the formal 'problem description' and 'evaluation' phases of the North Plaistow Project, and is complemented with additional observation and interviews carried out during the three years of fieldwork (1988–91). This 'problem description' phase comprises, first, data from the files of the agencies involved in the project collected using a standardized coding form. Although it was intended that all the agencies would provide data, eventually only those provided by the police could be used. Secondly, a series of twenty-three group interviews were conducted with about 200 staff of the local agencies. These included interviews with relief, Home Beat, and Newham Organized Racial Incident Squad (NORIS) officers, and mid-level mangers from the West Ham Division; public and private sector caseworkers and advisers, rents and benefits officers, and caretakers from the Housing Department; teachers, head teachers, non-teaching staff, and pupils from the schools system; and a small number of the social workers, probation officers, and residential care staff from the Social Services Department. Thirdly, a victimization survey was conducted by Harris Research using a questionnaire based on the Newham Crime Survey and the British Crime Survey.[1]

The 'evaluation phase' of the project offered the second opportunity to collect primary data on violent racism, policing, and the multi-agency approach. This involved further analysis of recorded incidents, interviewing officers from the agencies involved, and observing them during their work; this included the observation of two shifts each with relief PCs, Home Beat PCs, and the Newham Organized Racial Incident Squad. These formal observation and interview sessions were augmented with long periods of conversation with police officers of various ranks and from various specialisms.

In addition to this more formal data collection, I collected information from individuals connected with or affected by the project. This includes individual case studies of two victims of violent racism in North Plaistow, one of whom I interviewed twice, the other on five separate occasions. I also interviewed police officers in the Community Relations Branches of Scotland Yard and Newham (K) Division.

The Study Site

Before describing patterns of racial harassment, the police response to the problem, and the multi-agency approach in North Plaistow, something should be said about the geographic, social, economic, historical, and demographic characteristics of the study site and its environs.

Geography

The London Borough of Newham, one of thirty-three boroughs in Greater London, lies to the east of the City of London beyond the 'old' or 'inner-East End' neighbourhoods of Tower Hamlets. North Plaistow is one of Newham's twelve housing districts which is coterminous with the electoral wards of West Ham and Plashet. The boundaries of North Plaistow do not reflect those of a 'natural community' or 'natural area', in that it has no individual identity, no commercial or neighbourhood centre of its own, and has a heterogeneous population (Morris, 1958: 9). Rather, three of its boundaries are marked by physical barriers. A London Underground line (which

---

[1] See App. I for details of the survey design, methods, and the sample profile.

actually runs *overground* at this point) marks its southern edge and forms a boundary which divides Newham north–south; a British Rail line bounds the area to the west; West Ham Park cuts the area off to the north; and it narrows to a wedge to the east. Despite its physical distance from the heart of the East End, North Plaistow forms part of the 'outer' or 'extended' East End (Hobbs, 1988; Husbands, 1983). Dick Hobbs (1988) argues that to define the physical boundaries of the East End or east London more generally without attempting to define its culture is 'a mere exercise in cartography':

Not a street, borough or town, East London is a disparate community bonded by a culture rather than by any single institution or governmental agency. This one-class society locates its own boundaries in terms of subjective class definition, and east of the City of London you are either an East-Ender, a middle-class interloper, or you can afford to move sufficiently far east to join the middle classes of suburban Essex[2] [Hobbs, 1988: 87].

This may be an oversimplified characterization of a large geographical area with a population of diverse class and ethnic backgrounds. But Hobbs' view reflects a specific understanding of East End culture as exclusively working-class and white, and which identifies people from other class and ethnic groups as interlopers—by definition not 'one of us' (*ibid.*: 86–90).

Social and Economic Characteristics

Although North Plaistow is part of an outer London borough, it displays many of the characteristics of an 'inner city' area. It has a high degree of relative and absolute deprivation in terms of its local economy, housing, physical environment, and social facilities. A government survey based on 1981 census data identified the London Borough of Newham as the second most deprived local authority district out of 365 in England, after Hackney and only just ahead of Tower Hamlets, two of its neighbouring boroughs (Department of the Environment, 1983). Of Newham's twenty-four wards, the two that make up the study site—Plashet and West Ham—are the third and twelfth most deprived, respectively. Large sections of the project

---

[2] This 'subjective class-definition' is also a racially exclusive one. Hobbs informs us that many of the respondents in his study were racist; 'all Asians were "Pakis" and Afro-Caribbeans, "coons", "niggers", "macaroons" etc. Once, someone described their prospective next-door neighbours as "Pakis with turbans". Another explained how he had "clumped a lippy Paki". Another had moved out of an area because it was "over-run with niggers" ' (Hobbs, 1988: 12).

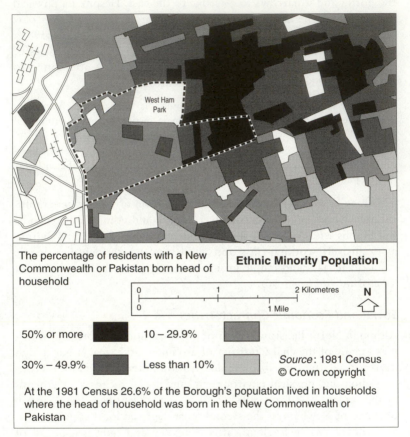

The percentage of residents with a New Commonwealth or Pakistan born head of household

Ethnic Minority Population

0 ————————— 1 ————————— 2 Kilometres   **N**

0 ——————————————————— 1 Mile

50% or more

30% – 49.9%

10 – 29.9%

Less than 10%

Source: 1981 Census
© Crown copyright

At the 1981 Census 26.6% of the Borough's population lived in households where the head of household was born in the New Commonwealth or Pakistan

Figure 6.1 *Ethnic minority population in Newham*

area were identified as 'extremely deprived' according government criteria, that is falling among the worst-off 2.5 per cent in England. The project area has a high level of unemployment; 14 per cent and 13 per cent of economically active residents of Plashet and West Ham respectively were unemployed at the time of the 1981 census.

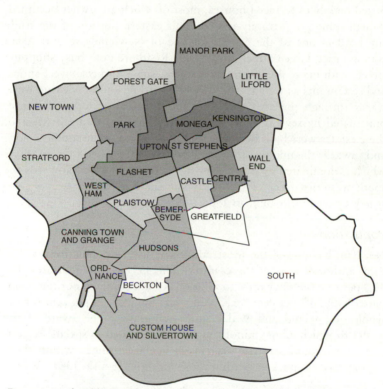

Percentage of residents with a New Commonwealth or Pakistan born head of household

- 0–9.9
- 10–19.9
- 20–29.9
- 30–49.9
- 50–59.9   Borough average:– 26.6%

Figure 6.2 *New Commonwealth and Pakistan residents by Ward, Newham*

Housing

The random sample of the survey indicated that 45 per cent of the area's residents rented from the council, 40 per cent were owner-occupiers, 3 per cent rented from housing associations, and 12 per cent rented privately or lived in some other type of housing.[3] Thirteen of Newham's 114 tower blocks (eight storeys and over) stand in the project area. The narrower, eastern end of the project area is comprised mainly of terraced houses, most of which are owner-occupied, though some are privately rented. This eastern portion of the study site borders one of the centres of one of Newham's several Asian communities. Green Street and Plashet Road are both busy shopping streets with many Asian-run food stores, supermarkets, sweet-shops, and restaurants as well as 'traditional' East-End shops. Moving westwards through the area there are more streets of terraced houses punctuated by several high- and low-rise housing estates.[4] Most of these estates were built between 1963 and 1967. On the southern edge and towards the middle of North Plaistow is the Chadd Green estate which is dominated by five fifteen-storey tower blocks.[5] Towards the south western corner of the study site stand a pair of twenty-two-storey tower blocks built in 1966.

Population

Newham has one of the most ethnically diverse populations of any local authority area in the country. The 1991 census indicates that 42.3 per cent of Newham's population is from ethnic minorities, compared with 20.2 per cent for Greater London and 5.9 per cent for the whole of England and Wales. It is important to be aware of the extent to which ethnic minorities are concentrated in specific regions and cities around the country, in particular localities within those regions, and in 'pockets' within those localities (Smith, 1989). Within

[3] This compares with 1981 census data which found that 59% of West Ham residents and 41% of Plashet residents, respectively, rented from the council.

[4] For the term 'housing estate' (which sounds rather grand to North Americans) read 'housing project'.

[5] The Chadd Green estate was built in 1967, and each block contains 56 flats. A recent proposal for environmental improvements listed the estate's problems as: crime, fear of crime, vandalism, racial harassment, squatting, noisy parties, rent arrears, and the alienation of the tenants from their environment. This proposal also noted that 20% of the estate's residents were unemployed and 44% of all tenants were claiming housing benefit. 61% of the tenants have current applications to transfer out of the estate.

the London Borough of Newham the ethnic minority communities are concentrated in pockets towards the north of the borough. Asian communities are concentrated mainly in East Ham, Upton Park, and Plashet, while Afro-Caribbeans live mainly in Forest Gate or in small pockets of Upton Park and Plashet (see Figures 6.1 and 6.2).[6] In the south of the borough there are far fewer ethnic minority resident as a result of a combination of factors, including former council housing allocations practices and a both perceived and actual local tradition of racial exclusionism, violence, and support for racist politics.[7]

The eastern end of Plashet ward forms part of Newham's Asian community, while the south western edge of West Ham ward borders Plaistow and is *en route* to Canning Town. The total population of the study site is 19,492 (1981 census estimate) and, like the borough as a whole, has an ethnically mixed population. Of the random sample of 751 residents of the study area generated by the survey, 65 per cent were white, 11 per cent Afro-Caribbean, 10 per cent Indian, 4 per cent African, 3 per cent Pakistani, and 1 per cent each Bangladeshi, Chinese, Filipino, 'other Asian', and 'other'. These figures compare with 1981 census data which suggest that 36 per cent of West Ham and 18 per cent of Plashet residents lived in households where the household head was born in one of the countries of the New Commonwealth and Pakistan.

Violent racism in East London

In east London, racial antipathy and exclusionism, and territorial defensiveness among the white community appear to be deep-seated and reflected in support for racist politics and violent racism (Husbands, 1982, 1983; Hobbs, 1988). Hobbs describes racism as 'part of East London's ideological inheritance . . . manifested in various ways including a long history of racist attacks on a variety of ethnic groups' (1988: 11). Husbands (1982) charts geographical continuities in racial vigilantism and extreme right-wing politics in the East End from 1900 to 1980. The British Brothers' League emerged in the inner-East End at the turn of the century and, in the pre-war years, agitated against 'aliens'—Jewish immigrants fleeing Eastern Europe (Husbands, 1982: 7–10). The anti-black and anti-Chinese rioting of 1919 in London focused on seafarers and others in

---

[6] See Newham Monitoring Project, 1991: 1; London Borough of Newham, 1986.
[7] See Husbands, 1983: 18–20; Newham Monitoring Project, 1991.

Limehouse, West India Dock Road, Poplar, and Cable Street, all in the East End (Fryer, 1984: 310).[8] In the inter-war years the inner-East End saw the rise of political parties such as the British Union of Fascists (BUF) and anti-Semitic agitation (Husbands, 1982: 14–15). The post-war Union Movement, built on the remains of the BUF, was also involved in anti-Semitic and anti-black agitation, and there is evidence of 'racial vigilantism' from the beginning of the 1950s (Husbands, 1982: 15). Anti-black rioting in 1958 affected parts of East London such as Hackney and Stepney, although this was not as widely reported as that occurring elsewhere in the country, such as Nottingham and London's Notting Hill (Fryer, 1984: 380, see also Chapter 2).

East London is cited as the geographical origin of the skinheads in 1969 (Mungham and Pearson, 1976:7). This development in the politics and style of British youth culture coincides with the coining of the term 'Paki-bashing' to refer to systematic attacks on ethnic minority individuals and communities in various localities in the East End and elsewhere (Mungham and Pearson, 1976; Husbands, 1982: 18). In a three-month period in 1970, 150 people from ethnic minorities were seriously assaulted and one stabbed to death in east London (Gordon, 1986: 2).

Politically organized racism also found a home in both the inner and extended East End during the 1970s with the emergence of the National Front (NF). In the mid-1970s, the National Front set up an 'advice centre' in Canning Town, in the south of Newham. In 1974, during the period in which the NF were campaigning for the forced repatriation of people from the New Commonwealth[9] and Pakistan, they polled 29 per cent of the vote in Hudsons ward and 25 per cent in Canning Town, both in the south of the borough.[10] In the 1977 Greater London Council election the East End provided nearly one third of the NF's total vote, with the party gaining more than 20 per cent of the vote in some constituencies.[11] During the late 1970s and early 1980s, East London continued to be the focus for both politi-

---

[8] Similar 'riots' occurred in South Shields, Liverpool, Glasgow, and south Wales (Fryer, 1984).

[9] Former colonies, primarily in Africa, the Caribbean, the Indian sub-continent, and South East Asia, most of which gained their independence in the post-war period. Distinct from the 'Old Commonwealth' countries of Canada, Australia, and New Zealand.

[10] See Husbands 1983: 9–10; Newham Monitoring Project, 1992: 28.

[11] See Miles and Phizacklea, 1984; Husbands, 1983.

cally organized racism and racist violence.[12] Clashes between the National Front and anti-racist demonstrators occurred regularly from 1978 until the collapse of the NF in the 1979 general election and local government elections in 1981 (Miles and Phizacklea, 1984: 104).

In the late 1970s, there appeared to be an increase in 'street-level' activity by organized and semi-organized racists (Husbands, 1982: 18; Layton-Henry, 1984). Of these, the most blatant was a 'rampage' down Brick Lane in the inner East End by 150 skinheads during which windows were smashed and people assaulted (Bethnal Green and Stepney Trades Council, 1978; Commission for Racial Equality, 1979). From 1978 until the end of the decade racial violence appeared to escalate in east London. Nine apparently racially motivated murders occurred in east London between 1978-81,[13] and in 1985 there were numerous arson attacks on the homes of Asian families in east London, some of which resulted in the death of the occupants (Hesse et al., 1992: 22–38). During the remainder of the 1980s and into the 1990s racial violence has continued to be directed against ethnic minorities in east London and elsewhere (Hesse et al., 1992: 38–45; Home Office, 1989, 1991; Gordon, 1990). However, there appear to have been no fatalities in east London until December 1991 when a Tamil refugee was allegedly 'beaten to death' by a 'racist gang' in Manor Park, Newham.[14]

This history of sporadic attacks against ethnic minority individuals and persistent campaigns of harassment against families forms the backdrop for the survey data which are presented below.[15] This context applies to east London in general, rather than specifically North Plaistow, though this locality has been the scene of some serious and well-known outbreaks of violence and campaigns of harassment.[16] If a micro-socio-geographical approach were adopted, however, North Plaistow might not be considered the most problematic area in east London in general or in Newham in specific. Other areas, such as neighbourhoods in the inner-East End and in the south of Newham were considered to be areas where racist sentiment was deepest and violence was more common (e.g. Husbands, 1982, 1983).

[12] See Husbands, 1982: 15–19; Layton-Henry, 1984: 108–21; Miles and Phizacklea, 1984: 118–35; Hiro, 1991.
[13] See Bethnal Green and Stepney Trades Council, 1978: 57; Gordon, 1986: 8; Newham Monitoring Project, 1991: 38; Hesse et al., 1992.
[14] Independent, 20 October 1992; Anti-Racist Alliance, Bulletin, December 1992.
[15] See also London Borough of Newham, 1987, 1988; Tompson, 1988.
[16] See Tompson, 1988; Newham Monitoring Project, 1991.

Nonetheless, in 1987, when the North Plaistow Racial Harassment Project was initiated, police statistics indicated that Newham had the highest rate of reported racial incidents in Greater London, just ahead of neighbouring Tower Hamlets.[17] At the time, Plaistow North Housing District had the highest number of recorded cases in Newham.[18] With this context firmly in mind, we now turn to the empirical study of victimization (Chapter 7) and policing (Chapter 8).

[17] In 1986 208 racial incidents were recorded in Newham and 189 in Tower Hamlets (House of Commons, written answers 92 and 93, 4 December 1986); in 1987, these figures had risen to 364 for Newham and 242 for Tower Hamlets (Metropolitan Police, 1989c; cited in Saulsbury and Bowling, 1992: 51).

[18] *Racial Attacks in Newham: Police Statistics for January/June 1987*. Report to London Borough of Newham Council Police Sub-Committee, 17 September 1987.

7

Racism and Victimization

Violence is like the 'white noise' of society. The incessant and myriad attempts to express an emotion, communicate a desire, or exert power over others may seem to the casual viewer like the hiss and crackle of a badly tuned television set. It is possible to see how, superficially, violence might be considered random, inexplicable, and unfocused. Survey research, like a tuner, attempts to distinguish signal from noise. It records moments of human experience in both digital and narrative forms and through tabulation and cross-tabulation seeks to reveal patterns of social action and interaction. Drawing on a victimization survey, official records, interviews with officers from local statutory agencies, and detailed case studies, this Chapter gives voice to experiences of violence and shows how they are patterned by 'race' and racism. The Chapter describes the extent and nature of violent racism, who the victims and perpetrators are, and where and when incidents occur. It examines how violence impacts on those who are targeted and explores the relationship between experiences of violence and the broader context of racist discourses and exclusion.

The Views of the Staff of Local Agencies

The first view of the problem was obtained from the officers from local agencies, such as housing officers, social workers, and teachers. The consensus was that Asian people, and particularly Asian women with children, were the most likely to be victimized. Some identified those living in local authority housing as especially vulnerable. Afro-Caribbeans were also thought to be potential targets, but were thought less likely to suffer harassment than Asians. People in mixed-race relationships, including the white partners of Afro-Caribbean and Asian people and mothers of mixed-race children, were also seen as targets. Perpetrators, it was believed, were usually groups of young white men and boys resident on the same estate as the victims or from nearby areas.

The officers believed that the harassment was usually directed at the victim's home or at his or her person when travelling along fixed routes, such as those between home, school, and shopping. The incidents were frequently described as being 'low level' but 'persistent' and included such incidents as criminal damage, graffiti, spreading rubbish, abusive behaviour, egg throwing, stone throwing, threatening behaviour, and 'knock-down-ginger',[1] often forming patterns of harassing behaviour. More serious incidents such as physical assaults and arson were believed to occur, though less frequently than mundane but persistent harassment. Interviewees mentioned that people were harassed by school children at the end of the school day and that harassment was most prevalent during school holidays and especially the summer break when the evenings were long and children and young people spent a lot of time playing and hanging about on the streets.

A number of specific locations were mentioned in group interviews[2] (see maps on page 174–5). These included a number of streets on the western edge of the study site (Rokeby Street, Skiers Street, and Paul Street), streets on the Chadd Green estate (Stratford Road, Lettsom Walk, Hunters Walk), and one of the main shopping streets on the eastern edge of the study site (Green Street). The areas around local schools, and especially Rokeby Street secondary school, were also mentioned. Although some officers considered North Plaistow to be a particularly problematic area, others believed that other locations—particularly in the south of the Borough—had far greater problems of both racism and violence.

These views, which are largely consistent with conventional wisdom about racial harassment and attacks emerged as the consensus among the officers from local agencies concerned to provide an 'operationally useful' description of the problem. There were, however, some contradictory views. The views of the police, specifically concerning the policing of racial incidents, will be returned to in Chapter 8.

The most outspoken views encountered in the interviews during the initial data-gathering phase were with groups of caretakers from

---

[1] Also known as 'knock and run', a 'game' the object of which is to 'wind up' the target by knocking on the door or ringing the door bell so that they come to the door and find no-one there, or shout abuse at them before running away.

[2] For descriptions of the locales mentioned in this section of the report, see the introduction to the case study.

the local authority housing estates.[3] These officers saw the problem of racial harassment not as one in which ethnic minorities were the victims of white racism, but where white people are 'victims' of different cultural practices of ethnic minorities. For example, racial harassment was conceived of as victimization by 'noisy' 'coloureds' and quiet, but 'smelly' Asians:

They put a coloured in and the first thing they bring in is speakers and loud parties. Ninety nine point nine per cent of racial harassment is parties. There ain't no other harassment. [The] racial problem isn't as much as it is made out to be.

[Racial harassment] only happens now and then. [The] smell of cooking can drive you crazy . My life is ruined. Makes you vomit. Call it racial harassment. If they are going to live in this country they should eat our food. . . . The smell of ghee oil comes up through the toilets. Let them all live together.

Immigrants will never be accepted in this country 'cos they were called over here as cheap labour. [There should be] separate blocks for coloureds and Asians otherwise there will never be racial harmony. Got to separate themselves. West Indians are music lovers, Asians are quiet.

These views are based on the assumption that the presence of ethnic minorities is illegitimate because they were invited to Britain only to meet a demand for cheap labour and without the consent of the white population. Their illegitimate presence is further exacerbated by their supposed unwillingness to eat 'our' food and adopt 'our' cultural practices. The implied course of action is that ethnic minorities should either be segregated or otherwise excluded (Hesse *et al.*, 1992, introduction).

Police-recorded Racial Incidents

In the eighteen-month period from 1 July 1987 to 31 December 1988, the police recorded 152 racial incidents[4]—an average of about two incidents a week on the study site (see Tables 7.1 and 7.2).

Three quarters of the victims recorded by the police were Asian, one-fifth African or Afro-Caribbean, 3 per cent were white, and 1 per

[3] Although the semi-structured questionnaire employed in the interviews was intended to collect 'operational' information about racial attacks (where and when they occurred etc.), the caretakers also provided us with their views on the nature of the problem.

[4] See Chap. 7 for a description of police racial-incident recording and monitoring procedures.

Table 7.1 *Racial incidents in North Plaistow*
1 July 1987–1 January 1989

Type of act	%
insulting behaviour	59
attempted or threatened assault	9
actual assault	9
attempted or actual damage to property	20

N = 152

Table 7.2 *Racial incidents recorded in West Ham for 1990*

Type of act	number
Abuse/other	60
Assaults	23
Criminal damage/burglary	21
Total	104

cent 'Mediterranean'. Nearly three-quarters were female and just under one quarter male. The victims recorded by the police tended to be adults; 83 per cent were aged 25–44, 13 per cent 45 or over, while only 11 per cent were aged under 24. The overwhelming majority were secure council tenants (93 per cent), the remainder being owner-occupiers or private renters. Where it was known, half of the addresses where the incident occurred were houses, 40 per cent were flats on upper floors and 9 per cent ground floor flats. 62 per cent of incidents were referred to them by the housing department and the remaining 38 per cent were reported directly.

Three-fifths of the incidents occurred between 2 pm and 10 pm and one-fifth each between 10 pm and 6 am and 6 am and 2 pm.[5] 59 per cent consisted of insulting behaviour, 20 per cent involved attempted or actual damage to property, 9 per cent were attempted or threatened assault, and 6 per cent were actual assaults. Of the ninety-five incidents in which the act was directed against the person, eighty-four resulted in 'non-physical injury',[6] eleven cases resulted in

[5] The survey indicated that incidents occurred at all times of the day and night; 13% in the morning, 29% in the afternoon, 11% sometime during the daytime (but could not be placed more accurately than that), 30% between 6 pm and midnight and 4% during the hours of darkness.

[6] 'Actual Bodily Harm' may be inferred if pain, tenderness or soreness results from the act, even if no physical injury is visible. It will be sufficient if the act merely causes *psychological injury* such as an hysterical and nervous condition: see Chap. 8.

physical injury, three required medical attention, and two hospital treatment. In forty-three incidents missiles were thrown and in three an offensive weapon was involved.

Police records showed that 94 per cent of suspects were male. 62 per cent were aged under 16, 24 per cent 16–24, and 11 per cent over 24. In 95 per cent of the incidents perpetrators were all white, while 5 per cent involved Africans or Afro-Caribbeans. The perpetrator was on their own in 19 per cent of the incidents, two were involved in 18 per cent, a group of between three and five in 28 per cent, and six or more in 18 per cent. In 55 per cent of the incidents the perpetrator was described by the victim and named in one third of them.

The police data largely confirm the conventional view of racial incidents in east London with respect to the characteristics of the event and of the protagonists.

Dispersion and entrenchment

The data from police records in North Plaistow may be analysed spatially using a method developed by Hesse *et al.* (1992). These authors argue that an investigation of the *dispersion* (configuration across various locations) and *entrenchment* (concentration in specific locations over time) is required to understand its 'spread' (1992: 129). In common with the findings of Hesse *et al.* (1992), a feature of the incidents recorded by the police in North Plaistow over this period is their concentration in particular places over time. Table 7.3 shows the streets in which the incidents of racial harassment recorded by the police occurred, and Table 7.4 the street in which the victims lived. It is important to bear in mind the selectivity of this sample of incidents.[7] These are only incidents recorded by the police, most of which were referred from housing. It is, therefore more likely that incidents targeted at local authority tenants will be included in the sample. This will probably have the additional effect of skewing the locations of the incidents to those in or around housing estates.

As can be seen from Tables 7.3 and 7.4 there is a concentration of incidents to the west of the study site where a greater proportion of the housing is owned by the local authority and where there are fewer ethnic minority households. Clearly, the fact that more recorded cases were targeted at tenants of the local authority reflects the

---

[7] Hesse *et al.* note a similar problem with their use of recorded racial incident statistics (1992: 149).

Table 7.3 *Address where incident occurred for police recorded incidents (1 July 1987–31 December 1988)*

Street	frequency	%*
Abbey Road	6	4
Ada Gardens	2	3
Arthingworth Street	1	1
Bates Point	2	1
Beardsfield Road	5	3
Brassett Point	3	2
Bridge Road	1	1
Caistor Park Road	1	1
David Lee Point	9	6
Dell Close	1	1
Dirleton Road	2	1
Eastbourne Road	1	1
Green Street	1	1
Harberson Road	1	1
Hubbard Street	1	1
Hurry Close	1	1
Leather Gardens	5	3
Leywick Street	2	1
Lucas Avenue	2	1
McEwen Way	1	1
Manor Road	2	1
Marcus Street	1	1
Meath Road	1	1
Milton Road	1	1
Napier Road	7	5
New Plaistow Road	1	1
Park Grove	1	1
Paul Street	10	7
Plashet Road	1	1
Richford Road	1	1
Rokeby Street	34	23
Skiers Street	21	14
Smith Point	6	4
Stephens Road	1	1
Stratford Road	2	1
Tanner Point	3	2
Terrace Road	1	2
Watts Point	7	5
West Ham Lane	3	2
West Ham rec. grd.	1	1

N = 152. missing = 2
* column does not = 100% because of rounding
Shaded area marks those addresses in an area of less than 10% ethnic minorities. This small area on the western edge of North Plaistow is the locality for 69% of racial incidents recorded by the police.

Table 7.4 *Victims' address for police recorded incidents (1 July 1987–31 December 1988)*

Street	frequency	%*
Abbey Road	2	1
Aida Gardens	3	2
Bates Point	4	3
Beardsfield Road	5	3
Brassett Point	3	2
Caistor Park Road	1	1
David Lee Point	9	6
Dirleton Road	2	1
Eastbourne Road	1	1
Harberson Road	2	1
Hurry Close	1	1
Leather Gardens	5	3
Lucas Avenue	2	1
McEwen Way	1	1
Marcus Street	1	1
Meath Road	1	1
Napier Road	8	5
Park Grove	1	1
Paul Street	13	9
Plashet Road	1	1
Rokeby Street	41	27
Skiers Street	21	14
Smith Point	5	4
Steele Road†	3	2
Sratford Road	2	1
Tanner Point	3	2
Watts Point	7	5

N = 152. missing = 12
* column does not = 100% because of rounding
† outside North Plaistow
Shaded area marks those addresses in an area of less than 10% ethnic minorities. This small area on the western edge of North Plaistow accounts for 65% of racial incident victims recorded by the police

process by which cases are recorded. Council tenants visit their housing offices to pay rent, collect housing benefit, report damage and the need for repairs, as well as to complain about their experiences of harassment. It is likely, therefore that cases affecting owner-occupiers towards the east of the study site are under-represented in the sample.

It is not certain that this pattern reflects that of the actual incidence of racial harassment, but we can at least say that this is how the problem presents itself to official agencies and examine the data further in this light. To this end it is interesting that police records tally with the perceptions from the officers from a range of local agencies; all of the specific localities mentioned in the group interviews had high concentrations of recorded incidents. The consistent findings when triangulating the data strengthen the evidence. However, it may be that opinions are formed on the basis of recorded incidents, thus creating a closed information loop within the local agencies.

It is also interesting to note that the racial incidents were recorded largely in areas of *low ethnic minority concentration*. As Tables 7.3 and 7.4 illustrate, about two thirds of the incidents occurred in and were directed against people living in or on the immediate borders of a few streets in the only part of the study site to have a concentration of less than 10 per cent ethnic minority households. By comparison, in very few cases indeed was the area to the east of the study site (with a concentration of ethnic minorities of over 50 per cent) either where the victim lived or the location for the incident.

On the face of it, this finding might seem to be contrary to expectations. One might think that the more targets for racially motivated violence in a given locality, the greater likelihood that some victimization will occur. There are three possible explanations for this finding. First, it may simply reflect the selectivity of reporting and recording referred to above. Secondly, it may be that, as local officers believed, young people from Rokeby, a large secondary school on the western edge of the study site, are responsible for many of the incidents—creating a concentration of reports in that area. This view is supported by the fact that Rokeby's catchment area includes areas south of the District Line, and that the route of children from these areas to school would take them through the streets with the greatest concentration of incidents.

Finally, this finding might support the work of such authors as Husbands (1982), Smith (1989), and Hesse *et al.* (1992) who point to the relationship between racial harassment and white territorialism and exclusionism. It may be that some areas have a low concentration of ethnic minorities as a result of formal and informal practices (violence being the most crucial) maintaining predominantly white neighbourhoods. Smith (1989) notes that:

attacks tend to cluster in areas where black people form a small minority of the population, but appear to be challenging the territorial preferences of whites (this trend was noted in the report of the Home Affairs Committee (1986)). . . . This prospect of violence and intimidation is a strong disincentive to black households who might other wise wish to move away from the poorer properties in which they are over-represented [Smith, 1989: 161–2].

An Episode of Victimization

Turning to the temporal nature of racial victimization, Table 7.5 is a list of racial incidents recorded by the police occurring in a twelve-month period in two streets on the western edge of the study site. These two streets consist primarily of (new) council housing in the area of low ethnic minority concentration referred to above. Again, it must be remembered that these recorded incidents are a product of the recording and monitoring practices of the police and housing department and cannot be taken, at face value, as evidence of a geographical focus of racial violence. Nonetheless, they do provide some insight into an episode of victimization in one locality and do suggest a pattern.

During the year January 1987 to January 1988, fifty-three incidents targeted against seven families in two streets were recorded by the police. As Table 7.5 shows, the overwhelming majority of the incidents consisted of verbal abuse and harassment, egg-throwing, damage to property, and door knocking. Conceived of as individual instances of offensive or threatening behaviour, and employing any kind of hierarchy of seriousness using legal categories, many of these incidents would be regarded as minor. However, in the context of the life of any individual family and most clearly in the life of a locality the repeated incidence of harassment is bound to have a cumulative effect.

Moreover, interleaved with the 'mundane but persistent' harassment of these Asian families and their property are instances in which the capacity for escalation is fulfilled and the incident turns into one of serious physical violence. The assault on Mr S in October 1987 might be seen as the crescendo of this violent episode. During this particular incident, the attackers smashed their way into the victim's home and attacked him with a pool cue. This incident led to police and court action, but did not end the ordeal of the S family. During the run up to the trial of the perpetrators, the family was subjected to persistent intimidation in the form of door knocking, egg

Table 7.5 *Reported racial incidents at Skiers Street and Rokeby Street*

January 1987–January 1988

Date of offence	Offence	Location	Victim
19.1.87	criminal damage	Rokeby Street	Mr P
26.1.87	racial harassment stones thrown	Rokeby Street	Mr P
24.2.87	criminal damage broken window	Rokeby Street	Mr P
25.2.87	racial harassment verbal abuse	Rokeby Street	Mrs S
27.2.87	theft of milk	Rokeby Street	Mrs S
18.3.87	common assault stones thrown	Rokeby Street	Mrs S
2.3.87	criminal damage broken window	Rokeby Street	Mrs K
25.3.87	racial harassment eggs thrown	Rokeby Street	Mrs J
7.4.87	racial harassment verbal abuse	Rokeby Street	Mrs J
15.6.87	racial harassment verbal abuse	Rokeby Street Paul Street	Mr H
30.5.87	racial harassment verbal abuse	Rokeby Street	Mrs J
5.6.87	theft of milk	Rokeby Street	Mrs. J
16.6.87	racial harassment eggs thrown	Rokeby Street	Mrs S
1.7.87	common assault water thrown	Rokeby Street	Mrs K
22.8.87	verbal abuse	Rokeby Street	Mrs P
16.9.87	eggs thrown	Rokeby Street	Mrs P
10.9.87	criminal damage broken window	Rokeby Street	Mrs J
13.9.87	racial harassment dog excrement placed on doorstep	Rokeby Street	Mrs J
11.9.87	racial harassment eggs thrown	Rokeby Street	Mrs J
13.9.87	racial harassment eggs thrown	Rokeby Street	Mrs P
16.9.87	racial harassment eggs thrown	Rokeby Street	Mrs P
24.9.87	racial abuse	Rokeby Street	Mrs S
3.10.87	racial abuse	Rokeby Street	Mrs S
7.10.87	attempted criminal damage	Rokeby Street	Mrs J
19.10.87	racial abuse	Rokeby Street	Mrs S
21.10.87	racial abuse	Rokeby Street	Mrs S
23.10.87	racial abuse	Rokeby Street	Mrs S
26.10.87	racial abuse	Rokeby Street	Mrs S
6.12.87	aggravated burglary	Rokeby Street	Mr A

Date of offence	Offence	Location	Victim
25.10.87	racial abuse	Rokeby Street	Mr L
28.10.87	stones thrown racial abuse	Rokeby Street	Mrs J
31.10.87	stones thrown racial abuse	Rokeby Street	Mrs J
7.11.87	eggs thrown	Rokeby Street	Mrs P
24.11.87	racial abuse	Skiers Street	Mrs L
8.12.87	knocking on doors	Rokeby Street	Mrs P
28.6.87	verbal abuse threats	Skiers Street	Mrs S
21.10.87	assault (GBH) criminal damage	Skiers Street	Mr S
1.11.87	knocking on doors	Skiers Street	Mr S
31.10.87	eggs thrown	Skiers Street	Mrs N
1.11.87	eggs thrown	Skiers Street	Mrs N
14.11.87	common assault bottles thrown	Skiers Street	Mrs S
5.11.87	eggs thrown at house	Skiers Street	Mr S
6.22.87	eggs thrown at house	Skiers Street	Mr S
7.11.87	eggs thrown at house	Siers Street	Mr S
9.11.87	eggs thrown at house	Skiers Street	Mr S
13.12.87	eggs thrown at house	Skiers Street	Mr S
14.12.87	eggs thrown at house	Skiers Street	Mr S
9.12.87	theft of milk	Skiers Street	Mr S
20.12.87	eggs thrown	Skiers Street	Mr S
1.1.88	criminal damage	Skiers Street	Mr S
7.1.88	verbal abuse	Skiers Street	Mr N
23.1.88	verbal abuse	Skiers Street	Mr S

Total 53 incidents (4–5 per week) on seven families.
Source: Newham Organized Racial Incident Squad, internal memorandum.
Note: incidents appear not in chronological order, but in the order that they were reported to the police.

throwing on their house, and verbal abuse and missile throwing on the street.

The North Plaistow Racial Harassment Survey

The third component of the initial data-gathering of the North Plaistow Racial Harassment Project was a victimization survey (see Appendix I for details of survey methods, samples, etc.). The survey was based on a random sample of 751 residents of the study area and a 'booster sample' of Asian residents, giving a total sample size of 1,174. These interviewees completed a short *general questionnaire,* which covered several general issues relating to crime and racial harassment and then ascertained whether the respondent had suffered a racial incident. This sample forms the basis for the analysis of the prevalence and incidence of the problem.

Of the 163 respondents who mentioned a racial incident, 114 (70 per cent) completed a *victim questionnaire*. It was intended that up to three incidents would be recorded in detail for each victim. In the event, not all subsequent incidents were recorded. The total number of incidents recorded in detail was 158. These form the basis for the analysis of patterns of incidents, the effects suffered, etc. The field-work was carried out by Harris Research using 'ethnically matched' interviewers during May and June 1989.

The Views of Survey Respondents

Views about the Locality

By almost any 'objective' criterion, North Plaistow is not the best place to live. In terms of its economy, the physical condition and cleanliness of its environment, the quality of its housing stock, its facilities for young and old people, and its rate of recorded crime and racial harassment, it is among the very worst-off localities in the whole of England and Wales. Despite this, many more respondents thought their area to be a good (60 per cent) rather than a bad one (28 per cent) to live in, and ethnic minority respondents rated the area considerably more highly than white ones. 55 per cent of white respondents said that the area was a good one, compared with 65 per cent of Asians and 70 per cent of Africans and Afro-Caribbeans.

Respondents were then read a list of things 'that are a problem in some areas', and were asked to what extent they themselves felt each were a problem. The things most likely to be seen as a big problem in the area were rubbish and litter (51 per cent), crime (44 per cent), and unemployment (32 per cent). 29 per cent of the sample thought that racial harassment was a problem—12 per cent thought it a big problem and a further 17 per cent a bit of a problem. As expected, ethnic minorities were more likely than white people to think that racial harassment was a problem.

Views about Racial Harassment in Relation to Other Problems

Respondents were also asked what they thought to be the three great-est problems in the project area (see Table 7.6). Crime was consid-ered the greatest problem, followed by rubbish and litter, unemployment, and housing conditions.

Table 7.6 *Respondents' opinion of the greatest 3 problems in the area (%)*

	All	WM	WF	ACM	ACF	AM	AF	V	MV
Crime	48	48	51	41	30	60	52	57	61
Rubbish/litter	43	44	52	30	40	31	28	31	30
Unemployment	24	26	22	25	28	20	20	14	11
Housing conditions	19	19	21	24	19	14	15	11	6
Youth facilities	18	18	25	11	19	9	6	12	11
Leisure facilities	15	19	15	11	12	10	6	12	12
Rowdy youths	14	16	10	14	15	31	14	14	11
Council services	13	11	14	17	18	13	9	18	21
Schools	12	11	11	14	15	13	14	14	11
Graffiti	12	16	13	8	9	4	6	11	13
Racial harassment	10	8	5	3	16	22	28	27	36
Police service	9	9	5	16	10	14	12	18	14
Race discrimination	8	7	3	6	15	17	23	16	15
Noisy neighbours	8	10	5	11	9	10	5	2	2
Public transport	6	7	6	6	10	4	3	2	2
Rank order of racial harassment	11th	13th	12th	15th	8th	3rd	2nd	3rd	2nd

Note: Tables 7.6–7.13
WM = white male
WF = white female
ACM = African/Caribbean Male
ACF = African/Caribbean Female
AM = Asian Male
AF = Asian Female
V = racial harassment victim
MV = multiply victimized

Ten per cent of the sample said that racial harassment was one of the three greatest problems in the area, ranking eleventh out of a list of fifteen problems. Racial harassment was for the sample *as a whole* more important only than police service provision, racial discrimination, noisy neighbours, and public transport. As expected, this picture changed substantially when desegregated by ethnic and gender group. Now, racial harassment emerged as a problem second only to crime and on a par with rubbish and litter for Asian women and as the third greatest problem for Asian men. Other ethnic and gender groups ranked racial harassment much lower—seventh for African and Afro-Caribbean women, thirteenth and twelfth for white men and women, respectively and fifteenth (bottom of the list) for African and Afro-Caribbean men.

Views about Problems Relating to Law and Order

Narrowing the focus somewhat, the survey next asked respondents to say whether or not they found specific forms of crime and disorder to be a problem in their area (see Table 7.7).

As might be expected, a large proportion of African and Afro-Caribbean and Asian respondents considered 'racial attacks on Afro-Caribbean and Asian people' to be a problem. Nearly two thirds of Asian women and men, about half of African and Afro-Caribbean women and men thought it was either a big, or a bit of a, problem in the area. However, there was also a considerable degree of concern among the white majority community about attacks on ethnic minorities; one quarter of white women and one third of white men said they thought that racial attacks *on Afro-Caribbeans and Asians* were a problem in the locality.

Table 7.7 *Respondents' opinion of the greatest 3 'crime' problems in the area (%)*

	All	WM	WF	ACM	ACF	AM	AF	V	MV
Burglary	55	49	57	57	61	57	61	63	68
Street robbery	39	40	39	30	39	50	39	37	37
Vandalism	35	37	34	43	36	31	21	35	32
Car theft	35	36	33	33	39	42	29	39	37
Sexual assault	21	19	29	25	7	13	14	21	22
Youth misbehaviour	17	18	15	19	9	18	20	21	25
Women pestered	16	14	24	13	15	6	7	18	20
Racial attacks[1]	15	7	11	11	25	28	33	27	28
Fights in street	9	11	9	6	6	8	9	5	3

[1] The question referred to 'racial attacks on Afro-Caribbean and Asian people'.

Views about Police Priorities

Views about policing priorities reflected, to some extent, beliefs about the greatest crime problems, although some forms of crime and harassment (e.g. sexual assault and pestering) were rated higher as police priorities than as crime problems (see Table 7.8).

Racial attacks were the third highest police priority for Asian men and women (after burglary and street robbery), fourth for African and Afro-Caribbean women, sixth for African and Afro-Caribbean

Table 7.8 *Which crime should the police concentrate on most?* (%)

	All	WM	WF	ACM	ACF	AM	AF	V	MV
Burglary	50	45	49	54	55	57	58	52	49
Street robbery	36	38	34	25	42	42	40	34	32
Sexual assault	32	30	39	32	31	20	20	24	22
Car theft	27	27	26	27	28	32	25	32	24
Vandalism	26	26	24	32	28	23	24	26	26
Women pestered	21	20	30	21	15	10	7	16	18
Racial attacks[1]	19	16	13	21	28	33	39	30	30
Youth misbehaviour	10	11	8	16	1	12	14	15	21
Fights in street	8	9	7	10	6	7	10	7	8

[1] The question referred to 'racial attacks on Afro-Caribbean and Asian people'.

men, and seventh for white men and women. Despite the differences in views among ethnic groups, some white people thought that racial attacks on African and Afro-Caribbean and Asian people were one of the three most important police priorities. The proportions of white people believing that racial attacks on ethnic minorities are a problem (32 per cent) and should be a policing priority (14 per cent) suggests that there is considerable concern about such attacks among the white majority community.

Fear of Racial Harassment

Fifty-eight per cent of Asian women worried either a great deal or a fair amount about being victimized, compared with 51 per cent of Asian men, 37 per cent of African and Afro-Caribbean women, 26 per cent of African and Afro-Caribbean men, 20 per cent of white women and 13 per cent of white men. Most white men (64 per cent), African and Afro-Caribbean men (57 per cent) and white women (54 per cent) did not worry at all about being victimized, compared with only 12 per cent of Asian women, 20 per cent of Asian men, and 29 per cent of African and Afro-Caribbean women. When asked whether they worried about the possibility of their families being victimized, the number of those fearful rose for each ethnic-gender group. Most worried of all were Asian women, only 10 per cent of whom claimed to live free from this anxiety (see Table 7.9)

Table 7.9 *Respondents' worry about themselves becoming victims of racial harassment (%)*

	All	WM	WF	ACM	ACF	AM	AF	V	MV
A great deal	10	5	6	10	18	19	29	35	39
A fair amount	15	8	14	16	19	22	29	25	27
Not very much	23	20	24	16	22	33	24	22	13
Not at all	50	64	54	57	39	20	12	18	19
Don't know/not stated	3	2	3	2	1	5	6	*	*

Experiences of Racial Harassment

Respondents were next asked about experience, if any, of racial harassment. Interviewers explained that the term racial harassment referred to 'any form of insult, threat, violence, damage to or theft of property, or any attempt to do any of these things which was racially motivated. By racially motivated I mean an act directed at you because of your race.'

Respondents were then read a list of some types of offences and were asked to say whether any of them had happened to them personally within the previous eighteen months (January 1988–June 1989). 163 of the 1,174 survey respondents said they had experienced some form of racial harassment, about one in five ethnic minority respondents—21 per cent of African and Afro-Caribbean women (14 respondents), 19 per cent of Asian men (57 respondents), 18 per cent of Asian women (43 respondents) and 17 per cent of African and Afro-Caribbean men (n=11). A small proportion of white people also said that they had experienced a racial incident—8 per cent of white men (n=14) and 7 per cent of white women (n=21).

Between them, these 163 victims mentioned approximately 831 actual incidents over the eighteen-month period.[8] This figure assumes that respondents' descriptions of the number of times they were victimized was accurate. They may not be able to recall the number and nature of incidents accurately over a period of eighteen months—some may be forgotten; others may have occurred longer ago and 'telescoped' forward into the reporting period; others may have

---

[8] Because Asians were believed, *a priori*, to be those most likely to be victimized, they were deliberately oversampled in order to have enough 'victims' in the sample for meaningful analysis. As a result, the number of incidents in the sample reduced to 724 when weighted to correct for oversampling.

occurred during the reporting period, but 'telescoped' backward and thus not been mentioned by the respondent. Because of the problem of defining racial harassment, discussed at some length in Chapter 2, some respondents may have defined incidents as *racial* when the motivation was arguable, or when they could not even be certain that a person from another racial group was responsible for the incident. Others may have ignored incidents they regarded as minor or unimportant.[9]

Despite this, it must be concluded that in the eighteen-month period in question, there were many thousands of incidents defined by the victim as racial harassment in North Plaistow. Given that roughly 10 per cent of the adult population of the area was interviewed, as many as 7,000 instances of insulting behaviour, threats of or actual violence, theft, damage to property (or attempts to do any of these things) where the victim believed that the incident was directed at him or her because of their race may have occurred in the eighteen-month period in question.

Detailed Description of Incidents

The preceding results are based on information supplied by the whole sample of 1,174 people. Of the 163 respondents who said that they had experienced one or more incidents, 114 agreed to provide details of 158 incidents.[10] These were between two thirds and three quarters of all those who stated that they had experienced a racial incident in the previous eighteen months. The information in the following section is based on their accounts of what happened. The victims detailing an incident were slightly more likely to be male than female, were much more likely to be under 45 than over, and were little different from the occupational class structure of the sample as a whole. Of the 158 incidents described in detail, the race–gender breakdown is as follows: fifty-eight Asian males, forty-five Asian females, thirteen

[9] An attempt was made to offset this problem by explaining to respondents that: 'I don't just want to know about serious incidents, I want to know about small things too. It is often difficult to remember exactly when the small things happened so please try to think carefully.' Nonetheless, the well-documented under-reporting of incidents to the police may also apply to reporting incidents to survey interviewers. The authors of the ICS, for example, concluded from one interview that 'some segments of the population are so over-exposed to [racist assaults] that it becomes part of their everyday reality and escapes their memory in the interview situation' (Jones *et al.*, 1986).

[10] 118 when weighted to compensate for oversampling Asians.

African and Afro-Caribbean males, thirteen African and Afro-Caribbean females, fourteen white males, twelve white females, and three others.

By far the most common form of harassment consisted of insulting behaviour or verbal abuse (42 per cent), which the majority of victims suffered (see Table 7.10). Next were actual damage to property (16 per cent), actual physical assault (10 per cent), and actual theft (7 per cent). There were a very large number of 'less serious' incidents and many 'very serious' ones. Some appeared to be one-off events, while others were said to be part of a pattern of repeated attacks and harassment. This is consistent with the views of officers from local agencies who said that persistent door-knocking, egg throwing, damage to property, verbal abuse, threats, and intimidation had a cumulative effect on victims, even though the events may not look serious as individual 'incidents'.

Table 7.10 *Types of harassment and numbers of incidents suffered by respondents over an 18-month period (weighted figures).*

Form of harassment	Incidents
Insulting behaviour/verbal abuse	303
Threatened damage or violence	98
Attempted assault	81
Actual assault	72
Actual and attempted damage to property	114
Actual and attempted theft	53
Actual and attempted arson	3

Unweighted n = 163

Nearly six out of ten incidents occurred in the immediate vicinity of victims' homes (see Table 7.11). This including incidents which occurred at the home address[11] (23 per cent), those that occurred in the street outside the victim's home (16 per cent), outside or inside the building in which their home was located (12 per cent and 4 per cent respectively), and near their garage (4 per cent).

Incidents happened at all times of the day and night, 29 per cent sometime during the daytime, and a further 13 per cent occurred in the morning, 30 per cent between 6 pm and midnight, 11 per cent

[11] This includes actual and attempted break-ins, damage to property (including window breakages), incidents on the doorstep, and offensive material through the letterbox.

Table 7.11 *Where the incident took place (%)*

Location	All	WM	WF	ACM	ACF	AM	AF	R[1]
In/around the home[2]	23	21	25	31	15	21	31	37
Street outside home	16	14	17	8	8	31	18	10
Inside own building	4	–	–	–	15	2	9	2
Outside own building	12	14	17	15	–	17	11	20
In garages for houses	4	21	–	–	8	4	–	8
All in vicinity of home	59	70	59	54	46	66	69	77
At work	7	–	–	–	31	7	–	3
All others[3]	33	29	42	39	23	28	17	17

[1] Incidents reported to an official agency (e.g. the police or the Housing Department)

[2] Includes attempted break-ins, incidents on the doorstep, material through the letter box.

[3] Includes school/college, in street near work, in/near a pub, at place of work out of doors and place of worship, and 'don't know'/not stated, all of which were very small numbers. The bulk (33% of the whole sample) were 'other' responses.

between midnight and 6 am, and 4 per cent sometime during the hours of darkness.

Patterns of Victimization for Each Ethnic–Gender Group

It is evident that a wide range of different experiences have been defined by respondents as racial incidents. The data suggest that there are very different experiences among the various ethnic and gender groups. Thus, it becomes impossible to speak of the *typical* case of racial harassment or attack. The experiences are so varied that one hesitates to include every instance in the same class of events, behaviours, or experiences.

In addition to differences between groups, there are differences *within* groups. Thus, the incidents mentioned in the survey by a single ethnic–gender group appear to cover a wide range of activities, with regard to the characteristics of the victim and perpetrator, or the context of the incident. In the following analysis, the quantitative data from the survey, *selected* quotations from the survey's open-ended questions are used to illustrate specific points as they emerge.[12]

[12] Most of the survey items were precoded, leaving open-ended only questions such as what actually occurred in the incident, why the respondent believed the incident to

Asian People

Of the 103 incidents mentioned by Asian respondents, no fewer that thirty-nine of them (38 per cent) were directed at Asian council tenants. Only 14 per cent of the Asians sampled were council tenants, suggesting that those living in council accommodation were almost three times as likely to have provided detail about an incident as Asians as a whole. The majority of council estates in North Plaistow are away from the eastern portion of the study site, which has a high proportion of Asian residents (more than 50 per cent). Council housing lies mainly in the centre of the area (e.g. the Chadd Green estate) or on the western edge of the area where there is a low proportion of Asian residents. These facts support the view that the geographical spread of racial incidents reflects the targeting of ethnic minorities living outside the areas of high ethnic minority concentration.

The survey showed that seven out of ten incidents mentioned by Asian women happened close to home, with three out of ten occurring directly on or immediately adjacent to their homes and a further four out of ten in the street, walkway, or passageway outside their home. The remainder occurred elsewhere. The pattern was similar for Asian men, though more were incidents which occurred in the street outside their homes.

Most recent incident:

I was watching TV at home, and a gang of kids come, shouted abuse, and started throwing stones, hitting and breaking windows in my house, and of my car. *What was it about the incident which makes you believe that the attack was racially motivated?* They call me a black fucking Paki, and they said I shouldn't be here, to go home.

Second most recent incident:

It was some kids I chased off earlier in the day, they come and threw stones at my windows breaking them, shouting 'Go away Paki'. *What was it about the incident which makes you believe that the attack was racially motivated?* The fact that they hate anyone who is a 'Paki' as they call us. They tell me to go away.

have been racially motivated, why the incident was not reported to the police and other local agencies (in cases where it was not), and what happened as a result of a police detection (in cases where perpetrators were detected). The responses to these questions as recorded by the interviewer were transcribed in full. Because details were not recorded in every instance and because of the poor quality of some of what was recorded it must be stressed that the quotations selected for inclusion in the text are intended only to *illustrate* the quantitative survey findings.

Third most recent incident:

We were at the back of our garden, and we heard a noise. We come out to find the windows of our car broken. *What was it about the incident which makes you believe that the attack was racially motivated?* Because I'd had trouble with racial harassment before [Indian man].

The survey found that many incidents consisted of racist abuse, graffiti, window smashing, and egg throwing. There are three reasons for considering what are sometimes referred to as 'low level' or merely 'nuisance' incidents, very serious in their impact and their effect on the security of the victim.[13] First, any type of incident becomes serious when it is repeated frequently enough. Repeated or persistent incidents undermine the security of the victim and induce fear and anxiety. The sense of the cumulative effects of repeated instances of stone throwing, name-calling, and harassment are evident from this example:

Most recent incident:

Came in and called me Paki and started throwing bricks at me. They didn't hurt me because I had thick coat on. They called me Paki before they started throwing the bricks at me.

Second most recent incident:

A gang of teenagers started shouting at me 'Paki' go home and abuse. Nothing else.

Third most recent incident:

It's happened so many times—they come up in groups and call me names—they call me rude names and call me Paki. I want to move away from here because I'm frightened to live here now because it happens so often.

A second reason for taking seriously the effect of repeated harassment directed specifically against ethnic minorities is the apparent exclusionary intent and impact of this form of victimization. The two examples cited above illustrate the exclusionary language and practice of the perpetrator. The phrases such as 'go home', 'go back to your own country' challenge the human rights of the people who are victimized (made into a victim) with the obvious effect of undermining their sense of security and sense of belonging (Hesse *et al.*, 1992). The eventual impact is to create fear about living in a particular

---

[13] See also FitzGerald and Ellis, 1990: 59; Hesse *et al.*, 1992; Sampson and Phillips, 1992.

locality and to inspire a wish to move away. This aspect of racism is what Hesse *et al.* refer to as the 'logic of white territorialism':

> What then is the context and objective of 'white territorialism'? . . . Consider the discursive resonances wrought by expressions like 'Pakis go home', 'go back to your own country', 'alien cultures swamping British identity', 'immigrants colonizing Britain', 'blacks ghettoizing the inner-city' or more recently 'Islamic fundamentalism sweeping the nation'. At least two things should be apparent from these spatial obsessions. First there is heightened anxiety about these 'subordinate', 'other' populations resisting regulation and getting out of 'our' control; and secondly, there is a sense in which 'our' British identity (for 'our' read 'white') is under threat because 'our right' to dominate is being questioned; this is the expressive logic of the desire for racial exclusion [Hesse *et al.*, 1992: 172].

Even the most mundane instances of racial abuse may be seen as an exclusionary practice, one which acts to 'defend . . . space against change and transformation' (Hesse *et al.*, 1992). In this way, spaces are created within which black people are made to feel unwelcome and vulnerable to attack, and from which they may eventually be excluded.

Finally, mundane but persistent attacks *on property* are also attacks on *those inside* the dwelling (whether or not they are present at the time of the incident). Graffiti, window breakages, and other forms of criminal damage on the fabric of the building and physical attacks nearby the building violate the security of the place where an individual is often considered safest. Although an Englishman's home is (metaphorically) his castle, in actual fact the physical fabric of a house (particularly those in localities such as Newham) provides only an illusion of defence against attack from without.[14] Being a static object makes a dwelling an easy target—one which is open to repeated and persistent attack, and one where the potential for escalation is tied specifically to a fixed location (Hesse *et al.*, 1992). Several respondents mentioned instances of attack which resulted in damage to property where their personal security was at great risk. Such instances include shooting a window with an air gun and attempted arson attacks using inflammable fluid squirted through the letterbox:

---

[14] Some of the quotations provided in this section illustrate the vulnerability of houses and flats to attack through windows, glass door fronts, letterboxes, etc. Local authority flats, in particular, have been shown to be quite penetrable. In several instances which came to the author's attention while working in Newham, flats had been entered by perpetrators jumping through the thin ceiling of top floor flats having gained access to the eaves.

A bullet came through the bedroom window and broke it bringing the bullet into the room. An air gun was used. *What was it about the incident which makes you believe that the attack was racially motivated?* It's happened several times [involving] the same person. I have got NF written outside my wall and I don't know what to do about it this time. I have been attacked right in my bedroom [Other Asian].

Someone put container of liquid through letter box. Failed to make a fire. Could have been serious. *What was it about the incident which makes you believe that the attack was racially motivated?* Because of the sort of attack putting fire through letter box. Neighbours had one similar incident [Pakistani].

In several cases documented during the study period attacks have occurred in which groups of assailants have smashed their way through the front door and assaulted the victim with weapons (including knives, a hammer, and a pool cue) inside their homes. In other instances, attacks which started in public space led to attacks on the victim's home:

My children went to the park, under the supervision of my sister, and they were set upon, by these white kids, when they finished beating my kids up they followed them to my address, and threw stones at my window, breaking it. *What was it about the incident which makes you believe that the attack was racially motivated?* Because they shouted, abusive names like Pakis and many other insulting words.

Many of the incidents described by Asians in the survey are of a type identified in the Home Office (1981) study and noted by Walmsley (1986 drawing on Brown, 1984):

Many attacks on Asians and West Indians are attacks in the street when there is clearly no background of a prior argument or misunderstanding. In such incidents strangers may simply approach others and hit them, kick them, throw stones at them or even use knives and bottles to assault them [Walmsley 1986: 26].

In North Plaistow, respondents described walking along the street near to their homes or while shopping, going to work or worship, and being unexpectedly verbally abused or being physically attacked or menaced:

Me and my husband were taking our children to mosque in the afternoon. Some young white man just said verbal abuse—'Paki' and things like that [Indian woman].

As I was coming home there were some kids playing on the road—16 or 17 years old. They said 'You Paki. Why don't you go away from here'. Sometimes when I move my car they are there and won't move to let me get out [Indian].

Guy was drunk, he hit me with a piece of [wire]. Line on my face straight through where he hit me then he ran away—I didn't have time to do anything to defend myself. It happened very quickly, he didn't say anything but he wouldn't have done it if I was white. *What was it about the incident which makes you believe that the attack was racially motivated?* We had no conversation—didn't know the guy—first thing that happened was that he hit me. He just wouldn't have done it if I was white. No [Iranian].

I was shopping once [when a] white young girl came and stood in front of me. I told her I am in the queue and you should wait for your turn. But instead she started saying racially names and slapped on my face as well. *What was it about the incident which makes you believe that the attack was racially motivated?* That is quite obvious. If there was another white woman, first thing she would not jump the queue and secondly in the case of white women, if she had protested, this white girl would never slap her or abuse her [Pakistani].

Some incidents mentioned by Asian men (7 per cent) occurred while at work.

Argument over prices. Bloody Indian, bloody immigrant. Fucking bastard! *What was it about the incident which makes you believe that the attack was racially motivated?* Wording racial. Bloody Paki. Bloody immigrant [Indian shopkeeper].

The only Chinese victim in the sample who gave details of their experience also suffered harassment at work:

Most recent incident:

[I work in a] Chinese fish and chip shop. I come to work the next morning to find our shop window smashed. *What was it about the incident which makes you believe that the attack was racially motivated?* Because they smashed my window without stealing anything. [I] must be someone they don't like.

Second most recent incident:

Two kids came in. Got a drink and tried to steal it. I went out of the counter and said 'You've got to pay for the drink'. They started arguing. Finally he paid for it and on his way out, he was very angry and said "I'm gonna put a brick through that door". *What was it about the incident which makes you believe that the attack was racially motivated?* I just felt it could have been because of us [Chinese] living here.

The majority of the incidents experienced by both Asian men and women involved groups of young white males who were unknown to the victim. Very few incidents targeted at Asian women were one-to-one confrontations, with 85 per cent involving more than one perpetrator. More than one third of the incidents involved a group of four or more perpetrators. Four out of ten incidents directed against Asian men were carried out by a group of four or more. Asian men and women were harassed by a group of males in two thirds of the incidents. Also in two thirds of the incidents the perpetrators were aged 16–25, and in one quarter were school age.

In just over one incident in ten the victim knew all or some of the people involved and, where they were known, they were not known well, most often by sight only. Two thirds of the Asian victims said that their assailants were white, one fifth that they were African or Afro-Caribbean, and one tenth a 'mixed' group.

The question of whether African and Afro-Caribbean people can exhibit racist attitudes or behaviour toward Asian people has been a recurrent one since the emergence of the problem of racial violence as a policy issue in the early 1980s, though many reports simply duck the issue altogether.[15] In North Plaistow there is no doubt that some of the Asians interviewed believed themselves to have been the victims of anti-Asian racism perpetrated by groups composed solely of young men of African or Afro-Caribbean origin, or groups of blacks and white acting together. In some instances, the belief that attacks by African/Caribbeans were racially motivated was simply because the assailant was black. In other instances, African/Caribbean young people were perceived by the victim to engage in anti-Asian racist behaviour that was not readily distinguishable from that perpetrated by their white counterparts:

---

[15] FitzGerald and Ellis (1990), for example, state that: 'Initial perceptions of the problem (which was first brought to light in respect of Asian communities in the East End of London) have tended to frame the assumptions on which discussion has taken place and to limited the categories covered by surveys. Political pressure (with a small "p") has also been brought to bear, with strong exception being taken in some quarters to the notion that black people can exhibit racial hostility either towards whites or towards each other. . . . With regard to the survey data, it will be noted that even the Home Office (1981) report does not cover harassment between Afro-Caribbeans and Asians, while most of the other surveys implicitly deny that whites could be victims of racial harassment at all' (*ibid*.: 58). Small notes that 'conflicts between subgroups, ethnically or otherwise, within the black population' are 'a topic of tremendous taboo' (1991: 525).

Most recent incident:

Graffiti. Very abusive and dirty words were written on both the . . . front door and refuse box. All over the front walls. Some words are still visible. It happen[s] . . . frequently. *What was it about the incident which makes you believe that the attack was racially motivated?* It must be done by white or black kids. We are only two [Asian] families in this block. Everybody know[s]. That is why making our life very hard.

Second most recent incident:

My husband was coming back. A group of young kids push my husband and started kicking him. *What was it about the incident which makes you believe that the attack was racially motivated?* Because the gang was mix[ed] group. Two white and one black youth. They were awaiting for him [Indian woman].

There are also instances of African/Caribbeans echoing the racist epithets more commonly associated with white racism:

A couple of whites and a couple of blacks called me racist names. They pushed me around . . . *What was it about the incident which makes you believe that the attack was racially motivated?* The verbal abuse. That's all [Pakistani].

Just came and asked me for money. They punched me—black and white gang—there were lots of them. They threatened me but I didn't give them anything. They were carrying knives and a screwdriver. *What was it about the incident which makes you believe that the attack was racially motivated?* Paki—they called me a Paki—if I'd been white I don't think they'd have stopped and asked me for money. Nothing else. No [Bangladeshi].

One Indian person said that he had been assaulted by 'eight black people' who held him to the ground and kicked and hit him. When asked what was it about the incident which made him believe that the attack was racially motivated, he said, 'because they told me it was. There you bloody Paki that will show ya'.

For both Asian men and women, the most common reason for believing that the incident was racially motivated—in 54 per cent of those directed against men and 40 per cent against women—was that the perpetrator had referred to their actual or supposed race. This racial ascription was very often wrong, with people of Indian origin frequently called 'Paki'. The second most common reason, in about one fifth of cases, was the victim's belief that such attacks would not happen to them if they were white. In one in ten incidents directed against Asian men, the victim was told to 'go back to where you came from', or 'to your own country'. Often these racist epithets were combined, such as '[t]hey call me a black fucking Paki, and they said I shouldn't be here, to go home'. In other instances, the victim ascribed a racial motive to the perpetrator because of the circumstances of the incident. This was sometimes because the incident had occurred without prior history, warning, or provocation: '[w]e had no conversation—didn't know the guy—first thing that happened was that he hit me. He just wouldn't have done it if I was white.' On other occasions, this perception stemmed from the fact the victim was one of a few or the only Asian family living in the block; that similar incidents had occurred to minority families living nearby; or that other expressions of racist antipathy had occurred in the past.

Africans and Afro-Caribbeans

About half of the incidents mentioned by African and Afro-Caribbean men (54 per cent) and women (46 per cent) took place at, around, or near their home addresses. All the incidents mentioned by African and Afro-Caribbean respondents involved white perpetrators. In common with the experience of the Asian respondents, most of these incidents consisted of insults and verbal abuse (54 per cent for women and 69 per cent for men) involved unprovoked abuse or harassment:

Most recent incident:

A white guy came out of a pub and started abusing me. He called me a 'wog' and a 'nigger'. He first called me a wog and when I challenged him he called me nigger. It nearly turned [in]to a fight but a police car drove by and we broke it up. It ended in just words between us. *What was it about the incident which makes you believe that the attack was racially motivated?* Well his words. Wog and nigger. If that isn't racial, what is?

Second most recent incident:

I was walking down this road. I had a suit on as I was going for an interview when a blue van drove past and a white guy threw an egg at me. It was a fresh egg. Well the egg broke and stained my suit. I . . . had to go back home to change. I was late for the interview and didn't get the job [African].

Two white boys in a car slowed down as they passed me and shouted 'get out of the way stupid nigger'. *What was it about the incident which makes you believe that the attack was racially motivated?* Well, they shouted nigger didn't they and they were white. So it's obvious isn't it [Afro-Caribbean].

A number of other incidents arose out of a conflict with neighbours:

We had a party. Neighbours were informed before hand. My neighbours threw a bag of rubbish at my guests. *What was it about the incident which makes you believe that the attack was racially motivated?* The person involved was white. The type of language used by the man [African].

The woman's [neighbour] dog kept on barking and barking that it was so loud my baby couldn't sleep so I went to the woman and complained. She told me to get lost, called me a black bastard and slammed the door in my face. The dog was so disturbing that I reported it to the council. *What was it about the incident which makes you believe that the attack was racially motivated?* She said I was a black bastard and that I shouldn't bother her. Yes, she's white so it was a racial thing wasn't it? [African].

African and Afro-Caribbean men were the most likely of all ethnic–gender groups to mention threatened or actual property damage (in 46 per cent of cases).

Petrol was poured through the letter box and set alight. That's all [Afro-Caribbean].

Came home from college and found damage on my door and it has been set on fire, with graffiti on the wall calling me names.

First Incident:

Someone smashed my car windscreen. Nothing was taken. It happened in the evening or night. *What was it about the incident which makes you believe that the attack was racially motivated?* All over the car was written 'Out, out Paki' [*sic*].

Second Incident:

I came back in my car with children from shopping. I parked my car. Then the youngest son from next door (about ten) went to my doorstep, took down his trousers and urinated in front of me and my children. *What was it about the incident which makes you believe that the attack was racially motivated?* In relation to all the other things that they had done like cutting my telephone wires at least twenty times, stealing my son's glasses and me and my children were racially abused every single day [African].

African and Afro-Caribbean men mentioned incidents perpetrated by other males either in a group (60 per cent) or alone (40 per cent). In just under half of the incidents (45 per cent) the perpetrators were aged between 16 and 25, one fifth were school age, and one in three older people.

When explaining the basis for their perception that the incident was racially motivated, African and Afro-Caribbean men most often said that the perpetrators had referred to their race (54 per cent). They also mentioned that damage had been done to their property with no apparent motive other than racism, that they were told to 'go back to your own country', and that they were the only black people in the neighbourhood and were being singled out as victims of crime. Three out of ten respondents said that they felt that the incident was racially motivated, but had no proof.

About one in three of the incidents mentioned by African and Afro-Caribbean women occurred in their place of work. They were also more likely than any other group to know the perpetrator involved, suggesting that some of these incidents involved co-workers. In six out of ten incidents they were harassed by a sole male perpetrator and in more than half of them they knew the perpetrator involved. In more than half of the incidents described by African/Caribbean women, their race was mentioned and in one incident in ten they were told to 'go back to your own country'. 15 per cent of the incidents were said to have been part of a process of harassment over a longer period.

White People

In many ways the incidents mentioned by white women were similar to those mentioned by Asian and Afro-Caribbean women. A large proportion occurred in the vicinity of their home; many involved unprovoked abusive language and insulting behaviour. However, one very important difference between the incidents mentioned by white women and other groups was the likelihood of it involving theft. Those mentioned by white women were twice as likely to involve theft as those mentioned by Asian women and four times as likely as those mentioned by African and Afro-Caribbean women.

A striking feature of the incidents described by white women is the large proportion of cases in which white perpetrators were involved. White people were said to have been involved as aggressors in more than four out of the ten incidents directed at white women when the race of the perpetrator was known. In three incidents the perpetrators were *all* white and one other involved a mainly white group. Of the remaining six cases, four involved African/Caribbeans, one Asians, and one involved a mixed but mainly black group.

It is evident from some of the things said by white women when asked to describe their experience that some, and perhaps all, of the incidents in which other whites were the aggressors were directed against them because of their association with black or Asian people. The question of violence directed against people in mixed race relationships is explored below.

The types of incidents mentioned by white men diverged considerably from those mentioned by other ethnic–gender groups. Just under half of the incidents described in full by white men (43 per cent) involved theft of property. People of all ethnic and gender groups mentioned incidents of theft from their person or home which they thought to have been racially motivated. However, the rate for white men was at least twice that for any other group and over five times that for African/Caribbean women. The extent to which an incident involving economic gain can also be said to be partly or fully motivated by racism is problematic. That so many of the incidents involving white men involved theft suggests that their experience of 'racially motivated' crime is rather different from those for which no such economic motive was involved. The majority of incidents mentioned by white men involved black perpetrators (78 per cent), a mixed but mainly black group (11 per cent), and Asian (11 per cent).

The transcripts of the open ended questions in the survey reveal a range of types of incidents. Some incidents involve theft from the person, burglary, and theft from cars where the victim did not know who the perpetrator was, but believed that he or she was black. The belief that the incident was perpetrated by a black person carried with it the ascription of racial hatred for several respondents, even when the race of the offender was not known:

Most recent incident:

Car window was smashed. Cassette was stolen. Car smashed. *What was it about the incident which makes you believe that the attack was racially motivated?* Car was parked in front of this block. . . . people know my car. I think it was done purposely.

Second most recent incident:

Somebody tried to break in. An attempt to break in through front door. When I came home the front door lock was [broken]. Nothing stolen. *What was it about the incident which makes you believe that the attack was racially motivated?* That I can't say. Not sure. But I think it may be racially motivated.

I'd had words with a black man earlier for trying to steal my geraniums. At 3 o'clock in the morning I had a brick put through my window. *What was it about the incident which makes you believe that the attack was racially motivated?* A lot of the young blacks in the area always hate whites. They whisper as you go by and I feel their hatred.

In some cases, a racial motive was ascribed simply because the offender was black:

About three of them. One of the pulled on my [chain]. [I didn't] have much money on me . . . they took my money, jewels, watch, beat me up. *What was it about the incident which makes you believe that the attack was racially motivated?* The group were all blacks. Nothing else.

In one case, the respondent complained of being wrongly accused of doing damage to the home of some of his black neighbours:

Most recent incident:

She just used to shout up the stairs. Things like you fucking white trash. All this type of thing, I can't remember every thing she call us. *What was it about the incident which makes you believe that the attack was racially motivated?* Because of the names she called us, white bastards and white trash. She said we did things to her home because we didn't like coloured people.

Second most recent incident:

Down stairs this time smashed the place up, tore light fittings wrote NF on her wall . . . said we done it because we didn't like black [people]. *What was it about the incident which makes you believe that the attack was racially motivated?* She blamed us because she said we were against her because she was black.

In several incidents detailed in full, white respondents described being unexpectedly set upon by a group of black people:

Eight people jumped out of a car and started hitting me and my mates. One of them had a bar. They just started hitting. With a bar. On my head and that. *What was it about the incident which makes you believe that the attack was racially motivated?* They had no other reason. I was just in the street and they started, with my mates, hitting you know, with a bar.

Three guys attacked me. Later took off and went to the pub. Physical damage. Cuts and bruises on my face and chest. What *was it about the incident which makes you believe that the attack was racially motivated?* Because the attackers were black people.

In another instance, the respondent complained about being harassed by the next-door neighbours' 'all-night party' and of being called names when they protested:

They had a very noisy all night party next door. They kept banging and making noise. When they saw I was disturbed by it they called me names. Whitey Honkey, etc. and started banging on my front door. *What was it about the incident which makes you believe that the attack was racially motivated?* They kept banging on my door and wall. Then they covered up my spy hole so I couldn't see them. They were all blacks and they called me honkey and that.

It is evident that a not insignificant group of white people perceived themselves to have been victim of racially motivated incidents. This finding contradicts conventional wisdom in a number of respects. First, even those official reports which have included white people as potential victims of racial attack have found that such experience is rare. The Home Office (1981) report found that white people were fifty times less likely that Asians and thirty-six times less likely than Afro-Caribbeans to be victims of a racial attack. This figure is the most widely quoted finding of the study and, arguably, on the subject more generally. A replication of this study conducted in 1987 found the differential victimization rate to be even more pronounced, with that for Asians being 141 times that for white and for black people forty-three time that for whites (Seagrave, 1989: 20). Secondly, the experience of violent racism must considered in the context of the historicity of violence against ethnic minorities in Britain, the connectedness of behaviour and experience to the ideas and practices of racism, and unequal power relationships between white and 'non-white' peoples.

White people's perception that crimes committed against them by blacks were 'racially motivated' cannot be dismissed out of hand, however. Rather, these findings present a challenge to orthodox definitions of violent racism. First, they suggest that *white people may be exposed to **anti-black** sentiment and violence because of their association with people from ethnic minorities*. Secondly, the data suggest that white people do perceive themselves to be vulnerable to offences committed against them by black people and that they do sometimes attribute 'racial' motives to such experiences. As one white survey respondent put it:

This harassment thing you are doing is too one-sided. How come you only ask about racial attacks on Asian or Afro-Caribbeans, how about on we whites? Anything could have happened that day [after complaining about a neighbour's party], fire, rape anything, the police should keep their eyes on the block.

Two linked explanations of the perceptions of white people may be developed. First, the ascription of a racial motive to black crime against whites may be, itself, simply a form of racism. Secondly, these experiences may reflect a real sense of vulnerability experienced by white working-class inner-city residents.

It is important to note that ideologies linking (black) immigrants with crime have a long history in British society (Solomos, 1988: 88–118), and since the 1970s the involvement of black people in 'street crime' has been an important theme in popular language and political and policy debates (Solomos, 1988: 106). The co-articulation of black people and crime was a theme propagated and developed in the speeches of Enoch Powell in the 1970s and was reflected in the 'marches against mugging' of the National Front in 1977 and 1978 in Lewisham. For example, when, the National Front organized a march through the East End in the 1970s, 'it was specifically directed against *black muggings*—no qualifications, no inverted commas, no hesitation' (Hall *et al.*, 1978: 333).

That many white people understand crime and disorder to be connected with the presence of black people is evident in McConville and Shepherd's (1992) study of neighbourhood watch, which found that although most of their respondents were unwilling to identify a 'criminal type', 'for many, crime is associated with black people, and respondents were without prompting quite willing to identify ethnic minorities as the principal sources of their crime concern' (McConville and Shepherd, 1992: 110).

This 'streak of racism' was most striking in London where 'some 36 per cent of white respondents in all areas spontaneously blamed black people for crime or made overt racist comments in the course of the interviews'. While some were diffident in expressing their views, others gave full vent to their feelings:

Black people are dangerous animals. I shouldn't say this, but when [a mugging] happens, I hate all blacks. I don't normally allow a black in this house . . . If you say to me who are the first football hooligans, I would say the British; they were the ones slung out of Europe. You say to a black that mugging is a black crime, crash! that's a red rag to a bull. They won't have it.

They have got no manners and no respect. . . . They still think that they are living in a jungle and they forget themselves that they are living in England.

. . . Half the white people have put their tail between their bloody legs and they've run, instead of staying put. Most of what the blacks do is mugging; they are 'steaming' and all that kind of stuff [McConville and Shepherd, 1992: 110–11].

The sense of *vulnerability* of white people to the presence of blacks was also articulated by Enoch Powell. In his infamous 'rivers of blood' speech on 20 April 1968, Powell suggested that '[d]iscrimination . . . was being experienced, not by blacks, but by whites—"those among whom they have come". This invocation—direct to the experience of unsettlement in a settled life, to the *fear of change*—is the great emergent theme of Mr Powell's speech' (Hall *et al.*, 1978: 246). It was also on this occasion that Powell spoke of 'the little old lady of Wolverhampton' (the one nobody ever found), who had 'excreta pushed through her letter box' and endured the racialist abuse of 'charming wide-eyed grinning piccanninies' (Hall *et al.*, 1978: 245; Gilroy, 1987: 87).

Mixed-race Families and Relationships

It was noted above that 40 per cent of the victimization of white women was perpetrated by other white people. It is not possible to explain this finding fully from the survey data, but it is evident that at least some of these incidents were directed at white women because of their association with black or Asian people.[16] Several of the comments made in interviews indicated that white women themselves or their children experienced racist verbal abuse because of the children's ethnic origin. One respondent also complained of the 'negative attitude', manner, and behaviour of a policeman on an occasion when she attended a police station. In this incident, the woman attributed the policeman's manner to the fact that she attended the station with a black male friend. One Afro-Caribbean man also com-

[16] See also the experience of Ms J described in detail below. Several cases of violence against mixed-race families have been reported in the media recently. Of these, the best known targets are the comic actors Lenny Henry and Dawn French. On 6 March 1991 the daily newspaper, *Today*, reported that the Ku Klux Klan had targeted the couple with offensive material. On this occasion the French-Henrys were sent a 'tile . . . with a picture of St George on the front of it and on the back it said "You have been visited by the Ku Klux Klan". According to the article, "The National Front has always lurked in the background, sending abusive letters and smearing slogans on Dawn and Lenny's home. Last year . . . bigots daubed the NF slogan above the couple's front door using human excrement". Dawn French commented, 'Just yesterday, I got a letter from somebody who writes to me regularly as a "Nigger Lover".'

mented that he had been 'given hassle' by a 'white gang' because he was 'with a white girl': 'as I was walking down the street a big posse of white kids said to me; eh! nigger shouldn't be walking with a white girl'.

That a large proportion of the experience of white women should be at the hands of other white people indicates the importance of recognizing the complexity of the problem of racial harassment, and the risk of throwing the baby out with the bath-water. However, given dominant attitudes towards 'racial-mixing', this finding should hardly be surprising. Negative attitudes are evident throughout the discussion of 'race' in Britain. For example, the reaction of parliamentarians to the 1965 Race Relations Act included warnings about the dangers of racial mixing, including the apocalyptic view that 'the English people have started to commit race suicide' (Cyril Osborne); that 'the breeding of millions of half-caste children would . . . produce a generation of misfits' (Mr Sandy), and 'in thirty years we would be a coffee-coloured nation' (Mr Cordle) (Hall *et al.*, 1978: 240). That such attitudes live on, at least among right-wingers, is evident in a leaflet distributed by the explicitly racist organization, English Solidarity, cited in the preface to this volume. Small's study of 'racialized relations' in Liverpool also points to deeply racist attitudes towards racially mixed people and white people who associate with blacks:

whites who live in Liverpool 8 [the area in which the majority of Liverpool's black population lives] are regarded as suspect, even 'white trash' by whites outside the area (Gifford *et al.*, 1989). . . . Sexual relations between black people and whites [are] viewed by whites as biologically and socially undesirable . . . the white women who are party to such actions—and it is mostly women—are seen as degenerate, even prostitutes, while the black men are seen as sexually wanton, even 'pimps'. . . . Attitudes to what might become of such relations are equally pronounced. 'Black people of mixed origins' are seen as an inferior species, biologically degenerate, psychologically unstable and socially maladjusted, attitudes which have often been systematically elaborated and which reveal deep historical roots. . . . Instead of viewing a pattern of inter-dating as evidence of 'racial harmony', it is better to note that it is confined to a small section of the white population, the participants are regarded with disdain, even disgust, by others and the attitudes and perspectives of black women are not taken into account [Small, 1991: 517–18].

With the exception of a small number of studies, however, the experiences of violence among racially mixed individuals and families have been overlooked. An exception is a survey conducted by the Department of the Environment (DoE), which found that in one local authority, nearly half of the white people living in mixed-race households who were interviewed said they or another member of their household had been racially harassed (see FitzGerald and Ellis, 1990: 54). These observations about the different experiences of white people, their relationships with and attitudes towards ethnic minorities echo the words of David Thomas, who argues that:

The effect of pursuing a more differentiated approach to the personal racism of whites is that beliefs about whites will cease to be blanket appraisals. Any blanket appraisals that 'racism is a white problem' and 'all whites are incurably racist' are just that—as blankets they keep myths and stereotypes warm, and smother contact, inquiry and exploration. They protect whites and blacks from encountering each other. How can our ideas and actions against personal and institutional racism have any cutting edge if they are based on superficial propositions that homogenise whites and ignore the complexity of their personal dispositions towards blacks? [Thomas, 1986: 83].

Effects of Victimization

Taking aggregated figures for all groups, racial harassment appears to be thought of as a relatively unimportant problem. It is not considered by many to be a priority for the police, nor does it comprise a particularly salient fear for the majority of residents. When these figures are disaggregated, however, the picture changes dramatically. Particularly striking is that one quarter of the Asian women thought racial harassment a big problem; they ranked it second only to crime and a police priority after only burglary and street robbery.

Some of the victims said that the experience had made little impact on them, while for others the experience, threat, and fear of racial harassment had a considerable effect. The most common emotional reaction to the incident among the sample as a whole was anger (70 per cent), followed by shock (44 per cent), and fear (27 per cent); about 10 per cent mentioned no emotional reactions. The pattern is similar for different ethnic groups, with the exception of Asian women, 60 per cent of whom said that they became fearful as a result of their experience. When asked how long the worst effects took to wear off, one quarter of the whole sample said they had worn off within a few hours and a further quarter within a few days. For more than one fifth, however, the effects were still continuing. Again, Asian women were more likely than any other ethnic–gender group to feel the effects for longer, nearly one third of whom stated *that the worst effects of the incident were still continuing* at the time of the interview.

The gender differences in fear of racial harassment and in the extent to which it is thought to be a problem observed in this survey broadly confirms existing research on fear of crime. However, such differences are not explained easily with survey data, as is evident in academic debate on this subject. In this survey, the small differences in victimization rates between sexes might account for a small proportion of the difference in concern between African-Caribbean men and women, the latter being somewhat more likely to be victimized and were more fearful. Among Asians, however, men were more likely to be victimized and yet they were less fearful.

Stanko, reviewing explanations of gender differences in fear of crime, notes that many focus on issues related to gender experience and gender role expectations (Stanko, 1987: 126). From this perspective, researchers speculate whether men are simply reluctant to report fear and feel less vulnerable to interpersonal violence and more secure than women because of the social expectations upon them to be brave and fearless. This speculation is, as Stanko suggests, 'squarely located in one gender expectation: men's bravado' (Stanko, 1987: 126), a display which is clearly linked to what men are supposed to live up to:

A 'real' man is a strong, heterosexual male protector, capable of taking care of himself and, if necessary, guarding his and others' safety aggressively. He is the man who will stand up in a fight, but will not abuse his power by unnecessarily victimising others. And, according to the mythology of the 'real man', he will do so fearlessly [Stanko, 1990: 110].

Alternatively, gender differences in fear of crime may be explained because of differences in perception of social and physical vulnerability (Skogan and Maxfield, 1981). For Skogan and Maxfield, physical vulnerability concerns 'openness to attack, powerlessness to resist and exposure to physical and emotional consequences if attacked'; and social vulnerability involves 'daily exposure to the threat of victimization and limited means for coping with the medical and economic consequences of victimization' . Thus fear is a logical assessment of the ability of women and the elderly physically to withstand violence. (Skogan and Maxfield, 1981: 77–8; cited in Stanko, 1987: 128).

Turning attention to feminist theory and the subjective reality of lived experience, Stanko argues that women's fear of crime is related to a fear of and vulnerability to rape (Riger and Gordon, 1981). It is also from feminist literature that the extent of under-reporting of women's experience of male violence to both official agencies and surveys is apparent. Thus, 'daily, commonly taken-for-granted experiences of women contribute to the hostile and intimidating atmosphere wherein women are presumably supposed to feel safe' (Stanko, 1987: 130). Throughout this work, emphasis is placed on the importance of understanding how different people experience their lives and how this is affected by where or how they live and who they are (Stanko, 1990: 6). For men, an additional sense of security and perhaps actual avoidance of danger: 'comes from strength, backed up by physical ability and enhanced by the advantages of economic, racial or sexual status' (*ibid.*).

The data from this survey go some way to supporting a theory based on actual risk of attack. Although it seems very likely that this survey will have been as unsuccessful as others in capturing the full extent of the experience of victimization (in terms of its estimate of the number of victims and the frequency of their victimization), it is evident that some people are more likely to become victim than others, and that this has an effect on their perceptions of themselves as vulnerable and in need of protection. Specifically, white people are at less risk of experiencing a racial incident, and this appears to be related to the extent of fear, concern about the problem, and beliefs about policing priorities. However, the data also suggest that vulnerability must also play a part, particularly when explaining gender differences.

Perpetrators

The survey found that the people involved in carrying out the harassment or attack were predominantly male, aged 16 to 25, and most often acted in a group.[17] Only 15 per cent of the victims interviewed in the survey said that the perpetrators were of school age, 57 per cent said they were aged between 16 and 25, while 27 per cent said their assailants were older. The analysis of incidents recorded by the

---

[17] In one fifth of the incidents detailed in full in the survey the victim had no idea who the perpetrator was (25 of 118). The following analyses are made on the basis of those where it was known.

police diverged somewhat from the survey findings, in that 57 per cent of the suspects identified were aged 11–15, 24 per cent were aged between 16 and 24, and 11 per cent were over 24.

There was some variation in the number that victims said were involved in the incident (see Table 7.12). In particular, some ethnic–gender groups were much more likely to have been harassed by a gang and less likely to have faced a sole assailant than other ethnic–gender groups. Thus, 83 per cent of the incidents mentioned by Asian men, 85 per cent by Asian women, and 91 per cent by Asian council tenants involved more than one perpetrator. Just fewer than half of the incidents mentioned by Asians involved a group of four or more aggressors. For both Afro-Caribbean men and women, more incidents involved lone aggressors than groups. 59 per cent and 40 per cent of Afro-Caribbean women and men, respectively, mentioned an individual perpetrator. One third of incidents involving white men and 40 per cent of those involving white women involved an aggressor alone.

The survey is inconsistent with the police view that the perpetrators of racial violence tend to be children known to the victim. Although police records suggest the involvement of mainly young

Table 7.12 *Number of perpetrators involved in the incident[1] (%)*

Number	WM	WF	ACM	ACF	AM	AF	ACT[2]
1	33	40	29	59	17	15	9
2	8	21	29	10	26	18	24
3	41	10	10	–	17	21	21
4	–	10	10	–	20	24	18
5	–	10	–	19	3	10	6
6	–	–	–	–	3	3	4
7	–	10	–	–	–	–	–
8 or more	16	–	19	10	13	10	18
Not stated[3]	14	17	23	23	22	27	15
Unweighted n =	14	12	13	13	58	45	39

[1] Those unable to state the number of perpetrators have been excluded from this analysis and the number falling into this category is noted at the bottom of the table (see also note 3). It should also be noted that older people were more likely to give a 'don't know/not stated' response than younger; 34% of respondents aged 60+ compared with 14% of those aged 16–24 respectively giving these responses.

[2] Asian council tenants.

[3] This will include those incidents (e.g. criminal damage) where the perpetrator(s) could not be known to the respondent.

people, the survey data contradict this: only 15 per cent were of school age. One half were young adults (57 per cent were aged 16–25) and one quarter older people (27 per cent were older than 25). Secondly, the perpetrators tended not to be known to the victim, and in the cases when they were known, they were not well known. For the sample as a whole, in only one quarter of the incidents was any of the perpetrators known (n=26), half of which were known just by sight. 39 per cent of the sample said they thought they could describe the people involved and 16 per cent could name them.

Racial Motivation: Experience and Context

The majority of instances of violence revealed by the survey consisted of verbal abuse and insulting behaviour. Much of this abuse was clearly *racialized,* through the use of racially derogatory epithets, slogans, and remarks. In order to comprehend the experience of this form of behaviour, it is necessary to distinguish between the denotative and connotative meaning of racial epithets. The difficult question concerns the objective or denotative meaning which may be attached to different forms of epithet directed against specific groups, how this is experienced, and how meaning is connoted to these epithets.

First, let us take simple references to 'race' or 'ethnicity' such as some aspect of physical appearance (e.g. skin pigmentation), national and geographical origin. To describe someone, for example, as black, white, English, Pakistani, European, African, Asian, Jewish etc. does not denote superiority or inferiority or carry, in and of itself, positive or negative meanings. These proper nouns or 'names' are commonly used in everyday speech to describe the person's appearance, parentage, or 'background'.

However, within the language itself, terms of race are not neutral in their connotations. The synonyms listed in *Chambers English Dictionary* for 'white' include 'of the light complexion characteristic of Europeans: pure: unblemished: innocent: purified from sin: auspicious, favourable: reliable, honest'. For 'white man', the dictionary offers: 'one of the white race: assumed to deal fairly with others' (colloquial). Despite its comprehensiveness, *Chambers* offers no definition for 'white trash'. 'Black', by way of contrast, means: 'dismal: sullen: horrible: dusky: foul, dirty: malignant: illicit: Negro, of African, West Indian descent (often *offensive; acceptable in US* . . . S. Africa): coloured, of mixed descent'.

In addition to the skew (built into the language, or at least *Chambers'* orthodox interpretation of it), these terms describing race or ethnicity may be given a negative connotation depending on the context within which they are used, by whom and to whom they are addressed. Obviously, the terms can be used as an insult. By adding an insulting comment or a swearword, a neutral term of identity may be turned into a racially derogatory remark. In the comments transcribed above, respondents referred to being called 'black bastard' or 'white trash'. Coupling a racial signifier with a common swearword creates a racialized epithet. Much of the racial abuse described above, however, is negative both in connotation and denotation. The epithets mentioned included 'Paki', 'black Paki', 'immigrant', 'wog', 'nigger', and, directed at a white person, 'honky'.

This brings us to the question whether calling someone 'white' is the same as calling someone 'black'. On the face of it, the answer seems to be yes. We can surely have no quarrel with the use of either word as a description of someone's physical appearance, and there seems to be no ground for arguing that references to 'white' skin are any more or less legitimate than references to 'black' skin. Nonetheless, because the two terms carry different significance in the context of Britain and the English language, the use of each cannot be said to be equivalent. To say 'the Brits are invading' carries different connotations, conjures up a very different mental image from 'the Pakis are invading'. 'Honky', as offensive as it may be, is nowhere near as powerfully insulting as 'nigger'. Attempting to insult a white English person with the phrase 'go back to your own country' would be meaningless in England. And yet, to make the same remark to a black or brown English person is profoundly exclusionary. Only if the geographical and social context is changed do anti-English terms of abuse, such as 'gringo', 'pom', 'limey', or even 'sasenach', have any real weight.

The Process of Racist Victimization and Surveys of Incidents

In Chapter 5, it was argued that attempting to break down the dynamic of violent racism into a set of discrete incidents and to disconnect them from other social processes is problematic. To illustrate this point, what follows is a description of the experience of one Asian family and of a white woman.

The A Family

The A family, comprising mother, father and eight children, have their origins in the Gujerat region of India though they were settled in East Africa for two generations. In 1973, following political and social upheaval in Kenya (Mr A's birthplace) and Uganda (Mrs A's birthplace), Mr. A gave up his job as an accountant and the family moved to London. After a period in which 'no one wanted to let [them] a flat', they found rented accommodation, but were harassed by their Pakistani landlord to the point that they were, effectively, evicted. In 1977 the family moved into their current home, then a new, council-owned three bedroom 'townhouse' in the south western corner of the North Plaistow area. Mr A believes they were the first black or Asian people to move into the neighbourhood, arriving some years before any other Asian families moved in. There were still very few Asian families living in this part of North Plaistow at the time of the study.

Immediately, some local people began to harass the family, making it clear that they did not want Asian neighbours. On the day that they moved in, a brick was thrown through a first-floor window. Over the period that they have lived in this house Mr and Mrs A and their children have suffered several physical assaults, have been threatened repeatedly, and have suffered regular racist abuse. People would bang on the door saying 'come out Pakis, we want to kill you'. On one occasion someone telephoned to say that they were going to put a bomb through the letterbox with the intention of killing the family. In 1977 Mr A was attacked from behind while in a public telephone box near his home by an assailant wielding a twelve-inch blade. Although a young man was arrested for the offence and the knife was recovered, the case was dropped after twenty white families gathered outside the local police station, calling for the boy's release, claiming that they were witnesses and that nothing had happened.

Local children and young people throw eggs and stones at family members and their home. They repeatedly kick a football against the front of the house and bang the garage door. The family have had rubbish thrown into their garden, external plumbing broken, and 'Pakis out' painted on their garage door. On one occasion a visitor to the house was beaten up and had his spectacles smashed. Mr A attributed many of the incidents to two 'hardened' and 'notorious' families (one next door and one across the street). The adults would abuse the family and encourage the children to throw stones at them and engage in nuisance behaviour. Over the past fourteen years their windows have been broken no fewer than twenty-six times. Now, Mr A says:

> we have to put a metal plate across our letter box every night. We can't leave the house empty, we are afraid to go out. We have been imprisoned in our own home. . . . When the police come they say they can't do anything. They ask 'have you been injured? then we can take action'. We have had 15 years' experience, how can we tolerate this? . . . No authority is prepared to help until someone is murdered. . . . The only time we tried to defend ourselves from boys throwing stones, both me and my wife were arrested [leaving their children alone in the house], locked up and charged with assault.

The outcome of the court case was that Mr A was bound over to keep the peace.

Counting Incidents: Attempting the Impractical

It is evident from this vignette that the attempt to count all the 'incidents' involved would, at the very least, be impractical. Initially, a somewhat arbitrary decision would have to be made about what constituted an 'incident'. Certainly a very large number of events which contravene the criminal law have occurred; there have been numerous incidents of 'assault', 'threat', and 'criminal damage'. The attempt to record as a series of incidents the experience of harassment which extends over a period of years would be impractical. Even if it were possible to record all these events it is highly unlikely that the 'victims' would be able, or prepared, to sit down with a survey researcher fully to detail each and every 'incident'. Most likely, many of these relevant 'criminal incidents' would not be disclosed to survey researchers and would simply be defined out of the investigative process.

In the event that respondents were able to recall and disclose all the events involved in their victimization the survey would face the choice of either accurately recording all these events or 'normalizing' the data. If all these 'incidents' were recorded they would have the effect of inflating 'average' rates of victimization which are, often, what surveys are aiming to produce. The alternative, and most frequently chosen, route is to place a limit on the number of incidents that can be recorded. For example, the BCS limits the number of

'series' incidents (i.e. involving the same people under similar circumstances) to an arbitrary five occurrences (see Genn, 1988). From
Mr A's perspective such a record of his victimization would be quite
meaningless.

Ms J

Ms J is a white woman who was born and grew up in the East End.
Her second marriage was to an Afro-Caribbean man and she has three
mixed-race children as well as one white daughter. Although her experience as a child and young adult was that of a white East Ender, in
later years she found herself victimized by white racism. Her first 'shattering' experiences of racial harassment were of verbal abuse, being
spat at, and pelted on one occasion with eggs and on another with golf
balls from passing car windows while in the company of black friends
or with her mixed-race children. One of the most serious incidents
which occurred during the life of the project was directed at Ms J and
a friend of African origin. What follows is a description of her experience as recorded by a local housing officer:

I moved into [a house in a road on the south western edge of the study area]
during late 1988 and moved out March [1990]. I did then, and still do live
with my four children. My first daughter aged 13 is white, and is from my
first marriage. My last 3 children aged 9, 8 and 6 are all mixed race and from
my second marriage.

From the beginning I was not welcomed and the neighbours made it obvious
to me that they did not like having me in the area. I could always sense tension in the atmosphere when I went out. They did not really talk to me or
smile back at me, but would give me bad looks, so I decided that it would
be best if I kept myself to myself. After some time some of the children would
shout out verbal abuse at me, because of my half West Indian children. They
would say things like 'wog meat, wog lover' and the like. On other occasions
they would say 'we don't want any niggers on our patch, this is our Manor
and we don't want those wogs here'. They were referring to my younger children, and my black friend who would visit from time to time.

When I would go and use the public telephone box, the boys in the area
would gather round and try to intimidate me, and be abusive. I soon learnt
that it was a close community of hardened racists, who had lived and been
brought up in the area, and did not take very kindly to new or black people
moving in.

My next door neighbour once invited me to her party, I knew that she
wanted me to attend, because she kept checking with me whether I was going

to be there. When I attended the party [the neighbour] was dressed up as a golliwog, and her grown-up children and a couple of others were dressed up in the full Ku Klux Klan uniform, with the lettering on their backs. I became afraid and wondered what was going on. They gathered round me and asked me what I was doing there, so immediately I left.

[In] March 1990, at about 6pm I was playing some reggae records, with the window open, but I kept the volume rather low. At this point Mr N from [several doors up the road], who I would classify as the ring-leader of the group of boys that constantly intimidate me, banged several times on my front door. I had previously noticed that he was working on a car directly outside my house. He was holding a hammer and said that, 'a wog friend of yours called my brother something'. He was referring to my friend called E, who used to visit me sometimes with his girlfriend. I had a mind that Mr N was making it up, and decided to disturb me because of the music I was playing. I did not like the fact that he repeatedly called E a wog, so I pretended not to understand what he was talking about. My children were standing behind me at this point and became threatened by his remarks. He then started to wave the hammer at my face and said, 'if I see any more wogs around here I will be back'. I then shut the door and he returned to the car.

At 7pm that evening E came round, and I told him about what had happened earlier, and he confirmed that he had never spoken to anyone around here, apart from me. Then all of a sudden I heard crashing and the smashing of glass, coming from the front of my house. Mr N and two other boys all bout the age of 19 or 20, smashed their way into my house. They were smashing everything in sight, with the hammers they were carrying. E and I quickly grabbed hold of the children and tried to take them upstairs. It was all happening very quickly. The boys got hold of E and was beating him about the head and the body with the hammers. E was hurt very badly, and my children were just screaming. [The next-door neighbour] informed the police, who came after the boys had left.

Before E was taken to hospital he was able to identify the perpetrators to the police, as they were still in the area. When the police returned [the neighbour] verbally identified the boys.

The day after the incident, I left the house with my children, as we were all afraid to live there. A couple of days later I returned to the house to collect a few things for the children. I noticed that the front door was open. I had been burgled and the whole house was in a mess, things were just thrown around everywhere and everything which remained had been smashed up. All our clothing had been ripped and cut to bits. The television, video and Hi Fi had all been taken, and all the other large electrical equipment had all been broken up. All the bedding and mattresses had been cut open. My children's jewellery had been taken. All my children and black friends had been cut out of my photographs, just leaving me, or any other white people behind. There was nothing in my house that was able to be re-used, due to the total destruction that had taken place. I called the police, and action is still pending[18] [Statement made by victim to Plaistow North Housing, July 1990].

These two incidents—the first assault on the house and the second aggravated burglary were, in and of themselves, traumatic for Ms J. However, the process of victimization was by no means concluded once the incidents had occurred. On the contrary, these incidents merely marked the beginning of an ongoing process which took more than eighteen months to resolve.

In the immediate aftermath of the attacks, Ms J felt 'devastated and bewildered' and as though her 'world was crumbling'. Having had her house invaded and eventually made uninhabitable by burglars in a context in which it had been made clear that her presence would not be tolerated, Ms J was, effectively, homeless. After two months, however, she was found a new home elsewhere in the borough.

When her case came to court initially, she had high hopes that 'justice would be done': The case appeared to her to be clear cut; the perpetrator had violated her house, smashed ornaments and furniture, and physically assaulted her friend. Moreover, the defendant was already in custody charged with six further offences. Although the police warned Ms J that the defence would almost certainly involve an assault on her character and allegations against her and E, Ms J recalls: 'I felt confident. I had nothing to hide. E was a law student attending Thames Polytechnic. What could go wrong. We were 100% in the right.'

In the event, however, it was not a clear-cut case. First, the defending barrister completely destroyed the credibility of Ms J and Mr E in the eyes of the jury. From the outset the defence stressed the assertion that Ms J had regular visits from Afro-Caribbean and African people. Throughout the trial, and particularly in his final speech, he referred repeatedly to the incident occurring in an 'unusual household' which 'instinctively' gave us, he said, some indication of the background to the case: '[t]he picture you get is of an unusual house-

---

[18] For some inexplicable reason, although the police visited the scene and recorded details of the incident, no forensic evidence was taken. It was not possible, therefore, to link the burglary with the perpetrators of the assault on Ms J's home and on her friend, E.

hold. . . . A large number of African or West Indian friends come and visit [Ms J]. This seems to be a fact. The inferences are up to you.'

Although Mr E was of good character and had never been in trouble with the police, he was alleged to have been a 'crack dealer' who had attempted to sell 'crack' and 'ecstasy' to Mr N's younger brother. It was inferred that the incident in question had occurred because Mr N was incensed about Mr E's behaviour and that Mr E had a crack-dealing accomplice with him at the time of the incident.[19] At one point the prosecution objected to the 'obvious attack on the character of the witnesses', arguing that it was now relevant that Mr N's character should also be assessed on the basis of his previous convictions and six outstanding charges, including offences against the person and misuse of drugs. The defence countered that since the allegation against Mr N was one of racism, he could produce the front page of a newspaper which showed him as a hero who had saved a family of Indians from burning alive in their home in March 1989. The judge commented that with regard to the defence defamation of the character of witness, 'technically the line may have been crossed [but] I will use my discretion to deny this application'. The effect was to give the prosecution licence to use explicit and coded references to the fact that Mr E was black and that Ms J had black friends in its presentation of the case.

Secondly, the defendant and defending counsel had an alternative version of events. In this version, 'coloured people' had, over the previous six or seven months, made sexual remarks to Mr N's stepmother, stolen a radio and tools from his car, and offered 'crack cocaine' to his younger brother. Rather than being an unprovoked attack on Ms J and E, Mr N described the incident as a fight resulting from Mr E saying 'come in the crack house'. According to Mr N, the fight started outside the house, involved Mr E and an accomplice, and the damage was caused by the struggle between him and his two black assailants. This version of events was assisted by an unexplained item of evidence—a cut on the top of Mr N's head. This was used by the defence as evidence that a fight had taken place during which Mr N himself was injured. Mr N's evidence included comments to the effect that he had been hit over the head from behind

---

[19] At one point the defending barrister went to far as to ask 'was the person who was there either of the other [black] people who were with you in the court room yesterday', referring to me personally and a plain-clothes black police officer who had been in court the day before.

by Mr E's accomplice. Although the attending police officers stated specifically that they had seen no blood on Mr N at the time of the offence, the evidence of the police surgeon who attended showed that Mr N did indeed have a cut by the time he was in custody. In fact, it appears that this injury occurred after the incident while he was in police custody.[20]

Thirdly, not only was the element of racism in Mr N's language and stated purpose not brought out in the case by the prosecution, it was explicitly down-played. Mr N and witnesses for the defence consistently denied that the incident was racially motivated, claiming to treat black people 'the same as everyone else'. The disappearance of racism from the case was assisted by the appearance in the witness box of a young man, described by the defence as 'mulatto, half-caste', who testified that he was 'best of mates' with Mr N who treated everyone the same and had no bias or hatred towards black people.[21] In his summing up the judge commented that racism was not relevant and questioned the need for a specialised racial incident squad. He commented that, '[w]e live in what is now a multi-racial society. This brings problems and we must work to overcome these problems. . . . I put it to you that the racial element should not loom too large in the case. . . . In anger many words are said.'

In sum, in the courtroom the case was by no means clear-cut. Rather, there were two competing accounts of events which were completely at odds with one another. The defence evidence was not strong and there were conflicts between that provided by Mr N, and his brother and another friend who were witnesses to the incident. But Ms J and Mr E had not been 'good' witnesses either. There were points at which their evidence conflicted (Ms J said there were three assailants; Mr E thought there were two). Their characters were destroyed by the defence. The police evidence was also not strong. There was no forensic evidence; no pictures of the damage done to the house. There was conflict between the police evidence and the evidence of the police surgeon with regard to Mr N's head injury. The defending barrister was sharp and used a range of subtle and blatant strategies to good effect. The prosecution, by contrast, was slow failed to bring out some important factors in the case, and concluded

---

[20] I was informed after the trial that the cut on Mr N's head had been a instance of 'summary justice' inflicted by the door of a police van.

[21] I have been informed by a number of police officers that this is a tactic used regularly by defending counsel in racial incidents.

its case weakly. The racial motive was deemed irrelevant and, indeed, was destroyed in the eyes of the court. As a result, it was not possible for the jury to be any more convinced that Ms J and Mr E were telling the truth than that Mr N was. They had to be sure beyond reasonable doubt that Mr E and Ms J's story was the true one before they could convict. In the event, they did not. Mr N was acquitted on all three counts of aggravated burglary, assault, and criminal damage.

As we left the court, the housing officer who had attended the case was in tears. The police officer was furious, although the outcome of the case had been apparent since the day before the end of the trial. He said:

its a total f—ing travesty of justice; that's the only words for it. The judge was totally biased. Allowing the defence counsel to defame the witnesses in this way was totally outrageous, disgusting. I feel very angry. Being called an unusual household simply because many of your friends are black shouldn't have been allowed. Basically, if you're black you are either a drug dealer or a whore.

Ms J's immediate emotional reaction was that of anger: 'tears welled in my eyes, anger burned within and Mr N grinned. If I had a gun, he would have died with that expression.' Later I asked Ms J how she felt about the outcome of the court case:

Immediately after it I kind of felt numb and felt that I had always been led to believe this was a democratic country and that justice would be done . . . I felt awkward about the fact that I was condemned for having black friends, cause that was what it felt like. It felt like, throughout the trial, that I had an 'unusual household' because I had black friends and I was condemned for that. It then made me worry about my own identity, and where I actually fitted in. And it also gave me an inward strength that made me feel like I was going to fight.

What about the court officials, how do they make you feel?

Particularly the defending barrister and the judge. Well, they made *me* feel like I had something to be guilty for. That I had done some terrible thing. That I wasn't a normal person. That's kind of how I felt. I felt very angry and very embittered.

Would you . . . I mean, maybe this is too much of a leading question, but . . . would you say that the courtroom experience was another form of victimisation?

Yeah. I was victimised. I was condemned for having black friends.

Conclusion

The two case studies presented above draw together some of the themes addressed in this Chapter and point to some of the issues to be examined in the analysis of policing in the next. The key point is that the experience of violent racism is not reducible to an isolated incident, or even a collection of incidents. Victimization and racialization—the processes by which a person *becomes* a victim of this form of crime are cumulative, comprised of various encounters with racism, some of which may be physically violent, some lying only at the fringes of what most people would define as violent or aggressive. Some of these experiences are subtle and amount to no more than becoming aware that someone is annoyed or disgusted by the presence of black people or fleeting instances such as a half-heard racist joke or epithet. At the other end of this continuum are the more easily remembered instances when racism is coupled with physical aggression or violence. Changing the emphasis from racial violence to violent racism allows the experience of becoming its victim to be connected to other process of racialisation and exclusion. As Paul Gordon (1993) argues:

A society that wishes to deal effectively with racist violence must face the uncomfortable and inconvenient fact that such violence, while a serious problem in and of itself, is also a manifestation of something larger: it is an expression of racism, in particular of white exclusionism or territorialism, and if it is serious about wanting to do something about it, rather than mere remedial work, then it must address that racism. In Britain, this is the racism that for more than three decades has defined black people as a problem for white society, whose entry must be controlled; which has time and again expressed its concern, in the clichés of the racist imagination, at possible 'swamping', 'flooding' and 'invasion' by Third World immigrants. Racist violence, on the streets, in the housing estates, at work and in schools and colleges, is the everyday expression—and consequence—of this policy of white exclusionism

It is evident from the discussion of the local context that the experience of living in Newham differs among different ethnic groups. For white East Enders, East London is their 'natural' home, one over which they are able to exert a territorial imperative and which they act to defend. The literature reviewed above bears witness to the sense of territoriality, racial exclusivity, and hostility to 'interlopers' felt among the white community in the area. This provides white East

Enders with a sense of place, identity, and security which does not automatically extend to North Plaistow's ethnic minorities. It must be added that hostility to 'interlopers' may extend to their white associates. Ms J's experience illustrates that white people are not immune to challenges to their identity and security as East Enders.

The opposite side of this coin for ethnic minority communities is the experience of being defined as 'out of place' in the neighbourhood where they live and, quite likely, were born. The language described by the ethnic minority victims in the survey—being told that they are 'not wanted here', to 'go home' or 'back to where you came from'— illustrates the point. Sadly, even at a time when the majority of the ethnic minority community in Newham will be *indigenous*, the very notion of a 'real East Ender' carries racially exclusive connotations.

The pattern of violent racism directed specifically against black and brown minorities[22] which emerges in the history and contemporary experience is dialectically related to racist ideologies. Black and Asian people have been identified as a problem (or more accurately a set of problems (Gilroy, 1987)) which justifies or promotes exclusionary practices including intimidation, harassment, and attack. The exclusionary racist rhetoric accompanying the incidents mentioned above by Afro-Caribbeans and Asians resonates with that of political and common-sense racism.

Some account must also be taken of the power relationship between white majority and ethnic minority communities. This cannot, however, consist in a reductionist notion of racism. In particular, the formulation that racism = power + prejudice in which black people can be the only 'victims' of racism and whites the only 'perpetrators' does not withstand empirical or theoretical scrutiny. This position and the 'municipal anti-racism' which was its author have been criticized from a number of perspectives and exposed as simplistic and impotent in terms of both politics and policy, however well-intentioned (Gilroy, 1987: 136–51; Gilroy, 1990). The problems with such a formulation, according to Gilroy, are that it endorses the idea that racial groups are *real* in the sense of being fixed and exclusive, as an unproblematic common-sense category which can be taken

---

[22] As Hesse *et al.*, found in their study of neighbouring Waltham Forest, 'there was absolutely no evidence of a historical pattern of attacks, abuse and violations of white communities. Furthermore, there was no particular region of the Borough which could be identified as a locale where racial harassment of people because they are white regularly took place' (Hesse *et al.*, 1992: 41).

for granted (Smith, 1989; Solomos, 1988). The political problems which attend it are thereby reduced to prejudice:

Races are political collectivities not ahistorical essences. 'Race' is, after all, not the property of powerful, prejudiced individuals but an effect of complex relationships between dominant and subordinate social groups. If whites have shared the same job centres, schools, police cells, parties and streets with blacks, in what sense can we speak of them having additional power? [Gilroy, 1987: 149].

Despite this critique of a reified notion of 'races' and racism, however, it is necessary to retain an understanding of power relationships between ethnic minority and majority communities. Most obviously, the fact that the ethnic minorites in Britain make up only a very small proportion of the population (6 per cent in total) place them in a vulnerable position. Even in Newham, with one of the highest concentrations of ethnic minorities in the country, white people are still in the majority. In North Plaistow, wherein some specific localities have more than 50 per cent concentration of ethnic minorities, white people remain the largest ethnic group. This experience of being a minority introduces an important element of experiential context:

In contrast to his or her black counterpart who encounters white majorities daily, the white person rarely, if ever, finds himself in a wholly black situation. The experience is not a comfortable one, at least not at first. One feels isolated and self-conscious and acutely aware of looks or glances cast in one's direction. One becomes extremely sensitive to half-heard comments or any suggestion that one is being mocked [Parkes, 1984; cited in Thomas, 1986: 80].

In addition to being a small minority of the British population, people of African, Caribbean, and Asian origin are economically weak relative to their numbers. Ethnic minorities are under-represented in national and local political institutions. Even in localities with a high proportion of ethnic minorities, political and economic resources lie mainly within sections of the white community. Land, industry, and commerce which are in private hands are owned principally by white individuals, corporations, and institutions. The local and central state bureaucracies which own or control a large proportion of economic resources are also controlled, by and large, by white people. Although Newham have pursued equal opportunities policies at the level of political representation and the composition of the workforce, the balance remains tipped in favour of white people. Newham's three parliamentary representatives are white and the elected members of the local council do not represent the ethnic mix of the locality. In 1986, the London Borough of Newham still employed only 300 black people out of a workforce of 11,000, most of whom were in the lower grades in the organization.[23]

Finally, power may also be seen in terms of access to a discourse which defines individuals as superior/inferior, insider/outsider, in/out of place, in/out of one's own country, one of 'us'/one of 'them', white/non-white. As Gilroy and others have argued black people have been historically, and are contemporarily, defined as other than European, British, English, or East Enders. Such inclusionary/exclusionary ideologies give rise to a form of personal power to which only white people have recourse. As Hall *et al.* suggest: '[t]he assumption of superiority over all other peoples is often a quiet, unspoken one, but it is largely unquestioning; and it is especially strong with respect to former "natives"—colonised or enslaved peoples, especially if they are black' [Hall *et al.*, 1978: 147].

What then of Gilroy's rhetorical question whether white people who have grown up alongside and enjoyed the same impoverished circumstances as blacks can be said to have additional power. The answer is that whites, however marginalized socially or economically, have the ability, by dint of their ethnicity, to connect with a form of discursive power from which black people are excluded. Some white people may be unaware of their recourse to racist discourses or the practices of racial exclusion. Others are aware of the discursive practices of racism but refuse to utilize them. What is significant is that such ideas and practices are available to be used at any time. That is, at any moment, racism, expressed most perniciously in violence, can exclude the 'other'. The question that remains to be addressed in Chapter 6 is the extent to which the police, having accepted that they must protect ethnic minority communites from violent racism, have been willing or able to meet this responsibility.

[23] Labour Research survey, May 1986, cited in Tompson, 1988.

8

Policing Violent Racism

One of the most contentious issues that the police had to face in the
wake of the 1981 disturbances was that they had failed to protect
minority communities from violent racism, and that this had given
licence to the feeling among the communities which were targeted
that they had no choice but to defend themselves. Despite strenuous
efforts by the police to deny this charge, this 'crisis of legitimacy' persisted well into the second half of the 1980s. By the time the North
Plaistow project was under way the police had established a racial
incidents policy which comprised recording and monitoring procedures, changes in interpretation of the law, and introduced the multi-
agency approach. Much has been said earlier in this book about these
policy developments, and now we turn to an examination of policing
violent racism on *the ground*. The Chapter begins by presenting the
views of survey respondents about the police response to reported
incidents, concluding the presentation of survey findings. It then outlines a theoretical framework used to analyse policing and describes
relevant aspects of police working culture, the operation of racial
incidents policy, and an analysis of the processing of a racial incident
through the police organization.[1] The Chapter concludes with com-

[1] This Chap. draws on the following data: (1) a description of the organizational
structure of policing in the study site. This was compiled by modifying existing organizational charts (e.g. GLC, 1986) and by collecting organizational charts from each
level of the police organization and by asking police officers at each level to draw an
organizational chart as they saw it. (2) A description of police racial-incidents policy
(legal and administrative) at the time of the study (this will be summarized only briefly
here because the development of this policy is described in more detail in Chaps. 1, 2
and 4). (3) A description of the aspects of police occupational culture which relate to
the policing of racial violence. This was based on group interviews with relief and
Home Beat officers, mid-level managers, and NORIS. This material is supplemented
by notes taken during observation of relief, Home Beat, and NORIS officers (2 s
hifts each) and during lengthy periods in the divisional headquarters. (4) A description
of the process by which a racial incident passes through the police system. This
was compiled by the formal observation referred to above, together with interviews

ments on the quality of the policing on the ground and the effectiveness of police racial incident policy in enforcing the law, maintaining order, preventing crime, and producing 'clear-up rates'.

The Views of Survey Respondents

In addition to asking about victimization, the survey (see Chapter 6; Appendix I) also included some questions on the quality of the police response to the reported incidents. The following section presents the key findings.

Police Attending the Scene

Of the 70 respondents who reported an incident to the police, 81 per cent said that a police officer had attended the scene (58 respondents). Many did not know which type of police officer had attended (44 per cent); of those who did, two thirds said they thought it was a Home Beat Officer, one quarter a detective from CID, 8 per cent a relief officer, and 4 per cent a member of Newham Organized Racial Incident Squad (NORIS). In only one quarter of all incidents was a second contact made to keep the victim informed about the progress of his or her case. A second contact was made more often for Asians (41 per cent for men and 46 per cent for women). In six out of fifty-eight incidents more than two contacts were made.

Satisfaction with the Police Response

Just under one in ten (9 per cent) of those who reported their experience to the police said that they were very satisfied with the way in which the police handled the matter and less than half were very or fairly satisfied (44 per cent) This contrasts sharply with comparable BCS figures of 22 per cent and 60 per cent respectively, suggesting

and periods of observation in the community contact office and interviews with officers in youth and community sections at borough and headquarters level. (5) A description of the experiences reported in the victimization survey. In conclusion, these bodies of descriptive data will be analysed to assess the outcomes or effect of police policy with respect to (i) order maintenance, (ii) law enforcement, (iii) protection, (iv) prevention, (v) information production and communication, (vi) 'service' to victims and community. The work conducted was by necessity flexible, eclectic, and pragmatic. The researcher had only limited control over sources of data and limited time to make as full and accurate records as would be optimal. Although unlimited access was agreed in principle by the Area DAC, access to personnel and records had to be negotiated and re-negotiated with each separate component of the organization.

that victims of racial incidents were substantially less likely to be satisfied with police service than victims of crime in general. Satisfaction varied with the ethnic and gender characteristics of the victim. Thus, 10 per cent and 29 per cent of white men and women respectively were either very or fairly dissatisfied, compared with 35 and 30 per cent of Asians, and 80 per cent and 60 per cent of Afro-Caribbeans. *All* the Afro-Caribbean women who expressed an opinion said that they were dissatisfied with the police response.

The most common complaints among those who were dissatisfied with the police response (23 respondents) were that the police did not do enough, that they failed to keep the respondent informed, and that they seemed not to be interested. In only 6 per cent of the reported incidents did the respondent feel that the police had kept them very well informed, compared with 66 per cent who said they were not well informed. In North Plaistow, fully nine out of ten respondents who expressed an opinion felt that the police should have kept them better informed. The frustration of not knowing what was happening with the incident reported (but assuming that nothing was happening) is evident from some of the respondents' comments:

'[u]p till the time of this interview I am still waiting for the police to give me the result of their inquiry after three months. Nothing came out of it' (Indian).

In 22 per cent of the incidents the police found out or were told who the perpetrator was. Of these, five were thought to have been prosecuted—two each mentioned by white men and women and one by an Asian man. A further two perpetrators were cautioned, one was arrested but the victim did not know what occurred afterwards. In the remainder, no further action was thought to have been taken. In one case mentioned by an Asian man, the result of reporting to the police was that the police took no action and the victim was threatened again by the perpetrators. '*What happened as a result of reporting to the police?*' 'Nothing. It was their word against mine. They all said they were somewhere else. I went to court but nothing was done to them. After the case they come back and threatened me for reporting them.'

Some respondents were very critical of the police response, pointing specifically to what they saw as police prejudice against Afro-Caribbeans and Asians:

On the phone they can distinguish your voice and it takes them a long time to arrive if you are coloured. And they are only up the road, but [by] the time they would arrive you could have gone there yourself and come back home [Afro-Caribbean].

They don't care about us. They say they are busy, and there's too many cases like mine for them to cope [Indian].

They don't get the offenders. And if they catch them they don't charge them. If I was to offend someone like this the police would harass me instead of turning a blind eye which is what I feel they do in case of white offenders. And the offenders feel they can do anything they like as they are always let off [Pakistani].

I haven't [as a victim support co-ordinator] come across anybody so far including myself, who would say that they are satisfied with the police. The way they were treated. When you try to tell them what's happening, they either ignored me or didn't believe me [African].

These ethnic variations in satisfaction with the police are consistent with the findings of the BCS, which indicated that while 22 per cent of white victims of crime in general were very satisfied with the police response, only 14 per cent of Afro-Caribbeans and 11 per cent of Asians were very satisfied. Table 8.1 shows that dissatisfaction expressed among victims of racial incidents in North Plaistow is rather greater than than among crime victims in the BCS. It is interesting to note that the respondents in North Plaistow were much more critical of the police than in the BCS with regard to 'doing enough' about the incident, keeping them informed, apprehending the offender, and in that they made mistakes or handled the matter badly. However, racial incident victims in North Plaistow were only slightly more likely than victims of all offences nationally to complain of the police being slow to arrive and were no more critical of the police officers' interest in the case or the politeness with which they dealt with it.

In only three cases (6 per cent) was the victim informed about Victim Support (64 per cent said that they definitely had not and 22 per cent could not remember). This probably reflects the police practice of referring only cases of recordable crime to NVSS at the time of the survey.

Respondents were asked whether they felt the police were sympathetic to their case and whether the victims of racial harassment got fair treatment compared with the victims of other forms of crime. Overall, 6 per cent of those who expressed an opinion said that the police were very sympathetic when dealing with the incident, while

Table 8.1 *Reasons for dissatisfaction with the police response-comparing the NPRHS with BCS 1984, 1988*

Reason for dissatisfaction	NPRHS 1989	BCS 1988	BCS 1984
Did not do enough	72	40	30
Failed to keep the respondent informed	44	34	21
Were not interested	38	39	38
Did not apprehend offenders	28	21	18
Made mistakes/handled the matter badly	24	6	5
Kept me waiting/were slow to arrive	11	7	9
Did not recover property	11	15	14
Were impolite/unpleasant	2	5	3

Percentages do not total 100 because multiple answers were allowed.
NPRHS Weighted data. Unweighted n = 23.
Source: 1984 and 1988 BCS core sample (see Mayhew *et al.*, 1989).

two thirds said that they were either very or fairly sympathetic. 52 per cent of respondents did not express an opinion about whether victims of racial harassment were treated fairly and equally compared to other people requesting services from the police. Of those who did express an opinion (twenty-eight incidents), 61 per cent said that such victims were treated fairly and 39 per cent said that they were not. For those that thought victims of racial harassment got unequal treatment, the most frequently cited reason was that the police did not take the problem seriously.

Finally, all respondents who had mentioned an incident of racial harassment (whether or not they had provided us with details) were asked a number of general questions about their general views on the way in which racial harassment was dealt with in the area. Of the 130 respondents who mentioned an incident, ninety-eight offered their opinion. Of these, only 5 per cent said that they were very satisfied with the way in which racial harassment was deal with in the area and less than one third at all satisfied. Half were dissatisfied and one fifth very dissatisfied.

Conceptualizing the Policing Response to Violent Racism

My starting point for conceptualizing the structure and process of policework, the impact of policy on this work, and the effect of policing on violent racism is the framework set out in Grimshaw and Jefferson's (1987) *Interpreting Policework* (see also Jefferson, 1990). This work has been useful in developing the arguments presented in this Chapter, both in its detailed analysis of forms of beat policing and policing policy and in its overall analytical framework. What follows is a brief summary of Grimshaw and Jefferson's theory of policework, modified and developed to take account of more recent literature and the specifics of policing violent racism.

Grimshaw and Jefferson (1987) identify two broad approaches to the study of the police and policing: sociological liberalism and class functionalism. Within sociological liberalism they suggest three variants, defined in terms of their conception of the organization: the 'machine', 'subcultural', and 'environmental' models.

The Machine Model

The 'machine' model, which relates closely to the work and ideas of 'rational scientific management', 'implicitly or explicitly conceives the organisation as a "machine" in which individual actors within the organisation simply execute the directives of a superior authority' (Grimshaw and Jefferson, 1987: 6). Thus, the normal functioning of the police can be understood by analysis of the administrative and criminal law, other formal rules, and the organizational structure of the police. An implicit 'machine model' is evident in the development of racial incident policies within the police and central government (see Chapters 3 and 4).

Using this perspective, 'rational scientific managers' have reviewed the relevant criminal and procedural law and systems for recording and monitoring racial incidents. The primary route to changing policing practice as it relates to racial incidents has been to issue policy directives intended to change the legal framework (albeit in only marginal ways) and to change the ways in which incidents are recorded and monitored. The 'machine model' can be criticized easily for its attention only to how organizations ideally *ought* to function rather than how they actually work in practice. Nonetheless, this approach draws attention to the importance of the structure of the police organization and the operation of the law. It is important to recognize, however, that law and administration do not *determine* policing practice, but exert a specific degree of influence in specific circumstances.

Subcultural Model

The 'subcultural model', stressing the importance of detailed obser-vation, documents the occupational milieu of policework, describing the norms, values, customs, and working practices of police officers (Holdaway, 1983, 1996; Hobbs, 1988). We learn a great deal from these studies about policing in action (mainly from the viewpoint of the police themselves), but the law, the formal police organization, its policies, and senior management remain unexamined. Thus the relationships between the organization and the law and between pol-icy, management, and practice are obscure. Researchers utilizing a subcultural model have identified the racism of the 'canteen culture' as the key to understanding the apparent failure of the police to act sympathetically or effectively to instances of violent racism (e.g. Pearson *et al.*, 1989). Police sub-cultural racism has also been the object of changes in policing policy in the form of 'race awareness' training (Bull and Horncastle, 1989).

The 'Environmental Model'

The 'environmental model' lies somewhere between the two previous models and takes into account the 'basic environmental features' of the organization—such as its management, organizational structure, and processes, and the constraints of the law. J. Q. Wilson (1968), for example, 'appears to have demonstrated . . . that there is an observable relationship between the working "style" of officers, departmental policies and organisational codes, and the prevailing political culture'. This approach 'flatly contradicts the findings of the subculturalists' in that it shows that managerial strategies and constraints imposed by the 'community' 'can affect at least some areas of police behaviour some of the time' (Grimshaw and Jefferson, 1987: 10).

Grimshaw and Jefferson argue that none of these models, on its own, provides a framework adequate to explain the complexities of policework:

the 'machine' model fails to contextualise the machine or examine its work-ing; the 'subcultural' model fails to examine the machine or the contexts in which it operates in anything like the detail it affords the working practices and meaning systems of the machine's agents; and the environmental model gives insufficient attention to the machine itself and to the operating norms and practices of organisational agents [*ibid.*: 11].

Moreover, as an academic community, sociological liberals 'define the police, if only implicitly, in an empirical or pragmatic fashion, while retaining idealistic normative assumptions, about law for example' (*ibid.*: 11).

Class-functionalism

Using the documentation of abuse and discrimination at the hands of the police as the key methodological approach, class functionalism prioritizes for analysis the ways in which policing impacts on the working class and other marginalized groups (Grimshaw and Jefferson, 1987: 31). Although these authors are evidently in sympathy with the aims of class functionalism to explain 'immediate empirical reality' and the fundamental historical processes underlying the apparent processes of social life, they criticize the Marxist paradigm as simplistic and 'reductive'. In its most simply stated form, empirical reality is said by Marxists to 'reflect' the economic class struggle. Thus, 'economic class domination is reflected in law, which is enforced by the police, who thereby reproduce existing relations of exploitation'. The problem with this perspective is not the lack of evidence of discrimination or exploitation, but the evidence that these processes are not simple and linear, but complex and contradictory.

The class functionalist approach has produced an important strand of analysis of police racism. Relying principally on the documentary method, independent research,[2] police monitoring groups,[3] ethnic minority community organizations[4] and labour-left local authorities[5] have produced a great deal of evidence of over-policing black communities as alleged offenders and under-protecting them as victims. While these studies are useful, particularly in their strong historical dimension, they suffer the weakness of reductionism identified by Grimshaw and Jefferson with reference to social class. Introducing an element of 'institutional racism' into Grimshaw and Jefferson's characterization of the class-functionalists argument as reductionist, we might say that the Marxist approach argues that class bias and racism are institutionalized in law, the legal system, and the police. The

---

[2] e.g. Institute of Race Relations, 1979, 1987; Dunhill, 1989; Mama, 1989.

[3] e.g. Newham Monitoring Project, 1991; Lewisham Action on Policing, annual reports; Southall Black Sisters, annual reports (see also Dunhill, 1989).

[4] e.g. Commission for Racial Equality reports, 1979–89.

[5] e.g. Greater London Council reports, 1981–6; London Strategic Policy Unit Reports. London Borough of Newham, 1987.

effect is, thus, that policing reproduces existing relations of class and race exploitation.

Grimshaw and Jefferson's Model

Grimshaw and Jefferson argue that what is needed to explain policing:

is an approach which is faithful to the profane details of daily policework, like that of the sociological liberals, but in a way which attempts to link these systematically, that is in relation to the system as a whole, which represents the merit of the Marxist approach. We need to consider policing as a *combination* of structures [Grimshaw and Jefferson, 1987: 13; original emphasis].

To this end, the authors build on the sociological concepts of formal structure, working practices, and environmental contexts, taking account of the importance of law, work, and the community. They retain the class functionalist attention to underlying historical and social processes and a recognition that social inequality is an important determinant on the pattern of policing. Rather than assuming that policing in an unequal society will have a simple repressive effect, however, they urge an investigation of *how* inequality impacts on policework.

This framework consists of three basic elements: law, work, and the community. Law is defined as the dominant (but not determinant) constraint on police work. To understand how it exerts effects in particular situations, it is necessary to know the 'formal structure' of the relevant law—the legal powers of the police, the legal demands made by the criminal law, the legal powers of citizens and legal authorities, and the uses made of them (*ibid.*: 18). Work is defined as a single structure with two dimensions: an 'organizational' one—referring to the vertical dimension of rules, policies, approved procedures, command, and control—and an 'occupational' one, referring to the horizontal dimension of the norms and practices of 'colleague groups' (*ibid.*: 19). Community is defined as the influence on policework of the actions of a heterogeneous public composed of individuals and institutions outside the police organization. Citizens encounter the police organizations in a number of different ways as individuals—as potential witness, injured party, complainant, caller, or refreshment spot—as representatives of the community (either elected or self-appointed leaders of community or pressure groups), or as members of organizations with which the police have institutional contact (e.g. social services, housing departments, schools, or the media). Forms of contact can vary in numerous ways (conflictual or co-operative, equal or unequal, sporadic or recurrent), each with a different actual or potential effect on police behaviour.

In order to comprehend, using this framework, how policy will affect policework in a given situation, it is necessary to review briefly the hypotheses offered by existing models of policework.

For the 'machine model', policy is taken as 'an authoritative statement of the organisation's specific goals, carrying a clear meaning and relevance for all subordinates which it is intended that they should automatically put into practice—*policy as rational authority*' (*ibid.*: 19). Any discrepancies between organizational requirements and operational practice are explained as 'communication blockage' (*ibid.*: 25). For the subculturalists, policy is 'merely a declaration of some orientation favoured by policy makers . . . issued in various degrees of good faith, which is in practice impotent'—*policy as irrelevance*. The rank-and-file subculture is seen as the key determinant of police behaviour and relatively impermeable to management values and policies. The subculturalists, therefore, explain the discrepancies between policy and practice as stemming primarily from a conflict between management and rank-and-file subculture (characterized by a 'managerial' and 'common-sense' professionalism, respectively). The environmental model hypothesises that the 'environment' shapes police behaviour, but 'works with an under-developed conception of the environment'. Similarly, the class-functionalist approach which hypothesises that 'class determines police behaviour' must be developed such that class, race, gender, age (and other factors) relate complexly to law and its enforcement (see also Brogden, Jefferson, and Walklate, 1988).

Using a theoretical case-study approach looking in detail at forms of beat policing (the unit-beat and resident beat systems), policy files, and policy-making systems in one police force area, Grimshaw and Jefferson provide evidence to support their model. In looking specifically at the policy-making process, they further refine their arguments. They provide a *specific definition of policy* as 'an authoritative statement signifying a settled practice on any matter relevant to the duties of the Chief Constable' (*ibid.*: 204).

With respect to the policy making process, they hypothesise that:

policies involving operational and related tasks will be characterised by the values of occupational common sense, and those involving administrative tasks will be characterised by rational scientific management values . . . the 'success' of policy in influencing practice [will be] task related. Thus, the impact of those policies bearing on operational and related tasks where occupational common sense is to the fore will be less decisively calculable and more unpredictable in effect than those policies bearing on administrative tasks where rational-scientific management values can come to the fore [Grimshaw and Jefferson, 1987: 199].

Utilizing the three structures outlined above, Grimshaw and Jefferson suggest three hypotheses to 'examine the alleged "gap", not between policy and practice, but rather between particular types of policy and practice'. These hypotheses may be summarized thus:

(1) Law is the dominant structure of policework; situations where the legal structure is in any way limited or permissive will enable work-related values to prevail; those tasks involving a substantial and precisely articulated legal structure will not be so open to the influence of work-related values. Because tasks involving different legal structures cross the rank structure of the police, the relationship between task, law and work will be relevant to any part of the police organisations.

(2) Tasks involving limited or permissive legal structures are those dealing with operational and related matters, and it is these tasks which will more often be subject to the operation of occupational, common-sense values than those dealing with administrative matters. The more discretionary and ambiguous the legal matter, the greater the opportunity for such common sense to enter.

(3) The effectiveness of supervision is related to task. Where the legal or work structure is limited or permissive, supervision will need to recognise rank-and-file values in order to be effective; but in others, where the task is strongly determined by law, administrative systems or managerial directives, supervision need not fail [Grimshaw and Jefferson, 1987: 26].

Police Occupational Culture: The Literature

There is a large and growing literature on police subcultural racism. An investigation of prejudiced attitudes and discriminatory behaviour among police officers has formed a component of several detailed studies based on ethnography, observation, or interviews and has formed the focus of numerous theoretical or speculative articles about the nature of police racism and what is to be done about it.[6]

[6] See, e.g., Smith and Gray, 1983; Graef, 1989; Pearson et al., 1989; Lea, 1987; Reiner, 1989.

Among these studies, those based on empirical data have described the endemic and pervasive racist stereotyping of Afro-Caribbean and Asian people and the routine use of racist language on patrol and in the canteen (although such language has rarely been observed by the researchers on the street). Most studies are concerned with the relationship between police racism and the tendency for black people to be stopped, searched, and arrested more frequently that their white counterparts,[7] though some have looked at police racism in the context of their response to racial violence (see Table 2.2, Chapter 2). Although studies such as that conducted by Smith and Gray (1983) failed (in their own terms) to establish a link between racist stereotyping and racially prejudiced behaviour, these studies do alert us to specific aspects of stereotyping which bear on the policing of violent racism.

Reiner (1985) argues that ethnic minorities are seen as 'police property' along with 'vagrants, skid row alcoholics [etc.]' and as 'rubbish' when they present themselves as victims of crime (1985: 95; 1989: 18; citing Lee, 1981). By 'rubbish' police officers mean 'people who make calls on the police which are seen as messy, intractable and unworthy of attention or the complainant's own fault' (Smith and Gray, 1983: 64–6). One case of racial harassment reported by Smith and Gray in their ethnographic study of the Metropolitan Police (circa 1981) illustrates the point. In this case stones were being thrown at the home of a family of Nigerian origin, the police being called when a bottle was thrown through a window. The alleged culprits were children aged 11–14, some of whom were wearing Union Jack badges (signifying for the authors that the young people involved had sympathy with NF). After informally warning the alleged culprits, the police left the scene. Half an hour later, the police officers were called back to the address because the stone-throwing had started again. On attending this time, the police officers told the Nigerians that there was little they could do, one officer saying that he felt sure that this had not happened to them simply because they were black. Nine days later the same family had their window smashed again. After this call one of the officers said: '[t]he PC who came with me the second time asked me if she [the Nigerian woman] wound the kids up. I told him that she did. She deserves to have her windows smashed if she talks to them that way' (Smith and Gray, 1983: 141).

[7] See, e.g., Stephens and Willis, 1979; Willis, 1983; Reiner, 1989; Skogan, 1990.

This case illustrates three important points. First, a call involving minor criminal damage and perpetrated by children was seen as 'rubbish'—intractable, the activity of children, and not worth investigation or taking formal action against perpetrators. Secondly, the victims were somehow not seen as 'deserving' or 'good' victims, and had in some way brought their victimization on themselves. Thirdly, the police appeared to be unwilling to ascribe a racial motive to attacks, even though the victims felt that they were being singled out for attack by young people who they felt were being violent towards them in a racist way.

The tendency on the part of the police to play down or deny a 'racial' motive recurs in other studies (see Table 2.2). This tendency appears also to be related to a stereotyped view of Asians, in particular, as prone to exaggeration and lying (Smith and Gray, 1985: 388–439). This view is vividly illustrated by an interview with a Superintendent interviewed by Roger Graef:

Two pigs' heads were thrown into the main mosque, smashed through the window. Immediately the senior Asian elders got together and spoke of racism. They paraded. There were hundreds of them. It created all sorts of problems. . . . As far as they were claiming it was a major racial incident against the Asian community. Turned out to be a couple of drunken yobs who didn't even know it was a mosque. They had gone down to the abattoir, got two bloody pigs' heads out of there, gone on had a good booze up, intending to drop them in the door of someone they had a disagreement with, decided against it, and just slung them through this window.

That's the problem with Asians: they make so many allegations that are totally a pack of lies [Graef, 1989: 131].

Racial Incidents and a 'Hierarchy of Police Relevance'

Grimshaw and Jefferson's work suggests that the dominant influence on the work of the police officer initially attending the scene of a call for service (a relief PC) is the legal structure (see Appendix II). The nature of their response to any given incident is influenced by the relationship of the incident to a 'natural agenda' of policework—an agenda constructed through a working common-sense understanding of the law (Grimshaw and Jefferson, 1987: 107). Thus:

A range of matters brought to police attention thus carry legal relevance, but not necessarily in terms which are interpreted as relevant to the police; incidents located in the territory of civil law by the officers in attendance can be seen as of reduced relevance. Debts, nuisances, domestic disputes and neigh-bour disputes can be regarded as falling into this zone, one of ambiguity and limited police relevance [cf. Reiss, 1971: 77; Grimshaw and Jefferson, 1987: 91].

legal work is conducted within a fixed agenda of police relevance, con-structed in relation to objective legal structures and influences, and under-taking in a pragmatic spirit not inconsistent with the legal realities of procedure for dealing with suspects [Grimshaw and Jefferson, 1987: 98].

legality becomes the prism for social censoriousness [*ibid*.: 95]

A constant stream of calls on police service is filtered into the orga-nization and categorized, first, by the dispatcher's definition of the incident as 'police relevant' (Manning, 1988). As officers answer these calls, and arrive at the scene they also make decisions about the rel-evance of the event to the police. They decide whether to complete an item of paperwork, to make an arrest, investigate further, or sim-ply exit from the encounter and move on to the next incident. Thus, Grimshaw and Jefferson suggest, when an incident is clearly defined in criminal law as 'police relevant', the outcome of the encounter will be predictable and will reflect legal reality; where legality is ambigu-ous, the outcome will be ambiguous, left open to the operation of common-sense values of the relief.

Numerous authors have noted the use of specific terminology to classify events into categories at various levels within the police 'hier-archy of relevance'.[8] At the top of the hierarchy is 'good crime'—criminal offences with a good victim ('innocent', high status, willing to testify), a real villain (a professional, or least experienced, crimi-nal), after which a 'good arrest' can be made (one likely to result in a conviction and the removal of 'chummy' from the streets). Further down the hierarchy come 'rubbish crimes'—those where either the victim or perpetrator are 'police property' (people of apparently 'low social status' who are routinely under police suspicion), where there is a low likelihood of detection or arrest, or where there appears to be a chance that the victim might withdraw the allegation at a later point. Further still down the hierarchy are other calls for police service, such as 'disputes' and 'disturbances'.[9] Such a hierarchy of

[8] See, e.g., Smith and Gray, 1983; Holdaway, 1983; Reiner, 1985; Grimshaw and Jefferson, 1987: 81–3; Shapland and Hobbs, 1989; Young, 1990; Hesse *et al.*, 1992.

[9] Other categories not of immediate relevance to this study would include: 'civil emergencies', 'traffic accidents', 'disturbed people', 'sudden death', etc. (Shapland and Hobbs, 1989).

relevance is evident in the police officers' categorization of 'racial incidents', described below.

Police Occupational Culture: Group Interviews

Racial Incidents as a 'Force Priority'

Before looking at how the rank and file police officers conceptualize racial incidents, it should be noted that senior managers were keen to get the message across that racial incidents were a 'force priority'. The police officers were instructed to attend the group interviews by the Chief Superintendent and by the borough Community Liaison Officer (CLO) by letters sent separately from each and were provided with the list of questions that would be asked in the interview. The CLO's short letter primed the interviewees: '[t]hese are the questions which you will be asked to discuss in the group interview sessions. The reduction of racial attacks and harassment is a force priority and a divisional objective for West Ham. Your careful consideration of answers to these questions will be greatly appreciated.'

The officers were clear, therefore, that racial incidents were a 'force priority' and made made aware that they should comment on the problem and the police response to it with this in mind. The occasion of these interviews was not the first time that the force priority to reduce racial incidents was brought to the attention of the reliefs, however. On the contrary, the prioritization of racial incidents in the police organization had been apparent to them for some time. In the recent past a high-profile media campaign had been conducted by Headquarters Youth and Community Section (YACS) (see Appendix II) to advertise this prioritization and to encourage reporting of incidents (Metropolitan Police, 1989a). The Newham Organized Racial Incident Squad (NORIS) worked part of the time from the police station in which the reliefs were located. In particular, the *Force Orders* of 1986 and 1987 required the reliefs to complete specific items of paperwork in instances where any person alleged racial motivation.

Racial Incidents as 'Crime'

When the officers in the group interviews were asked what type of incidents came to their attention, some racial incidents were defined clearly as 'crime':

Many [are] muggings of middle-aged or elderly [Asian] women. Perhaps it is because they are an easy kill. They are also an easy kill because they wear expensive jewellery. It's not a racial attack—the gold's there for the taking, it's just there for the taking.

groups of black or white youths attacking Asians, . . . mugging of an Asian lady by West Indians—this is not necessarily racial . . . obviously West Indians pick on Asians because they are an easy target. Is this racialist or just because they are easy victims.

[Attacks on] shopkeepers [are] not necessarily racial—it could be burglary or theft. They call to show a police presence but are unwilling to follow it up. Most of the shops around here are Asian run, so it is difficult to tell what is racial and what is not.

These examples illustrate the tendency to define 'racial incidents' which fall into the police relevant category of crime strictly within 'operational' categories. The legal relevance of the criminal offences of robbery,[10] assault, and theft is clear (see Hesse *et al.*, 1992: 64). It is worth noting also that legal categories of crime and disturbance were seen by the police officers interviewed to be much more important than the category of 'racial'. Indeed, with only a rare exception officers of all ranks consistently questioned or denied the relevance of racism or racial motivation to these crimes (see below).

Racial Incidents as 'Yobishness'

When asked who the perpetrators of racial violence were, police officers pointed first to 'yobs' or 'hooligans', shorthand for members of the dangerous classes, also referred to in the literature as 'toe rags' and 'slags' (Smith and Gray, 1983), 'prigs' (Young, 1991), and 'police property' (Lee, 1981: 53–4; Reiner, 1985: 95). Throughout the interviews with the police, the predominant view of the perpetrators of racial violence was of a group of streetwise youths with low intelligence and bad education. It was believed that they came from criminal backgrounds and despised both ethnic minorities and the police. One relief sergeant described the 'yobs' like this: '[t]hese are the ones who are doing all kinds of stuff. They are the young trouble makers. [Racial harassment] is another facet of anti-social behaviour. Its parents letting them become too streetwise. We will keep on dealing with them—probably throughout their lives.'

[10] Although the term 'mugging' does not exist within criminal law it is synonymous with the category 'robbery and other violent theft'.

The continuity between the behaviour of these young people and their parents was also something stressed by the police officers we interviewed. For some, criminality was part and parcel of the locality. One officer summed up this viewpoint: 'the whole area has a criminal mentality, they're all at it'. For others, perpetrators had an inherited, pathological tendency to offend and engage in 'anti-social behaviour'. These comments illustrate this viewpoint:

These are people who are arrested for all manner of things—twelve to eighteen year olds often those whose parents are in trouble, or even their grandparents. They come from a criminal background. [Their] parents are more anti-police than the kids are anti-ethnic.

you can't stop [yobishness] because it is hereditary. They inherit it from their mums and dads.

For other officers, racial incidents were part of a more recent problem connected with a shift among young people towards becoming 'streetwise' and disrespectful of authority and tradition:

[the] yob problem [is] a gradual decline in respect for the police over the last 25 years. [They] lack . . . respect—for Asian traditions—and for police officers.

A home-beat officer described how he thought "yobishness" would result in a racial incident:

Usually it's a small group of youths ten to sixteen years old . . . idling, unemployed or truant. . . . If they see an Asian female they will shout abuse. [It is] mainly racial abuse—'gestured assault'. With the vast majority it is difficult to say what is in their mind—generally they will not assault. It is important to bear in mind that these youths will abuse any target. Groups of very idle youths . . . are quite likely to abuse anyone who passes . . . especially the vulnerable people—ethnic minorities, especially women. [They] only pick on vulnerable people; less likely to pick on stronger people.

The stereotypical perpetrator of racial incidents appears to fall into the category that Lee (1981: 53–4; cited by Reiner, 1985) describes as 'police property'. Officers from the Newham Racial Incident Squad (NORIS) explained that the people who carry out racial attacks are not 'normal Mr. Niceguy all week and only do a bit of racial violence at the weekends', but those responsible for a whole range of petty crime and minor disorder. According to this view, the 'yobs' had to be contained, and wherever possible removed from the street. If it was not possible to 'get' a yob on one particular occasion that he or she appeared in court (for a racial incident or any other offence), he or she would 'come again'. Eventually, a case against a yob would be a 'good one', he or she would 'fall hard' and 'go down' for a few years. That racial attack perpetrators were, for the police, indistinguishable from ordinary yobs was expressed by one of the NORIS officers, whose role, officially, was to target organized racially motivated crime: 'our mission is to seek and destroy yobs'.

Racial Incidents as Disputes and Disturbances

A step down from the offensive and criminal behaviour of the yobs in the police 'hierarchy of relevance' one finds events defined as 'neighbour disputes' and other forms of dispute or disturbance. In these cases, racial motivation was seen as irrelevant by the relief officers interviewed:

[It's] more usually when two households are against each other [an inspector].

[It's often] neighbours who fall out. We take more notice of these incidents because people are of opposite races [sic].

Some [victims] will say it is racial when it [the victim's race] was never raised in the first place.

You get kids and parents claiming [incidents at school are] racial [but] this is normal schooling.

These incidents occurring between neighbours are less likely to be categorized as 'crimes' than those in which the 'yobs' are involved, because, from a police perspective, they routinely fall short of the criteria which would enable them to be classified as crime. While some of them are certainly criminal offences—assault and criminal damage in particular—they are classified by the police as 'anti-social acts' or 'unpleasantness rather than crime'—in short, 'rubbish'. If the incident fails to meet the police criterion of legal relevance to classify it as a crime, there can be neither victim nor offender.

Racial Motivation

The view that the police tend to deny the existence of a racial motive in incidents perceived by the victim as racially motivated crops up throughout the history and research reviewed above. Ethnic minority community organizations and academic studies have consistently found that the police are unwilling to admit the existence of racial motivation. Pearson *et al.* (1989) for example, noted that 'unless there was evidence of organised racial motivation, then it could not count as a "racial" incident'. As a result, what were racist attacks for victims were neighbourly disputes [*sic*] or a 'form of troublesome crime' involving 'just bravado lads, people who've been drinking too much' and not 'real policework' (Pearson *et al.*, 1989: 124).

The tendency to deny the presence or relevance of racism or a racial motive emerged clearly in the interviews conducted in the present study. Consistent with Pearson *et al.* (1989) it was found that unless there was clear evidence of involvement of extreme right political groups or some form of 'premeditated racial motivation' officers consistently said that incidents should not be classified as 'racial':

We should reclassify racially motivated incidents. They should be classed as 'racial' when there is some evidence that the incident was racially motivated—that is with clear *premeditated racial motivation.*

In inter-racial incidents, do we have to look deeper into it, or just get on with it—do we have to treat it differently? . . . we do have to, but we shouldn't.

Because racist political parties and their members were not seen as the perpetrators of racial violence, the existence of a racial motive was denied: '[t]here is no nationalist or extreme right activists involved. The National Front is virtually extinct in the area.' Thus, many incidents reported by victims as 'racial incidents' were defined by the police simply as neighbour disputes: 'much of it is instantaneous verbal abuse or loss of temper. I've never been to an incident where it is a premeditated racial attack.' In other incidents, it was suggested that a 'racial motive' was fabricated by the victim for ulterior motives; in particular so that he or she might be rehoused by the council:

Many [Asian] neighbours claim that they are racially abused so that they can get out of the area. Some are genuine but many do it to get moved.

We get a number of malicious allegations . . . a number of spurious allegations come forward for re-housing purposes. This results in a blunting of the effect of officers [an inspector].

With premeditated or organized racism being defined as the only *bona fide* form of racism, and then its existence denied, the officers effectively removed 'racial motivation' from their understanding of the problem in North Plaistow. Clearly, this fails to match the victim's perception of racism and the sense in which racial harassment is a process with a wider experiential context (see Chapters 2–6 above).

Paradoxically, however, evidence of the wider processes of racialization and victimization *did* emerge from the interviews with the rank-and-file PCs. Specifically, the explanations of 'racial incidents' were suffused with racist categorizations and assumptions.

The Causes of Racial Incidents

A first set of explanations of the causes of racial incidents revolved around observations about a 'natural' and inevitable resentment felt towards the presence of ethnic minorities in what had been at one time 'white areas'. One source of this resentment was the existence of racial equality or equal opportunities policies: '[w]hile racial equality has such a high profile the problem will remain. It won't make resentment disappear [and] will make people more resentful. There's too much positive discrimination—if there weren't then resentment would go.' The argument that policies aiming to improve equality of opportunity and respond to racism (characterized as the 'Race Relations Industry') are themselves a cause of racism has been a common theme among the discourses of the tabloid media and commentators of the New Right (Gordon and Rosenberg, 1989). This natural resentment, it was suggested, would lead to spontaneous expressions of violence:

You have to treat it as the next man. He might have spent years building up his house over these years. He will resent his area being taken over.

Motivation is jealousy. Asians are business like. The system which should be working for them [the perpetrators] isn't and they become resentful.

It's a spontaneous expression of how they are feeling.

Throughout the group interviews, police officers of all ranks expressed views that reflected the logic of white territorial ownership of the locality and its resources. The areas belonged to the white community—it was 'theirs', while ethnic minorities—an illegitimate presence—were seen to be 'taking over'. Similarly, the economic and political 'system' should have been working for the white youths, but instead allowed ethnic minority business to succeed. This is not to say that the police condoned violent attacks, but the interviews indicated that the police officers identified with the viewpoint of the white community, seeing its resentment and its expression in violence as 'natural' and understandable. The interviewees did not question this territorial logic, or express the view that the ethnic minorities had an equal right to live in the locality.

A second, related set of explanations revolved around a belief in a conflict between the cultural practices of whites and ethnic minorities. These relied principally on familiar racist stereotypes of Afro-Caribbeans liking loud music and Asians cooking smelly food:[11]

Lots of white people don't like Asians; they don't like curry; they don't like them taking over their areas; they are moving out further and further. I don't think blacks like Asians any more than whites do.

[The perpetrators] don't like their customs; [the victims] don't accept our culture or our way of life so there's resentment.

It depends how much they have had to drink, how strong the smell of curry is, how loud the West Indian music is. Usually an ordinary incident develops into a racial incident.

Again, the police respondents identified clearly with the white community. 'Our' culture was being rejected, 'their' customs were unacceptable, and resentment was the natural outcome. Cultural practices of dress and language were also mentioned as contributing to the resentment:

A fair proportion of the first generation have poor command of English—28 years in England and could not speak English—I found this despicable—if these people won't accept us . . . it is very difficult for people to accept them.

Bengali women are often victimised, especially the traditionally dressed ones. The way they dress, their lack of English. They look a bit threatening, a bit different . . . [They are victimised because they are] not adapting to English customs and because they are vulnerable.

Thus, the targeting of ethnic minorities for attack was not a consequence of racial prejudice, but of the rejection of the English language and failure to adapt to English customs, diet, and style of dress. This failure to 'accept' Englishness made ethnic minorities at once threatening and vulnerable to attack. Racism and victimization are, as Gilroy (1987) puts it, pushed outside social and historical processes into the realm of natural and inevitable events.

---

[11] See also the views of the housing department caretakers described in Chap. 5.

A third set of explanations, also evident in the last example, turned on the notion of the victims' inherent vulnerability. In particular, the brunt of violence committed by 'yobs' was explained in terms of a supposed natural vulnerability of the victims:

[Victims] are discernible by their vulnerability—mainly Asians—youths have a hierarchy of respect—they do not respect Asians, but do respect Afro-Caribbeans—an odd allocation of respect.

Perpetrators have a healthy respect for Afro-Caribbeans, but have contempt for Asians.

Pakistanis . . . sorry, Asians . . . are the least likely to fight back . . . they just accept it. As a culture they tend to be more philosophical about it. Shopkeepers just accept it to allow trade to continue.

It comes down to vulnerability—the jackal mentality . . . when they see a woman with shopping or a pram . . . it's like a wolf pack will pick on a wounded animal.

These views revolve around twin pathologies—the natural vulnerability of the victim (like a wounded animal) and the natural hostility of the perpetrators (the jackals) rather than being seen as rooted in socially and historically constructed patterns of dominance and subordination on the basis of race and gender. The process of victimization becomes fixed in the very nature of being young and white and being female and Asian.

It is interesting to note that, while the officers were keen to register that the yobs would abuse *anyone*, that they also stated that it was *vulnerable* people who were actually abused. Indeed, the officers were able to identify likely victims—Asians, and particularly Asian women, on the basis of their 'vulnerability'. Rather than 'vulnerability' being seen as the consequence of an ongoing historical process of economic and social marginalization (of which violence is a part) it is seen as fixed in the physical characteristics of the victim. Being Asian, in and of itself, was an explanation of their victimization. This seems to be an example of the reinforcing logic of racism.

Although the views presented above were typical of the relief police constables (see Appendix 2: 342) and were evident across the interviews, some Home Beat and NORIS officers did identify perpetrators' racial prejudice as a feature of their actions. One Home Beat officer suggested that the perpetrators had a 'latent racial hatred' which would give rise to a 'set of responses triggered by the identity of the victim'. In general, however, respondents did not see racial hatred as a relevant factor, speaking instead of cultural conflict and resentment arising from the 'take-over' of white areas and conflict between 'our' (white) culture and the supposedly noisy and smelly cultural practices of ethnic minorities.

Rank-and-file Police Culture and Racial Incidents as a Force Priority

The 'top-down' view of racial incidents as a force priority referred to at the start of this section is evidently in conflict with the operational common-sense conceptualization of the problem employed by rank and file police officers. As a group, the experience of the rank and file is of random and isolated incidents, the 'racial' motivation of which they explicitly refute. They fail to see patterns of harassment experienced by the victim and his or her community, seeing instead a random scatter of flare-ups caused by the routine 'anti-social behaviour' of the 'yobs' and friction between defensive and resentful indigenous whites and their neighbouring ethnic minority interlopers—the cause of which is cultural conflict. These 'spontaneous' (and apparently random) events are responded to in the context of myriad other calls on police resources defined within the police natural agenda of 'crime', 'disputes', and 'disturbances'. They are thereby stripped of their meaning from the victim's point of view (see Chapter 5), and are translated into objects for policing, reified in the form of an incident record (see Chapter 4). In 'crime' incidents, the most police-relevant of all incidents, any racial motive is irrelevant to how the police do their job, except for the completion of an additional item of paperwork. Most of the remainder of the incidents are seen as 'rubbish'—of little or no practical interest to the police.

The interviews suggested two ways in which the rank and file solved the conflicting paradigms of 'managerial' and 'common-sense professionalism'. First, they argued that the management prioritization of the problem was not a response to a genuine policing need, but arose from 'politics':

There are more important things going on, mugging for example. Compared with other crimes, racial harassment is given a lot of attention because it is political.

It's all political. [Racial harassment] is given as a police problem when it should be someone else's problem. The easiest point would be for people not to report it then we wouldn't have to deal with it.

The fact is, of course, that the issue of racial incidents *is* politicized. That the issue rose from irrelevance to prominence during the 1980s had not escaped these officers. The local politics of racism had been intense at times over the previous few years, involving the bitter exchange of accusations in the local media and actual physical conflict between the protagonists (see Chapters 3 and 4). The political struggle engaged in by ethnic minorities for the violence and intimidation inflicted on them to be recognized and responded to was fresh in their minds. What the rank-and-file officers were pointing to, however, is the *illegitimacy* of the arguments presented by individual black and Asian people, pressure groups, local authorities, central government (and even their own management!), that violent racism is a problem which is widespread, damaging to local community life, and requires a vigorous response. Clearly, this perspective is quite at odds with that of the ethnic minorities, and particularly those of Asian origin, interviewed in the survey, who saw racial attacks as a high police priority.

A second means that the rank and file used to resolve the contradiction between their views and those of management was to suggest that the wishes of management could be put into effect if it had more resources and legal powers than it had at present: 'If we had enough people on the street we could combat all acts of hooliganism.' 'We need more powers. Verbal abuse, minor things, we can't act—we need to increase our powers.' With such increased powers the officers believed that it would be possible simply to 'remove' the 'yobs' from the streets and thereby solve not only racial incidents, but all the anti-social behaviour of these young people.

Racial Incidents, Law and Policy

In July 1987, the police issued a *Force Order* concerning racial incidents. Standing Orders, according to Grimshaw and Jefferson, are the standing instructions of the force, governing its organization, basic policies, and systems, and 'are intended to be a series of guidelines, to advise and help officers better to perform their duties' (1987: 209). This order can be seen, therefore, as the principal means of communicating policy—an authoritative statement signifying a settled practice—to police officers charged with its implementation. The 1987 Force Order is cited in full below:[12]

Minimum requirements:

1. The Divisional Chief Superintendent will assume overall responsibility for ensuring that all reporting, recording, monitoring, investigative and follow-up procedures are properly carried out. This will include reviewing all papers at the completion of the investigation, or in non-crime cases, when all appropriate action is complete.

2. All racial incidents which fall within the definition of Instruction 1/86 must be reported to the Community Liaison Officer. The Community Liaison Officer is responsible for informing the Divisional Chief Superintendent, notifying Headquarters branches in accordance with GO [General Orders] Section 49, paragraph 70A, and informing TO30 Branch [Headquarters YACS] of *all* incidents by submitting form 3424B weekly.

---

[12] At the time of the start of the North Plaistow Racial Harassment Project (16 August 1988), West Ham division had in operation a slightly different version of the *Force Order* which is outlined below.

(1) A Racial incident is defined as: 'Any incident in which it appears to the reporting or investigating officer that the complaint involved an element of racial motivation; or any incident which includes an allegation of racial motivation made by any person'.

Strong emphasis is placed on a liberal interpretation of this definition to ensure than accurate assessment of the overall problem can be made.

(2) INITIAL ACTION

All Officers reporting or investigating an incident or complaint involving an element of racial motivation are required to report the matter immediately on form 3424 in addition to any other reports which may be relevant to the incident or complaint being investigated. Allegations of crime are normally required to fulfil a minimum requirement criterion before full investigations are conducted. This criterion does not apply to crime allegations involving an element of racial motivation and will be fully investigated by a CID Officer. Matters of assault will be processed by s. 47 Offences Against the Person Act 1861 and the minimal requirements of 'actual bodily harm' will suffice to satisfy proceedings being considered under this s. of this Act. Racially motivated cases which do not display any technical evidence of assault or where no actual bodily harm has resulted are carefully examined for evidence of behaviour contrary to s. 5 Public Order Act 1986 and in appropriate cases offender charged accordingly.

SECONDARY ACTION

All victims of racial incidents will be visited by the Home Beat officer, independently of any investigation in order to report progress to ensure a sufficient level of communication is maintained and generally to support the original investigation

This document also notes that 'it is not possible to practically detail Police responsibilities directed to Racial attacks since the application of Police powers in respect of criminal law are applicable to the community as a whole and not directed to any particular group. It can only be stated that the Commissioner's directive places the prevention and investigation of racial incidents as one of the forces highest priorities.'

3. At the completion of all investigations the papers must be forwarded to the Divisional Chief Superintendent through the Community Liaison Officer. In non-crime cases a final report must be submitted to the Divisional Chief Superintendent.

4. All victims of racial incidents will be visited by an officer of appropriate rank, independent of any investigation, in order to report progress and explain difficulties and to ensure a sufficient level of communication is maintained.

5. The Community Liaison Officer will be responsible for maintaining and monitoring local records of racial incidents and for drawing the attention of the Divisional Chief Superintendent to any trends or significant developments.

An examination of the cases *R. v. Miller* (1953), *Taylor v. Granville* (1978) and *R. v. Reigate Justices, ex parte Counsel* (1983) and the results of a pilot study have shown that so long as an 'assault' has occurred, any 'actual bodily harm', however slight, is sufficient to establish an offence under Section 47 Offences Against the Person Act 1861. 'Actual Bodily Harm' may be inferred if pain, tenderness or soreness results from the act, even if no physical injury is visible. It will be sufficient if the act merely causes psychological injury such as an hysterical and nervous condition.

Therefore, with effect from 1 July any case of assault which has been aggravated by racial motivation will be processed by virtue of Section 47 of the Offences Against the Person Act 1861, provided that there is some 'actual bodily harm' as defined above. Racially motivated cases which do not display any technical evidence of assault, or where no actual harm as defined, has resulted, must be carefully examined for evidence of behaviour contrary to Section 5 of the Public Order Act 1986 and in appropriate cases the offender prosecuted accordingly.

The next section examines the operation of this policy in practice in terms of the framework offered by Grimshaw and Jefferson (1987). As a first step, it is necessary to distinguish between *administrative* and *operational* forms of policy and between those aspects of the policy directed at *relief* and *community* officers.

Table 8.2 distinguishes elements of the 1987 force order on racial attacks between those directed at changing operational and at administrative practices of relief and community officers. The administrative aspects are framed in the language of rational science complete with reference to recording and monitoring, channels of communication, and has objective performance measured as an end-product. This aspect of the policy is designed not to change the way in which racial incidents are dealt with by either immediately responding

Table 8.2 *The 1987 Force Order on Racial Incidents: operational and administrative policy for relief and community officers.*

	Unit at which policy targeted	
	Relief officers	*Community officers*
Aspect of policy		
operational	Treat all assaults aggravated by racial motivation as s. 47 assaults. Seek evidence that an offence contrary to s. 5 of POA 1986. Charge offender in appropriate cases	Visit victims 'independent of investigation' to keep victim informed, explain difficulties, and maintain communication.
administrative	(As reporting officer), report incident to CLO on form 3424.	(As reporting or investigating officer) report incident on form 3424. Copy of form to be passed to Chief Superintendent (CS). Submit form 3424B weekly to TO30 (via Area YACS). Maintain records and inform CS of trends and developments

police officers, or those charged with investigation or other 'secondary' action, but merely to change the way in which racial incident paperwork is produced and processed through the system.

On the other hand, the operational aspect of the policy for relief officers is framed in the legal term of 'managerial professionalism' and aims to use the law to change the way in which the immediately responding police officer deals with reported racial incidents—to deal with them as crime (i.e. section 47 assault), rather than as non-crime offences (i.e. common assault). The operational aspect of the policy directed at Home Beat officers is framed in the managerial/professional language of community policing—in terms of 'information', 'explanation', and 'communication'. That this aspect of the policy relates specifically to community relations is signified by the instruction that the actions of the 'officer of appropriate rank' (specified in West Ham as a Home Beat officer) is to be conducted *independent of investigation.*

Policing Practice—Processing a Racial Incident

Thus far, this Chapter has presented data concerning the occupational common-sense understanding of racial incidents and the formal policies directed at controlling the way in which two components of the police organization respond to reported racial incidents. Appendix II describes the formal structure of the components of the police organization responsible for some aspect of the response to racial incidents, the style of work of these units and sections. This Appendix will be referred to in order to explain the role and function of each organizational unit as it appears in the narrative presented in the next section.

What follows is a narrative account of how racial incident records are processed through the police organization in practice. The intent is to map this process, noting where decisions are made and on what basis, and where and how policy exerts an effect. The means used to present this material will be a series of flow diagrams, based on those presented by Manning (1983:178; 1988). Instead of Manning's detailed semiotic approach, however, the notion of organizational processing is employed.

The flow diagram shown in Figure 8.1 illustrates the entire processing of a racial incident from entry into the system through the various points at which it will exit from the system. This process may be broken down into five distinct stages, based on the point in time at which the relevant events occur, the nature of the decisions made, the administration of different forms of paperwork, and the component of the police organization most likely to be involved. In essence, the process consists of the following stages: *Stage I*—input into the police system by the informant/victim and its initial processing by the despatcher; *Stage II*—the initial response and reporting of the incident by a 'mobile unit' or relief officer; at *stage III* the incident may be processed in one of two ways—either as a 'racial incident' by the Community Contact Team (stage IIIa), or as a 'crime' by the Crime Desk and CID (stage IIIb), or both. *Stage IVa* follows the processing of racial incidents through the Youth and Community Section administrative system and *stage IVb* the processing of crime incidents through the investigative process to court action.

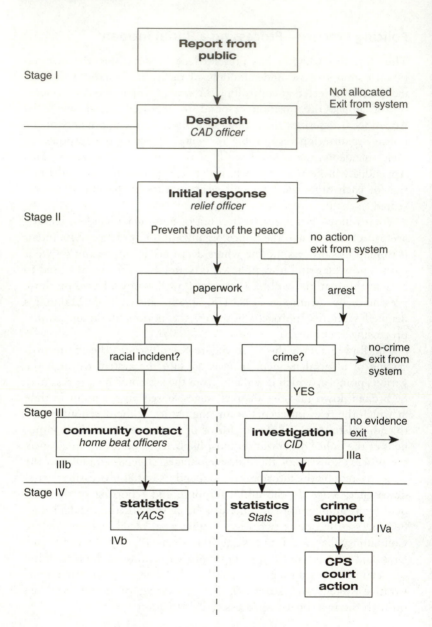

Figure 8.1 *Police Processing of a Racial Incident (Outline)*

Stage I: Input and Initial Processing (Figure 8.2)

The input of a racial incident into the police system may come from a range of sources, of which four make up the bulk in the locality observed. These are from the complainant by telephone (by dialling 999 or calling the local station), by a visit to the police station, by stopping an officer on the street, or by referral from another agency

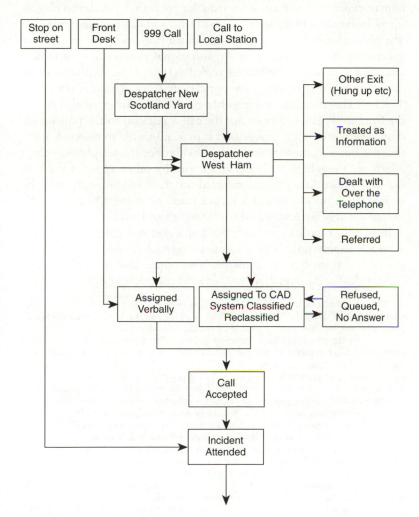

Figure 8.2 *Stage I: Input and Initial Processing*

(see Manning, 1988). Most accounts of policing in general identify the bulk of reports entering the police organization by telephone, a finding which is supported by the victim survey data collected in North Plaistow.[13] The incidents recorded by the police, however, show a preponderance of incidents referred from the housing department.[14] (See also pp. 273–5, below)

The input into the police organization is a point at which complex human experience and personal troubles are transformed into objects for policing. Manning describes the transformation as one in which 'the phenomena of interest are transformed from everyday or primary experience into secondary or organisationally encoded experience; and the life experience becomes reified', (1983: 173). At the moment that an incident is reported a set of classificatory decisions are made. The first classification, made either by the despatcher or the PC on the front desk, is whether or not the call is relevant to the police and, thus, whether or not a mobile unit is to be allocated to respond. Calls that are not allocated might be dealt with over the telephone; others which are thought to be better dealt with by other agencies (such as the ambulance service) are referred to them. Some calls may be treated as information and a record made of them. Others may be judged entirely irrelevant and no formal record made.

If the call is 'police relevant', the despatcher will enter the call onto a visual display unit (VDU) using a range of 'police relevant categories' based on type of event (such as crime, dispute, disturbance, sudden death, etc. noted above), seriousness (such as extent of phys-

[13] Three-quarters of the incidents said to have been reported were reported by telephone, either by using the 999 service (40%) or by calling the local station (34%). 22 per cent of the incidents were reported by visiting a local station.

[14] 38% of the racial incidents occurring in North Plaistow recorded by the police came direct from members of the public, while 62% were referred by the local housing office. The incidents referred from the housing office were already defined as racially motivated prior to being recorded by the police. The majority of these reports arrived with the police by letter (a pro forma letter—RH4), in accordance with Newham council's housing policy to refer all incidents to the police where the victim consents. This letter, signed by the district housing manager, was addressed to the Divisional Chief Superintendent, and sent immediately to the divisional CCT to deal with as part of police policy. This bureaucratic process was inevitably a time-consuming one. The data indicate that of the 94 incidents referred to the police by housing, only 3 arrived with the police on the day that the incident occurred. Within 7 days of the incident occurring still only 44% had come to the attention of the police. It is not possible to pinpoint precisely where delay occurred, but there are undoubtedly instances in which there are delays in reporting by the victim (when attending the local office for some other reason), in processing the paperwork through the housing department, in processing the paperwork through the police organization.

ical injury), urgency of the call (such as 'incident in progress' v. incident discovered long after its occurrence). As noted above, there are a very large number of calls being processed by this complex system. When an incident is classified onto the VDU it is given a classification code, an identifying number, the name of the caller, the location of the incident, and a variable number of lines of additional information on the nature of the call (this could be anything from two lines to two pages). The calls in which we are interested could not be identified easily as they passed through the operator of the computer-aided despatch (CAD) system or 'despatcher' because there was no CAD classification number specifically for racial incidents. Clearly, there is scope for this, notwithstanding the problems with overcoming the occupational common-sense resistance to defining incidents as racially motivated.

All calls processed by the despatcher are temporarily 'parked' on the system, awaiting the dispatcher's decision whether or not to assign an officer to the call. A graded-response system operated, wherein calls were allocated according to 'operational priority' rather than chronological order. Those judged to be of high priority (e.g. robbery in progress) were likely to be allocated immediately; those judged to be of low priority will remain 'parked' on the system until an officer is available to respond to the call. This might give rise to a delay of anything from a few minutes to a few hours.

Stage II: Attending the Scene (Figure 8.3)

Having been allocated to a call a mobile unit will proceed with varying degrees of haste to the location of the incident, primed to deal with it only with the snippet of information provided by the despatcher over the radio. This information may extend no further than an indication that the call is a crime, dispute, or disturbance. It is unlikely that officers attending an incident defined by the victim as racially motivated will conceptualize it as such. The incident is, therefore, responded to solely in terms of its police relevance. As an inspector put it: 'officers turning up at the scene view things in terms of crime'. That is, their ultimate concern was whether or not an arrestable offence had occurred (see Sheptycki, 1993: 44–78).

Although the eventual outcome of the call depends on how the incident is defined, at the point of arrival, the initial role of the 'attending officer' is that of 'peace officer' tasked with the 'emergency

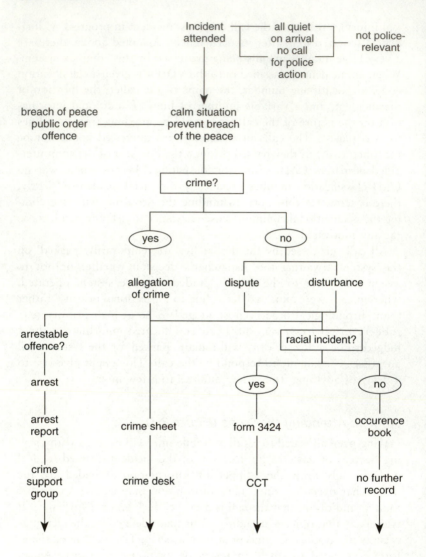

Figure 8.3 *Stage II: Attending the Scene*

maintenance of order' (Reiner, 1985: 116). The officer thus assesses whether or not a 'breach of the peace' (Public Order Act 1986) has occurred or is likely to occur (Sheptycki, 1993: 49–50); and, if so, the police officer may decide to arrest one or more parties to the incident. The racial incidents recorded by the police suggest that this action occurred rarely (see pp. 278–9, below).

Having dealt with the practicalities of what could well be a volatile situation and having ensured that 'order' is maintained for the immediate future, the attending officer must make a range of classificatory decisions. These decisions can be identified in terms of the completion of specific items of paperwork. Relevant to the present discussion are the decisions whether or not to classify the incident as a 'crime' and whether or not to classify it as 'racial'. If the officer decides that the incident is neither a crime nor racial (nor any other of the categories that would merit a formal record, such as a 'domestic'), the officer may only make a record of the incident in his or her individual notebook which may or may not be written up subsequently in the station's occurrence book.

Defining an Event as a Crime

The decision to classify the event as a crime (and therefore to complete a 278 'crime form') is 'done by the book' according the first-line managers (sergeants and inspectors) interviewed; that is, according to the formal rules of the law and criminal procedure. However, the interpretation of the law depends on occupational factors including the officer's knowledge of 'the job' and his or her judgement of what has occurred in the incident. In particular, this interpretation is based on judgements about the likely course of events if a crime form is completed (e.g. the chances of securing a criminal conviction) and if a crime form is not completed (e.g. the chances of management discovering that the law was interpreted too narrowly). Decision-making at this point is also influenced by the officer's view of the protagonists involved. If an incident meets the criteria necessary to merit its recording as a 'crime', the first section of a crime form will be completed by the attending officer at the time of the incident. This will include details of the allegation, date and time of the offence and when it was reported, details of the scene, of the victim, and of the informant (where someone other than the victim reported the offence). After being checked by the relief inspector, this form is passed to the Crime Desk.

It is relevant in looking at this decision-making process to draw a distinction between 'property', 'personal', and 'public order' offences. The classification of property and personal offences hinges on the basis that, for an offence to have occurred, there must be a 'victim' and a 'suspect'. For property crime (including criminal damage) the decision to 'crime' the incident (i.e. complete a crime record) is straightforward. If there is evidence of damage or a witness stating that (non-accidental) loss or damage has occurred, a crime can unequivocally be said to have occurred. The victim is the person complaining of the loss or damage; the suspect is either identified or said simply to be 'person or persons unknown'.

In the case of an offence against the person, however, this initial classification is made problematic if the victim seems at all unwilling to sustain his or her allegation against the suspect. In order for a 'crime' to have occurred and for the event to *sustain* that definition the victim must be willing, and appear to be willing, to 'substantiate the allegation'. If at any point the victim becomes unwilling unequivocally to reiterate his or her allegation against the suspect (throughout investigation and on to court), the 'crime' literally ceases to exist and will be 'no-crimed' (Sheptycki, 1993: 56).

This point in the process determines whether or not the law enforcement function of policing is triggered. If a reported incident is not recorded as crime at this point, it is very unlikely that it will be defined as such at a later point. Thus, if an incident is defined initially by the attending officer as a 'dispute' rather than a crime, it is unlikely that law enforcement will follow, unless the incident were to escalate while the officer was present at the incident. From the officers' point of view, crime is defined by the legal framework. Their decision-making is guided first by objective evidence of what has occurred.

In theory, an incident may be defined as a section 47 assault if there is only psychological injury (see the 1987 *Force Order*, quoted above). However, I was informed consistently that only in instances where there was physical injury would such a classification be made. Thus, for an event to be defined as a section 47 assault in practice there must be a clearly identifiable victim—that is someone with a *physical* injury and clearly identifiable suspect—someone whom the victim and preferably an 'independent witness' is willing to identify as his or her assailant (Sheptycki, 1993). Without injury and 'independent evidence' that the alleged assailant is responsible, the officer will tend not to define the event as a crime. The decision is affected, secondly, by the attending officer's knowledge and beliefs about what will occur later in the criminal process—such as the decisions taken by first-line management, the Crown Prosecution Service (CPS), and courts. If the officer thinks that, ultimately, the evidence is insufficient for the CPS to think that a prosecution is justified, it is unlikely that he or she will complete a crime form.

Where the legal position of the incident is, from the officer's point of view ambiguous—for example, where there is no physical injury or where there is only the word of the alleged victim (or a member of his or her family) against that of the alleged perpetrator—it is unlikely to be recorded as a crime. Decisions where legality is ambiguous also allow the norms and values of the officers' occupational culture to come to the fore. Of particular relevance to the definition of racial incident as 'crime' are beliefs about the 'innocence' of ethnic minority victims and the extent to which they are thought culpable for their victimization, beliefs about the validity of the perpetrators' resentment of the presence of ethnic minorities, and their 'threatening' cultural practices and beliefs about the tendency of ethnic minorities tendency to be 'compulsive liars' (see 248–256 above).

Implementing the Operational Policy

What, then, can be said about the instruction of the 1987 *Force Order* to treat all allegations of assault with injury, however slight, which are perceived by the victim to be racially motivated as section 47 assault?

It is evident from police records that this 'operational' aspect of the policy was not implemented. Despite the attempt to tighten the legal framework in this regard, attending officers, by and large, continued to apply the quasi-legal decision-making process of traditional operational common-sense policework. Thus, despite the existence of a policy which elevated racially motivated common assaults to actual bodily harm (ABH), it remained the case that unless there was bruising or a cut, racial incidents (like any other incident) would, from an enforcement point of view, be defined as an 'offence' (common assault), but not a 'crime' (ABH) (Young, 1991).

Defining an incident as 'racial' had no bearing on the officer's view of enforcement. This observation is closely related to the irrelevance of motive to the definition of a crime in criminal law. As Smith and Hogan put it:

if either the *actus reus* or the *mens rea* of any crime is lacking, no motive, however evil, will make a man guilty of a crime . . . motive, by definition, is irrelevant to criminal responsibility—that is, a man may be lawfully convicted of a crime whatever his motive may be, or even if he has no motive [1983: 66–7].

However, as *evidence* motive is always relevant, (Smith and Hogan, 1983: 67)—if we know that a suspect has a motive for committing a crime, then this makes it more likely that he or she committed it. Even here, with regard to racial incidents, there remain problems in identifying a specifically racist motive—that is concrete evidence that the perpetrator had singled out this particular victim on the basis of 'race' or racism—a point noted by police officers above. In actually deciding whether or not an offence has been committed and how it is to be categorized in law and defined by the police, a racial or any other motive is quite irrelevant. As the Community Contact Team (CCT) office informed the North Plaistow project at its outset 'it is not possible to practically detail Police responsibilities directed to racial attacks since the application of Police powers in respect of criminal law are applicable to the community as a whole and not directed to any particular group'. In other words, as Grimshaw and Jefferson point out, effective *operational policy* (authoritative statements signifying settled practices of law enforcement) did not exist. The universality of constabulary independence makes operational policy effectively redundant (1987: 291). Or, as the Home Beat sergeant put it, 'definitions of crime spring from the legal framework; the only way to make these offences appear as crime would be to pass a law making these specific incidents criminal offences' (see also Forbes, 1988).

Defining an Incident as 'Racial'

The principal criterion on which an incident would be formally defined as 'racial' (and therefore for a racial incident form to be completed) is that it appeared to the reporting or investigating officer or any other person to include an element of *racial motivation*. This would, therefore, include such 'objective' criteria as the use of racist language or the presence of racist graffiti. It would also be based on the victim's perception that the incident was racially motivated.

It is evident from police records that racial incident forms are completed, though it is not possible to estimate the proportion of incidents where an allegation of racial motivation is made but not recorded as 'racial' by the police. There is evidently a conflict between the requirements of the organization for additional paper to be completed and the occupational common-sense understanding of what constitutes a racial incident. Given that the only requirement of the attending officer is to complete a racial incident form in instances when racial motivation is alleged, there is reason to think that this procedure is completed in most cases.

With respect to law enforcement, however, the completion of a racial incident form has little or no influence on the way in which the incident is dealt with at the scene. As we shall see in the next section, following the police attendance at the incident, 'crime' and 'racial incident' paperwork follow quite separate and independent routes through the police organization.

Stage IIIa: Investigation (Figure 8.4)

The role of the *crime desk* is to screen the vast volume of crime reports produced by the reliefs (see Appendix 2: 343) and coming through the front desk. The kernel of the decision-making process concerns the value of investigation: is there enough evidence to justify the investment of additional time in the case? Those cases which are deemed not to merit any further investigation are 'screened out'. They then simply exit from the investigative system and are filed. After the implementation of the Plus Programme all victims of crime were sent a word-processed letter of commiseration, a case reference, and contact name.

Crimes that are 'screened in' are passed back to detectives and other operational officers, who will 'develop the investigation of the case' and seek further evidence by, for example, interviewing the victim (in their status as witness), interviewing any suspects, independent witnesses, seeking forensic evidence, etc. (see Hobbs, 1988). The case might be allocated to the Criminal Investigation Department (CID) in the case of serious crimes, to Home Beat officers (in the case of 'beat crimes'); or to members of special squads or other dedicated officers (such as the Domestic Violence Unit, Drug Squad, NORIS, etc.).

For present purposes, these officers can be grouped together under the title of 'investigating officer'. This officer decides whether or not a 'crime' has actually occurred in the same way that the attending officer makes a decision at the scene. Again, the decision whether or

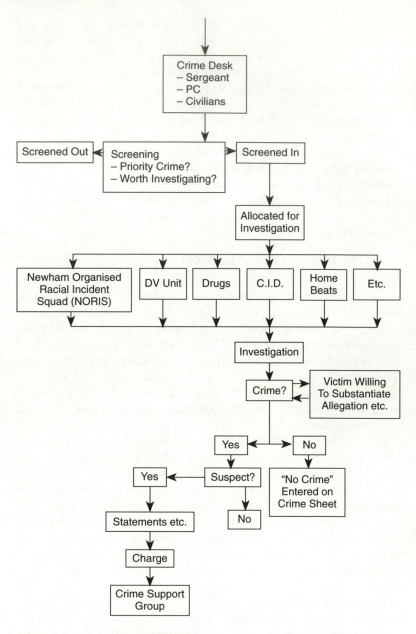

Figure 8.4 *Stage IIIa: Investigation*

not to 'no-crime' an incident hinges on the willingness of the victim to substantiate the allegation (Sheptycki, 1993: 55–6). If, on investigation, the complainant says that he or she was mistaken about what had occurred, or if it appears to the investigating officer that he or she was mistaken, drunk, or lying, the allegation of crime is effectively nullified and the incident is 'no-crimed'.

Stage IVa: Preparing a Prosecution (Figure 8.5)

In those incidents which are crimed and in which a suspect is detected, the paperwork will be passed to the Crime Support Group, which will prepare the papers for prosecution. The final decision whether or not to prosecute lies with the Crown Prosecution Service.

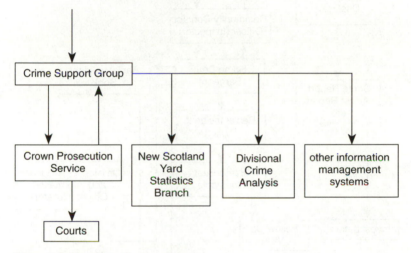

Figure 8.5 *Stage IVa: Prosecution*

Stage IIIb: Follow-up on Racial Incidents (Figure 8.6)

The paperwork for those incidents defined as 'racial' by the attending officer is passed to the Community Contact Team (CCT). Joining the process at this point are also incidents referred to the police by other agencies. The records referred from housing are pre-classified as racial incidents and, thus, pass directly to the CCT. On receipt of a referral from housing, the CCT sergeant completes a racial incident form (a copy of which is also sent to the Chief Inspector (operations))

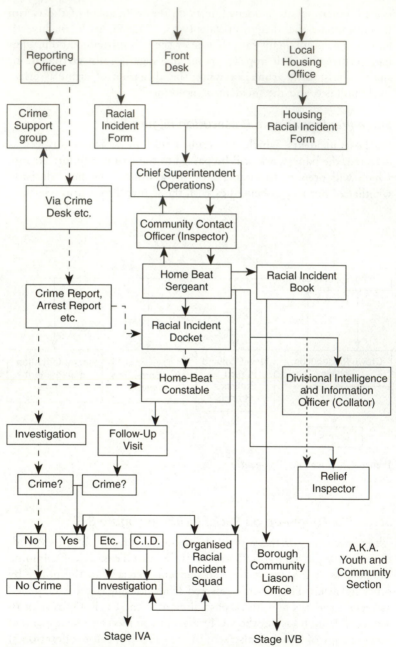

Figure 8.6 *Stage IIIb: Racial Incident Follow-up*

and from this point reports from the two sources flow into the same channel of processing.

The CCT sergeant assigns an identifying number to the racial incident form, files one copy in a 'racial incident book', and places one copy into a docket which will also be used to file any other relevant papers. The incident is then passed to the Home Beat officer on whose beat the incident occurred. In both official policy and operational practice, the Home Beat officer's role is to conduct a follow-up visit to explain why (in most cases) no prosecution will result, to maintain communication with the victim. Although the main remit of the Home Beat officer is not to investigate, he or she is able to record further details of the case and has the potential for spending time with individual victims.

Stage IVb: Monitoring Racial Incidents (Figure 8.7)

The subsequent stages of processing a racial incident move completely away from operational policing. The Home Beat sergeant passes the racial incident form (together with a checklist of actions taken) to the borough Community Liaison Officer (CLO) for the attention of the borough information officer. The form is then logged in a book of incidents which have occurred in the borough.

One of the primary roles of the borough information officer was the collation and dissemination of weekly and monthly racial incident statistics. Monthly statistics were produced for local dissemination. Two reports (one for the month and one for the year to the end of the relevant month) were sent to NORIS and to the two Divisional Information and Intelligence Units (DIIU) at Plaistow and West Ham divisions. These statistics were broken down by type of offence and contained details of persons identified and the clear-up rates. These reports were also made available to the local authority and to the local council for racial equality (see Table 8.3).

The borough information officer finally passed weekly statistics to the Area information office. The Area information office calculated clear-up rates for the area by police division and passed the records up to TO30 at Scotland Yard for publication as quarterly reports which were made available to such organizations as the Commission for Racial Equality (CRE) and Greater London Action for Racial Equality (GLARE) (see Table 8.3). The final resting-place of racial incident reports was in annual aggregated data which are presented in the Commissioner's year-end report.

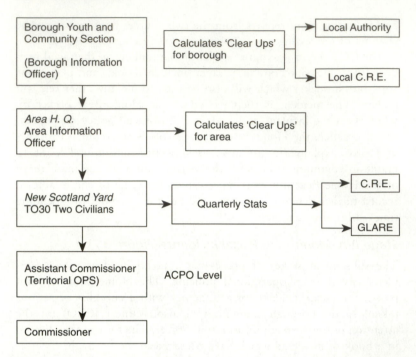

Figure 8.7 *Stage IVb: Final Processing of a Racial Incident*

The Outcomes of Policing Practice

In 1986 racial incidents were established as a police priority by the Association of Chief Police Officers (ACPO) and the Commissioner of London's Metropolitan Police. As the Government Inter-departmental Racial Attacks Group (RAG) report stated, the police were at the forefront of the state response to racial incidents:

Given their responsibility for maintaining the peace, for crime prevention, and for apprehending those who break the law, the police have primary responsibility for responding to racial incidents. This responsibility is recognised by both chief officers of police and by the Government [Home Office, 1989: paragraph 64].

Symbolically at least, racial harassment had reached a high level of prioritization. This is in itself important. To prioritize a form of crime, acknowledge past deficiencies, and take steps to make

Table 8.3 *Racial incidents recorded by the Metropolitan Police by type of incident (1980–92)*

Year	Serious assaults	Minor assaults	Abusive language/ behaviour	Criminal damage	All racial incidents
1980	–	–	–	–	77
1981	–	–	–	–	727
1982	–	–	–	–	1346
1983	–	–	–	–	1276
1984	322	189	–	–	1515
1985	350	243	–	–	1945
1986	220	282	–	–	1733
1987	270	397	–	–	2179
1988	250	–	–	–	2214
1989	186	–	–	–	2697
1990	12%	18%	38%	23%	2908
1991	17%	14%	25%	29%	3373

Year	violence against the person	criminal damage	inciting racial hatred	racial abuse etc.	civil/ neighbour disputes	common assault	other	Total
1991	583	952	252	835	105	–	105	3373
1992	517	997	273	770	86	421	163	3227

Notes
1. Definition of racial incident: ACPO.
2. The figures given include the following types of incident: serious assaults, minor assaults, arson, criminal damage, leafleting, abusive behaviour, and slogan-writing.
3. Figures are not available on the number of persons arrested.
The way in which racial incidents were categorized was changed in 1991.

improvement, in theory, signal to actual and potential perpetrators that such crimes will not be tolerated and promise protection to ethnic minority communities. What is far more important, however, is that symbolic prioritization is translated into effective action.

But what is meant by effective action?[15] Quality of service?[16] In order to answer these questions we must first establish what *effects* policing is intended to achieve. The RAG report quoted above offers three effects to which police action should be directed: (1) law

[15] *Chambers English Dictionary* defines 'effective' (adj.) as 'having power to effect: causing something: successful in producing a result or effect: powerful'.
[16] *Chambers English Dictionary* defines 'quality' (adj.) as 'high grade of excellence'.

enforcement, (2) order maintenance, and (3) crime prevention. One might add to this list (4) the improvement of performance indicators and (5) increase community consultation. To conclude this Chapter, the effect of the police in each of these capacities will be examined using the evidence presented in this study.

Law Enforcement

The police are the central agency charged with law enforcement—the 'gatekeepers' of the criminal justice system. With regard to racial incidents, the police have emphasized their role as law enforcers: '[i]t is Metropolitan Police policy to treat any racially motivated incident as a high priority. This means that where the evidence exists appropriate action will be taken in respect of *initiating prosecutions* against the perpetrators of such offences' (Metropolitan Police, 1989a: 10).

This definitive statement places racially motivated incidents squarely in the domain of crime and of law enforcement. The Met's *London Racial Harassment Action Guide*—of which 100,000 copies were distributed in 1989—states that the police are 'most likely to initiate the prosecution process' when called to: acts intended or likely to stir up racial hatred; cases of assault, even those which inflict only psychological harm, 'such as an hysterical or nervous condition' (1989a: 3); threatening abusive or insulting words or behaviour; and damage to property.

As the case study illustrates, however, in general the police considered only the most serious racial incidents as 'crimes'; and in only the most serious of those was prosecution initiated. Cases of minor assault, threats, or abusive behaviour—whether or not they psychologically harmed the victims—were not even defined as crimes, much less were they prosecuted. Of the 152 incidents recorded by the police in the eighteen-month period from 1 July 1987 to 31 December 1988, in only ten incidents were interviews with offenders conducted and in only two cases were charges brought. This amounts to a prosecution rate of 1.3 per cent (see Table 8.4).

We may conclude that the implementation of the *operational* aspect of the 1987 *Force Order*, which aimed to orient the response of the relief and CID officers towards law enforcement in racial incidents, appears to have failed. Despite the reading of the law offered in the *Force Order,* operational common sense of the rank-and-file PC identified racial incidents as existing in an area of legal ambiguity. Despite the victim's perception that incidents were racially motivated,

Table 8.4 *Action taken by the police in racial incidents in North Plaistow*

1 July 87–1 January 89

Action taken	%	n
Against the suspect:		
referral to housing	0.7	1
arrests	1.3	2
charges brought	1.3	2
In support of the victim		
Home beat visit	99	150
Other action		
Increased patrol	55	84
Observation	42	64
Victim diary	1.3	2
Referrals		
None	90	137
Victim Suport	6	9
Community group	3	5

N = 152

reporting officers' operational common sense led to a tendency to deny such motivation or to consider it irrelevant. Operational common sense came to the fore and those racial incidents which did not fall into the category of 'crime' were generally neither investigated nor prosecuted.

Law enforcement may be advocated for numerous reasons, among them punishment of the perpetrator, specific deterrence of the individual prosecuted, general deterrence of potential offenders; and (through deterrence) the prevention of the recurrence of the offence and protection of the victim. Without effective law enforcement, it would follow, these functions cannot be fulfilled.

Order Maintenance

Police research indicates that the police rarely 'enforce the law' in most reported incidents, so it is hardly surprising that this is also the case for racial incidents. Many studies find evidence of the tendency of the police to 'negotiate order', rather than 'enforce the law'. Robert Reiner, for example, argues that most policework is order-maintenance—the settlement of conflict by means other than formal

law enforcement. As Reiner and others have noted, by skilfully bal-ancing the recourse to legally sanctioned coercive force, the police act as peace keepers, arbiters, and maintainers of order.[17] Clearly, the first priority of a policing response to a reported instance of racial violence is the prevention of any (further) violence, injury, or dam-age from occurring. Up to a point we can concur, therefore, with Reiner's view that order-maintenance is the 'core mandate' of the police and is a function 'which is both necessary and capable of fullfilment by the police' (1985: 116).

Crucial to this discussion, however, is Reiner's observation that 'order maintenance is just as problematic in terms of social and polit-ical justice as the higher-profile issues of crime control' (Reiner, 1985: 115). What this means from the point of view of the victim of racial harassment is that 'order-maintenance' may serve simply to maintain the ongoing process of their victimization. If the threat of violence and occasional use of actual violence is used to intimidate, exclude, or terrorize, the balance of power between victim and perpetrator remains. Such action, therefore, may be perceived by the victim as a failure of police protection and by the perpetrator as sanctioning his or her actions (Hesse et al., 1992). That the victims generally view police intervention to be ineffective is evident from the survey (see 235–8, above).

Crime Prevention

Although it is generally agreed that 'the police have a major respon-sibility in relation to the prevention of racial incidents' (Home Office, 1989: paragraph. 75), how exactly this responsibility is to be met is far from clear. The policing process described above appears to hold little scope for prevention, nor indeed does any aspect of the opera-tional policy actually hold out the promise of any such prevention. Prevention, inasmuch as it is addressed at all, is considered to fall in the domain of 'the multi-agency approach' to which we will return in Chapter 9.

Information Production and Distribution

Although the Met's racial incident policy appears to have made little impact on the front-line operational response to racial violence it is not the case that the policy changed nothing. On the contrary, it

---

[17] Reiner, 1985: 111–16; Shapland and Hobbs, 1989: 22–3.

changed some aspects of policework quite dramatically. Specifically, racial incidents policy has introduced a large information, production, and distribution process and with it a bureaucracy to administer it. It is evident that the implementation of the *administrative* policy of the 1987 *Force Order* directed at the reliefs was successfully implemented. Although the rank-and-file police officers were reluctant to define an incident as 'racially motivated' the instruction to complete an item of paperwork when racial motivation was alleged, while it might be irksome to them, was strongly determined by the managerial directives and administrative system which it set in place. It is not possible, however, to be certain what proportion of all reported instances of violent racism is recorded. The survey data presented in Chapter 7 indicate that many more incidents are occurring than official records suggest. It may be that this discrepancy is explained in part by non-recording on the part of the police.

The implementation of the *operational* policy directed at Home Beat officers appears to have been largely successful. The task was defined within the terms of the occupational common sense of community-relations policing (which is common to both police constables and managers) and was strongly determined by the instructions contained in the *Force Order* and the routine supervision of paperwork which it set in place. The implementation of *administrative* policy directed at Home Beat officers and the YACS at levels between the divisional and headquarters levels was also largely successful. Here, Youth and Community sections formed *in themselves* an administrative system and were able to respond almost automatically to the requirements of the Force Order of which it was, itself, author.

For some Home Beat officers the administration of racial incident forms took up a considerable portion of their time. Monitoring this paperwork was an important feature of the work of the CCT sergeant and dedicated personnel in YACS at borough, Area, and Headquarters levels. The Metropolitan Police can rightly point to all of these officers as providing a response to racial harassment and to the costs of implementing this policy. But these officers respond principally to the problem in a bureaucratic sense—filling in and collating forms, report-writing, and presenting the police case to outside bodies. There is no evidence that this monitoring has any effect on how police officers (either Home Beat or relief) respond to reported instances of violent racism. Rather, the evidence points to the changes in practice going no further than completing a racial incident pro forma.

The Home Beat officers who provide a service in the most meaningful sense may be seen as a resource for the community. It is with the Home Beat officers that the greatest potential for providing support for racial attack victims and engaging in preventive work lies However, the work of these officers was unfocused and there was little evidence of successful preventive initiatives being taken either by individual officers or the 'team' as a collection. Moreover, what these officers were also, in this locality at the time of the study, was a reserve army of personnel available as 'mutual aid' to other divisions for the policing of public order in which a large number of officers were deployed.

Performance Indicators: The Clear-up Rate

The information produced and distributed by the community relations bureaucracy produces a measure of police performance—the clear-up rate—which is at odds with the indicators of performance from the victim survey or the analysis of police records presented above. In common parlance, a crime cleared up may be equated with a crime 'solved'; the term implies that a suspect has been apprehended and prosecuted. In 1988, 31 per cent of the racial incidents recorded by the police in Area 2 of the Metropolitan Police were 'cleared up'. At a public meeting in 1989, the divisional CLO for West Ham division claimed that 35 per cent of the incidents in the division were cleared up in the previous year. How then is a clear-up rate of 35 per cent reported for the division as a whole to be reconciled with the prosecution rate of only 1.3 per cent observed in the study site? The answer is that a clear-up includes not only those incidents in which an arrest was made, but also those in which 'victim and suspect are known to the police and appropriate action taken'. Thus, in those incidents defined by the police as 'disputes', 'appropriate action' would simply be to have 'advised' both parties. As the Home Beat sergeant put it, 'if a clear up rate of 35 per cent is being given, then its a little bit, well, tongue in cheek'. As an illustration of the extent to which credibility was being stretched, the sergeant pointed to borough-wide clear up rates of 45 per cent which had been calculated for some months.

This process of artificially inflating the clear-up rate also occurs on a London-wide basis—as published figures demonstrate. Between 1984 and 1986 the Met's performance indicator for their response to racial harassment was a 'clear-up rate' representing 'racial incidents in which an arrest was made'. As Table 8.5 shows, this 'clear-up rate' remained relatively constant from 13 per cent in 1984 to 12.5 per cent in 1986. In 1987, the definition of a clear-up changed to include not only those in which an arrest was made, but also those in which 'appropriate action' was taken. While the arrest rate remained constant at 12.8 per cent, the proportion of incidents 'cleared up' rose dramatically to 30.8 per cent. Without police performance changing in the slightest, the new performance indicator demonstrated a two and half fold improvement over the previous year. In 1988 the arrest rate was no longer published, leaving the redefined clear-up rate at 33 per cent.

The importance of the clear-up rate as an indicator of police performance should not be underestimated. While in 1986 the Home Affairs Committee commented that at 12.5 per cent the Met's clear-up rate was 'worryingly low', the 1989 House of Commons Home Affairs Committee reported that: '[t]he clear up rate for racial incidents in the Metropolitan Police Area has risen from 15 per cent in 1985 to 33 per cent in 1988 (Commissioner's report for 1988). We welcome this advance which we expect to see sustained in future years' (House of Commons 1989: vii).

Thus, the new clear-up rate acquired a life of its own as a performance measure. The data produced by the Youth and Community structure and published by Scotland Yard are taken at face value as a hard-and-fast performance measure. It became a social fact. It

Table 8.5 *Racial incidents recorded by the Metropolitan Police: arrests and clear-ups*

Year	Recorded racial incidents	Incidents in which arrests made	Incidents cleared up
1980	277		–
1981	727		–
1982	1346		–
1983	1276		–
1984	1515	13.0%	–
1985	1945	14.7%	–
1986	1733	12.5%	–
1987	2179	12.8%	30.8%
1988	2214	n/a	33.0%
1989	2697	n/a	–
1990	2908	n/a	–
1991	3373	n/a	–
1992	3227	n/a	22.0%

appears to claim that one third of racial incidents were solved in 1988—a noteworthy 'advance' over previous years. Given that, for recorded crime as a whole, clear-up rates have been declining slowly to around the 10–15 per cent mark, the Met's racial-incident clear-up rate is impressive. However, a closer look at this impressive improvement reveals it to be a falsehood. The data produced in the Commissioners report and reproduced by the House of Commons are entirely misleading. The increase is attributable solely to a change in the definition of a crime cleared up.

Conclusion

This Chapter has attempted to unravel a paradox of policing violent racism: that is, 'performance' has improved while practice remains unchanged. It is clear that, as claimed by the police managers, racial incidents were made a 'force priority', a consequence of which is that all incidents so defined are given personal attention by an inspector and a Home Beat officer. Recording and monitoring have improved. Contact with the community has increased. Clear-up rates have risen. As a consequence of these 'improvements' and the introduction of the multi-agency approach, the crisis of police legitmacy which threatened to engulf the institution in the mid-1980s has receded. And, yet, *operational* practice remains largely unchanged. For deep-rooted legal, organizational, structural and cultural reasons, the police still do not prevent violent racism; they offer little or no protection for victims and tend not to enforce the law against perpetrators. Meanwhile the rank and file tend play down the problem and deny the relevance of racism. *Plus ça change, plus c'est la même chose.* The implications of this depressing conclusion are drawn out in the final chapter.

9

Conclusions

'All our silences in the face of racist assault are acts of complicity' (bell hooks, 1996).

In a nutshell, it is argued here that while violent racism is a *social process,* the police and criminal justice system respond to *incidents,* and in this contradiction lies an explanation of why the targets of violent racism feel unprotected and remain dissatisfied with the police response despite apparent improvements in police policy.

When 'racial' characteristics—that is: features of the body (skin pigmentation; eye- or hair-colour; width of nose or lip), cultural or geographical origins—inform or justify the practice of discrimination, insult, harassment, and physical violence, this does not occur in a moment, but is ongoing, dynamic, embedded in time, space, and place. It cannot, therefore, meaningfully be reduced to an isolated 'incident', but must be kept in context if it is to be understood and responded to effectively (see Chapters 5 and 7). Context refers to: historical patterns of xenophobia; the lived experiences of the individuals, families, and communities targeted; local population dynamics (especially balances of numerical, political, and economic power); the attitudes and behaviour of offenders, their families, and communities; and the wider context of local, national, and global discourses and practices of race and nation. In particular, violent racism must be seen in the context of discursive practices of racial exclusion. Becoming a victim of any crime—particularly of one as complex as violent racism—does not occur in an instant or in a physical or ideological vacuum. Victimization—with the emphasis on the suffix *-ization*—denotes a dynamic process, occurring over time. It describes how an individual *becomes* a victim within a specific social, political, and historical context (see Chapter 5).

The other half of the argument is that in opposition to the experience of violent racism, the process of law enforcement—policing and

the administration of criminal justice—is constituted in the response
to tightly-defined *incidents*. An incident is a one-dimensional, narrowly restricted time-slice, within which only the actions of the
immediate protagonists are of relevance. So, for example, English
criminal law understands crime only as a single event—a 'guilty act'
(*actus reus*) committed by an individual with criminal intent, or
'guilty mind' (*mens rea*). The incident become isolated, detached
from the wider context of racism and racial exclusion. Incidents are
describable and measurable but appear random and inexplicable.
When context is drained from lived experience, it becomes impossible to understand the significance of the event to the individual or
community targeted, or how and why the event occurred. As the incident is transformed from the world of the victims' experience into an
object for policing it is placed in the new context of the police organizational and cultural milieu. This new environment is commonly
antithetical to that of the victim (see Chapter 8).

The consequence of this contradiction between the process of victimization and the police response to incidents is that while police
officers may believe that they have responded effectively in general or
in any given case, the survivors are frequently left unsatisfied, unprotected, and fearful (see Chapters 7 and 8).

The Failure of the Police to Protect the Targets of Violent Racism

Criminal justice statitistics—such as victim surveys and police
records—show that many criminal offences are never reported, and
in only a small minority is a suspect detected and prosecuted. Many
offenders will be informally warned or formally cautioned by the
police, and when charges are brought, many cases will be discontin-
ued by the Crown Prosecution Service or result in an acquittal. As a
result, in only about 2 per cent of all 'notifiable' criminal offences is
an offender caught and convicted (Home Office, 1996a). This study
shows that attrition in 'racial incidents' is greater than for the 'average' offence. Chapters 5 and 6 indicated that between 2 and 5 per
cent of all incidents are recorded by the police. Of those recorded by
the police in North Plaistow in the eighteen months following the
introduction of a new racial-incident policy aimed at increasing law
enforcement, prosecution occurred in only 1.3 per cent of cases (two
out of 152). Calculated on the same basis as the Home Office figure

refered to above, about four racial incidents in 10,000 resulted in prosecution.[1]

If the extent of law enforcement is indicative, it seems clear that policing and the criminal justice system do not offer protection from violent racism. The historical record shows that police managers for many years insisted that violent racism was an intractable problem the solution to which was beyond their remit; and when they changed their minds and elevated racial incidents to the status of 'force priority' they did so reluctantly (see Rose, 1996: 68–9). The view that the police rarely enforce the law in instances of violent racism has been expressed by many people inside and outside the police organization. Any claims that the police are routinely effective (using 'clear-up rates', for example) must be treated with great scepticism (see Chapter 6).

Perhaps the focus on enforcement misses the point. Robert Reiner (1992), for example, argues that policing must be seen principally as order maintenance—irrespective of beliefs about what the function of policing *ought* to be. As 'order maintenance', police intervention is geared towards stopping or reducing levels of violence in an immediate sense; the police's primary concern is to prevent a breach of the peace. The violence itself may desist or persist after police intervention, but the ability of the police to impinge on the status quo between victimized and victimizing parties is limited indeed. Policing as order maintenance offers little protection to those affected by violent racism.

The limits to policing were identified by the police officers interviewed in North Plaistow. Many felt that there was little they could do to for the targets of violent racism, a feeling reflected in a 1985 *Police Review* editorial, which stated that the victims of 'systematic violence' perpetrated by 'white youths' and 'racialist neighbours' were 'still beyond effective help from the police'. This points not just to a lack of will on the part of the police, but a recognition that their ability to prevent racial incidents from happening, to enforce the law in any but the most serious incidents, and, therefore, to protect individuals and families from violence, is fundamentally constrained. The

[1] Of course, North Plaistow is an atypical example, if only because it has an unusually high rate of racial incidents. However, the national picture is probably broadly similar, if less marked. Of the estimated 130,000 incidents occurring in England and Wales in 1992, 7,734 were recorded by the police, less than 6%. There is no national record of the number of cases in which arrests were made or the number of cases for which prosecutions were initiated.

traditional incident-based reactive 'fire-brigade' response to 'racial incidents' holds little promise in preventive terms. Police policy documents indicate that the work of community police officers—the 'Home Beats'—was never really intended to be preventive, but aimed simply to 'maintain communication' with the victim, 'independent of investigation'.

This apparent failure of policing is reflected in the subjective experience of the survivors of violent racism interviewed in North Plaistow (Chapters 5 and 6). The victimization survey indicated that fewer than one in ten people were very satisfied with the police response when they called the police to report a racial incident. Respondents said that the police did not do enough, appeared uninterested, and kept them ill-informed about what happened after the initial response. The survey showed that people were more likely to think things were going to get worse than better. The small minority of victims who did report an incident to the police were also aware of the attitudes towards ethnic minorities common among the rank and file, even when these were not expressed directly. Victims were also aware of the widely-held police view that nothing could be done to protect them. As one Indian respondent put it, 'They don't care about us. They say they are busy, and there's too many cases like mine for them to cope.' All of this evidence supports the volumes of academic accounts, reports from community relations councils, local government agencies, and others which point consistently to the routine failure of policing.

Impact of Police Policy on Policework

Despite united opposition to racial violence—from the police, local, and central government—and a stated commitment to prevention, little difference appears to have occurred in many aspects of the police response in practice during the 1980s and early 1990s, particularly in 'front-line' police operations. This may partly reflect a lack of political will (Hesse *et al.*, 1992), (despite a decade and a half of strong words from police, central, and local government officials), but the evidence presented here suggests that there is more to it than that. Translating police *operational* policy into practice requires an understanding of three interlocking structures—law, work, and democracy each of which have a bearing on attempts to change operational policing (Chapter 6).

However, to say that the Metropolitan Police policy had little impact on the day-to-day response to racial incidents 'on the ground' does not mean that their policy changed nothing. While operational policy and practice remain largely unchanged, the production of information and its distribution throughout the organization and elsewhere have changed quite substantially with two observable consequences. First, administrative policy on racial incidents—recording, monitoring, and communication—has added a large information production and distribution bureaucracy, namely the Youth and Community Sections (YACS). Divisional community police officers (from PCs to inspectors) amounted to a large dedication of personnel and resources, in addition to which YACS at Area and Headquarters level have had an annual budget of about £20m since 1990 (See Metropolitan Police, 1991–6). The contribution of YACS to racial incidents largely comprised recording, monitoring, and processing incident report forms and disseminating information to outside bodies. The impact that resulting recording rates and improved clear-up rates have in changing perceptions of policing practice is described in Chapter 6.

Racial incidents policy has also provided an additional item to the brief of Home Beat officers. The formal brief of community police officers concerning racial incidents was restricted to maintaining contact with victims 'independent of investigation'. In theory, they had the potential for providing support for victims and acting in a range of creative ways which might usefully have prevented violent racism. In practice, however, there were few ideas (either within or outside the police organization) about how these Home Beat officers should have gone about such preventive work. They were neither trained nor resourced in ways which would allow them to fulfil the potential that their relative autonomy holds. Instead, in the main, they were doing 'hegemonic work', intended to maintain or rebuild the legitimacy of the police organization in the eyes of victims and the wider public (Grimshaw and Jefferson, 1987). These officers are also a reserve army of personnel available for the policing of public order. Home Beat officers in North Plaistow commented that they tended not to be on their beats at the weekends, when, one might have imagined they would be needed most. Rather they were on 'other duties'— most often on 'mutual aid', assisting other parts of the force with public order responsibilities.

In conclusion:

Reducing either violence or racism is not a task to which the police organization is suited. The relief and Home Beat police officers who are called to help are aware of their impotence in this regard. The data presented in Chapter 6 indicate that the rank and file are cynical about demands that they should be seen to be able to act effectively—considering the issue 'political'. Most incidents are not considered to be 'real policework'. Consequently, the protection offered to the targets of violent racism and those who are actually victimized is precarious at best.

Constraints on Changing Policing

The evidence presented in this book suggests that the reason the police organization holds out only limited hope of being able to reduce violent racism is a result of the combined weight of legal, occupational, and cultural limitations on the ability of the police to reduce *either* violence *or* racism, together with the limitations on victimized communities to influence these factors.

Legal and Organizational Constraints

Crucial to an understanding of the apparent failure of policing to respond effectively to violent racism is the concept of the 'racial incident', which undermines the ability of the police to understand the cases to which they are called. Devoid of political, historical, and experiential context from the victim's perspective, the incidents are ascribed new meaning to fit the specific subjectivity of the police officer called to intervene. The result, as Chapter 6 suggests, is an ineffective response to violent racism.

Law is the *dominant, but not determinant* structure of policework—'the prism of social censoriousness' (Grimshaw and Jefferson, 1987). In other words the law defines what is and what is not an object of policing, but does not determine how the police will act in any given unlawful situation (see also Lustgarten, 1986). Consistent with Grimshaw and Jefferson's argument, the present research found that the police response to reported incidents unfolded within a legalistic framework. From the time that the initial report of the incident was taken by the police its 'police relevance' was categorized in a quasi-legal hierachy with serious crimes—such as murder—placed at the top, followed by other less serious crime, then other incidents such as disputes and disturbances. On arriving at the scene, officers are concerned with whether a serious crime has ocured and think how the incident will be reconstructed before a court.

The optimum 'result' when a serious crime has been committed is that when the incident proceeds to court, it will be presentable in an unambigious way with an unambigiously villainous offender, virtuous victim, and independent witnesses. The ideal incident is packaged with clear and unambiguous eye-witness evidence which cannot be muddied by any attempts to discredit the victim or other witness. It comes with an unambigous confession from the perpetrator which does not cast doubt on the victim's or witnesses' credibility, or appear to justify the perpetrator's action. The case is preferably backed up with physical evidence from expert witnesses such as forensic scientists and doctors. Of course, few criminal incidents contain these ideal elements. The point is that the further that the incident departs from that ideal, the more ambigous any element becomes, the muddier the case appears to be, the less likely that the case will be won, and, for the responding police officer, the less justifiable the processing of the case beyond the initial response.

Criminal Evidence

In prosecuting a case, the first test which must be met is that there must be sufficient evidence that an offence has been committed *and* that there is clear evidence of the offender's guilt. In Chapter 6, the distinction was drawn between crimes, offences, and other incidents (see also Young, 1991). If the incident to which the police are called is not considered an offence, but rather a neighbour dispute, a disturbance, or some other in the class of events falling either into a grey area of legal ambiguity outside police definitions of an offence, then no further action towards prosecution will be taken. Even though all racial incidents, concerning crime or not, are now supposed to be recorded, non-crime incidents will not result in further legal action.

Apart from the question whether an offence has been committed there must be sufficient evidence of the offender's guilt before prosecution to proceed. Obviously what constitutes 'sufficient evidence' is open to interpretation. However, what is required at least, is a victim (in his or her capacity as witness to the crime) willing to substantiate the allegation in a criminal court. But there should also preferably be independent witnesses or a confession.

Seriousness

The police organization brings to bear its full resources only when hatred, anger, and aggression have reached a critical mass and have exploded into violence. And even then, they invoke the powers of law only if the 'incident' to which they are called sits towards the top of a hierarchy of police relevance—in other words when it is unambiguously a 'serious crime'. This appears to be the case whether one looks at violence against women and children in the home or strangers in the streets.

There *are* racist murders (Table 2.1) and serious assaults (Table 9.1), but these make up a tiny minority of either all murders or all instances of violent racism. Violent racism is often of a much more ordinary, 'everyday' nature (Stanko, 1990). Strictly from the point of view of the criminal law, racial incidents are rarely of the most serious type. All the research on the police response to 'non-serious crimes' would predict that instances of grafitti, vandalism, harassment, and abuse, and even assaults occasioning injury, are likely to be seen by the police as 'rubbish' and are unlikely to result in a strenuous law-enforcement response. Thus, in 'everyday' acts of violent racism—verbal abuse, threat, intimidation, and minor assault—the police are unlikely to act. Leaving aside, for a moment, the racial motive, it seems plain that a number of hurdles need to be jumped before a prosecution will occur. To summarize, *a prosecution is unlikely without clear evidence that a relatively serious offence has been committed, there are 'reliable' witnesses, and there is a strong likelihood of conviction. Without these criteria being met, reported crimes are unlikely to be prosecuted.*

Table 9.1 *Racial incidents recorded by the police in Newham (1990–5)*

Tye of incident	1990 (%)	1991	1992	1993	1994	1995
Serious assault	2 (1.0)	15 (3.0)	13 (2.5)	20 (3.0)	18 (3.0)	11 (2.0)
Common assault	64 (25.5)	155 (31.0)	153 (29.0)	195 (31.0)	191 (32.0)	147 (25.5)
Criminal damage burglary	62 (24.5)	127 (25.5)	140 (26.5)	166 (26.5)	139 (23.5)	148 (25.5)
Theft	2 (1.0)	1 (0.5)	13 (2.5)	8 (1.5)	10 (1.5)	7 (1.0)
Robbery	1 (0.5)	6 (1.0)	3 (0.5)	10 (1.5)	9 (1.5)	7 (1.0)
Racial abuse	117 (47.0)	175 (35.0)	163 (31.0)	193 (30.5)	219 (26.5)	252 (43.5)
Arson	1 (0.5)	9 (1.5)	19 (3.5)	31 (5.0)	13 (2.0)	5 (1.0)
Other	– (–)	10 (2.0)	21 (4.0)	6 (1.0)	– (–)	3 (0.5)
Total	249 (100)	498 (99.5)	525 (99.5)	629 (99.5)	599 (100)	579 (100)

The Racial Motive

Crown Prosecution Service (CPS) guidelines state certain criteria that might increase the gravity of criminal offences and therefore increase the likelihood of a prosecution. Those that are relevant to racial incidents are as follows: *impact on victim* (the victim is vulnerable; victim caused considerable distress concern or other shock, or psychological injury; attack was personal and involved considerable damage or disturbance); *discrimination* (victim's race, ethnic origin, religous beliefs, or sexual orientation are significant motivating factors); *prevalent offence* (if the offence, although not serious in itself, is widespread locally, and it is agreed with the local CPS that the offence can be treated as a prevalent offence and could amount to an additional aggravating factor). Additional aggravating factors also relevant to racial incidents are, for offences against the person and criminal damage, that the incident involved group action or deliberate action without provocation and was premeditated. If the offenders have previous convictions this can also be an aggravating factor.

The problem with the notion of racial motivation is that of having *concrete evidence* that the incident was 'motivated by race'. Clearly, the use of racist language provides some indication of motive, but it may not be taken by a court to be evidence of motive. Interviews with police officers indicate that, for the CPS to prosecute, they must have direct evidence that can be 'seen'. Even if an offender uses racist language at the time of the incident, and even if this is heard and reported by an independent witness, this still may not be taken in court as proof of the *intent* of the individual. In other words, simply because someone uses racist language it does not necessarily mean that the offender selected the victim on the basis of his or her race or was motivated to use violence because of his or her race. It might, so the argument goes, be simply 'incidental' to the offence.

There has been an increasing recognition of the relevance of racially motivated incidents by the CPS after a long period of reluctance. Under current guidelines, the CPS can take a common assault to court if there is clear evidence of racial motivation. The problem, the police argue, is that the CPS will discontinue if they do charge. A detective sergeant gave examples of assaults involving serious injury which the CPS subsequently down-graded from wounding to common assault. Common assault, officially 'rubbish' can only be tried in a magistrates court. Technically, it is the case that common assaults, where there is evidence of 'psychological injury' can be upgraded to actual bodily harm (ABH), but it must have supporting evidence from a doctor. So, for exmple if the victim is suffering post-traumatic stress, or is suffering headaches, or cannot sleep, or the vic-timization is having that kind of effect on children within a family, and a doctor has made reference to this within case notes that can be read out in court, then this would constitute evidence of psychologi-cal injury. The problem, according to the police, is gaining evidence of this type, and so they are reluctant to charge and forward the case to the CPS unless there is material evidence which meets the criteria the CPS expects.

Cultural Constraints

According to Reiner (1992), 'cop culture'—how police see the social world and their role in it—is crucial to an analysis of what they do because the rank-and-file officer defines what policing means on the street (see also Lustgarten, 1986). An idealist might argue that police officers need to be 'anti-racist' in order to provide a fair response to ethnic minoritiy victims in general and to victims of violent racism in particular. The police do need, at least, to be 'race-neutral', by which I mean that their actions do not discriminate on the basis of race. This is different from a 'colour-blind' approach. Being blind to skin colour is not only difficult (perhaps impossible) to achieve, but ignores the fact of cultural diversity; different people have different histories and experiences and face different problems. So-called 'colour-blindness' also ignores the fact that racism exists and that a person of colour is likely to have expeienced this first hand. Obviously, if police officers actually hold racist values and sympathies, use racist stereotypes in the organization of their work, and act on the basis of these beliefs, it is likely that their response to violent racism will be affected.

Since the mid-1960s it has been alleged by ethnic minority com-munities and by numerous independent researchers using documen-tary evidence that the police hold racist views, that these views are reflected in the language used to describe ethnic minorites (in and out of their hearing) and in their behaviour towards them. It has also become commonplace in the criminological literature to find refer-ences to racial prejudice within police culture. David Smith, for example, cites evidence from his observational study of police and peope in London in the early 1980s showing that 'racial prejudice and racialist talk . . . are pervasive: they are, on the whole expected, accepted and even fashionable. Senior officers seldom try to set a different tone (though they do on occasion) and there were some cases where they initiated racialist talk and kept it going' (Smith and Gray, 1983: 355). It is common, however, to find the assertion among some police officers and academics that this racial prejudice does not result in discriminatory police behaviour towards minorities. Despite the extent and pervasiveness of racist language within the police service, Smith argues that this was not reflected in police behaviour towards ethnic minorities. Take, for example, this statement from an area car driver in the PSI study: 'I freely admit that I hate, loathe and despise niggers. I can't stand them. I don't let it affect my job though' (Smith and Gray 1985: 403). Smith concludes that 'there is no widespread tendency for black or Asian people to be given greatly inferior treatment by the police' (Smith, 1983: 128; also cited in Smith, 1994: 1091; Smith and Gray, 1985: 404). Smith concedes that there have in recent years been a number of cases in which racist police conduct was proven, it remains his view 'based on research evidence that racial antagonism does not substantialy influence the *pattern* of behaviour among working groups of police officers' (Smith, 1994: 1093).

The relationship between prejudiced attitudes and discriminatory behaviour has been the subject of much debate within social psychology (see Allport, 1954; Hewstone and Brown, 1986; Kleg, 1993; Brown, 1995). The literature draws a distinction between attitudes of mind (which may be prejudiced) and forms of behaviour (including discrimination, scapegoating, and other acts of hostility). The nub of the argument employed by those seeking to down-play the significance of police prejudice is that 'prejudiced attitudes do not always result in discrimination. Individuals may hold strong prejudices against certain groups at a universal or general plane, but when confronted with face-to-face situations, they may restrain their hostile feelings and not discriminate' (Ajen and Fishbein, 1977; cited by Kleg, 1995: 158). Nonetheless, as Allport (1954) suggests, attitudes have a directive and dynamic influence on behaviour (Kleg, 1995). Attitudes create a 'readiness to respond' or 'set the stage' for action. Thus, prejudice may be 'acted out' in the form of discrimination that reflects and reinforces attitudes. In the case of Smith and Gray's data on the Metropolitan Police it is abundantly clear that prejudice *was* acted out in the presence of researchers in a number of ways, most clearly in the use of racially prejudiced and discriminatory talk or 'banter'. Utterance, far from being simply an attitude of mind, is a form of behaviour, a 'speech act'. The use of racially derogatory language does not offend everyone; racist conversation among consenting adults does not necessarily comprise abuse. But simply because racist language was used in the presence of white researchers or police officers does not make it any less a racist act, and the conversation itself is a *patterned* form of behaviour. Racist attitudes are obviously reflected in police behaviour if only in how they *speak* to one another.

Despite documenting racist behaviour 'in private', Smith and Gray did not observe explicitly racist conduct on the street (although respondents to the survey of Londoners report racist abuse), and it is this which leads them to the conclusion that there is no relationshp between police beliefs and behaviour. But this is obviously questionable evidence that such behviour does not occur occasionally or even regularly. The 'Hawthorne effect', where the presence of an observer affects the behaviour of the observed, is well documented, especially regarding prejudice and discrimination. Indeed the social psychology of prejudice has been reformed to deal with the tendency of people to respond in 'socially desirable ways in the presence of researchers' (Brown, 1995). It would be naïve to believe that hosting two outside researchers will not impact on the extremes of police misconduct, and Smith and Gray are aware of this (1985: 305–7). Expressing racist beliefs in the presence of Smith and Gray lies on the border of acceptable conduct, but it seems obvious that their presence would curtail the use of racist language or blatantly discriminatory behaviour towards ethnic minorities on the street. Although researchers have rarely observed the use of racist language or clear racial discrimination in street encounters between police and ethnic minorities, the racist expressions documented in the canteen mirror precisely the experience of black communities documented in voluminous reports published since the 1960s.[2] The obvious missing link between police attitudes, verbal expressions of hostility, and behaviour towards ethnic minorities is routine police conduct *unobserved* by social scientists.

In Chapter 6, the evidence indicates that specific racially prejudiced attitudes pervaded the police culture in Newham. In formal and informal interviews with police officers, specific stereotypes about

---

[2] Hunte, 1966; Institute of Race Relations, 1978, 1987; Howe, 1988; Gilroy, Pryce, Kettle and Hodges, 1982; Gordon, 1984; Graef, 1989; Surprisingly, David Smith fails to cite any of these papers.

Asians and Afro-Caribbeans were evident. Of course, such attitudes are not held by each and every individual officer, but this study confirms that racist views remain pervasive and accepted. One of the numerous racist jokes I heard during the fieldwork illustrates the point: 'what do you get if you cross an IC3 (black) with an IC4 (Asian)? A car thief who can't drive.' Or, after arresting a suspected 'illegal immigrant', 'the country's full of illegals these days . . . Where's your passport, Ben?' More pertinently, racist stereotypes formed a central component of police explanation of the causes of racial incidents. Thus, ethnic minorities' loud music and smelly food, simultaneously threatening and vulnerable physical appearance brought victimization upon them. What was peceived as a rejection of English language and customs, and the 'take-over' of specific localities was said to form a source of 'natural resentment', aggression, and violence. Racial prejudice and racial incidents were seen as inevitable events in which ethnic minorities—especially Asians—were 'natural victims'. Why did racial incidents occur? Simply, the officers seemed to suggest, because the blacks and Asians were there. Ultimately, the presence of ethnic minorities themselves was seen as *the* cause of racism.

The extent of sympathy with the perpetrators and the belief that the problem is intractable and relatively impervious to police intervention obviously hinder the development of an effective response to violent racism. Despite the prioritization of racial incidents by senior management, officers 'on the ground' tended to deny or play down the presence or relevance of racial motives for the incidents reported to them as 'racial'. The attribution of a racial motive to such incidents was seen, in the main, to be the consequence of 'politics', the paranoia of victims, and the use of fabricated 'racial' 'allegations' for ulterior motives such as re-housing (see Chapters 4 and 6).

As a result of racist stereotypes, the victims are unlkely to be seen as 'good witnesses'. It is a widely-held belief within the police service that Asian people tend to lie. The police officer in Roger Graef's study, *Talking Blues*, who was quoted in full in Chapter 6, illustrates the point: 'That's a problem with Asians: they make so many allegations that are totally a pack of lies' (Graef, 1989: 131). Different stereotypes exist for Afro-Caribeans, who are seen as naturally excitable, aggressive, lacking brainpower, 'anti', having drugs, giving trouble, and being 'tooled up'. These stereotypes mean that for many police officers ethnic minorities are not 'good' victims. Offences committed against them are more likely to be seen as 'rubbish'—

messy, intractable, and partly the complainants' own fault—specifcally because of perceptions of what it is to be Asian or black. Something similar is true for ethnic minority witnesses other than victims. In addition to which, it has been noted in several reports that, if witnesses to racist incidents are themselves from ethnic minorities, particulary if they belong to the same ethnic group as the victim, they are sometimes perceived not to be 'independent', even if they would otherwise be viewed as such (i.e. with no ties of family or friendship) (see Institute of Race Relations, 1987).

To summarise:

There is clear evidence that racially prejudiced attitudes are reflected in racist utterances (irrespective of who hears them), and these utterances contain racist stereotypes which suggest a course of action. The widely-held belief among police officers that ethnic minorities are untruthful (especially, but not exclusively, Asians), encourages the practice of disbelieving allegations they make. Consequently people from ethnic minorities find that the police have consistently seen them as 'unreliable' and untruthful. This patterning is clear evidence that a relationship exists between police attitudes and police behaviour and that these undermine an effective response to violent racism.

Democracy and the Limits of the Multi-agency Approach

There are only limited means to bring about change in the way in which the police respond to violent racism through the application of pressure from the local community. The criticisms levelled at the police during the 1980s that the police were not accountable to the local community in regard to racial incidents were intended to be resolved by the 'multi-agency approach'. It had the stated aims of improving police effectiveness and response to community concerns and became central to the police policy in the mid-1980s (Chapter 4). In order to gauge the impact of the new approach on policework, it is necessary to be clear what the aims and objectives of the approach were. Chapter 3 described the different stated objectives of the key players in the consensus around the idea of the multi-agency approach to racial harassment, which are summarized in Table 3.1.

It is appropriate begin an examination of the impact of the multi-agency approach by looking at its aims as the police saw it. First, the multi-agency approach was intended to 'establish confidence and understanding between agencies and establish common ground'. The evidence presented in the book indicates that this goal has, largely, been achieved. As a result of the introduction of the multi-agency approach:

the working relationship between the police and Housing Department, and indeed between all the agencies involved in the project, improved over the study period. For the sake of clarity, however, it is important to consider what is meant by an 'improved working relationship'. On one hand it may be improved because inter-agency conflicts are recognised, held in abeyance, and not allowed to prevent communication. It can be improved through contact in a forum such as this project's Working Group, or simply through the compatibility of personalities. On the other hand, a relationship may be improved because of an identifiable and lasting change in organisational arrangements between the agencies in question which brings about an enhancement, or greater co-ordination, of procedures. In the case of this project, there is clear evidence of an improved working relationship in the former sense. There is less evidence of it in the latter [Saulsbury and Bowling, 1991].

In short, conflict between the agencies was mediated by the existence of the multi-agency approach, such that it is less publicly visible.

A second aim, to increase 'the exchange of information between agencies', was also achieved. Collecting information from other agencies—the local housing department in particular—had the effect of improving police performance indicators, specifically the recording and clear-up rate (although these indicators do not meaningfully assess police effectiveness: see Chapter 8). Recording more incidents from other agencies may assist in demonstrating that a problem exists, but does not mean that the response will be improved. The clear-up rate is too inclusive a category for any judgement to be based upon it. A racial incident 'cleared-up' is unlikely to be one in which an arrest, prosecution, and conviction occurred. But, if incidents are defined as non-crime, as they frequently are, any 'appropriate action' taken by the police at the scene would mean that the incident could be counted as cleared up. As demonstrated in Chapter 8, 'appropriate action' was far more likely to be that where both parties were 'advised' than that where legal action resulted.

The third objective, to 'release the police from position of sole or main responsibility for the problem', was also achieved. The explicit intention of the North Plaistow project was to identify how the local authority and other agencies could contribute to reducing violent racism and to co-ordinating that contribution with that of the police. It is true to say that the police response remains primary even within the discourse of the multi-agency approach, but the police are now not seen as having sole responsibility for dealing with racial incidents.

Whether the final police objective— to 'solve the problem'—has been achieved would depend on how the problem facing the Metropolitan Police was defined. If it were to solve the problem of violent racism (which implicitly it was), then the evidence gathered in North Plaistow would indicate that this has not been achieved. It the 'problem' was one of being *seen* to be failing to deal effectively with violent racism and the resulting crisis of police authority and legitimacy that this engendered, then this has been achieved to some degree. Policies designed to establish common ground and understanding between agencies and to be released from having sole or main responsibility for making racial incidents less likely have been successful.

The aims stated by central government have not been achieved to the same extent as those of the police. The evidence collected in North Plaistow indicated that the multi-agency approach did not really bring about an improvement in the effectiveness of action against racial incidents. Residents of North Plaistow are not really any safer on the streets and in their beds as a result of the introduction of the new approach.

The aim to make police more aware of the problem is one which has been pursued since the issue first appeared on the formal political agenda at the beginning of the 1980s. The implementation of the multi-agency approach seems to have contributed to this process, but has affected only certain parts of the police organization. Certainly, the Community Contact team at divisional level and the Youth and Community Sections up and down the organization have become more aware of the problem. Looking to the top of the organization, the content and tone of the Metropolitan Police booklet and policy statement, *Working Together for Racial Harmony* (Metropolitan Police, 1990), is a far cry from the language used by police management at the end of the 1970s when police managers would go to great lengths to deny the significance of racism in the face of strong evidence and community protest. Among rank-and-file police officers— where an 'awareness' of the problem really counts—change is less easily identifiable (Chapter 8).

The Home Office aim to promote action by other agencies has also been achieved to some degree, though the effectiveness of that action is uncertain. Whatever the action of other agencies, evidence from

North Plaistow indicated little success in achieving the ultimate aim of the project—to prevent violent racism. Although recorded racial incidents declined during the life of the project, the final report concluded that:

Overall, there was little evidence that either the style of preventive policing or the quality of the physical environment were significantly changed from that which existed before the start of the project. As a consequence, the decline in levels of recorded incidents cannot reasonably be attributed to the project's preventive strategies [Saulsbury and Bowling, 1991].

The stated aims of ethnic minority community groups such as the CRE were to persuade the police to take action against violent racism. The weight of evidence indicates that the North Plaistow multi-agency approach, by and large, persuaded the police to take action only to the extent of participating in such a project. There is no evidence to suggest that it affected, or indeed could affect, the police decision to take action in individual instances of violent racism or the decision to take action in general. With respect to prosecuting perpetrators 'interviews with management and ground-level officers during the implementation phase revealed very little by way of change in operational practices from what occurred during the problem description phase' (Saulsbury and Bowling, 1991). The most optimistic view of the community organizations was that a co-ordinated response was a means to combat racism and overcome the causes of racial harassment and attacks. These objectives cannot be said to have been met. Indeed, the evidence presented in the book supports the conclusion that quite fundamental change in the mode of policing is required before such goals can be achieved, if at all.

The attempt by community orgainzations to change the police operational response to racial incidents in London during the 1980s has strong parallels with the process documented by Grimshaw and Jefferson in another Metropolitan force in 1970s (1987: 256–62). The 'problem' of racial incidents, they show, was defined by the police as 'one of communication: a failure to consult and to explain police actions'. As a result, it was decided that 'there had been insufficient attention to communications and explanations; that the improvement of community relations required more consultation; that certain failings required attention; but that some success was evidenced by the arrest and charge of those responsible for incidents'. 'Implementation' took the form of consulting with local community groups, attending meetings to answer critics, and avoiding the groups most critical of the police. However, since the specific allegations made by the various community representatives were 'not admitted, but consistently rebutted', the influence of the community on specific policy with respect to racially motivated offences was nil. Thus, there was 'no policy commitment to give special attention to racially motivated attacks; rather there was an insistence that there was nothing special about such attacks, which, as criminal attacks, would be dealt with in the normal way' (*ibid.*: 260).

This apparent paradox is explained by Grimshaw and Jefferson thus: '[a]n issue of burning concern to particular minority groups, expressed through appropriate democratic channels, is taken very seriously by the force—but not in a way which lead to the inauguration of policy (that is, new policy) in the area causing initial concern' (*ibid.*: 261). Most importantly, despite the fact that policy consideration and development occurred in this instance, there remained an absence of operational policy—that is an authoritative statement relating to how police officers should actually act—when dealing with offences involving a racial motivation.

Racial Incidents and Police Resources

Many avenues suggested by commentators across the political spectrum for improving the police response to violent racism—increasing legal powers, involvement in multi-agency panels, increased enforcement in less serious offences—imply increasing police resources. It was certainly the view of police officers interviewed that more personnel and legal powers were required before they could deal with 'all acts of hooliganism' including racial incidents.

There are reasons to proceed only very cautiously down the route of urging more financial and legal resources for the police. Any increase in police resources 'earmarked' to deal with violent racism cannot be 'ring-fenced' to deal with the victims and perpetrtors of this form of crime. An increase in policing powers would be used more generally. Any arguments for increased resources to deal with violent racism would inevitably be co-opted to form part of a more general argument for more resources to deal with crime and 'anti-social behaviour' because such incidents are relatively rare when compared with all crime recorded by the police. Moreover, they are overwhelmingly experienced by a group of people which comprises less than 6 per cent of the population of England and Wales.

To summarize:

While it is tempting to urge that the police do more and be given more to do it with, much of what has been said in this book about the failure of policing and the criminal justice system and of the fundamental constraints on change would suggest that increasing police resources would not have the effect intended. The response to violent racism probably would not improve. It is also possible that there would be unintended, but predictable, consequences of such an increase in police powers, including a more legalistic and punitive approach to offending by ethnic minorities, including acts committed in self-defence against perpetrators of violent racism (see Bridges, 1993).

Shifting the Focus From Victim to Offender

Understanding violent racism from the perspective of those who are its targets is a necessary, but not sufficient, basis for responding effectively to it. A victimological perspective was required to move the issue from the margins to the centre of political and policy debates. A conceptual and practical shift is now required.

Until 1981, the black and Asian experience was excluded from official thinking, as 'unreliable'. In 1981 it was possible for the then Home Secretary to express surprise that racist incidents could be found recorded by the police. The reason that the problem had not been recognized or responded to earlier, he claimed, was because of a 'lack of reliable information'. Now, no Home Secretary could possibly say this; the evidence is overwhelming.

The study of 'racial attacks' in Britain emerged from a broader concern about the position of the victim in the criminal justice process, and has remained almost entirely on that terrain until very recently. Violent racism emerged fully as a public issue in the late 1970s and early 1980s, 1981 being the defining moment when it explicitly achieved public recognition as a legitimate concern of government. This moment also is defined by the ascendancy of what might be termed the 'victims movement' in the United Kingdom, and indeed worldwide. In the late 1970s, for the first time, certain categories of victims (or survivors) were either drawn into, or forced themselves into, public recognition. Thus, sexual and physical violence against children, domestic violence against women, sexual harassment, homophobic violence, violence against disabled people emerged onto the public agenda for the first time (see Rock, 1990).

The emergence of violent racism into the political sphere has, of course, its own history, and black and anti-racist activism continues (see Newham Monitoring Project 1991, *Annual Reports* Sivanandan, 1982). In 1981, parts of it became fused with the victims movement, which sought to secure rights for victims of all crimes (Chapter 4).

The victims movement within the sphere of political activism had its analogue within criminology, and indeed a former moribund sub-discipline appeared—that of victimology. The victimological project which was embarked upon in 1981 has now probably taken us as far as it can because of two inter-related problems. First, victimology seeks to explain crime through an analysis of the characteristics of the victim. This does not necessarily lead to 'victim-blaming' (e.g. Von Hentig's 'victim precipitation', in which the behaviour of the victim is said to be a major explanation, or cause, of their victimization). However, the focus on the victim inevitably leads to the question: what is it about this person or this class of people which helps us to explain their victimization? The consequence is that the wrong kinds of questions are asked and the wrong kinds of conclusions reached. One of the most obvious examples may be found in the British Crime Survey which concluded that, 'Afro-Caribbean [and] Asian women, saw more of the threatening situations in which they had been involved as *caused by their race*' (Mayhew *et al.*, 1989: 48, emphasis added). Perhaps this is simply an unfortunate choice of wording, since elsewhere in the report the authors express the problem differently. And yet this quotation demonstrates the tendency for the characteristics for the victim to be seen as an explanatory, or *causal*, factor. It thus becomes the victims' *African/ Caribbean/Asian/other/ness* which *explains* the violence and its focus on ethnic minorities, rather than aspects of the perpetrator or the broader context of racist discourses and practices. This kind of thinking resonates with the views of police officers set out in Chapter 8 wherein Asian women were believed to be victimized because of their simultaneously vulnerable and threatening physical appearance, their failure to learn English or to adapt to British customs, and other characteristics which trigger the violence of young white people.

The second, related, problem with the victimological approach to violent racism is that it fails to problematize the perpetrators of violent racism. At present racist expression and intent are assumed on the basis of other people's experience of it. The perpetrator is unknown and, consequently, the possibility for any understanding or interpretation of his or her behaviour becomes impossible. Thus we have no idea about perpetrators' backgrounds, their relationships to politically organized or disorganized racism or the relationship between instrumental and expressive elements of their motives.

An effective response to violent racism now requires a shift away from the victimological perspective which has characterized the development of policy thus far. This is not to say that the victim's perspective should not inform this development. On the contrary, understanding the experience of victimization and of police intervention in this process must remain central to the whole enterprise. What is needed for the purposes of explaining violent racism, however, is for attention to be turned away from an analysis of the characteristics of victims to focus on the characteristics of offenders: their relationship with those they victimize; the social milieux in which anger, aggression, hostility, and violence are fostered; and the social processes by which violence becomes directed against ethnic minorities. At present, analysis of racist offenders and their offending might be characterized as *theoreotyping:* the re-creation of simple stereotypes about racism and offending into the form of supposedly credible academic theories (Pitts, 1995).

When asked who the perpetrators of racial incidents were, police officers said they were local 'yobs' or 'hooligans'. King (1991) notes a similar language employed in political discourse and provides examples of the 'degrading epithets used by politicians and the tabloid press to distinguish law-breakers from law abiders. They include "louts", "thugs", "brutes", "hooligans", "monsters" '. (King, 1991: 95). These identically named folk devils have plagued the body politic throughout modern history (Pearson, 1983; Cohen, 1972).

The correspondence between the police perception of the typical racist perpetrator and the young people who form part of 'police property' poses a moral dilemma for the development of progressive policing and criminal justice policies. In the efforts to focus our attention on preventing racist violence, young people (themselves marginalized socially, politically, and economically) have ended up yet again as the point in the process at which our attention is directed. As Brogden *et al.*, suggest:

youth suffer a *double discrimination*: the offences they tend to be involved in (minor disorderly acts, mundane property offences, fighting etc.) are subject to police 'overattention' in the first place; the results of this over-attention provide the justification for yet more attention, with all the potential for amplification this entails. It is this double discrimination which enables us finally to conclude that the social division of age is unjustly overpoliced, and that 'troublesome' youth constitute one category of police property [Brogden *et al.*, 1988: 112].

Yet criminologists operate with scant evidence about what is going on in the lives of these young people (from where do their racist attitudes and rules of behaviour spring, on whose behalf do they think they are acting). Instead, we have only a devilish effigy for symbolic sacrifice.

In the wider discussion of offending, two main tendencies are discernable, over-simplified as 'conservative' and 'liberal'. The conservative tendency would urge a more punitive response, firm police action, increases in prosecution rather than diversion, harsh sentences, and punitive prison regimes. This would also require that victims be urged to report incidents to the police. The liberal position distinguishes 'non-serious' from 'serious' offenders and argues for diversion from court and custody for the former and, for the latter, the minimum necessary punishment together with strategies to reduce re-offending.

However, when discussing violent racism 'something strange happens to Left-Liberal critics. . . . Liberals and radicals find themselves making calls for more active policing, more vigorous prosection: for crime control, not due process' (Rose, 1996: 73). The label 'racist' also works to depersonalize perpetrators. The solution is therefore unproblematic. A consensus has formed between conservatives, liberals, and radicals (who might otherwise be expected to be at odds with one another) that punishment and deterrence are the primary means to ameliorate the problem of racial violence. As David Rose puts it, '[o]n the Right, crime in general is blamed on the individual evil of demonised young thugs. For the Left, racist violence is simply the acts of demonised racist thugs' (Rose, 1996: 86). This begs the question whether racist offenders are so *essentially* different from their peers who offend without recourse to racist discourse and practice that they require an entirely more punitive response? Are they irredeemable? Is their racism reason enough to justify liberals and radicals abandoning such principles as due process, minimum intervention, diversion from court and custody, and swing towards a punitive, carceral approach which seeks, as John Major would have had it, to 'condemn a little more and understand a little less'?

The police should of course continue to try to improve their response to reported incidents, especially more serious incidents such as murder and serious assault. Failure to take racial incidents seriously, to treat victims on the basis of their rights rather than appearances, to collect evidence systematically and thoroughly needs still to be adressed. However, the fact is that it is not only instances of violent racism which only rarely lead to prosecution. This suggests that the limits on policing are general limits, not specific to violent racism. If so, that attempt to increase the detection and prosecution of racist crimes is likely to be no more fruitful than for other crimes. Neither the conservative nor liberal approach, it seems to me, actually offers much of a solution to the apparent failure of enforcement, prevention, or protection or the legal, cultural, and organizational constraints on police action. It is perhaps better to admit this failure and to consider alternatives.

Shifting to an Analysis of Violent Racism

One possibility is to separate violence from racism and to think both theoretically and strategically about each in its own terms. Conceptually it seems easier to see both the problems and potential for dealing with racism once it has been separated from violence, and conversely to think about ways of dealing with violence once it has been separated from racism.

The shift to an analysis of attacks targeted specifically against ethnic minorities *as a form of racism* rather than a form of violence shifts attention to its roots in broader forms of racist discourse and practice. In my view, racist utterances—'go back to your own country', for example—are not the result of the individual pathology of the offender, but reflect and reinforce accepted discourses of race and territorial ownership that are shared by a large proportion, perhaps even a majority, of the white English population. If violent racism is simply an aggressive distillation of wider discourse and practices then perhaps the most important strategic response is to challenge the production and reproduction of these discourses and practices.

Expressive and Instrumental Racism

One of the biggest bugbears of policies aiming to respond to violent racism is the problem of perpetrator's motive or motivation. It is often argued that the only real way to understand this motive is to get inside the head of the perpetrator. In my view, the idea of 'racial motivation' is at best a red herring and at worst an idea which can entirely undermine the conception of violent racism and the experience of being subjected to it. A way forward, theoretically, may be to draw a distinction between instrumental and expressive racism. Thinking about the inter-connections between these two aspects of violent racism suggests that identifying motivation is inherently problematic. It is nonetheless important to understand the dynamics of offenders who commit racist acts. It is clearly part of a wider problem of violence but one that has a specific focus. The question is what lies at its roots? Limits to our understanding of racist behaviour inevitably undermines attempts to tackle it.

Distinguishing between the remark made simply to express the anger of the protagonist with no specific object in mind, and that which was intended specifically to exclude or undermine can only ever be a subjective assessment, not made solely on the basis of the details of any specific event, but also on the basis of past experience. No two actors will share precisely the same cognition of events. It is possible, however, to identify elements of racial discourses of exclusion and expulsionism in the experiences of those people interviewed in North Plaistow: one commented, for example, '[a gang of teenagers] called me Paki and started throwing bricks at me . . . shouting . . . "Paki" go home. It's happened so many times . . . I want to move away from here because I'm frightened to live here now because it happens so often' (see Chapter 7). The verbatim quotations from the survey are only snippets of the experiences of a number of people who have experienced violent racism. Despite their limitations, these accounts provide a window into these events which enable insight into the way in which racism is expressed in violence.

The expression of racism, whether it is in the form of a political tract or violent action, may be seen as either as expressive or instrumental (Bjorgø and Witte, 1993). It may be expressive of many things—frustration, boredom, alienation, anomie are among those offered by sociologists and social psychologists. They may also be seen as expressions of racialized hostility. Racist discourses that cast black and Asian people as 'the other', antipathetic to Englishness, Britishness, Europeanness, or simply whiteness, and argue for exclusion and expulsion inform popular consciousness and give form to the expression of these feelings. In some instances violent racism is explicitly instrumental. Obvious examples are the London marches in support of Powell in the 1960s, the National Front marches of the 1970s, and activities of the BNP, Choice, English Solidarity in the 1990s, which have at the centre of their actions the intent to stop the arrival of black people or expel them from neighbourhood and the country as a whole. Neo-Nazis have frequently used their violence as a means both to express and to further their goal of a whites-only locality. Note also the continuous violence experienced in the case studies set out in Chapter 7 and their consistent undercurrent of racial exclusionism. Take, for example, Ms J's experience of being told of her mixed-race children 'we don't want any niggers on our patch, this is our Manor and we don't want those wogs here',—followed by a hammer attack and a thoroughly destructive burglary. In no specific instance is it possible to tease apart the expressive and instrumental aspects of violent racism; clearly it will often have an element of both, and indeed elements unrelated to 'race' (FitzGerald and Hale, 1996).

To summarize:

Attempting to define motivation in individual instances, particularly in a legal setting, is particularly problematic. A better understanding of the dynamic relationship between wider forms of racism and the specific acts of individuals may provide more fruitful avenues for research and practice.

Violent Racism and Police Legitimacy

Police Legitimacy During the 1980s

Commentators on the relationship between the police and public during the 1980s agree that, during this period, the police faced a crisis of police legitimacy (Robert Reiner), a breakdown of accountability (Eugene McLaughlin), and a challenge to the idea of policing by consent (Rod Morgan) (see Chapter 4).

During the late 1970s and early 1980s political pressure was applied by local government and black and anti-racist organizations campaigning for more effective control of violence directed specifically against ethnic minority communities and of police racism. From 1981, pressure from central government was also applied to shift police policy and practice towards an effective response to violent racism. The failure to meet this demand led to the formation of self-defence organizations which gained widespread public support. The introduction of a Private Member's Bill by Labour MP Harry Cohen

in 1985 to make racial harassment a specific criminal offence indicated a challenge to the legal legitimacy of the police with respect to
their response to this form of crime. From this perspective, the police
cease to be legitimate protectors as a consequence of an inadequacy
of the law.

With respect to attitudinal consent, it is evident that, during the
1980s, the opinion that the police were failing to deal effectively with
violent racism was widely expressed in both documentary accounts
and victimization surveys. Monitoring groups, local authorities, and
pressure groups engaged critically with the police in the media and in
central and local political processes. In the mid-1980s in particular,
news sources across the political spectrum were outspoken in their
criticism of the police response to racial violence. Arif Ali, editor of
the *Asian Times,* wrote an open letter to Margaret Thatcher: 'If the
authorities will not protect us we will be reluctantly forced to defend
ourselves. This has nothing to do with becoming "vigilantes"—it is
simply about survival'. Self-defence organizations had widespread
media sympathy and came close to being sanctioned after lenient sentences were imposed on young Asians who had confronted white
racists. These indications of a challenge to the legitimacy of the police
in public attitudes were reflected in surveys of the police response to
racial violence which showed very low rates of reporting and satisfaction with police intervention. Declines in public confidence in the
police throughout the 1980s on the part of whites and ethnic minorities left rates of support among the latter very low indeed (see
Skogan, 1990).

It is also clear that, for some social groups at least, operational
legitimacy had reached crisis point. Young Asians—mobilized around
the case of the Newham Seven—were on the streets claiming that the
police were failing to protect them. The police responded with paramilitary force. The result was that Asian youth and the police fought
pitched battles on the street, and on one occasion in Newham in
1985, fifty demonstrators were injured and thirty-three arrested. It
was at these moments that the police use of force was declared illegitimate (see Chapter 4). The protection offered by the police was
exposed as 'precarious' to the point where it could not be relied upon
(Rawlings and Stanko, 1991). In these instances, the willingness of
demonstrators to be marshalled by the police was withdrawn. From
the point of view of the policed in these instances, police officers
cease to be protectors and emerge as aggressors.

Impact of Police Policy on Police Legitimacy

It is evident that the policy-making process set in train by the police and government in the early 1980s was intended to rebuild the idea of 'policing by consent' and to re-establish the legitimacy of the police institution without making radical changes in existing systems of accountability (Reiner, 1992; McLaughlin, 1991, 1994; Morgan, 1989). Part of the process was the move made by the police to respond more effectively to racial incidents. At the beginning of the 1980s, police decision-makers referred to the issue of racial incidents as one which required no specific policy, but would be dealt with on a 'general level' (see Chapter 3). By mid-decade, official policy had been reversed and the problem became a 'police priority'.

The prioritization of racial incidents by the police and the introduction of new polices for recording, monitoring, changing operational practices, and fostering the multi-agency approach have been effective in rebuilding police legitimacy to some extent. The Metropolitan Police and the Association of Chief Police Officers (ACPO) have been successful in neutralizing challenges to the contractual consent which exists between them and government (McLaughlin, 1991: 120). In London, where the Metropolitan Police are accountable to Parliament through the law and to the Home Office (as sole police authority), the police have defended the quality of their response to racial incidents to the extent that their refutation of the allegations made against them were accepted by Parliament (see Chapter 8). Notwithstanding the Commons Committee comment that 'despite police efforts the incidence of racial attacks and harassment among minority ethnic communities remain unacceptably high' (House of Commons, 1989: 4), the necessity or utility of legal reforms has been successfully refuted by the police and government (cf. McLaughlin, 1991: 123).

Other challenges to the legal and political legitimacy of the police which emanated from local government agencies and pressure groups have also been successfully deflected by the police. The development of the multi-agency approach has taken much of the conflict out of the relationship between the police, Newham Council, and Newham Council for Racial Equality. In the place of conflict is a degree of consensus built around the idea of the multi-agency approach. In this process, those most critical of the police—the Newham Monitoring Project—were effectively marginalized. The Newham Monitoring

Project (NMP) shared many of the goals stated above—to combat racism and see the police response to reported incidents improved. However, the organization was consistently of the view that the multi-agency approach was simply a means of pushing ethnic minority concerns about policing to the margins of political debate. The NMP Annual Report for 1988 commented on the North Plaistow project:

although the police and government continuously emphasise that tackling racial harassment is not just the responsibility of the police, it is they alone who determine the action taken by all. This scheme is a more obvious example of a police/Home Office initiative—controlled by them and yet demanding support from the community. . . . Apart from Newham CRE, few local groups had agreed to have anything to do with this scheme. Desperate approaches are now being made to other groups to come forward, to 'participate' and basically lend this shameful exercise some official credibility [NMP, 1989: 29].

It is not really possible to say how far such a 'crisis' of operational legitimacy remains. There has been little recent open conflict between the police and ethnic minority communities in Newham, certainly not of the ferocity of the mid-1980s. Reported racial incidents are still very high, among the highest in England; reports of the most serious forms of violent racism—murders and firebombs—are also less prevalent in this locality than in the mid-1980s. Although there is no clear answer to why this is the case, there are some pointers: the politics of racism in Newham is not as explicit as it was in the 1970s and 1980s; minority representaton has increased in local politics; fascist political parties and racist social movements are less active; there is no current moral panic about race; and minority communities are significantly stronger politically, certainly than they were in the 1970s and early 1980s.

To summarize:
Whatever changes may have occurred in levels of either violence or racism seem likely to have occurred independently of what the police have done. The evidence presented above indicates that the police are unable to deal effectively with reported instances of violent racism or to prevent their occurrence. This suggests an interesting paradox. The legitimacy of police as the sole possessor of the right to use violence depends upon a belief that they are able and willing to protect the public. Legitimacy, challenged in the 1980s because of a perceived failure

*to protect ethnic minorities from violent racism, has been restored
without changing operational practice.*

Alternatives to Policing and the Criminal Justice System

This Chapter has shown how policy initiatives have changed the way
in which the police respond to violent racism and the extent of the
constraints on attempts to influence policework. These findings,
together with those of other recent empirical studies of the influence
of policy and politics on policework, point to more careful consideration of the sites to which the politics and policy analysis of policing
must be addressed (Grimshaw and Jefferson, 1987; Stanko and
Rawlings, 1991; Hesse *et al.*, 1992; Sheptycki, 1993). They also point
to the need to seek alternative and supplementary means of challenging racism and offensive and violent behaviour expressed by
young people on the streets and by one neighbour against another.
This is not to say that the aim to ensure the universal rights of individuals and communities to security and justice regardless of race or
ethnic origin should be abandoned. Rather, the limits of the law and
of existing policing arrangements must be recognized and strategies
adapted accordingly (Gordon, 1993).

The evidence and arguments made in this book point to developing aspects of the criminal law that can move away from the *actus*
to the act in context. Not all criminal law is constrained by the
notion of the incident. 'Continuing offences' come close; the notion
of harassment also implies a series or sequence of events. In terms of
prevention, the way in which the police organization is constituted
allows no time or space for the type of 'legal casework' which would
be required. As Grimshaw and Jefferson suggest:

In other legal areas involving public complaint, such as disorderly disputes
requiring sensitive judgement, the avoidance of partiality based on attitudes,
reputation or character can probably be achieved only be encouraging sustained and recurrent contact with complainants—a sort of legal casework—
a practice which would help prevent the insidious and recurrent 'minor
complaint' disappearing into the routine case-load (for example, vandalism
against ethnic minority households). If intimate knowledge in the individual
case results from sustained contact, such knowledge in relation to the pattern of attention to offences generally can come only through monitoring.
Such monitoring is the necessary pre-condition of ensuring that particular
groups or communities do not suffer the fate of either 'over' or 'under-atten-
tion' with respect to police activity [1987: 293–4].

It is possible, though not common, to prosecute offences that are part of a pattern of harassment. The new intentional harassment section of the Criminal Justice and Public Order Act 1994[3] might offer some potential in this regard. The courts might accept a string of incidents that would amount to evidence that someone was abusing the victims. It seems clear that the development of creative legal strategies is important (Forbes, 1988), but will not resolve some of the problems set out above.

There are interesting possibilities in the use of crime-pattern analysis using on-line data where such systems exist. Patterns to confirm whether incidents occur where minority settlement is small but increasing (challenging white territory) to identify repeat victimization and offending locations, to improve targeting of preventive and responsive resources might all provide possibilities for policing developments.

There is a clear need to improve provision of victim support. Police officers, however well-intentioned, do not have the requisite skills or remit for providing support to people who have suffered violent racism. There should be a victim support worker on a statutory basis in areas where violent racism is either prevalent or entrenched. In the London Borough of Newham there has been victim support work for some years (see Kimber and Cooper, 1991), but this has always been funded on a short-term basis. The present worker is funded from National Lottery money. There are a range of innovations in victim support including preventive strategies based on preventing re-victimization (e.g. Farrell, Phillips and Pease, 1995; Sampson and Phillips 1993, 1996).

The failure of enforcement and of policing in general means that new ways will need to be found to deal with offenders outside the criminal justice system. It seems clear that in order to deal with violent racism, strategies to deal with *both* violence *and* racism are necessary. However, as set out above, before recommendations in this regard can be made, more needs to be known about perpetrators (e.g. Sibbitt, 1997). There seems to be potential in strategies based on preventing re-offending emerging from probation practice. Since there is a point of connection between repeat victims and repeat offenders,

---

[3] The 1994 Criminal Justice and Public Order Act amends the 1986 Public Order Act to create a new offence of intentionally causing harrasment, alarm, or distress through using threatening, abusive, or insulting words, behaviour, or displays. It carries a maximum penalty of 6 months imprisonment or a £5,000 fine, or both.

some consideration needs to be given to strategies based on the nexus between repeat victimization and repeat offending.

We know far too little about offenders' backgrounds, motives, motivations, relationships with communities, and relationships with expressive and instrumental aspects of racism. Further research is needed on the support for violent racism among the offender's peers, parents, and wider community. Research on racist murders seems an obvious area for research, perhaps using prison interviews. It is equally important to examine the successes as well as 'failures'. This means investigating how changes in the lives of white people have resulted in a shift from a racist to an non- or anti-racist perspective. In particular, there is potential in examining changes in families which have accepted black people into their lives. Those cases where individual racists have denounced racism are also worth examining.

We need to know more about members of extreme-right-wing groups and followers. It is clear that racist literature is an important vehicle for producing, reproducing, and circulating racist ideas. More work is needed on schools and the way in which racist literature and discourse filters into the education system (see Troyna and Hatcher, 1992); on the relationship between violence, racist and fascist propaganda, and in particular the development of global racist networks, on the internet, for example. Monitoring of the actions and outcomes of intervention by the criminal justice system is required. In addition to a record of the number and types of incidents coming to the attention of the police, the number of arrests, cautions, and convictions should be publicly available. The 'clear-up rate' is a meaningless measure of police performance and should be abandoned. Action research on strategies aiming to deal with offenders is needed. In particular, more needs to be known about the creative legal strategies and the work of such agencies as probation, prison, the CPS, and the police.

Strategies aimed at reducing racism more generally (separate from violence) are required in schooling, and through education in a more general sense. This might also include programmes of non-racist work within play schemes, schools, and youth work, and work with families. Some European strategies have been extraordinarily creative in this regard, such as anti-racist youth work and anti-racist public education.

* * *

If the authorities will not, or cannot, protect ethnic minorities, individuals can only survive through strategies of self-defence. Those strategies of last resort have been successful in earlier periods, despite the obvious risks involved. In the Notting Hill riots of 1958 self-defence strategies were the only option open to those people under attack. Workers organized to defend their homes and provide escorts to and from work. In the 1970s Afro-Caribbean and Asian communities formed self-defence organizations and took to the streets to defend their homes, places of worship, and communities from attack (Sivanandan, 1982). In each case, individuals and communities have expressed a willingness to meet violence with violence if necessary. In the mid-1980s, campaigns around the Newham Seven, Bradford Twelve, and others were built on the principles of self-defence. These strategies were born out of necessity. Self-defence, simply stated, is unproblematic. The right to defend one's life or property from attack is obviously central to any discussion of a social response to crime. The problem is in defining where the boundaries of self-defence lie. Any acts or arguments which legitimate vigilantism are a risky strategy and one which has been used by racists to justify racist attacks.

Given the history and contemporary reality of racism directed against black and other ethnic minority people in England, it would hardly be surprising if some black radicals were distrustful of white people. Malcolm X, for example, argued for separate development, stressing that when white people become involved in black organizations, the development of black self-organization is inhibited, slowing black people's discovery of what they need and can do for themselves. Such organization would inevitably become dependent on whites who would, because of their greater access to resources, become controllers of the organization (Malcolm X and Alex Haley: 364–82). However, Malcom, after his pilgrimage to Mecca, regretted ever saying that there was 'nothing' a white woman could do in the struggle against racism. The conclusion he reached at the very end of his brutally shortened life was that white people had a crucial role to play in the struggle against racism:

I tried in every speech I made to clarify my new position regarding white people—'I don't speak against the sincere, well-meaning, good white people. I have learned that there *are* some. I have learned that not all white people are racists. I am speaking against and my fight is against the white racists. I firmly believe that Negroes have the right to fight against these racists, by any means necessary' [*ibid*: 367].

The British situation in the 1990s is, of course, quite different politically and socially from that of the United States in the 1960s.
Although many black Americans are 'mixed-race', the division
between white and 'non-white' is clearer than in the United Kingdom.
Here, many more people are conscious of the fact of their mixed
parentage, with an increasing proportion of the Afro-Caribbean, and
to a lesser extent the Asian population marrying white people and
having children who are not clearly either black or white.
Consequently, an increasing proportion of the white English population has a personal interest in the safety of 'non-white' people, as they
form family ties with them as their own children, grandchildren,
cousins, and in-laws. This makes it all the more important to recognize the potential contribution of 'non-black people' to the struggle
against racism.

*   *   *

It could be argued that the stage has been set for the development of
a comprehensive and proactive response to violent racism. Arguments
about the prioritization of the problem have been won. The police,
central, and local government no longer deny that the problem exists
or that it requires a serious response. Most agencies that have some
responsibility for prevention, victim support, and dealing with
offenders have acknowledged that they have a role to play and have
begun to act accordingly. Conditions may be set for change. We must
hope so, and that no one becomes complacent during those periods
when the extent and ferocity of violent racism wanes. The historical
record shows that violent racism waxes and wanes with social, economic, and political forces. It would not take much concerted action
by a resurgence of extreme-right political and street-level activity to
escalate what is already a grave situation. The police and organizations involved in the multi-agency approach, the anti-racist movement, ethnic minority communities, and, most importantly, the white
majority community, must be prepared to confront racism and its
expression in violence wherever and whenever it occurs.

Epilogue

In November 1996, I visited Newham to find out how much the nature and extent of violent racism, the nature of the police response, and the relationships between the police and other agencies had changed since completing the fieldwork. I travelled out from Victoria by Underground in the morning rush-hour. The District Line train was packed, passengers barely able to stand, much less sit down. It remained that way past Westminster (the centre of government), Temple (the Law Courts), and the stations serving the City of London. By Aldgate East (the last stop in the City) the carriage was almost empty, leaving me and five other passengers. Next stop Whitechapel and into the East End, historically poorer and dirtier, and soon, at Bow Road, the train runs above ground. The scene is bleak; grey high- and low-rise housing projects stack one upon the other, receding into the flat distance, interspersed by the decaying grandeur of spired Victorian buildings and gas works. I notice that New York-style graffiti lines the tracks as I pass through the quaint-sounding stations that attest to Newham's early history as a series of villages in the flat marshes of the Thames flood plain—West Ham, Plaistow, Upton Park, East Ham.

The economic position of Newham remains largely unchanged from the time that field study was conducted; if anything it has worsened, relatively at least. It is now *the* most deprived local authority area in England, based on an index which takes into account a range of economic factors; 56 per cent of its enumeration districts (the smallest sampling unit for the census) are within the most deprived 7 per cent in England.[1] In July 1996, 23 per cent of economically active men and 10 per cent of women were unemployed and seeking work. In May 1995, 38 per cent of residents living in private-sector housing and half of local authority residents claimed housing benefit. In 1991,

---

[1] Department of the Environment, cited in London Research Centre, 1996: 180.

35 per cent of the borough's dependent children—19,560 of them—lived in a household where there were no wage earners. Nearly 5 per cent of all Newham's households (27 per cent of those living in furnished rented accommodation) lived in housing without basic amenities. 23 per cent of Newham's local authority stock and 40 per cent of private-sector dwellings were assessed as statutorily unfit in April 1995.[2]

Although it is still economically desperate, Newham has changed in some ways since the late 1980s. The 1991 census showed that there had been a demographic shift, with white people only just in the majority, and the various ethnic minority communities continue to grow. Projections based on the 1991 census suggest that Newham may, by the time of writing, be the first borough in England and Wales where white people comprise less than 50 per cent of the population, although they remain the largest of the ethnic group.

Inevitably there have been some changes in the organizational structure of policing (see Appendix II). There was a shift to borough-based policing in which the two Newham divisions were amalgamated to create one division in one reorganization, then split apart again in another. Consequently, the actual structure reported on in this book still applies, with an area based structure (now 3 Area), and a divisional structure, with certain elements—notably Youth and Community—operating at a borough level. The process of dealing with incidents has undergone some changes as a consequence of the introduction of the Crime Reporting Information System (CRIS). Now, all incidents are recorded directly onto a computer. These incidents are then screened by the crime desk. All incidents categorized as 'racial' are 'screened in' and allocated to the Newham Organized Racial Incident Squad (NORIS) or Community Safety Unit for investigation. Once investigated, the docket is passed to the borough YACS which compiles statistics and then passes the case to the sector inspector or sector manager who will despatch a local sector PC. *Despite these technical/technological changes, however, the description in this book of the police response to racial incidents remains broadly accurate at the time of writing.*

---

[2] London Borough's HIP submissions, cited in London Research Centre, 1996: 178.

The Community Safety Unit

One ironic change in the five years that had elapsed since the field-work is that the police formed a Community Safety Unit, while the local authority which pioneered the concept no longer had one. This is a paradoxical testament to both the success and the failure of the local authority. In the 1986 Home Affairs Committee report on racial attacks and harassment, the London Borough of Newham was con-gratulated by the committee for forming a Police and Community Safety Unit (PCSU) with the specific remit of co-ordinating crime pre-vention across authority's service-delivery and for promoting part-nerships with other agencies. The notion of community safety was a relatively new one, and one which caught the imagination of central government and other local authorities. At the time, however, the language of community safety was entirely new to the local police and was, to a large extent, resisted. It was thus a success of the local authority that the notion of community safety and the kinds of strate-gies which were implied by it should have been embraced so whole-heartedly by the police. It was a failure in that the resources which could have flowed into the local authority for the purposes of crime prevention disappeared as local government funding shrank. The sit-uation would clearly have been different if community safety had become a statutory responsibility of local authorities (if the recom-mendations of the Morgan report had been implemented, for exam-ple). In Newham, the police Community Safety Unit comprisesd a detective sergeant, one detective constable, two 'accredited investiga-tors', four constables, and two administrative officers. Its remit included dealing with domestic violence, racial incidents (NORIS), homophobic incidents, and missing persons. The unit was mainly reactive, dealing with reported incidents as they came in, but also had a 'proactive role', though what this consists in is not defined.

There is some evidence of a cultural shift in the police organiza-tion. On my first visits to Newham there was a Chief Superintendent and a Divisional Community Officer who set the tone for policing in Newham and who were both very much of the 'old regime' (Rose, 1996). Towards the end of the field study there was a transition to a new group of officers who were willing to make changes to the way the police 'did business', to listen to the community, and to try to take seriously what they heard. The current generation of senior management seems to be a step further than that. A fast-track police officer once characterized his senior colleagues as falling into two groups in terms of their evolutionary level: dinosaurs and 'dinosaurs with fur'. When I was first in Newham, the dinosaurs ruled, only a few of whom were at all furry. Now explicitly scaly creatures are few and far between, at least at the senior management level. It appears that mammals are in the ascendancy, but more evidence is needed before drawing firm conclusions. There is an urgent need for more survey and observational research into police culture; a replication of the Policy Studies Institute (PSI) study would greatly assist an assessment of whether racist attitudes and behaviour have changed since the early 1980s.

As a consequence of this shift from the top, it is probable that awareness has increased at all levels in the police organization in recent years, with the likely result that police officers have become more likely to record an incident as 'racial'. What would once have been written off as 'advice given, ongoing neighbour dispute' is now recorded as a racial incident. The current senior managers undoubtedly understand the issues much more clearly than did their predecessors, and they are able to articulate the issues—to the researcher at least—in ways which appear not only to show a deeper understanding, but also a greater degree of belief in what they are saying.

Senior police officers still feel that it is very difficult to deal with racial incidents because, they argue, members of the Asian community are strongly reluctant to report. As an example of this I was told that a family requested the local authority to provide an escort (which had been granted) to school because they feared for their child's safety. And yet no incidents had been reported to the police because the family feared reprisals. The police could not reassure the family and the officers felt that they were 'fighting against perceptions all the time'. However, public dissatisfaction with the police response and the risk of reprisal are matters of fact, not simply perception.

Police and Local Authority Partnerships

The relationship between the police and local government in Newham gradually shifted from conflict in the early 1980s towards consensus, or at least a state of 'negotiated co-existence',[3] by the end of the decade. The North Plaistow project unfolded at a time of some

---

[3] Thanks are due to Alice Sampson (personal communication) for this phrase.

acutely painful transitions which were largely complete by 1991. There is little doubt that a sea-change occurred in the late 1980s within individual agencies involved and in the relationship among them. The police adopted the issue of violent racism, as well as a whole range of 'community issues' including homophobic attacks and violence against women. The police also shifted in terms of their relationship with local state and community organizations. At the time of the Newham Seven case, police officers were publicly antagonistic to both ethnic minority organizations and the local authority which supported anti-racist campaigns. At all levels within the police, local authority officers were often seen as left-wing trouble makers intent on driving a wedge between ethnic minorities and the police.

The local authority also made a significant shift, taking a less combative posture in its dealings with the police. At the beginning of the 1990s, the police and local authority have reached a 'comfort-zone' or plateau on which they now are resting. The situation might be considered one of containment. They have managed to work together to deal *reactively* with problems as they arise, which was only just beginning to happen in the mid- to late 1980s. So in the case where a racial incident is not handled well by the police, the issues involved can be 'sorted out' in a comfortable multi-organizational environment.

For example, on the day of my visit, there had been a meeting between the local authority chief executive and the police borough liaison officer to discuss arrangements for dealing with security of polling stations in the 1997 general election. The issues of concern, apart from normal security arrangements, were that the boundary commission reorganization had created a new parliamentary constituency from the Isle of Dogs (Tower Hamlets), Canning Town, and Silvertown (Newham), all of which had significant support for the National Front and British National Parties. The British National Party fielded fifty candidates in the 1997 General Election which gave it, at the taxpayers' expense, television coverage and the distribution of leaflets. Consequently, the polling stations were thought to be likely sites of conflict between fascist and anti-fascist demonstrators. It was the view of both the police and the local authority that, for reactive purposes and for planning for very concrete events, multi-agency co-ordination was now the norm.

In the recent period, the police and local authority have moved out of a volatile relationship into one where conflict can be handled 'constructively'. A council representative characterized the relationship between the police and local authority as being like a marriage, where there is an acknowledgement that relationships have to be worked at and where one can fight without anyone having to walk out. A police officer confirmed the existence of 'good mature partnership arrangements'. A council officer suggested that the North Plaistow Racial Harassment Project contributed significantly to the process of *détente* between the council and the police. However, the same officer commented that 'the litmus test is how far do you take it? You should go as far as you can, refuse to accept the notion that there is an acceptable level of harassment, or that the problem is only solvable by an impossibly large commitment of resources.' The issue now is how to 'shift from reactive to proactive mode'. Over the past five years, partnership arrangements have become formalized, principally in terms of reactive operational co-ordination. With partnerships, the police and local authority have got past the phase where they have reluctantly 'got to do it' to a point where it is accepted that this is simply the way they work. To take the most obvious example, if the local authority or the police want to get central government money for a local project, they have to have a partnership because money cannot be bid for otherwise.

The shift to crime prevention, to dealing with perpetrators, working in any way proactively has not yet occurred. There are some clear obstacles such as the following: (i) a lack of clarity about what proactive, preventive, or offender-oriented strategies would consist of, or even how such strategies would be defined; (ii) a pull towards the immediate demands of day-to-day work and the need to provide an immediate responses to incidents; (iii) a need to work to meet performance targets or 'key performance indicators' that are usually quantitative and do not allow for an assessment of the quality of response; (v) an inability to find shared goals,[4] (vi) limited resources; (vii) an attempt to work strategically on a grant-giving basis. Each of these factors forces the organizations back into 'containment mode'. Containment is based on a 'repertoire of responses from joint experience'; but strategic, proactive responses which might allow the development of preventive and supportive strategies cannot get off the ground because the people responsible are dealing with the day-to-day problems. As Bill Saulsbury and I have noted, 'it is hard for

---

[4] There are shared goals, but the way in which they are approached can vary widely. As the council representative put it: 'if we wait till we have ideological synonymity, we'll be waiting for the rest of our lives'.

people to pay much attention to draining the swamp when they are up to their knees in alligators' (Saulsbury and Bowling, 1991: 28). Dealing with acute symptoms prevents agencies from dealing with chronic causes.

The partnership remains fragile. Earlier in 1996 the police and the local authority planned to issue a joint statement of intent on racial harassment, particularly vis-à-vis perpetrators. However, shortly before the statement was due to be issued, there was a death in police custody. Within three weeks of the issue of CS gas to police officers a Gambian man, Ibrahima Sey, died in police custody in nearby Ilford shortly after having been sprayed with CS gas. The police would not comply with various requests from the local authority and consequently the joint statement was never made.

And what of community organizations active in Newham, specifically the Newham Monitoring Project? NMP was formed out of the Newham 7 Defence Committe, which was itself a product of the self-defensive response to police underprotection. Its remit, to monitor police racism, racist attacks, and the police response to them, meant that throughout the 1980s and into the 1990s, NMP consistently highlighted the failings of both the police and the local authority response to violent racism. As this book shows (in Chapter 4) part of the reason that the multi-agency approach developed was the crisis of legitimacy—shared by both the police and local authority—which was intensified by community organizations highlighting their failure to deal effectively with violent racism. As one commentator put it: the police and local authority have 'a common enemy— the campaigning wing of NMP. Both agencies want to get rid of NMP and this "unites" them.' Consequently, it may be that the relationship between the police and local authority appears consensual because they are simply complacent and look to each other for mutual support for the 'we've got this in hand', or 'contained' position. As both police and local authority representatives noted, their response goes no further than to react to incidents as they are reported. Concerning dealing with the underlying processes of victimization, they are doing little or nothing. Meanwhile, recorded incidents of violent racism remain high. Although there has been a slight fall in the last year or so, there were still between 500 and 600 racial incidents recorded in Newham each year in the 1990s (see Table 9.1). As this book has demonstrated, these reported incidents form simply the most intolerable moments in the process of racist victimization.

*   *   *

It seems that the general picture painted in the main body of this book remains largely unchanged, though certain developments have occurred. The consensus view was that policy and practice have, after radical changes in the 1980s, reached a 'plateau' with only 'consolidation' since the turn of the decade. This, in effect, means that racism remains a potent force in Newham; that it is regularly expressed in violence, with the result that many families and individuals are at risk of attack and live in fear for their safety. The protection offered by the police is 'precarious' at best. Although it is clear from this book that government has not always acted in either a forthright or candid way, this book ends by reflecting on the most recent House of Commons opinion on the state of violent racism in Britain: '[r]acism, in whatever form, is an evil and destructive force in our undeniably multi-racial society. We are in no doubt that racial attacks and harassment, and the spread of literature which preaches racial hatred, are increasing and must be stopped. More can be done' (House of Commons, 1994: p. xxxviii).

Robert Miles (1994) warns against exaggerating claims that there has been a 'rise of racism and fascism in contemporary Europe' (see Ford, 1993); and I agree that exaggerating racism benefits no one. This observation should not be seen as grounds for complacency, however. The historical and contemporary record shows that whatever the extent of violence at any one time, the *potential* for escalation is ever-present. The stock of racism which exists in diverse cultural forms in the United Kingdom should not be underestimated. For those who doubt, examine Bill Buford's (1991) *Among the Thugs*, an account of football violence in the late 1980s and its close links with racist subculture and the National Front, or the detailed evidence examined by the 1994 Home Affairs Committee referred to above. 'Race' provides a powerful expressive and motivating force, and a direction for exclusionary and sometimes violent practices. There are too many examples of extraordinary violence in the history of ethnic minorities in Britain and elsewhere in the world today to think that 'it could never happen here'. It has happened, and it will again. More *must* be done.

Appendix I

Survey design and methods

This appendix briefly describes several aspects of the survey design and methods. It covers questionnaire design, sampling, some methodological problems encountered, ethnic matching, weighting, and a demographic profile of the sample.

1. The Scope of the Survey

The survey aimed to guide the thinking of the North Plaistow Racial Harassment Project—a co-ordinated action project involving Newham Council, the Metropolitan Police, local voluntary agencies, and the community. It aimed to guide the formulation of action strategies targeted at the following broad goals:

1. Preventing racial attack and harrassment;
2. Assisting victims of racial attacks and harassment;
3. Identifying and taking action against perpetrators;
4. Tackling under-reporting;
5. Identifying good practice for involved agencies.

In order to ensure as great a degree of comparability as possible with the British Crime Survey (BCS) and Newham Crime Survey (NCS), the questions and methods employed in those were adapted to elicit information to address the goals of the project. The product was a survey which aimed to: illuminate patterns of harassment, identify the most victimized groups, identify the groups which were most frequently perpetrators, estimate the extent and patterns of reporting, and examine agency responses and citizen satisfaction.

2. The Questionnaire

In order to ensure comparability with the BSC and NCS to the extent possible, the majority of questions (and coding frames) were adapted straight from the two existing questionnaires.

The questionnaire came in five distinct sections:

(i) *The General Questionnaire* administered to all respondents;

(ii)   *Victim Questionnaire* 'most recent' incident;
(iii) *Victim Questionnaire* 'second most recent';
(iv)   *Victim Questionnaire* 'third most recent';
(v)   *Racial harassment Questionnaire* administered to all respondents

On average, the *General Questionnaire* took about fifteen minutes to administer and each detailed incident questionnaire took fifty to sixty minutes.

3. Sampling

3.1 Sample Design and Selection

The survey aimed to gather as much detail about the experience of racial harassment as possible. It also aimed to root this within the experience of the population of the area as a whole. To gather information about the experience of racial harassment and to illuminate patterns of victimization a sample of 'victims' had to be identified. In order for these responses to be located within the experience of the wider population a random sample had also to be drawn. In order to accommodate these twin aims, a two-stage sample design was used.

3.2 Random Sample

Interviewers were allocated a list of addresses chosen at random from the Rates Valuation List. A random sample of 1,521 addresses was drawn. Interviewers were instructed to call back at least four times in the event that they should receive no response at any of the addresses allocated. These call backs were to take place at different times of the day and on different days to ensure that all respondents had an equal chance of being contacted and in order to achieve as high a hit rate as possible.

Within each household contacted, the random selection of the interviewee was by use of the 'Birthday Rule'. This method required the interviewee to select the member of the household over the age of 16 who next had a birthday.

The breakdown of the random sample is as follows:

Table A1. Breakdown of the random sample

Total addresses approached		1,521
Deadwood	Empty	52
	Sick	18
	Not found	48
	Business	5
Total available to be interviewed		1,398
No response	417	
Refusals	230	
Interviews achieved		751

The response rate of 54 per cent (excluding deadwood) is lower than, for example, the BCS. In particular, the 'no response' rate (for example, no one found in, no one opening the door) was higher than might be expected.

The completed random sample consisted of 482 white people, 130 Afro-Caribbeans, 126 Asians, and 13 'others'.

3.3 The Booster Sample

The main aim of the survey was to gather information from people who had experienced racial harassment. A problem anticipated was the size of the sample of 'victims' needed to perform reliable statistical analyses on the detail and patterns of victimization. Even with a high victimization rate a random sample would yield few victims. Based on the findings of the NCS, it was thought that no more than 20 per cent of the black population would have suffered racial harassment in a twelve-month period. This would yield a victimization rate of around 8 per cent for the population of the area as a whole.

Obviously, there are problems in designing a sampling frame to identify the victims of any crime. In an attempt to overcome this, a booster sample intended to identify the largest number of victims as possible was drawn. The pragmatic decision was to choose the group which existing evidence suggested most frequently suffered racial harassment—namely, Asian people.

A targeted sampling method was used in which interviewers were given a quota to fulfil which ensured a range of age and gender, but left them free to interview in-home in those areas where Asian residents were concentrated. A total of 399 Asian respondents were interviewed in this way.

Section 8, below, consists of a full presentation of the sample profile.

4. Pilot Study

In advance of the main stage of the survey, four interviewers were employed on a small pilot study. Three of these interviewers were Asian. Each interviewed eight respondents within the study area.

The purpose of the pilot study was to test the effectiveness of the questionnaire. The interviewers reported that the aim of eliciting detail of up to three incidents might be excessive, given the length and detail of the questionnaire. In an attempt to accommodate this problem, a number of questions were dropped and parts of the questionnaire were rationalized. In the event, however, a number of problems were encountered which are discussed in sections 5.1, 5.3, and 5.4 below.

5. Methodological Problems

5.1 Selecting an Incident to Detail in Full

An attempt was made (following the methodology of the BCS) to capture in the *Victim Questionnaire* the detail of a selection of the 'incidents' experienced by victims. This, it was hoped, would be achieved by asking victims to provide details of the 'three most recent incidents' which they had experienced. The Newham Crime Survey (NCS) asked for details of the 'most important incident', arguing that this would give a better picture of the magnitude of the problem.

In practice, it is far from clear that the information respondents gave as 'the most recent incident' was in fact this incident. Several features of the material recorded (e.g. rates of reporting; see 5.4 below) cast doubt on this. Moreover, most respondents provided the details of only one incident, and refused to detail any more than this.

It is unclear exactly why this was the case, but there are several possibilities. It could simply be that the *Victim Questionnaire* was too long and too detailed to sustain the respondents' attention and willingness to participate. That there is no evidence that this was the case for the BCS (which employed a similarly long questionnaire), however, suggests that the problem might stem from other factors.

One possibility arises from the difficulty in pinpointing an 'incident' in the process of racial harassment (see Chapter 5). Many of the crimes recorded by the BCS might profitably be viewed as unusual, one-off events in an otherwise orderly life. These events, being rare, will not complicate a method which records the detail of up to only three 'incidents'. On the other hand, if a respondent has been harassed on a large number of occasions over a period of time it may be difficult to pinpoint which was, exactly, the most recent. Additionally, if the incidents were similar (even if they could not actually be said to form part of a 'series') it is not surprising that respondents were reluctant to detail three incidents.

Given these difficulties, it cannot be said for certain that the incidents detailed in full were a random sample of all the incidents mentioned at the end of the *General Questionnaire*. It is possible that they were the most important, the most memorable, or some other victim-selected incident. Nonetheless, this set of incidents reveals patterns of victimization, perpetrators, reporting, and agency responses which are interesting and of practical utility in their own right.

5.2 Incidents Outside the Project Area

The survey aimed to explore the experience of racial harassment and attack specifically within the project area. However, a large proportion of the incidents mentioned by Afro-Caribbean women occurred in the workplace and outside the North Plaistow area. This experience of workplace harassment is important in its own right and is discussed in the main body of the text.

Table A1.2 Whether the incident occurred in North Plaistow or elsewhere (%)

	All	WM	WF	ACM	ACF	AM	AF
North Plaistow	63	64	75	46	38	78	71
Elsewhere	37	36	25	54	62	22	29

5.3 Attrition of Sample Size

There was some attrition of the cell sizes for analysis at each stage of the survey. All 1,174 respondents answered the *General Questionnaire*, of whom 163 (130 weighted) said that they had experienced at least one incident of racial harassment. It is upon the brief detail of victimization provided by these respondents that estimates of the extent of the problem are based.

Of these, 70 per cent (96 incidents when weighted) agreed to answer the detailed *Victim Questionnaire* for what was intended to be the 'most recent' or only incident that they had experienced. Of these a further 41 per cent (21 incidents when weighted) went on to describe a second incident, and a further 2 per cent the details of a third incident. The analysis of the detail and patterns of incidents, effects suffered, patterns of reporting, etc. was based on this sample of 158 *incidents* (118 when weighted).

Of these 158 incidents, seventy-seven (sixty-five when weighted) were reported to official agencies. Of these seventy were reported to the police, thirty-two to the Housing Department, four to Newham Council for Racial Equality (NCRE), two to the Social Services Department, and ten to other agencies (including the Fire Service, local bus depots, the Education Department and schools). Clearly, while the sample size of those reporting to the police and Housing is amenable to some form of analysis, the low numbers reporting to other agencies preclude detailed analysis.

There was further attrition of the sample size when it came to the *Racial Harassment Questionnaire* at the end of the survey. For the 130 (weighted) incidents, the questions relating to general satisfaction with local responses were completed in only seventy-five (57 per cent). Drop-out rates were highest for incidents mentioned by white women (62 per cent), Afro-Caribbean men (50 per cent), and Asian men (49 per cent).

6. Ethnic Matching

Attempts were made to ensure that interviews were ethnically matched. That is, Asian respondents were interviewed by Asian interviewers and so on. This was attempted because it has been suggested that in a survey on a sensitive subject, respondents would feel more comfortable and be more forthcoming when interviewed by a member of their own ethnic group.

For the booster sample this was straightforward, as Asian interviewers only were employed on this part of the survey.

The random sample set more difficulties; interviewers could not know in advance to which ethnic group the residents of their allocated households might belong. This was overcome by the use of a referral system. If an Asian respondent was identified by the random process of selection, and proved willing to be interviewed, an appointment was made for a visit by an Asian interviewer.

7. Weighting

In order to obtain a representative total figure in the computer tabulations (for the experiences of the sample as a whole), the over-sampling of Asians had to be corrected. This raised the question of what the actual ethnic mix of the area was to which to weight the data. The two immediately apparent alternatives were to use the local digest of the 1981 OPCS census or the random sample of the survey itself.

It became clear that both estimates were subject to methodological flaws, the magnitude of which undermined their utility for weighting. It was decided that the random sample of the survey, being the most recent estimate, was the most appropriate.

8. Demographic Profile of the Random Sample

Table A1.3 *Ethnic Origin of the Random Sample*

Ethnic origin	%
White	65
Afro-Caribbean	11
African	4
Other 'black'	*
Indian	10
Pakistani	3
Bangladeshi	1
Chinese	1
Philipino	1
Other Asian	1
Other	1
Not stated	1

Table A1.4 Age by Race and Gender (%)

Age	Total	WM	WF	ACM	ACF	AM	AF
16–24	18	15	13	27	16	28	35
25–34	24	22	19	29	43	26	33
35–44	18	16	18	21	16	20	16
45–54	11	9	11	11	12	12	12
55–59	5	7	4	5	6	8	2
60–64	5	5	8	2	1	2	1
65+	18	26	27	3	4	4	1

N = 1174
WM   = white male
WF   = white female
ACM = Afro-Caribbean male
ACF = Afro-Caribbean female
AM   = Asian male
AF   = Asian female

Table A1.5 Number of People Younger than 16 in Household by Race and Gender (%)

No. of children	Total	WM	WF	ACM	ACF	AM	AF
None	60	75	64	60	51	30	24
1	16	12	18	17	22	15	17
2	11	4	10	8	18	21	23
3	6	5	2	10	6	16	15
4	3	1	3	–	1	7	12
5	1	–	–	–	–	7	12
6–10	1	–	–	1	–	5	1
Not stated	2	1	2	3	1	2	*

Table A1.6 Housing Tenure by Race and Gender (%)

Housing tenure	Total	WM	WF	ACM	ACF	AM	AF
Home owner	40	37	29	43	22	77	78
Rent (council)	45	46	56	44	58	14	14
Rent (Housing assn)	3	2	3	3	6	1	–
Rent (private)	10	12	11	6	10	6	5
Other/not stated	2	*	*	3	3	1	1

Table A1.7 Length of Time at Current Address (%)

Length of time	Total	WM	WF	ACM	ACF	AM	AF
Up to one year	16	15	13	25	28	13	11
1–5 years	26	24	21	37	30	29	30
5–10 years	19	18	17	16	21	27	25
10–20 years	21	18	23	17	16	26	28
20 years or more	18	25	26	5	4	5	5
Not stated	*	–	*	–	–	*	1

Table A1.8 Employment Status by Race and Gender (%)

Employment status	Total	WM	WF	ACM	ACF	AM	AF
Work full-time	40	54	22	51	43	63	30
Work part-time	7	2	12	6	9	1	4
Unemployed and seeking work	11	8	11	14	16	12	13
Long-term illness or disability	3	5	2	5	3	3	2
Retired	22	29	32	3	6	5	3
Non working	11	•	17	5	10	3	35
Full time education	5	1	1	14	4	12	10
Other	6	–	*	–	3	*	1
Not stated	2	1	2	2	4	2	2

Appendix II

Police Organizational Structure

Introduction

It is now commonplace to criticize theories which treat the state as mono-lithic—it is evident that central and local government are highly differenti-ated, diverse, and diffuse activities. Moreover, while the police may be said *literally* to be the 'coercive arm of the state' in some theoretical formulations, it is evident that numerous sites of conflict exist in the relationships among the police, central and local government. Similarly, the police organization is not monolithic. It too is sub-divided into components organized at central and local levels and with its own specialisms and organizational schisms and conflicts. The organization, even at the local level, is quite complex. It is composed of numerous smaller and smaller organizational units, each with its own specific *modus operandi* or style of work and, arguably, working cul-ture. Only an obsessive organizational cartographer would want to attempt to create a chart which encompassed the entire Metropolitan Police admin-istrative and operational structure; but the idea of such an exercise points to the danger in over-generalization about what the police function is, and what it is supposed to be. What follows is a brief description of the structure of policing in London at the time the study was conducted.

The Metropolitan Police is a highly differentiated and complex statutory agency. It is organized into formal hierarchies based on rank, geographical areas of responsibility, and specialization. In 1990 it comprised 44,000 police officers and civilians and cost £1.2 billion a year to run. It had a huge work-load, including the recording and response to some 834,000 notifiable offences, together with practically innumerable calls to disputes and distur-bances, and other calls on policing force and services.

Geographical hierarchy

Figure A2.1 illustrates the geographical hierarchy of the Metropolitan Police, showing the division of responsibility for specific policing tasks. Force headquarters, based at New Scotland Yard in central London, has responsi-bility for force-wide policy-making, management, personnel, training, specialist operations, and financial management. The Metropolitan Police

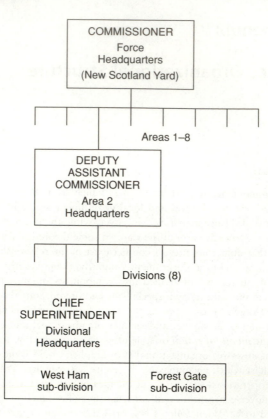

Figure A2.1 *Metropolitan Police Geographical Hierarchy*

organization is decentralized into eight relatively autonomous Areas. Each Area (with the exception of Westminster) reaches from the centre of the metropolis out to the fringe suburban boroughs and beyond. A Deputy Assistant Commissioner (DAC) heads each Area, and has overall responsibility for the policing in that locality. The DAC has direct responsibility for specialist policing, while day-to-day operational responsibilities are decentralized further to the police divisions. Each Area has a number of divisions; Area 2, in which the study site was located, for example, had eight divisions, two of which covered the London Borough of Newham (East Ham and West Ham).

Figure A2.2 illustrates the division of police responsibilities at the local level. The divisional Chief Superintendent, with the assistance of the Superintendent, has responsibility for all local operational and administrative duties. These are divided among two Chief Inspectors ('operations' and 'support'), a detective Chief Inspector (responsible for the CID), and a civilian (responsible for traffic and administration). The largest of the police stations in the division (West Ham) acts as divisional headquarters. This houses civilian and police officers engaged in a wide range of activities organized into separate departments and units. For the purposes of this study, the components at the local level of most specific interest are the 'reliefs' and the 'community contact team'.

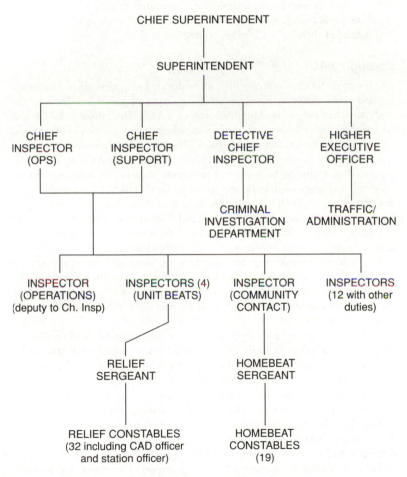

Figure A2.2 *The Structure of a Police Division*

Youth and Community Sections

Before looking in more detail at policework at the local level, it is necessary to look briefly at the location of 'community policing' within the police organization as a whole (see Figure A2.3). At the time of the study, Youth and Community Sections (YACS) existed at headquarters, Area, Borough, and Divisional levels. Among a wide range of 'youth'- and 'community'-related issues, the YACS at Scotland Yard had responsibility for developing, implementing, and managing on a day-to-day basis force-wide policy on racial incidents. Headquarters YACS as a whole was headed by a Commander, with a Chief Inspector responsible for 'Care and Trust', which included racial incidents policy. A similar arrangement existed at Area level, with the YACS headed there by a Chief Superintendent.

Borough YACS

The borough YACS requires a little more detailed attention since its personnel had more direct involvement in the policing of racial incidents in the study site than either Headquarters or Area YACS. The borough YACS had responsibility for administration of force policies on racial incidents, juvenile crime, schools involvement, and for dealing with all 'community relations matters'. This included a general public relations role. As one YACS PC explained in response to a general telephone inquiry, its role was 'to be involved with the community and to show another side to the police than just arresting people all the time. To show that the police do have a human face.' Although the officers interviewed considered themselves to be 'Newham's Police Public Relations Office', they were quick to point out that they were not engaged in 'the type of PR that is bullshit'.

The senior manager for the duration of most of the study was a Superintendent known as the borough Community Liaison Officer (CLO). This officer was responsible for maintaining contact with representatives of the local community at the highest level, including elected members and officials of the borough council and representatives of tenants' associations, victim support, school governors, community organizations, and the media. He played a central role in the formal police–community liaison structures, such as the Police Community Consultative Group (PCCG), the steering group of the North Plaistow Racial Harassment Project, and the management committee of the local victim support group. His remit also extended to representing the police in a range of official duties, such as supervising visits from Royalty and senior police officers from other forces and abroad. The duties of the YACS were carried out by eight constables, a sergeant, an inspector, and a civilian secretary. The PCs were engaged in a variety of tasks including visiting schools, referrals to and from other agencies, and processing information concerning racial incidents.

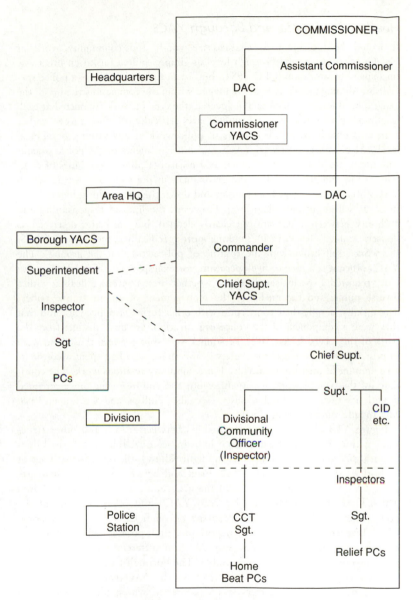

Figure A2.3 *The Structure of the Metropolitan Police Illustrating the Location of Youth and Community Sections (YACS)*

Headquarters, Area, and Borough YACS

It would be too blunt to characterize youth and community work at Headquarters, Area, and borough level as simply 'bolted on' to an otherwise unchanged organization (GLC, 1984), but it can rightly be seen as a police specialism. Although the YACSs are managed within the command structure of the geographical level at which each is located, the type of work conducted at each level more closely resembles its counterparts vertically (in other YACS), rather than horizontally (with other forms of policework at any given geographical level). Also, linkages between YACS and other elements of the police organization operate in a vertical as much as a horizontal dimension. Lines of communication and responsibility and resonances in the style of work in which YACS officers are engaged operate up and down the geographical hierarchy as much as within an individual level. However, the lines of responsibility and authority between YACS are not clearly defined, but are better described as 'loosely coupled' (Rock, 1990). Looking more specifically at the borough YACS, the work itself broke with the routine of policework 'on the ground'. The YACS office was a nine-to-five operation, for example. Youth and community work required a specific sets of skills, whether these concerned dealing with a diverse public and the media or the management of administrative policy. These skills, despite their connection with other forms of policework and that they were a component of the police organization, are quite distinct from the work of the reliefs or detectives. Personnel were split between those who were in post for short periods ('for the c.v.') and those who had spent a considerable amount of their service involved in community relations work. The continuity of the type of work, its organization, and culture of the office provided it with its own specialized identity (see also Phillips and Cochrane, 1988; McConville and Shepherd, 1992).

Figure A2.3 illustrates the relationships between YACS and other structures within the Met. The unbroken lines indicate well defined, formal lines of authority and responsibility. As the figure shows, the only formal lines of authority existed *within* each YACS itself and between the senior manager of YACS and the senior manager of the geographical area of responsibility. Thus, lines of communication between YACS and other elements of the police organization (such as between the borough CLO and the divisional Chief Inspectors) are informal, negotiable, and poorly defined. Lines of authority and responsibility between YACS at different geographical levels were also poorly defined and negotiable. The borough CLO was responsible most directly to the Area 2 DAC. It was from the DAC that any direct orders concerning operational matters would come, to whom the borough CLO would defer difficult decisions, and who would have a veto over any actions taken by the borough CLO. The borough CLO would also receive instructions from TO30 at headquarters, particularly in administrative matters such as the recording and monitoring of racial incidents.

The lines of communication, responsibility, and authority between the borough CLO and the divisional Chief Superintendent were far from clearly defined. Although the Chief Superintendent outranked the borough CLO he appeared to have little formal or direct jurisdiction over his actions, even though the work of the borough YACS might affect directly what occurred on 'his' ground.

The borough CLO had some authority over the divisional Community Contact Team and, thus, over the actions of the Home Beat officers on the ground. This authority was not defined clearly, however, and it is unlikely that any direct orders would be issued to the Community Contact Team to be instituted by the Home Beat officers. The Divisional CCT, as a divisional resource, fell under the command of the Divisional Chief Superintendent within the structure shown in Figure A2.3.

The Divisional Community Contact Team

Uniformed beat policing at the local level is divided into two systems—the 'reliefs' or unit beat system, and the 'home beats' or resident beat system. The division between the two forms of policework has its origins in the introduction of the 'unit beat system' in the mid-1960s (Weatheritt, 1986; Reiner, 1985: 63; McCabe and Sutcliffe, 1978: 83). The role of Home Beat policing evolved from the pre-unit beat form of policing known as the 'fixed-point system'.[1] When computer-aided dispatch, two-way radios, and police cars were introduced in the mid-1960s (and with them the ability for mobile police officers to respond immediately to calls for service over a wide area (the unit beats)), resident beat officers retained a beat for which they had 'geographical responsibility'.

Organization and Management

In West Ham, the divisional Community Contact Team (CCT) comprised nineteen Home Beat constables, each with a relatively small, fixed 'permanent' beat. North Plaistow comprised two police beats. The CCT was managed by two sergeants, each working from one of the sub-divisional police stations, and an inspector who was based at divisional headquarters. The main responsibility of the CCT inspector (also known as the Divisional Community Officer) was to maintain formal and informal contact with a range of statutory and voluntary agencies, community groups, and individuals. For example, the CCT inspector had regular meetings with local government officers (particularly in the housing department), the local council for racial equality, neighbourhood watch co-ordinators, tenants' associations, schools, and youth clubs. These contacts ranged from the most

[1] This system involved the patrol of a beat moving from one fixed point to another from which the officer would call in to the police station.

formal—such as the PCCG—to the most informal—such as fêtes, festivals, and other community events.

The main responsibility of the CCT sergeant was to supervise the activity of the Home Beat constables. This first-line supervision mainly consisted of organizing work schedules, monitoring and processing the paperwork produced by the PCs, and acting as a source of advice and encouragement (see also Grimshaw and Jefferson, 1987: 158; Phillips and Cochrane, 1988). The sergeant also acted as aide to the CCT inspector, accompanying him to community meetings or those with local housing officers, for example. The sergeant, with his knowledge of the 'ground' and with his routine supervision of reported incidents, follow-up calls, referrals, and other case notes, was often in the best position to provide details of cases and of the police response to them which members of the community might request at meetings.

As police 'representative' the CCT management had to speak for the police and was the recipient of information from individuals and organizations. Providing information to the public was one of the principal objectives of the work, and formed an essential component of the community relations specialism (Phillips and Cochrane, 1988). These officers (and their colleagues in YACS at higher levels) were engaged in the production and dissemination of information on a range of policing issues of concern to the community. With respect to racial attacks, they had details of the outcomes of, and constraints on action taken by, the police in individual cases and also on the volume of recorded incidents, clear-up rates and details of force policy, etc.

Home beat policing

The responsibilities of the Home Beat PCs can be divided into three main tasks: to patrol their beat on foot, to retain contact with a range of individuals, and to conduct follow-up calls to victims of offences allocated to them by the crime desk (see also Horton, 1989). Patrol of the beat is intended primarily to provide a visible presence on the street in order to deter crime and create the perception of a safe environment. In two observation sessions conducted with the Home Beat officers, this patrol entailed a circuit from the police station to the far end of the beat and back again in the duration of half a shift. Thus, one circuit was conducted before lunch and one afterwards. Maintaining contact with the public comprised visits to an old people's home, schools, and colleges on the patch, to neighbourhood watch co-ordinators, and to past victims of racial attacks. In addition to contacts with these individuals—characterized by Grimshaw and Jefferson as members of the 'respectable' public, *en route* the officers also had brief encounters and exchanges with contacts who were 'known' to the police (as alleged perpetrators of racial incidents, for example) (Grimshaw and Jefferson, 1987: 149). The offences allocated to the home beats comprised mainly 'beat crimes': offences defined as 'crime', but which did not merit investigation by CID (Grimshaw and Jefferson, 1987: 161). In North Plaistow, a large proportion of racially motivated incidents were classified in this way.

As Grimshaw and Jefferson demonstrated in their detailed study of the 'resident beat system', confirmed by the limited observational work conducted in this study, Home Beat policing tends not to be 'law enforcement' work, but rather 'operates in a borderline sub-legal domain consisting of public nuisances and minor complaints' (Grimshaw and Jefferson, 1987: 179). The absence of legal work gives rise to autonomous 'styles' of working within which individual PCs have great deal of freedom (*ibid.*: 153–6). The constables observed had few constraints on their working practices. With the exception of rostered starting and finishing times (between 8 am and 10 pm), appointments with crime victims, and contacts with other members of the public, there appeared to be few factors which influenced their work schedule and the nature of the tasks carried out (see also Horton, 1989). In particular, the officers were free of the continual calls for service from the dispatcher that characterized 'relief' work (see below). On one of the observation sessions the Home Beat PC carried no personal radio and, on the other, the radio was switched on at low volume but not used during the patrol. Moreover, because of the nature of the management of the community contact team described above, there was an almost complete absence of opportunities for direct supervision of the work of the Home Beat officers by the CCT management.

The Relief

Organization and Management

The 'relief' or unit beat officers provide a twenty-four-hour immediate response to emergency calls over the whole division (see Smith and Gray, 1983; Grimshaw and Jefferson, 1987: 41–117; Shapland and Hobbs, 1989). They work on a rotating three-shift basis—alternate blocks of early, late, and night shifts with a rest period in between. Each relief comprises thirty-two constables and is managed by a sergeant and an inspector. The relief is a coherent unit, often with its own specific identity or tradition (see also Foster, 1989).

Relief Policing

Relief work has far less autonomy than Home Beat policing, principally because of the external control exerted by its main source of work—the computer-aided despatch system (CAD) (see Manning, 1988). This system processes, categorises, and despatches calls coming into the station to mobile units which are otherwise engaged in random preventive patrol. The flow of calls from the dispatcher is a key determinant of relief police activity. In quiet periods the officers engage in random patrol, and many engage in more proactive policing (stop and search of suspicious vehicle or pedestrians, for example). During busy periods in particular, relief work is characterized by continuous movement from one incident to the next. The volume of calls for service relative to the number of officers available at any one time means that for much of the time, demand runs considerably ahead of supply. In the last quarter of 1989 the division dealt with 11,010 incidents and 10,557 messages (*West Ham Divisional Report for 1990*). The resulting 200 to 400 calls per day are dealt with by only approximately fifteen officers on the ground at any one time.[2]

On attending an incident, the relief constable's job is to ensure that order is maintained, where possible through negotiation but with the possibility of force held as a resource. With these immediate tasks resolved, the next concern of the attending officer was 'getting the paperwork right'—ensuring that victims provided him or her with all the information necessary for the crime form—to close the encounter as quickly as possible, and move on to the next call. The relief officers and their first-line managers interviewed complained consistently that they had too little time per call to do their job effectively, with the result that they had become mere 'messengers'. The other side of the coin was that the victims became providers of fact for the officers to complete their paperwork, or mere 'form filling machines'. As one relief PC put it '[n]ow the police are little more than messengers. They are continually running from one incident to the next, not spending enough time investigating or providing victim support. And it's getting worse.'

The working structure set in place by the CAD system gives rise to a particular pattern of work, described in case study and ethnographic accounts of policework (e.g. Holdaway, 1983; Smith and Gray, 1985; Grimshaw and Jefferson, 1987) and which were confirmed by the limited observational work of the present study (I observed two shifts in the Area Car). Grimshaw and Jefferson describe the fragmentation of work which results:

Unit policework seems formed out of a myriad of incidents each of which may well be unrelated to the next one, or to any other. A quick call here, a few words, an entry in report or pocket book: these together constitute a fragmented texture of events. [. . .] Typically several unconnected members of the public, often widely separated in space, enter the officer's field of operation during a shift. The relevance of each contact also seems limited, so that completion of the business in hand appears the principal objective of the officer; there is often little development or articulation of contacts opening up new ground or casting fresh light on what has gone before [1987: 70].

---

[2] Of the 32 PCs on relief, one was in the CAD room and one on the front desk at each sub-divisional police station. Of the remaining 28, some will be on meal breaks, on leave, sick, and at court. If an arrest is made, processing the detainee will detain the officers for long periods.

This style of police work limits the ability of officers systematically to make connections between the incidents that come to their attention (Goldstein, 1990). With respect to racial harassment, the inability to make connections between instances has important implications for how each individual call for service is viewed and handled by the attending officer..

Bibliography

AJEN, I. and FISHBEIN, M. (1977), 'Attitude-Behaviour Relations: A Theoretical Analysis and Review of Empirical Research', *Psychological Bulletin* No. 84: 888–928.

ALDERMAN, G. (1972), 'The Anti-Jewish Riots of August 1919 in South Wales' *Welsh History Review* No. 6.

ALDERSON, J. (1979), *Policing Freedom*, (Plymouth: Macdonald and Evans).

—— (1982), 'The Case for Community Policing' in D. Cowell, T. Jones and J. Young, *Policing the Riots* (London: Junction Books).

ALLPORT, G. (1954), *The Nature of Prejudice* (Reading, MA: Addison-Wesley).

ASSOCIATION OF CHIEF POLICE OFFICERS (1985), *Guiding Principles Concerning Racial Attacks* (London: ACPO).

AYE MAUNG, N. and MIRRLEES-BLACK, C. (1994), *Racially Motivated Crime: A British Crime Survey Analysis* (Home Office Research and Planning Unit Paper 82).

BANTON, M. (1983), *Racial and Ethnic Competition* (Cambridge: Cambridge University Press).

—— (1985), *Promoting Racial Harmony* (Cambridge: Cambridge University Press).

BARKER, M. (1981), *The New Racism* (London: Junction).

BAUDRILLARD, J. (1989), *Selected Writings* (edited by M. Poster) (London: Polity Press).

BELL, C., and NEWBY, H. (eds.) (1977), *Doing Sociological Research* (London: Allen and Unwin).

BENYON, J. (1987), 'Interpretations of Civil Disorder' in J. Benyon and J. Solomos (eds.) (1987), *The Roots of Urban Unrest* (Oxford: Pergamon).

—— and SOLOMOS, J. (eds.) (1987), *The Roots of Urban Unrest* (Oxford: Pergamon).

BETHNAL GREEN and STEPNEY TRADES COUNCIL (1978), *Blood on the Streets* (London: Bethnal Green and Stepney Trades Council).

BIDERMAN, A. D. (1973), 'When Does Interpersonal Violence Become Crime—Theory and Methods for Statistical Surveys' in R. G. Lehnen and W. Skogan (1981), *The National Crime Survey*: Working Papers (Washington, D.C.: National Institute of Justice), 48–51.

BILLIG, M. (1978), *Fascists: A Social Psychological View of the National Front* (London: Academic Press).

BITTNER, E. (1970), *The Functions of the Police in Modern Society* (Chevy Chase, Maryland: National Institute of Mental Health)

BJORGØ, T., and WITTE, R. (eds.) (1993), *Racist Violence in Europe* (London: Macmillan).

BLAGG, H., PEARSON, G., SAMPSON, S., SMITH, D. and STUBBS, P. (1988), 'Inter-agency Cooperation: Rhetoric and Reality' in T. Hope and M. Shaw (eds.), *Communities and Crime Reduction* (London: HMSO).

BOTTOMS, T. (1990), 'Crime Prevention Facing the 1990s', *Policing and Society*, Vol. 1, 3–22.

BOWLING, B. (1991), Ethnic Minority Elderly People: Helping the Community to Care, *New Community*, Vol. 17, No. 4, July, 645–54.

—— (1993a), 'Racial Harassment and the Process of Victimization': Conceptual and Methodological Implications for the Local Crime Survey', *British Journal of Criminology*, Vol. 33, No. 1 Spring.

—— (1993b), 'Racial Harassment in East London' in M. S. Hamm (ed.), *Hate Crime: International Perspectives on Causes and Control* (Academy of Criminal Justice Sciences/Anderson Publications).

—— and SAULSBURY, W. E. (1992), 'A Multi-Agency Approach to Racial Harassment', *Home Office Research Bulletin* No. 32.

—— and —— (1993), 'A Local Response to Racial Harassment' in T. Bjorgø and R. Witte, *Racist Violence in Europe* (London: Macmillan).

BRIDGES, L. (1993), 'The Racial Harassment Bill: A Missed Opportunity', *Race and Class*, March, 69–71.

BROGDEN, M., JEFFERSON, T., and WALKLATE, W. (1988), *Introducing Policework* (London: Unwin Hyman).

BROWN, C. (1984), *Black and White Britain: The Third PSI Survey* (London: Heinemann).

BROWN, R. (1995), *Prejudice: Its Social Psychology* (London: Blackwell).

BROWNLIE, I. (1992), *Basic Documents on Human Rights* (Oxford: Clarendon Press).

BUFFORD, B. (1991), *Among the Thugs* (London: Mandarin).

BULL, R. and HORNCASTLE, P. (1989), 'An Evaluation of Human Awareness Training' in R. Morgan and D. J. Smith (eds.) *Coming to Terms with Policing: Perspectives on Policy* (London: Routledge).

BUTLER, D., and STOKES, D. (1974), *Political Change in Britain* (London: Macmillan).

CAPA (1988), *CAPA Annual Report* (London: CAPA).

CASHMORE, E. (1984), *No Future: Youth and Society* (London: Heineman).

—— and McLAUGHLIN, E. (1991), *Out of Order?: Policing Black People* (London: Routledge).

CLARKE, J. (1973), *The Skinheads and the Study of Youth Culture,* paper presented to the 14th National Deviancy Conference, University of York.

—— (1975), 'The Skinheads and the Magical Recovery of Working Class Community', *Cultural Studies*, vols. 7 and 8, 99–102; also in S. Hall and T. Jefferson (eds.) *Resistance Through Rituals* (London: Hutchinson).

—— and JEFFERSON, T. (1976), 'Working Class Youth Cultures' in G.

Mungham and G. Pearson, *Working Class Youth Culture* (London: Routledge).

COHEN, S. (1972), *Folk Devils and Moral Panics: the Creation of the Mods and Rockers* (London: MacGibbon and Kee).

COMMISSION FOR RACIAL EQUALITY (1979), *Brick Lane and Beyond: An Inquiry into Racial Strife and Violence in Tower Hamlets* (London: Commission for Racial Equality).

—— (1981), *Racial Harassment on Local Authority Housing Estates* (London: Commission for Racial Equality).

—— (1987a), *Living in Terror: A Report on Racial Violence and Harassment in Housing* (London: Commission for Racial Equality).

—— (1987b), *Racial Attacks: A Survey in Eight Areas of Britain* (London: Commission for Racial Equality).

—— (1988), *Learning in Terror: A Survey of Racial Harassment in Schools and Colleges in England, Scotland and Wales, 1985–87* (London: Commission for Racial Equality).

CONSTANTINE, L. (1954), *Colour Bar* (London: Stanley Paul).

COOK, D. (1978), *A Knife at the Throat of Us All: Racism and the National Front* (London: Communist Party).

—— and HUDSON, B. (1993), *Racism and Criminology* (London: Sage).

COOPER, J., and QUERSHI, T. (1993), *Through Patterns Not Our Own: A Study of the Regulation of Racial Violence on the Council Estates of East London* (University of East London: New Ethnicities Research and Education Group).

COWELL, D., JONES, T., and YOUNG, J. (eds.) (1982), *Policing the Riots* (London: Junction Books).

CRAWFORD, A., JONES, T., WOODHOUSE, T., and YOUNG, J. (1989), *The Second Islington Crime Survey* (Middlesex: Middlesex Polytechnic Centre for Criminology).

CROWN PROSECUTION SERVICE (1988). 'Code for Crown Prosecutors', Annex to Director's *Annual Report* to the Attorney General 1987/88 (London: HMSO).

—— (1996), *Offences Against the Person: Charging Standards: Agreed by the Police and the Crown Prosecution Service* (London: Crown Prosecution Service).

CUTLER, D., and MURJI, K. (1990), 'From a Force into a Service?: Racial Attacks, Policing and Service Delivery', *Critical Social Policy,* March/April.

DEAKIN, N. (1970), *Colour, Citizenship and British Society* (London: Panther).

DEPARTMENT OF THE ENVIRONMENT INNER CITIES DIRECTORATE (1983), *Information Note No. 2 1981 Census, Urban Deprivation* (London: DoE).

DUNHILL, C. (1989), 'Women, Racist Attacks and the Response from Anti-Racist Groups' in Dunhill, C. (ed.) *The Boys in Blue: Women's Challenge to the Police* (London: Virago).

ECK, J. E., and SPELMAN, W. (1987), *Problem Solving: Problem-oriented*

Policing in Newport News (Washington, D.C.: Police Executive Research Forum).

EDGAR, D. (1977), 'Racism, Fascism and the Politics of the National Front', *Race and Class*, Vol. 19, 2, Autumn.

EKBLOM, P. (1979), 'Police Truancy Patrols' in J. Burrows, P. Ekblom, and K. Heal, *Crime Prevention and the Police* (Home Office Research Study No. 55, London: HMSO).

—— and SIMON, F. (with BIRDI, S.) (1988), *Crime and Racial Harassment in Asian-run Small Shops: The Scope for Prevention* (Crime Prevention Unit Paper 15, London: Home Office).

ELLIS, E., and FLAHERTY, M. G. (1992), *Investigating Subjectivity: Research on Lived Experience* (London: Sage).

EMSLEY, C. (1983), *Policing and its Context 1750–1870* (London: Macmillan).

EVANS, N. (1980), 'The South Wales Race Riots of 1919', *Journal of the Society for the Study of Welsh Labour History*, III/1, Spring.

FACTOR, F., and STENSON, F. (1989), *Community Control and the Policing of Jewish Youth*, Paper presented to the British Criminology Conference, Bristol, July.

FARRELL, G. (1982), 'Multiple Victimisation: Its Extent and Significance', *International Review of Victimology*, Vol. 2, 85–102.

——, PHILLIPS, C., and PEASE, K. (1995), 'Like Taking Candy: Why Does Repeat Victimization Occur?', *British Journal of Criminology*, Vol. 3, 384–99.

FEAGIN, J. R., and SIKES, M. P. (1994), *Living with Racism: The Black Middle-class Experience* (Boston, Mass.: Beacon Press).

FIELDING, N. (1981), *The National Front* (London: Routledge).

FIENBERG, S. E. (1977), 'Deciding What and Whom to Count' in R. G. Lehnen and W. Skogan (1981), *The National Crime Survey: Working Papers* (Washington, D.C.: National Institute of Justice), 48–51.

FITZGERALD, M. (1989), 'Legal Approaches to Racial Harassment in Council Housing: The Case for Reassessment', *New Community*, Vol. 16 (1), 93–106.

—— and ELLIS, T. (1990), 'Racial Harassment: The Evidence' in C. Kemp (ed.) *Current Issues in Criminological Research*. British Criminology Conference Vol. 2 (Bristol: Bristol Centre for Criminal Justice).

—— and HALE, C. (1996), *Ethnic Minorities, Victimisation and Racial Harassment* (Home Office Research Study No. 154, London: HMSO).

FORBES, D. (1988), *Action on Racial Harassment: Legal Remedies and Local Authorities* (London: Legal Action Group and London Housing Authority).

FORD, G. (1992) (ed.) *Fascist Europe. The Rise of Racism and Xenophobia* (London: Pluto).

FOSTER, J. (1989), 'Two Stations: An Ethnographic Study of Policing in the Inner City' in D. Downes (ed.), *Crime in the City* (London: Macmillan).

FOUCAULT, M. (1977), *Discipline and Punish: The Birth of the Prison* (trans. Alan Scheridan) (Harmondsworth: Penguin).

FRYER, P. (1984), *Staying Power: The History of Black People in Britain* (London: Pluto).

GAY, P., and YOUNG, K. (1988), *Community Relations Councils: Roles and Objectives* (London Policy Studies Institute/Commission for Racial Equality).

GENN, H. (1988), 'Multiple Victimisation' in M. Maguire and J. Pointing (eds.) *Victims of Crime: A New Deal?* (Milton Keynes: Open University Press), 90–100.

GIFFORD, LORD (Chair) (1986), *The Broadwater Farm Inquiry* (London: Karia Press).

GILL, B. A. G. (1985), *Towards Genuine Consultation: Principles of Community Participation* (London: Commission for Racial Equality).

GILROY, P. (1987), *There Ain't no Black in the Union Jack: The Cultural Politics of Race and Nation* (London: Hutchinson).

—— (1990), 'The End of Anti-Racism' in W. Ball and J. Solomos (eds.) *Race and Local Politics* (London: Macmillan).

—— (1993), *Small Acts: Thoughts on the Politics of Black Cultures* (London: Serpent's Tail).

GINSBURG, N. (1989), 'Racial Harassment Policy and Practice: The Denial of Citizenship", *Critical Social Policy* No. 26, 66–81.

GLADSTONE, F. J. (1980), *Co-ordinating Crime Prevention Efforts* (Home Office Research Study No. 62, London: HMSO).

GLARE (1988), *A Fair Cop?: Policing and Racial Equality* (London: Greater London Action for Racial Equality).

GLASS, R. (1960), *Newcomers: West Indians in London* (London: Allen & Unwin).

GOLDSTEIN, H. (1979)., 'Improving Policing: A Problem-Oriented Approach', *Crime and Delinquency*, April, 236–58.

—— (1990), *Problem-oriented Policing* (New York: McGraw-Hill).

GORDON, P. (1984), *White Law* (London: Pluto).

—— (1986), *Racial Violence and Harassment*, Runnymede Research Report (London: Runnymede Trust).

—— (1987), 'Community Policing: Towards the Local Police State?' in P. Scraton (ed.), *Law, Order and the Authoritarian State* (Milton Keynes: Open University Press).

—— (1990), *Racial Violence and Harassment* (2nd edn., London: Runnymede Trust).

—— (1993), 'The Police and Racist Violence in Britain' in T. Bjørgø and R. Witte (eds.), *Racist Violence in Europe* (London: Macmillan).

—— and ROSENBERG, D. (1989), *Daily Racism: The Press and Black People in Britain* (London: Runnymede Trust).

GRAEF, R. (1989), *Talking Blues: The Police in Their Own Words* (London: Collins Harvill).

GREATER LONDON COUNCIL (1983), *A New Police Authority for London: A Consultation Paper on Democratic Control of the Police in London*, GLC Police Committee Discussion Paper No. 1 (London: GLC).

—— (1984), *Racial Harassment in London,* Report of a panel of inquiry set up by the GLC Police Committee (London: GLC).

—— (1985), *Guide to the Metropolitan Police* (London: GLC).

—— (1986), *Policing London: Collected Reports of the GLC Police Committee* (London: GLC).

GRIMSHAW, R., and JEFFERSON, T. (1987), *Interpreting Policework* (London: Allen and Unwin).

HALL, S. (1992), 'New Ethnicities' in J. Donald and A. Rattansi, *'Race', Culture and Difference* (London: Sage).

HALL, S., CRITCHER, C., JEFFERSON, T., CLARKE, J., and ROBERTS, B. (1978), *Policing the Crisis: Mugging, the State and Law and Order* (London: Macmillan).

HAMM, M. S. (ed.) (1993a), *Hate Crime: International Perspectives on Causes and Control* (Academy of Criminal Justice Sciences/Anderson Publications).

—— (1993b), *American Skinheads: The Criminology and Control of Hate Crime.* (Westport, Conn.: Praeger).

HANNA, M. (1974), 'The National Front and Other Right-wing Organisations', *New Community*, Vol. 3, No. 1–2, 49–55.

HARROW COUNCIL FOR RACIAL EQUALITY (1991), *Racist Violence in Harrow* (London: Harrow Council for Racial Equality).

HARTLEY, B. (1973), *Son of Alf Garnet: Riot in Leeds,* paper given to conference on working class culture, University College, Cardiff, November.

HESSE, B., RAI, D. K., BENNETT, C. and McGILCHRIST, P. (1992), *Beneath the Surface: Racial Harassment* (Aldershot: Avebury).

HEWSTONE, M. and BROWN, R. (eds.) (1986), *Contact and Conflict in Intergroup Encounters* (London: Blackwell).

HIRO, D. (1991), *'Black British White British: A History of Race Relations in Britain'* (London: Grafton).

HOARE, M. A., STEWART, G., and PURCELL, C. M. (1984), *The Problem Oriented Approach: Four Pilot Studies,* Metropolitan Police Management Services Department, Report No. 30/84.

HOBBS, D. (1988), *Doing the Business* (Oxford: OUP).

HOLDAWAY, S. (1983), *Inside the British Police* (Oxford: Basil Blackwell).

—— (1996), *The Racialisation of British Policing* (Basingstoke: Macmillan).

HOLMES, C. (1988), *John Bull's Island: Immigration and British Society, 1871–1971* (London: Macmillan).

HOME OFFICE (1965), *Report of the Committee on the Prevention and Detection of Crime* (Cornish Committee) (London: Home Office).

—— (1976), *A Review of Criminal Justice Policy, 1976* (London: Home Office).

—— (1978), *Circular 211/1987 Juveniles. Co-operation Between the Police and Other Agencies*, jointly issued with Department of Health and Social Security, Department of Education and Science and the Welsh Office.

—— (1980), *Circular 83/198 Juveniles. Co-operation Between the Police and Other Agencies* (London: Home Office).

—— (1981), *Racial Attacks: Report of a Home Office Study* (London: Home Office).

—— (1982), *Crime Prevention: A Co-ordinated Approach. Proceedings of a Seminar on Crime Prevention, Police Staff College, Bramshill House 26–29 September 1982* (London: Home Office).

—— (1984), *Circular 8/84 Crime Prevention*, issued jointly with Department of Education and Science, Department of Environment, Department of Health and Social Security and the Welsh Office.

—— (1986), *Home Office Good Practice Guide for the Police: The Response to Racial Attacks* (London: Home Office).

—— (1987), *A Multi-agency Initiative for the Prevention of Racial Attacks. A Paper prepared by the Home Office Research and Planning Unit* (unpublished).

—— (1989), *The Response to Racial Attacks and Harassment: Guidance for the Statutory Agencies,* Report of the Inter-Departmental Racial Attacks Group (London: Home Office).

—— (1991a), *Safer Communities: The Local Delivery of Crime Prevention Through the Partnership Approach,* Report of the Home Office Standing Conference on Crime Prevention (London: Home Office).

—— (1991b), *The Response to Racial Attacks and Harassment: Sustaining the Momentum,* 2nd. Report of the Inter-Departmental Racial Attacks Group (London: Home Office).

—— (1996a), *Digest 3: Information on the Criminal Justice System in England and Wales* (London: Home Office Research and Statistics Department).

—— (1996b), *Taking Steps: Multi-agency Responses to Racial Attacks and Harassment,* The Third Report of the Inter Departmental Racial Attacks Group (London: Home Office).

hooks, b. (1995), *Killing Rage: ending racism* (Harmondsworth: Penguin).

HOPE, T. (1985). *Implementing Crime Prevention Measures*, Home Office Research Study No. 86 (London: HMSO).

—— and MURPHY, D. (1983), 'Problems of Implementing Crime Prevention: The Experience of a Demonstration Project', *The Howard Journal*, Vol. XXII, 38–50.

—— and SHAW, M. (eds.) (1988), *Communities and Crime Reduction* (London: HMSO).

HORTON, C. (1989), 'Good Practice and Evaluating Policework' in R. Morgan and D. Smith (eds.) (1989), *Coming to Terms with Policing* (London: Tavistock).

HOUGH, M., and MAYHEW, P. (1983), *The British Crime Survey: First Report*, Home Office Research Study No. 76 (London: Home Office).

—— (1985), *Taking Account of Crime: Key Findings from the 1984 British Crime Survey*, Home Office Research Study No. 85 (London: Home Office).

HOUNSLOW COMMUNITY RELATIONS COUNCIL (1986), *The Nature and Extent of Racial Harassment in the London Borough of Hounslow* (London: Hounslow Community Relations Council).

HOUSE OF COMMONS HOME AFFAIRS COMMITTEE (1982), *Racial Attacks,* Second Report from the Home Affairs Committee, Session 1981–82, HC. 106 (London: HMSO).

—— (1986), *Racial Attacks and Harassment*, Third Report from the Home Affairs Committee, Session 1985–6, HC. 409 (London: HMSO).

—— (1989), *Racial Attacks and Harassment*, First Report from the House of Commons Home Affairs Committee (London: HMSO).

—— (1994a), *Racial Attacks and Harassment*, Vol. 1: Report, together with the Proceedings of the Committee, Home Affairs Committee, Third Report (London: HMSO).

—— (1994b), *Racial Attacks and Harassment*, Vol. II: Minutes of evidence and appendices, Session 1993–4 Home Affairs Committee, Third Report (London: HMSO).

HOWE, D. (1988), *From Bobby to Babylon: Blacks and the British Police* (London: Race Today Publications).

HUMAN RIGHTS WATCH (1997), *Racist Violence in the United Kingdom* (London: Human Rights Watch/Helsinki).

HUNTE, J. (1965), *Nigger Hunting in England?* (London: West Indian Standing Conference).

HUSBANDS, C. (1982), 'East End Racism 1900–1980: Geographical Continuities in Vigilantist and Extreme Right-wing Political Behaviour', *London Journal*, Vol. 8, No. 1.

—— (1983), *Racial Exclusionism and the City: The Urban Support for the National Front* (London: Allen and Unwin).

—— (1992), 'Hate in a Cold Climate', *New Statesman and Society*, 24 April.

INSTITUTE OF RACE RELATIONS (1979), *'Police Against Black People'* Evidence submitted to the Royal Commission on Criminal Procedure (London: IRR).

—— (1987), *Policing Against Black People* (London: IRR).

JEFFERSON, T. (1990), *The Case Against Paramilitary Policing* (Milton Keynes: Open University Press).

JENKINSON, J. (1985), 'The Glasgow Race Disturbances of 1919', *Immigrants and Minorities*, Vol. 3, No. 3, November.

—— (1996), 'The 1919 Riots' in P. Panayi, *Racial violence in Britain* (2nd edn.) (London: Leicester University Press).

JESSOP, B. (1990), *State Theory: Putting Capitalist States in Their Place* (Cambridge: Polity Press).

JOINT COMMITTEE AGAINST RACIALISM (1981), *Racial Violence in Britain* (London: JCAR).

JONES, T., MacLEAN, B. D., and YOUNG, J. (1986), *The Islington Crime Survey: Crime, Victimisation and Policing in Inner-City London* (Aldershot: Gower).

JONES, NEWBURN, T. and SMITH, D. (1994) *Democracy and Policing* (London: Policy Studies Institute).

KEITH, M. (1991), 'Policing a Perplexed Society?': No-go Areas and the Mystification of Police–Black Conflict' in E. Cashmore and E. McLaughlin, *Out of Order?: Policing Black People* (London: Routledge).

—— and MURJI, K. (1990), 'Reifying Crime, Legitimising Racism: Policing, Local Authorities and Left Realism' in W. Ball and J. Solomos, *Race and Local Politics* (Basingstoke: Macmillan).

—— (1993), *Race, Riots and Policing: Lore and disorder in a multi-racist society* (London: UCL Press).

KELLING, G. L., PATE, T., DIECKMAN, D., and BROWN, C. E. (1974), *The Kansas City Preventive Patrol Experiment: A Technical Report* (Washington, D.C.: Police Foundation).

KELLY, L. (1987), 'The Continuum of Sexual Violence' in J. Hanmer and M. Maynard (eds.) *Women, Violence and Social Control* (London: Macmillan), 46–60.

—— (1988), *Surviving Sexual Violence* (London: Polity).

KIMBER, J., and COOPER, L. (1991), *Victim Support Racial Harassment Project* (London: Community Research and Advisory Centre, The Polytechnic of North London).

KETTLE, M., and HODGES, L. (1982), *Uprising!: The Police, the People and the Riots in Britain's Cities* (London: Pan).

KING, M. (1991), 'The Political Construction of Crime Prevention: A Contrast between the French and British Experience' in K. Stenson and D. Cowell (eds.) *The Politics of Crime Control* (London: Sage).

KINSEY, R., LEA, J., and YOUNG, J. (1987), *Losing the Fight Against Crime* (Oxford: Blackwell).

KLEG, M. (1993), *Hate Prejudice and Racism* (Albany, N.Y.: State University of New York Press).

KLUG, F. (1982), *Racist Attacks* (London: Runnymede Trust).

LAPIDO, D., (1996) *Human, All Too Human: The Resurgence of the American Prison,* Research paper (Cambridge: University of Cambridge).

LAYTON-HENRY, Z. (1980), *Conservative Party Politics* (London: Macmillan).

—— (1984), *The Politics of Race in Britain* (London: Allen and Unwin).

LEA, J. (1987), 'Police Racism: Some Theories and their Policy Implications' in R. Mathews and J. Young (eds.) *Confronting Crime* (London: Sage).

LEE, J. A. (1981), 'Some Structural Aspects of Police Deviance in Relations with Minority Groups' in C. Shearing (ed) *Organisational Police Deviance* (Toronto: Butterworth).

LEE, W. L. M. (1901), *A History of Police in England* (London: Methuen).

LEEDS COMMUNITY RELATIONS COUNCIL (1986), *Racial Harassment in Leeds 1985–6* (Leeds: LCRC).

LEGAL ACTION GROUP (1982), 'Why Consultation is not Enough' (editorial), *Legal Action Group Bulletin* (London: Legal Action Group).

LEHNEN, R. G., and SKOGAN, W. (1981), *The National Crime Survey: Working Papers Volume 1: Current and Historical Perspectives* (Washington, D.C.: US Department of Justice Bureau of Statistics).

LEMOS, G. (1993), *Interviewing Perpetrators of Racial Harassment: A Guide for Housing Managers* (London: Lemos Associates).

LIDDLE, M. A., and BOTTOMS, A. (1991), *Implementing Circular 8/84 A Retrospective Assessment of the Five Towns Crime Prevention Initiative*, Research report submitted to the Home Office.

LITTLE, K. (1943), 'Colour Prejudice in Britain', *Wasu* 10/1 May.

LONDON BOROUGH OF CAMDEN HOUSING INVESTIGATION ADVISORY PANEL (1988), *Racism in Camden Housing*, Report of the Housing Investigation Advisory Panel (London: London Borough of Camden).

LONDON BOROUGH OF NEWHAM (1986), *Planning Newham: Handbook and Atlas of Development and Planning Proposals in the Borough* (London: London Borough of Newham).

—— (1987), *Crime in Newham: The Survey* (London: London Borough of Newham).

—— (1988), *Written Evidence Presented to the Inter-Departmental Racial Attacks Group (RAG)* (London: London Borough of Newham).

—— (1989), *Social Services Department Interim Procedures for Dealing With Racial Harassment Cases* (London: London Borough of Newham).

—— (1990), *Responding to Racial Harassment: Guidelines for Schools* (London: London Borough of Newham).

—— (1991), *In-service Training Pack: Responding to Racial Harassment for Primary and Secondary Teachers* (London: London Borough of Newham).

—— (1995), *Racial Harassment in Newham 1990–1994* (London: London Borough of Newham).

—— (1996), *Racial Harassment in Newham 1995* (London: London Borough of Newham).

LONDON BOROUGH OF WALTHAM FOREST (1990), *Beneath the Surface: An Inquiry into Racial Harassment in the London Borough of Waltham Forest* (London: London Borough of Waltham Forest).

LONDON RACE AND HOUSING FORUM (1981), *Racial Harassment on Local Authority Housing Estates* (London: Commission for Racial Equality).

LONDON STRATEGIC POLICY UNIT (1987a), *Policing London: Collected Reports of the LSPU Police Monitoring and Research Group* (No. 2) (London: LSPU).

—— (1987b), *Police Accountability: A New Strategic Authority for London Police*, Monitoring and Research Group briefing paper No. 2 (London: LSPU).

LUSTGARTEN, L. (1986), *The Governance of the Police* (London: Sweet and Maxwell).

McCABE, S., and SUTCLIFFE, F. (1978), *Defining Crime: A Study of Police Decisions* (Oxford: Oxford University Centre for Criminological Research).

McCONVILLE, M., and SHEPHERD, D. (1992), *Watching Police, Watching Communities* (London: Routledge).

MACDONALD, I., BHAVINI, R., KHAN, L. and John, G. (1989), *Murder in the Playground. The Burnage Report* (London: Longsight Press).

McLAUGHLIN, E. (1991), 'Police Accountability and Black People: Into the 1990s' in E. Cashmore and E. McLaughlin *Out of Order?: Policing Black People*. (London: Routledge).

—— (1994), *Community, Policing and Accountability: The Politics of Policing in Manchester in the 1980s* (Aldershot: Avebury).

MACLEAN, B. D. (1986), 'Critical Criminology and Some Limitations of Traditional Inquiry' in B. D. MacLean (ed.) *The Political Economy of Crime: Readings for a Critical Criminology* (Scarborough, Ontario: Prentice-Hall).

—— (1991), 'In Partial Defence of Socialist Realism: Some Theoretical and Methodological Concerns of the Local Crime Survey', *Crime, Law and Social Change* 15, 213–54.

MAGUIRE, M., and POINTING, J. (eds.) (1988), *Victims of Crime: A New Deal?* (Milton Keynes: Open University Press).

MALCOLM-X and HAYLEY, A. (1965), *The Autobiography of Malcolm X* (New York: Grove Press).

MAMA, A. (1989), *The Hidden Struggle: Statutory and Voluntary Sector Responses to Violence Against Black Women in the Home* (London: London Race and Housing Research Unit and the Runnymede Trust).

MANCHESTER CCR (1986), *Racial Harassment in Manchester and the Response of the Police (1980–1985)* (Manchester: Manchester CCR).

MANNING, P. K. (1983), 'Organisational Control and Semiotics' in M. Punch (ed.) *Control in the Police Organisation* (Cambridge, Mass.: MIT Press).

—— (1988), *Symbolic Communication* (London: MIT Press).

MAY, R., and COHEN, R. (1974), 'The Interaction between Race and Colonialism: A Case Study of the Liverpool Race Riots of 1919', *Race and Class* 16, 2, 111–26.

MAYHEW, P., ELLIOTT, D., and DOWDS, L. (1989), *The British Crime Survey*, Home Office Research Study No. 111 (London: HMSO).

METROPOLITAN POLICE (1978), *Force Order on Racial Incidents* (London: Metropolitan Police).

—— (1982), *Racial Attacks,* Police Order 29, 30 April (London: Metropolitan Police).

—— (1985), *The Principles of Policing and Guidelines for Professional Behaviour* (London: Metropolitan Police).

—— (1986a), *Recording and Monitoring Racial Incidents Guidelines,* A7 Branch, January (London: Metropolitan Police).

—— (1986b), *Report of the Commissioner of Police of the Metropolis for the Year 1985.* (issued each year as a Command Paper) (London: HMSO).

—— (1989a). *London Racial Harassment Action Guide* (London: Metropolitan Police).

—— (1989b), *Guidance on the Initial Investigation of Crime: Report of the Crime Investigation Priority Project* (London: Metropolitan Police).

—— (1989c), *Racial Incidents 1988: 2 Area (East)* (London: Metropolitan Police).

—— (1990), *Working Together for Racial Harmony* (London: Metropolitan Police).

—— (1991), *Report of the Commissioner of Police of the Metropolis for the Year 1990* (issued each year as a Command Paper) (London: HMSO).

—— (1996a) *Police Order 14/96 Guidelines on the recording of non-crime racial, homophobic, domestic, and child care incidents* (London: Metropolitan Police).

—— (1996b) *Police Order 14/96 Racial incidents—Sharing Information with Other Agencies* (London: Metropolitan Police).

MILES, R. (1984), 'The Riots of 1958: Notes on the Ideological Construction of "Race Relations" as a Political Issue in Britain', *Immigrants and Minorities*, 33, 252–75.

—— (1994), A Rise of Racism and Fascism in Contemporary Europe?: Some Sceptical Reflections on its Nature and Extent, *New Community*, 20(4) July, 547–62.

—— and PHIZACKLEA, A. (1984), *White Man's Country: Racism in British Politics* (London: Pluto).

MILLIBAND, R. (1969), *The State in Capitalist Society* (London: Weidenfeld and Nicholson).

MOORE, C., and BROWN, J. (1981), *Community Versus Crime* (London: Bedford Square Press).

MORGAN, R. (1989), 'Policing by Consent: Legitimating the Doctrine' in R. Morgan and D. J. Smith (eds.) (1989), *Coming to Terms with Policing: Perspectives on Policy* (London: Routledge).

—— and SMITH, D.J. (eds.) (1989), *Coming to Terms with Policing: Perspectives on Policy* (London: Routledge).

MORRIS, T. P. (1958), *The Criminal Area: A Study in Social Ecology* (London: Routledge and Kegan Paul).

—— (1989), *Crime and Criminal Justice Since 1945* (London: Blackwell).

MULLARD, C. (1973), *Black Britain* (London: Allen and Unwin).

MUNGHAM, G., and PEARSON, G. (1976), *Working Class Youth Culture* (London: Routledge).

—— (1976), 'Troubled Youth, Troubling World', introduction to G. Mungham and G. Pearson, *Working Class Youth Culture* (London: Routledge).

NEWBURN, T., and JONES, T. (1996), *Policing and Disaffected Communities*, Paper for the Standing Advisory Commission on Human Rights (London: Standing Advisory Commission on Human Rights).

NEWHAM MONITORING PROJECT (1985), *Racism and Resistance: Annual Report, 1985* (London: NMP).

—— (1988), *Still Fighting: Annual Report, 1988* (London: NMP).

—— (1989), *From Strength to Strength: Ten Years of the Newham Monitoring Project: Annual Report 1989* (London: NMP).

—— (1989), *Annual Report 1989.* (London: NMP).

—— (1990a), *Keeping The Fight Alive: Annual Report 1990* (London: NMP).

—— (1990b), *Racism and Racist Violence in Schools* (London: NMP).

—— (1991), *Forging a Black Community: Asian and Afro-Caribbean Struggles in Newham* (London: Newham Monitoring Project/Campaign Against Racism and Fascism).

—— (1993), *Annual Report 1992/3* (London: NMP).

NEYROUD, P. (1992), 'Multi-agency Approaches to Racial Harassment: The Lessons of Implementing the Racial Attacks Group Report', *New Community*, Vol. 18, No. 4, July.

NICHOLSON (1974), *Strangers to England: Immigration to England 1100–1945* (Leyland).

NORTH PLAISTOW RACIAL HARASSMENT PROJECT (1990), *Co-ordinated Action Plan* (unpublished).

NUGENT, N., and KING, R. (1977), *The British Right* (London: Saxon House).

OAKLEY, R. (1991), *Racial Violence and Harassment in Europe* (Council of Europe).

PAGET, G. L. (1984), 'Racially Motivated Violence and Intimidation: Inadequate State Enforcement and Federal Civil Rights Remedies', *Journal of Criminal Law and Criminology*, Vol. 75, No. 1, 103–38.

PANAYI, P. (1996), *Racial Violence in Britain* (2nd edn., London: Leicester University Press/Pinter).

PARKES, N. (1984), 'Part-time Work with Black Youth' in G. John and N. Parkes. *Working with Black Youth: Complementing or Competing Resources?*, Extension report 2 (Leicester: Leicester NYB).

PEARSON, G. (1976), ' "Paki-bashing" in a North Eastern Lancashire Cotton Town: A Case Study and its History' in J. Mungham and G. Pearson (eds.),*Working Class Youth Culture* (London: Routledge).

—— (1983), *Hooligan: A History of Respectable Fears* (London: Macmillan).

——, BLAGG, H., and SMITH, D. (1988), *Crime, Community and the Inter-agency Dimension*, End of Award Report to the Economic and Social Research Council.

——, SAMPSON, A., BLAGG, H., STUBBS, P., and SMITH, D. J. (1989), 'Policing Racism' in R. Morgan and D. J. Smith (eds.) *Coming to Terms with Policing: Perspectives on Policy* (London: Routledge).

PHILLIPS, C. (1987), *The European Tribe* (London: Faber and Faber).

PHILLIPS, S. V., and COCHRANE, R. (1989), *The Role and Function of Police Community Liaison Officers*, Research and Planning Unit Paper No. 51 (London: Home Office).

PILGER, J. (1988), Preface to K. Tompson, *Under Siege: Racial Violence in Britain Today* (Harmondsworth: Penguin).

PILKINGTON, E. (1988), *Beyond the Mother Country: West Indians and the Notting Hill White Riots* (London: I.B. Taurus).

PIMPINELLA, G. (1995), *Most Severe Racially Motivated Attacks: 1992, 1993, 1994*, compiled February. Commission for Racial Equality: Commission for Racial Equality Library Press Cuttings..

PIRSIG, R. M. (1974), *Zen and the Art of Motorcycle Maintenance* (London: Corgi).

PITTS, J. (1993), 'Theoreotyping: Anti-racism, Criminology and Black Young People' in D. COOK and B. HUDSON, (eds.) *Racism and Criminology*, (London: Sage).

POPE, D. (1976), *Community Relations—the Police Response* (London: Runnymede Trust).

PRASHAR, U., and NICHOLAS, S. (1986), *Routes or Road-Blocks?: Consulting Minority Communities in London Boroughs* (London: Runnymede Trust).

RADELET, L. A., and CARTER, D. L. (1994), *The Police and the Community* (5th edn., New York: Macmillan).

RAWLINGS, P., and STANKO, B. (1991), *Precarious Protection: Policing Crime Prevention and Personal Safety*, British Criminology Conference, York (Law Department, Brunel University).

REES, T. (1982), 'Immigration Policies in the United Kingdom' in C. Husbands, *Race in Britain* (London: Hutchinson/Open University).

REEVES. F. (1989), *Race and Borough Politics* (Aldershot: Avebury).

REIN, M. (1983), *From Policy to Practice* (London: Macmillan).

—— (1976), *Social Science and Public Policy* (Harmondsworth: Penguin).

REINER, R. (1985), *The Politics of the Police* (London: Harvester Wheatsheaf).

—— (1989), 'Race and Criminal Justice', *New Community*, Vol. 16, No. 1, 5–22.

—— (1992), *The Politics of the Police* (2nd edn., London: Harvester Wheatsheaf).

REISS, A. J. (1971), *The Police and the Public* (New Haven, Conn.: Yale University Press).

RICHMOND, A. H. (1954), *Colour Prejudice in Britain: A Study of West Indian Workers in Liverpool, 1941–51* (London: Routledge and Keegan Paul).

—— (1955), *The Colour Problem: A Study of Racial Relations* (Harmondsworth: Penguin).

RIGER, S., and GORDON, M. (1981), 'The Fear of Rape: A Study in Social Control', *Journal of Social Issues*, Vol. 37, No. 4 (fall), 71–92.

ROCK, P. (1988), 'Crime Reduction Initiatives on Problem Estates' in T. Hope and M. Shaw (eds.) *Communities and Crime Reduction* (London: HMSO).

—— (1990), *Helping Victims of Crime* (Oxford: OUP).

ROOT, M. P. P. (ed.) (1992), *Racially Mixed People in America* (London: Sage).

ROSE, D. (1996), *In the Name of the Law: The Collapse of Criminal Justice* (London: Vintage).

ROSE, R., AND ASSOCIATES (1969), *Colour and Citizenship: A Report on British Race Relations* (London: Oxford University Press).

SAFETY FROM HARASMENT AND RACIAL ATTACKS (SaHaRa) (1993), *Out of Order: a Local Study of the Reporting of Experiences of Racial Harassment in South West London and the Response by Public Services* (London: SaHaRa with The Race Equality Council in Wandsworth).

SAMPSON, A., STUBBS, P., SMITH, D., PEARSON, G., and BLAGG, H. (1988), 'Crime, Localities and the Multi-agency Approach', *British Journal of Criminology*, Vol. 28, No. 4, Autumn.

—— and PHILLIPS, C. (1992), *Multiple Victimisation: Racial Attacks on an East London Estate*, Police Research Group Crime Prevention Unit Series Paper 36 (London: Home Office Police Department).

—— and —— (1996), *Reducing Repeat Victimisation on a London Estate*, Police Research Group Paper 67 (London: Home Office Police Department).

SAULSBURY, W. E., and BOWLING, B. (1991), '*The Multi-Agency Approach in Practice: The North Plaistow Racial Harassment Project*, Home Office Research Study No. 64 (London: Home Office).

SCARMAN LORD (1975), *The Red Lion Square Disorders of 15 June 1974*, Cmnd. 5919 (London: HMSO).

SCARMAN, SIR LESLIE (1981), *The Brixton Disorders: 10–12 April 1981: Report of an Inquiry: Presented to Parliament by the Secretary of State for the Home Department*, November (London: HMSO).

SCRATON, P. (1985), *The State of the Police* (London: Pluto).

SEABROOK, J. (1970), 'Pakie Stan', *New Society*, 23 April, No. 395, 677–8.

SEAGRAVE, J. (1989), *Racially Motivated Incidents Reported to the Police*, Home Office Research and Planning Unit Paper 54 (London: Home Office).

SEARCHLIGHT (undated), *The Murderers are Amongst Us: The Criminal Records of Britain's Racists* (London: Searchlight).

SHAPLAND, J., WILLMORE, J., and DUFF, P. (1985), *Victims in the Criminal Justice System* (Aldershot: Gower).

—— and HOBBS, D. (1989), 'Policing Priorities on the Ground' in R. Morgan and D. J. Smith (eds.) *Coming to Terms with Policing: Perspectives on Policy* (London: Routledge).

SHEPTYCKI, J. W. E. (1991), *An Investigation of Policing Policy in Relation to 'Domestic Violence' in London in the 1980s*, PhD Dissertation (London: London School of Economics).

—— (1992), 'The Limitations of the Concept of the "Domestic Violence" Incident in Policing and Social Scientific Discourse' in D. Farrington and S. Walklate (eds.) *Offenders and Victims: Theory and Policy British Criminology Conference 1991. Vol. 1* (London: British Society of Criminology/Institute for the Study and Treatment of Delinquency).

—— (1993), *Innovations in the Policing of Domestic Violence; Evidence from Metropolitan London.* (London: Ashgate).

—— (1995), 'Transnational Policing and the Makings of a Postmodern State' *British Journal of Criminology*, Vol. 35, No. 4, 613–35.

SIBBITT, R. (1997), *The Perpetrators of Racial Harassment and Violence*, Home Office Research Study 176 (London: Home Office).

SIVANANDAN, A. (1982), *A Different Hunger: Writings on Black Resistance* (London: Pluto).

—— (1993), 'Millwall and After', *New Statesman*, 15 October 1993.

SKED, A., and COOK, C. (1993), *Post-war Britain: A Political History* (4th edn., London: Penguin).

SKOGAN, W. G. (1986), 'Methodological Issues in the Study of Victimisation' in Fattah (ed.) *From Crime Policy to Victim Policy* (London: Macmillan), 80–116.

SKOGAN, W. (1990), *The Police and Public in England and Wales: a British Crime Survey Report*, Home Office Research Study 117 (London: Home Office).—— and MAXFIELD, M. (1981), *Coping with Crime* (Beverly Hills Cal.: Sage).

SMALL, S. (1983), *A Group of Young Black People: Police and People in London* (London: PSI), Vol. 2.

—— (1991), 'Racialised Relations in Liverpool: A Contemporary Anomaly', *New Community*, Vol. 17, No. 4, July.

SMITH, D. J. (1983a), *A Survey of Londoners: Police and People in London* (London: PSI), Vol. 1.

—— (1983b), *A Survey of Police Officers: Police and People in London* (London: PSI), Vol. 3.

—— (1994), 'Race, Crime and Criminal Justice' in M. Maguire, R. Morgan and R. Reiner, *The Oxford Handbook of Criminology* (Oxford: OUP).

—— and GRAY, J. (1983), *The Police in Action Police and People in London* (London: PSI), Vol. 4.

—— and —— (1985), *Police and People in London* (London: Gower).

SMITH, J. C., and HOGAN, B. (1983), *Criminal Law* (London: Butterworths).

SMITH, S. J. (1989), *The Politics of 'Race' and Residence: Citizenship, Segregation and White Supremacy in Britain* (Cambridge: Polity).

—— (1993), 'Residential Segregation and the Politics of Racialization', in M. Cross and M. Keith, *Racism, the City and the State* (London: Routledge).

SOLOMOS, J. (1988), *Black Youth, Racism and the State: The Politics of Ideology and Policy* (London: Cambridge University Press).

—— (1989), *Race and Racism in Contemporary Britain* (London: Macmillan).

—— and RACKET, T. (1991), 'Policing Urban Unrest: Problem Constitution and Policy Response' in E. Cashmore and E. McLaughlin, *Out of Order?: Policing Black People* (London: Routledge).

SOUTHALL BLACK SISTERS (1989), 'Two Struggles: Challenging Male Violence and the Police' in Dunhill, C. (ed.), *The Boys in Blue: women's challenge to the police* (London: Virago).

STANKO, E. A. (1987), 'Typical Violence, Normal Precautions: Men, Women and Interpersonal Violence in England, Wales, Scotland and the USA' in Hanmer and M. Maynard (eds.) *Women, Violence and Social Control* (London: Macmillan).

—— (1988), 'Hidden Violence Against Women' in M. Maguire and J. Pointing (eds.) *Victims of Crime a New Deal?* (Milton Keynes: Open University Press), 40–6.

—— (1990), *Everyday Violence* (London: Pandora).

STENSON, K. (1993), 'Community Policing as a Governmental Technology', *Economy and Society* 22, 3, 373–89.

—— and COWELL, D. (eds.) (1991), *The Politics of Crime Control* (London: Sage).

—— and FACTOR, F. (1993), 'Youth Work, Risk and Crime Prevention', Paper presented to the British Criminology Conference, Cardiff, July.

STEPHENS, P., and WILLIS, C. F. (1979), *Race, Crime and Arrests,* Home Office Research Study No. 58 (London: HMSO).

SUTTON RACIAL EQUALITY COUNCIL (1992), *Survey into Racial Harassment and Attacks in the London Borough of Sutton* (London: Sutton Racial Equality Council).

TAYLOR, S. (1982), *The National Front in English Politics* (London: Macmillan).

THOMAS, D. N. (1984), *White Bolts Black Locks: Participation in the Inner City* (London: Allen and Unwin).

TOMLINSON, J. (1981), *'Left, Right: The March of Political Extremism in Britain'* (London: Platform).

Tompson, K. (1988), *Under Siege: Racial Violence in Britain Today* (Harmondsworth: Penguin).

Troyna, B. and Hatcher, R. (1992), *Racism in Children's Lives: a Study of Mainly White Primary Schools* (London: Routledge).

Virdee, S. (1995), *Racial Violence and Harassment* (London: Policy Studies Institute).

Walker, M. (1977), *The National Front* (Glasgow: Collins).

Walklate, S. (1989), *Victimology: The Victim and the Criminal Justice Process* (London: Unwin Hyman).

—— (1990), 'Researching Victims of Crime: Critical Victimology', Social Justice, Vol. 17(3) 41, Fall.

—— (1992), 'Appreciating the Victim: Conventional, Realist or Critical Victimology?' in R. Mathews and J. Young (eds.) *Issues in Realist Criminology* (London: Sage).

Walmsley, R. (1986), *Personal Violence,* Home Office Research Study 89 (London: HMSO).

Walsh, D. (1987), *Racial Harassment in Glasgow* (Glasgow: Scottish Ethnic Minorities Research Unit).

Weatheritt, M. (1986), *Innovations in Policing* (London: Croom Helm).

Webster, C. S. (1993), 'Process and Survey Evaluation of an Anti-racist Youth Work Project' in P. Francis and R. Mathews (eds), *Tackling Racial Attacks* (Leicester: University of Leicester).

—— (1994), 'Racial Harassment, Space and Localism', *Criminal Justice Matters*, No. 16, Summer.

—— (1995), *Youth Crime, Victimisation and Racial Harassment* (Bradford: Bradford and Ilkley Community College).

—— (1997), *Local Heroes: An Empirical Study of Racial Violence Among Asian and White Young People*, Unpublished PhD Thesis (Leicester: University of Leicester).

Webster, M. (1980), *Submission of Evidence from the National Front to the House of Commons Select Committee on Home Affairs 1979–80: In Respect of Possible Changes to the Public Order Act, the Representation of the People Act and the Race Relations Act* (National Front).

Weeraperuma, S. (1979), *'So You Want to Emigrate to England Mohandas: Letter to a Coloured Emigrant'* (Colombo: Lake House).

Willis, C. (1983), *The Use, Effectiveness and Impact of Police Stop and Search Powers*, Home Office Research and Planning Unit Paper 15 (London: Home Office).

Wilson, J. Q. (1968), *Varieties of Police Behaviour* (Cambridge, Mass.: Harvard University Press).

Witte, R. (1996), *Racist Violence and the State* (London: Longman).

Yin, R. K. (1989), *Case Study Research* (London: Sage).

Young, M. (1991), *An Inside Job: Policing and Police Culture in Britain* (Oxford: Clarendon Press).

Index